ALL-TIME GREATS OF BRITISH ATHLETICS

ALL-TIME GREATS OF BRITISH ATHLETICS

Mel Watman

SPORTS BOOKS

Published by SportsBooks Ltd

Copyright: Mel Watman ©
April 2006

SportsBooks Limited
PO Box 422
Cheltenham
GL50 2YN
United Kingdom
Tel: 01242 256755
Fax: 01242 254694
e-mail   randall@sportsbooks.ltd.uk
Website www.sportsbooks.ltd.uk

Photographs for cover, colour section and of Ken Matthews, Mary Peters, Mary Rand,
Ann Packer, Lynn Davies, David Hemery, Brendan Foster and David Bedford in the
black and white section by Mark Shearman

Cover by Kath Northam

Typeset in Garamond Premier Pro

A CIP catalogue record for this book is available from the British Library.

ISBN 1899807 44 6

Printed by Cromwell Press

FOREWORD
by Sebastian Coe

Athletes are a discerning breed – no more so than when sniffing out the journalistic fraud from the real McCoy. Those who write about my sport tend to fall into two camps: the specialist who is equally at home watching the Yorkshire track championships at Cudworth just outside Barnsley as when reporting world records in an Olympic stadium and there are those who come hotfoot from a champion's league final and three days later become instant experts on the finer points of lofting a javelin or kicking for home in a 10,000 metres.

There is not one person I know of any credibility in my sport who would have any difficulty in pigeon holing the author of this book. Mel Watman is no instant expert, his insights and credentials to have set about this seminal work have been honed over significantly more than half a century. While some journalists have actually asked me how many laps there are in a 1500 metres, Mel would discuss each 100 metre split and every tactical nuance of the race.

Not for him the irritating rush to groundless hyperbole - 'this is the greatest race I have ever seen' or the 'greatest exponent of the particular discipline' and when Mel has ever bordered on such eulogy he will have 10 unanswerable reasons to back up his case. Sadly in my sport, the Watmans are a dwindling breed. His choice of great British athletes leaves little room for argument. From Walter George to Paula Radcliffe, all his choices have distinguished my sport and dignified the arena. And given that many of them are close friends, Watman has not just recounted their statistical claim to fame but placed them in a human and social context. I smile at his observation that Daley Thompson and I are separated only by a 100th second over 400 metres. Alas – that is where all comparisons end.

Steve Ovett, one of the most (if not the most) naturally talented athletes I ever competed against, and whose athletics club my neph-ews now compete for (it's a strange old world), is rightly given his place in Watman's firmament. And there are little insights into the author's exploration into his career that are new, even to me although his reply in an *Athletics Weekly* – the bible for many in British athletics – to a question in an interview 'Do you have a hunger for the world mile record?' 'no, I don't think so, it seems a bit pointless to me' I know from my own experience falls some way short of Ovett's full ambition at the time.

All Time Greats of British Athletics has been compiled by somebody who if we compiled a list over the last fifty years of great athletic writers would fall comfortably into that pack and would be close to heading it. He has lovingly and painstakingly chronicled those individuals who have left a nation with some of the most breathtaking moments in our sporting history like the four minute mile, great head to heads, Olympic glory and world records. I know that this book will relive those moments for everybody that reads it.

Sebastian Coe

ACKNOWLEDGEMENTS

In collecting material for this book I have drawn heavily on many magazine sources, notably *Athletics Weekly*, *Athletics Today*, *Athletics International*, *Track Stats*, *Athletics World*, *Athletics Arena*, *World Sports* and *Track & Field News* (USA), British Olympic Association Olympic Reports and a multitude of publications by the National Union of Track Statisticians (NUTS) and the Association of Track & Field Statisticians (ATFS). I am indebted also to Britain's foremost athletics photographer Mark Shearman, who has provided most of the illustrations, and to Dave Terry, who supplied some of the earlier photos. I would also like to thank Travis Marsh, for facts and figures on Muriel Cornell, and Randall Northam of SportsBooks for his help and advice with this project.

Among the books I have consulted and sometimes quoted from are:

Bailey, E McDonald – *If It's Speed You're After* (Stanley Paul, 1953)

Bannister, Roger – *First Four Minutes* (Putnam, 1955)

Barrett, Norman & Watman, Mel – *Steve Cram & Daley Thompson* (Virgin Books, 1984)

Black, Roger with Rowbottom, Mike – *How Long's The Course?* (Andre Deutsch, 1998)

Blue, Adrianne – *Queen of the Track: The Liz McColgan Story* (H F & G Witherby, 1992)

Booth, Dick – *Gordon Pirie: The Impossible Hero* (Corsica Press, 1999)

Brasher, Chris (ed.) – *The Road to Rome* (William Kimber, 1960)

Buchanan, Ian – *An Encyclopaedia of British Athletics Records* (Stanley Paul, 1961); *British Olympians* (Guinness Publishing, 1991); *Who's Who of UK & GB International Athletes 1896-1939* (NUTS, 2000)

Capes, Geoff with Wilson, Neil – *Big Shot* (Stanley Paul, 1981)

Christie, Linford – *To Be Honest With You* (Michael Joseph, 1995)

Coe, Sebastian with Miller, David – *Running Free* (Sidgwick & Jackson, 1981)

Coote, James – *The Dave Bedford Story* (Penta Publications, 1971)

Duncanson, Neil – *The Fastest Men On Earth* (Willow Books, 1988)

Duncanson, Neil & Collins, Patrick – *Tales of Gold* (Queen Anne Press, 1992)

Emery, David – *Lillian* (Hodder & Stoughton, 1971)

Folley, Malcolm – *Jonathan Edwards: A Time To Jump* (HarperCollins, 2000)

Foster, Brendan & Temple, Cliff – *Brendan Foster* (Heinemann, 1978)

Gunnell, Sally & Priest, Christopher – *Running Tall* (Bloomsbury Publishing, 1994)

Hadgraft, Rob – *The Little Wonder: Alf Shrubb* (Desert Island Books, 2004)

Harrison, Ted – *Kriss Akabusi On Track* (Lion Publishing, 1991)

Hemery, David – *Another Hurdle* (Heinemann, 1976)

Hill, Ron – *The Long Hard Road* (Ron Hill Sports, 1981 & 1982)

Holmes, Kelly with Blake, Fanny – *Black, White & Gold* (Virgin Books, 2005)

Hyman, Dorothy – *Sprint to Fame* (Stanley Paul, 1964)

Hymans, Richard – *Progression of World Best Performances & Official IAAF World Records* (IAAF, 2003)

Jackson, Colin – *The Autobiography* (BBC Books, 2003)

Lewis, Denise with Kervin, Alison – *Personal Best* (Century, 2001)

Lovesey, Peter – *The Kings of Distance* (Eyre & Spottiswoode, 1968)

Matthews, Peter – *Who's Who in British Athletics* (Archive Publications, 1989)

Matthews, Peter & Buchanan, Ian – *All-Time Greats of British & Irish Sport* (Guinness Publishing, 1995)

McWhirter, Norris & Ross – *Get To Your Marks!* (Nicholas Kaye, 1951)

Miller, David – Sebastian Coe: *Born To Run* (Pavilion Books, 1992)

Moon, Greg – Albert Hill: *A Proper Perspective* (1992)

Moorcroft, Dave & Temple, Cliff – *Running Commentary* (Stanley Paul, 1984)

Ovett, Steve with Rodda, John – *Ovett: An Autobiography* (Willow Books, 1984)

Pallett, George – *Women's Athletics* (Normal Press, 1955)

Pascoe, Alan with Hubbard, Alan – *Pascoe: The Story of an Athlete* (Stanley Paul, 1979)

Peters, Jim & Edmundson, Joseph – *In The Long Run* (Cassell, 1955)

Peters, Mary with Wooldridge, Ian – *Mary P* (Hutchinson, 1974)

Phillips, Bob – *Honour of Empire, Glory of Sport: History of Athletics at the Commonwealth Games* (The Parrs Wood Press, 2000); *3:59.4: The Quest for the Four Minute Mile* (The Parrs Wood Press, 2004)

Pirie, Gordon – *Running Wild* (W H Allen, 1961)

Quercetani, Roberto – A *World History of Track & Field Athletics* (Oxford University Press, 1964)

Radcliffe, Paula with Walsh, David – *Paula: My Story So Far* (Simon & Schuster 2004 & 2005)

Rand, Mary – *Mary Mary* (Hodder & Stoughton, 1969)

Rix, Martin & Whittingham, Rob – *British All-Time Lists* (Umbra Software, 1998)

Rowe, Arthur – *Champion in Revolt* (Stanley Paul, 1963)

Rozin, Skip – *Daley Thompson: The Subject is Winning* (Stanley Paul, 1983)

Sanderson, Tessa with Hickman, Leon – *Tessa: My Life in Athletics* (Willow Books, 1986)

Sheridan, Michael – *A Gentle Cyclone: Sydney Wooderson* (1998); *British Athletics 1950* (2000); *British Athletics 1946-1949* (2004)

Shrubb, Alf – *Running & Cross Country* (Health & Strength, 1908)

Thurlow, David – *Sydney Wooderson – Forgotten Champion* (1989)

Tomlin, Stan (ed.) – *Olympic Odyssey* (Modern Athlete Publications, 1956)

Watman, Mel – *The Ibbotson Story* (Athletics Weekly, 1958); *The Encyclopaedia of Athletics* (Robert Hale, 1964, 1967, 1973, 1977 & 1981); *History of British Athletics* (Robert Hale, 1968); *Who's Who in World Athletics* (Athletics International & Shooting Star Media, 1997, 1998, 1999, 2000); *Olympic Track & Field History* (Athletics International & Shooting Star Media, 2004)

Watman, Mel (ed.) – *The Coe & Ovett File* (Athletics Weekly, 1982)

Webster, F A M – *Athletics of Today* (Warne, 1929); *Great Moments in Athletics* (Country Life, 1947); *Olympic Cavalcade* (Hutchinson, 1948)

Whitbread, Fatima with Blue, Adrianne – *Fatima* (Pelham Books, 1988)

Whittingham, Rob, Jenes, Paul & Greenberg, Stan – *Athletics at the Commonwealth Games* (Umbra Athletics, 2002)

Williams, Peter – *Lynn Davies: Winner Stakes All* (Pelham Books, 1970)

M W

INTRODUCTION

ALTHOUGH I BEGAN assembling and writing the material for this book at the end of 2004, the project in effect started decades earlier. Ever since I left school in 1954 – four years after I got hooked on the sport at the age of 12 – I have been writing professionally about athletics. My early heroes included McDonald Bailey, Arthur Wint, Roger Bannister, Chris Chataway, Gordon Pirie, Jim Peters, Diane Leather, Dorothy Tyler and Sheila Lerwill, but I was just as enthralled by the exploits of such champions of the past as Walter George, Alf Shrubb, Albert Hill, Harold Abrahams, Eric Liddell, Douglas Lowe, Lord Burghley, Godfrey Brown and Sydney Wooderson as I devoured every athletics book I could lay my hands on. Two that stand out were *Great Moments In Athletics* by Lt-Col F.A.M.Webster (published in 1947) and *Get To Your Marks!* by Ross and Norris McWhirter (1951). Such works fired my imagination and sparked off a lifelong compulsion. Not only did I want to report the deeds of contemporary athletes; I aspired also to keep alive the memory and example of those who had gone before. This book, which combines much of my previously published work (revised and updated where applicable) with many totally fresh biographies, is my tribute to 78 of the all-time greats of British athletics ... in the hope that new generations of athletics followers will come to appreciate the brilliant achievements of men and women they may never have heard of before, and that older readers will rekindle fond memories of athletes and contests from their earlier days in this wonderful sport of ours.

I have been incredibly lucky to have spent half a century as an athletics journalist, statistician and historian; it's something I would gladly have done as a hobby. While working as a trainee reporter on a suburban weekly newspaper I also began to contribute to *Athletics Weekly*, a magazine I had read and loved since 1950, and it was my good fortune that when that publication needed a new overseas news compiler I just happened to be in the right place at the right time. Founding editor Jimmy Green – a major influence on the shape of my career – offered me the freelance position. Soon afterwards, in 1958, I covered single-handed the Commonwealth Games in Cardiff for *AW* and helped establish the National Union of Track Statisticians, or NUTS to you.

I was thus joyously immersed in athletics journalism when the Queen decided it was time for me to defend the realm and I was called up for two years' National Service in the RAF. That should have put a stop to my writing career, but somehow or other I still managed to file copy for *AW*, save up enough leave to get to my first Olympics (Rome 1960) and even edit a new monthly magazine, an *AW* offshoot entitled *World Athletics*.

On demob in 1961 I was invited to join *AW* full-time as Jimmy Green's assistant editor and I spent 25 happy years working alongside him, succeeding him as editor – and thereby fulfilling a boyhood dream – in 1968. During those years I was privileged to report on everything from club and schools meetings to the Olympics, steadily expanded the magazine's overseas coverage and feature articles, and interviewed several of the athletes included in this volume. Among the books I wrote was *History of British*

Athletics (1968), and much material on the earlier all-time greats has been reprinted from that source.

Following a change of ownership and a consequent erosion of my editorial influence, I parted company from *AW* in 1988 and along with Randall Northam (whose company SportsBooks is the publisher of this book) and with the generous financial backing of Sir Eddie Kulukundis I co-edited *Athletics Today*, which from 1989 set new standards for a weekly athletics magazine. That publication expired in 1993 and so, nearly, did I with a heart attack. However, I was keen to maintain the worldwide results service which had been a popular feature of *AT* and, in collaboration with Peter Matthews (who was overseas news editor of *AT* along with his TV commentating and fantastic work editing the ATFS Annual), I began publishing *Athletics International*, a newsletter which has continued to this day.

Over that half century of documenting the sport I have written countless profiles (and, regrettably, obituaries) of leading British athletes and some years ago I resolved to collect, expand and update them to form a book. It would be my retirement project. Well, as my long suffering but ever supportive wife Pat will testify, that retirement always tends to be deferred for just another year or two, so at the end of 2004 I decided I would get on with it while still involved with other work.

The most difficult aspect of this book was deciding who to include and exclude. How can you define who is, and who isn't, an 'all-time great'? The answer is that you can't; there is no definitive qualification. Ultimately it's a subjective choice based on facts, figures, historical perspective ... and a gut feeling. Originally I settled on the admittedly arbitrary figure of 80 biographies, which I later reduced to 78 as I felt that two of the more recent athletes I had chosen had not quite fulfilled the criteria for inclusion. I would guess that most athletics enthusiasts with a grounding in the sport's history would agree with around 70 of my selections but vehemently disagree with the others.

How could I possibly omit early Irish stars like Peter O'Connor and Tim Ahearne who, before the Republic came into existence, had no option but to represent "Great Britain and Ireland"? I took the view that those athletes were proudly Irish, not British, and therefore not qualified for inclusion – although their achievements are featured in the 'Honours List' at the end of the book. Similarly, I have omitted Zola Budd. I admired her as a runner and for her exploits on the track and over the country she certainly merits a biography, but she was never truly a British athlete. More as a newspaper stunt than anything else, and with traumatic consequences for her personal and family life, she was granted British nationality in record time but she was always really a South African bearing a flag of convenience and returned to her homeland after a fairly short time.

Conversely, I have included McDonald Bailey from Trinidad and Arthur Wint from Jamaica, both of whom joined the RAF and made their homes here after the war. There can't be any argument over Bailey, as he ran for Britain in two Olympics and spent the whole of his long career in senior competition as a member of Polytechnic Harriers. If anyone was a symbol of and ambassador for British athletics in the early

Introduction

post-war years it was 'Mac'. In Wint's case, he did represent Jamaica in the Olympics but he ran several times for Britain in international matches and, like Bailey, was for many years an integral part of the domestic club scene.

Other decisions were very difficult. Take the marathon runners. I included Jack Holden, Jim Peters, Basil Heatley, Ron Hill and Steve Jones ... but what about the likes of Sam Ferris, Ernie Harper, Tom Richards, Brian Kilby, Jim Hogan, Bill Adcocks, Jim Alder, Ian Thompson and Charlie Spedding? In a perfect world all of these would have been profiled, but with an equivalent expansion in other events the book would have become too massive a project. In any case, no matter where you set the boundaries there are always going to be those on the borderline. Believe me, I went through agonies before finalising my list. However, a brief summary of the main achievements of every athlete since 1900 with a claim to all-time great status can be found in the 'Honours List'.

The 78 biographies appear in date of birth order, which has led to some anomalies. For instance, Tommy Green – who won Olympic gold at a mature age in 1932 – precedes men like Harold Abrahams and Eric Liddell of *Chariots of Fire* (1924) fame. Jack Holden, who won Empire Games and European marathon titles in 1950, appears before 1932 Olympic 800m winner Tom Hampson, while Joyce Smith – a UK marathon record breaker as late as 1982 – is profiled before Peter Radford whose world 220 yards record was set in 1960.

The length of each entry varies considerably, ranging from around 500 words in the case of some of the 'old timers' to more than 4000 words for a few of the more modern legends. This is not meant to reflect the relative merit of the athletes concerned; it's just that there is more material of significance available on those athletes who have had long careers in the professional ranks with all the major championships and international competition open to them.

I am indebted to so many authors and publications in my research for this book. A detailed list of sources can be found in the acknowledgements but a special mention for *Athletics Weekly*, which was the home for so much of my work over a 30-year period. My thanks to the current publisher Matthew Fraser Moat and editor Jason Henderson for enabling me to reprint material from past issues.

More than 30 years ago, while I was *AW* editor, my Yorkshire correspondent Granville Beckett tipped me off about a promising young lad by the name of Sebastian Coe. I have followed his career every step of the way since then and am deeply honoured that he has contributed a generous foreword to this book.

Finally, as I stated early in this introduction, this book is my personal tribute to the brightest stars of British athletics. I consider it vital for the champions of past eras to be remembered and honoured. Some of their performances may look fairly ordinary today but one has to evaluate them in the context of the standards which prevailed at that particular time. One day, perhaps in connection with staging the 2012 Olympics in London, we may have a 'Hall of Fame' for British athletics. Until that happens, this is my contribution to preserving a rich heritage in the hope that future generations will be inspired and encouraged to follow in such distinguished footsteps.

Mel Watman March 2006

AUTHOR

Mel Watman's involvement with athletics spans more than half a century.

He was hooked as a 12 year-old after attending the 1950 AAA Championships at the White City and he has been writing professionally on the sport ever since he left Hackney Downs Grammar School in 1954. That was when he first started contributing to *Athletics Weekly*; he joined the staff in 1961 after completing National Service in the RAF, served as Jimmy Green's assistant editor for several years and succeeded him in 1968. He was consultant editor from 1985 to 1988.

From 1989 to 1993 he co-edited another weekly magazine, *Athletics Today*, and for the past 12 years he has co-edited and published *Athletics International* with Peter Matthews.

He has attended eight Olympic celebrations between 1960 and 1996 and reported on (via TV coverage) four others up to and including 2004. His previous books include *The Encyclopaedia of Athletics* (in five editions), *History of British Athletics, The Coe & Ovett File*, several editions of *Who's Who in World Athletics, Olympic Track & Field History* and (with Roberto Quercetani and Alain Billouin) *The Magic of Athletics: A Century of Great Moments*. As well as being a member of the ATFS (Association of Track & Field Statisticians), he is a co-founder of the British off-shoot, the NUTS (National Union of Track Statisticians), and the British Athletics Writers Association, and a member of the Track & Field Writers of America.

His own athletics career was resolutely mediocre, although he was undefeated as a steeplechaser (ran one, won one!) and he is proud to have completed the New York and London Marathons.

He and his wife Pat live in the north-west London suburb of Stanmore.

ALPHABETICAL LIST OF BIOGRAPHIES

Kelly Holmes (1970)	209
Thelma Hopkins (1936)	68
Dorothy Hyman (1941)	87
Derek Ibbotson (1932)	57
Colin Jackson (1967)	199
Derek Johnson (1933-2004)	60
Steve Jones (1955)	120
Diane Leather (1933)	62
Sheila Lerwill (1928)	42
Denise Lewis (1972)	219
Eric Liddell (1902-1945)	16
Douglas Lowe (1902-1981)	18
Ken Matthews (1934)	66
Liz McColgan (1964)	176
Dave Moorcroft (1953)	117
Paul Nihill (1939)	78
Steve Ovett (1955)	123
Ann Packer (1942)	89
Alan Pascoe (1947)	97
Jim Peters (1918-1999)	34
Mary Peters (1939)	76
Gordon Pirie (1931-1991)	54
Paula Radcliffe (1973)	222
Peter Radford (1939)	80
Mary Rand (1940)	84
John Regis (1966)	191
Arthur Rowe (1937-2003)	69
Tessa Sanderson (1956)	128
Alf Shrubb (1879-1964)	3
Joyce Smith (1937)	70
Ian Stewart (1949)	106
Arnold Strode-Jackson (1891-1972)	9
Daley Thompson (1958)	142
Don Thompson (1933)	63
Dorothy Tyler (1920)	36
Allan Wells (1952)	115
Fatima Whitbread (1961)	167
Harold Whitlock (1903-1985)	20
Arthur Wint (1920-1992)	38
Sydney Wooderson (1914)	29
BRITISH HONOURS LIST	231

WALTER GEORGE

Born 9.9.1858 Calne (Wiltshire). Died 4.6.1943.
Club: Moseley H

OF ALL THE great British athletes celebrated in this book, W.G. George was the one most in advance of his time. When he, a 19 year-old novice race walker, announced that one day he would run the mile in 4:12, made up of quarters of 59, 63, 66 and 64, his claim was met with amusement if not ridicule. The year was 1878 and the world's best by an amateur stood at 4:24.5 by Walter Slade in 1875 although the professional record was far superior at 4:17¼ by William Lang and William Richards in 1865. But Walter George would have the last laugh, for in 1886 he would set a record of 4:12¾ which would remain unbeaten by anyone until 1915 ... and it wasn't until 1935 that another Briton, Sydney Wooderson no less, would run faster!

It was later in 1878 that George won his first mile race, a handicap event, in a time of 4:29.0 off 45 yards – equivalent to about 4:36 for the full distance. It was the only time in his career that he would not start from scratch for he developed at such a remarkable rate that the very next season he became English champion at the mile (4:26.2) and 4 miles (20:51.8). That was the year in which two rival English championship meetings were staged: one organised by the Amateur Athletic Club, the other by the London Athletic Club. George's successes came at the LAC promotion.

There was no dispute in 1880, for at the inaugural AAA Championships George won both titles in 4:28.6 and 20:45.8. Still only 21, he rounded off that season by lowering Slade's mile record to 4:23.2 with terribly uneconomical quarter-mile splits of 59.0, 65.2, 69.8 and 69.2, and he also set new 4 miles figures of 19:49.6 – over half a minute faster than Slade's previous best. Illness (he was plagued throughout his career by asthma and hay fever) held him back in 1881 and he was beaten in the AAA mile by B.R. Wise, but later in the year he recovered sufficiently to produce a world 3 miles record of 14:42.4.

The lightly built apprentice chemist, just under 6ft tall at 1.82m and weighing but 136lb (62kg), carried all before him in 1882. He began his record spree as early as March with a 30:49.0 6 miles during a 7 miles race (he won the English cross country title the same month); in May he ran 10 miles in 52:56.5 and in June he slashed his mile time down to 4:19.4 after reaching halfway in 2:04.5 and three-quarters in 3:08¾, itself a world best. At the AAA Championships he won the half (1:58.2), mile (4:32.8) and 4 miles (although he ran only one lap as there was no challenger) on July 1 and added the 10 miles (54:41.0) two days later. At the end of July he reduced the 2 miles record to 9:25.6 (4:30.4 first mile) ... but that was not all. In November he journeyed to New York to meet the equally celebrated American, Lon Myers, in a series of three races. Myers, holder of the world record at 1:55.6, won the half-mile in 1:56.4 with George only three yards behind in a

British best of 1:57.0. One week later George levelled the score with an easy mile win in 4:21.4 and in the decider, a three-quarter mile event watched by a heavily wagering crowd of over 50,000, the Englishman clinched the rubber with a 3:10.5 victory on a snow-covered track. No doubt about it now ... Walter George was the world's greatest runner.

Ill health struck again in 1883, with the result that George met with a triple defeat at the AAA Championships, but by November he was fit enough to improve his 10 miles mark to 52:53.0. It was an indication of what was to follow. A contemporary described George as "a tall thin man with a prodigious stride, which arises from his bringing his hips into play more than any distance runner we have ever seen, and years of practice and training cultivated his staying power to an extraordinary degree." Extraordinary is certainly the word to use to describe his activities in 1884.

As in 1882 he started off with victory in the English cross country championship. Here, in cold facts and figures, is what followed: April 7: World records at 6 miles (30:26.0) and 10 miles (51:20.0), the latter mark surviving for 20 years. April 26: World record at 2 miles of 9:17.4 which lasted for 19 years. May 17: World records at 3 miles (14:39.0) and 4 miles (19:39.8). June 21: AAA titles at 880y (2:02.2), mile (4:18.4) and 4 miles (20:12.8), the mile time standing as an amateur world record for nine years. June 23: AAA 10 miles title in 54:02.0. July 28: World records for 6 miles (30:21.5) and one hour (11 miles 932 yards or 18,555m), the latter unbeaten for 20 years.

Having achieved everything open to him in the amateur field, George looked around for new worlds to conquer. His gaze alighted on William Cummings, a Scottish professional who had beaten 4:20 on five occasions with a best of 4:16.2 in 1881. George applied to the AAA for permission to race Cummings: half the gate money to be donated to the Worcester Infirmary, the other half to be handed over to Cummings. George asked nothing for himself, although he was in financial difficulties after having failed to complete his pharmaceutical studies. He would be happy to remain an amateur just as long as he was given the chance to prove himself the best miler of the day. Predictably, the AAA turned down George's request. Under no circumstances, stated the governing body, could an amateur compete with a professional. There was only one course open to George ... he turned 'pro'.

Their first clash, for what was dubbed "the mile championship of the world", came about at Lillie Bridge Grounds in London on 31 August 1885. Such was the popular appeal of the match (not to mention the opportunity for a little flutter) that 30,000 people fought their way into the stadium and it is said that George had to climb up a ladder from the coalyard next door in order to reach his dressing room at the top of the grandstand! George was in superb form, as testified by a truly sensational 4:10.2 time trial (laps of 58.2, 60.4, 68.4 and 63.2 ... and remeasurement indicated he covered six yards more than a mile!), and in the race he proceeded to burn off his tiny opponent from Paisley. He led from the start at a tremendous clip, passing the quarter in 58.6 and the half in 2:01.0. The pace slackened to 3:07.5 at three-quarter mile but it was still too fierce for Cummings, who was tailed off in the final furlong. George won by over 60 yards, easing up, in 4:20.2.

Lillie Bridge was the scene of their second miling duel on 23 August 1886. George was a clear favourite but the 20,000 spectators were afforded more of a race this time. George undertook the pacemaking and practically duplicated the speed of the first race: 58¼ at 440y, 2: 01¾ at 880y. With a quarter-mile to go the pair were level in 3:07¾, the signal for Cummings to draw away to a six-yard lead. George's supporters were stunned, but only momentarily, for their hero quickly caught and passed the Scot, who went on to collapse some 60 yards from home. George broke the tape alone in 4 minutes 12 and three-quarter seconds (in shorthand 4:12.75, although that gives a misleading impression that the race was electrically timed), easily the fastest mile run in competition and one of the outstanding sporting exploits of the 19th century. Just how far ahead of his time was George can be gauged by the fact that no man ran faster until Norman Taber (USA) clocked 4:12.6 in 1915 and no Briton bettered his time until Sydney Wooderson returned 4:12.7 in 1935! Note also how close George was to the schedule he had hit upon eight years earlier with laps of 58¼, 63½, 66 and 65.

George's fame is primarily as a miler but he was also the outstanding long distance runner of his generation. As mentioned earlier, he set world bests at numerous distances up to 10 miles and the hour although his most extraordinary performances came in time trials and in 1886 he claimed to have run 10 miles in 49:29 – a time which was not achieved in competition until 1946 – and 12 miles in 59:29.

George was a pioneer in so many ways. He invented and practised the '100-Up' Exercise, a system of home exercise and training which took the form of exaggerated running on the spot with the knees brought up to the level of the hips, while another aspect of his innovation is that at the time of his death, in 1943 when aged 84, the Swedish milers Gunder Hägg and Arne Andersson were approaching very close to four minutes for the mile, nurtured on a system of training known as 'fartlek'. And on what did Gosta Holmer, the system's originator, base 'fartlek'? Why, on the training methods of one W.G. George.

ALF SHRUBB

Born 12.12.1879 Slinfold (Sussex). Died 23.4.1964.
Clubs: Horsham Blue Star H, South London H

ALF SHRUBB, then aged 19, could thank a stack of blazing straw for his introduction to athletics. One evening he heard the clanging of a firebell and together with Fred Spencer, captain of Horsham Blue Star Harriers who happened to be passing, he ran three miles to the scene of the fire. The athlete was so impressed by the running of his companion – who was dressed in his working clothes and heavy boots – that he persuaded him to join the local club. That was in June 1899. Shrubb, a small man of 5ft 6.5in (1.69m) and 118lb (54kg) with a short, shuffling stride, was endowed with unusual powers of endurance, perhaps attributable to his habit as a boy of following foxhunts on foot. Improvement came swiftly and in order to further his career Shrubb joined South London Harriers in September 1900.

The first major honour to come his way was the English cross country title in March 1901, and the following month he won the 10 miles track title in 53:32.0. A second AAA championship (4 miles in 20:01.8) followed in July. He succeeded in the same races in 1902, and in the autumn started his record collection with English standards of 6:47.6 for 1.5 miles and 19:31.6 for 4 miles. Earlier, he had broken all known records for 15 miles when he clocked 1:20:15.8 but on that occasion he had to play second fiddle to Fred Appleby (1:20:04.6). In 1903 Shrubb demonstrated his versatility by, on the one hand, winning the English and inaugural International cross country championships and, on the other, defeating British record holder Joe Binks for the AAA mile crown in 4:24.0. He also retained his longer distance titles but his supreme achievements that year were world records at three (14:17.6) and two (9:11.0) miles within the space of nine days. That 3 miles time remained the British record for all of 33 years.

His exploits in 1904 overshadowed all that had preceded; without reservation Shrubb, who always delighted in running from the front, established himself as the greatest distance exponent the world had so far encountered. In bare figures here is a catalogue of his most outstanding successes: March 5: Won fourth consecutive English cross country title. March 26: Won second consecutive International cross country title. April 9: Won fourth consecutive AAA 10 miles title. May 12: Set world 5 miles record of 24:33.4. June 11: Set world 2 miles record of 9:09.6, which survived until 1926, the 880 yards splits being 2:06.0, 2:21.0, 2:31.4 and 2:11.2. Note the first and last half miles totalled 4:17.2 – only just outside the British mile record! June 13: Set world 4 miles record of 19:23.4, which survived until 1924. July 2: Won AAA mile in 4:22.0 (first and last laps totalled 2:01.4) and fourth consecutive 4 miles title in 19:56.8 an hour and a quarter later. August 27: Set unratified world 3 miles record of 14:17.2. November 5: Set world records of 29:59.4 for 6 miles (which stood as a British record until 1936), 31:02.4 for 10,000m, 35:04.6 for 7 miles, 40:16.0 for 8 miles, 45:27.6 for 9 miles, 50:40.6 for 10 miles (which survived as the world record until 1928), 56:23.4 for 11 miles and 11 miles 1137 yards (18,742m) in the hour. That last mark remained the British record until 1953. He began the race at an incredible rate, covering the first quarter in 64.8 and the half in 2:14.2!

This last race, at Glasgow's Ibrox Park on Guy Fawkes Day, was Shrubb's masterpiece for during its course he blew up every available world mark from 6 miles onwards. The event was a sealed handicap and conditions were far from ideal: the track was sodden and a lively wind was blowing. But nothing could hold back the 24 year-old Sussex tobacconist. Inspired, as he related afterwards, by the skirl of bagpipes he began lapping runners after a couple of miles and caught the last of his rivals before the final mile. Once the 10 miles record was secure (that was the one he coveted, having twice failed to beat Walter George's 1884 figures of 51:20.0) Shrubb was content to slacken off and thus the professional Harry Watkins' 1899 distance of 11 miles 1286 yards (18,878m) eluded him. At the conclusion of 11¾ miles (reached in 60:32.2) Shrubb was hoisted shoulder high from the track and, to a heartfelt rendering of 'Will Ye No Come Back Again', carried in triumph to the pavilion. Following that race, "The Little Wonder" as he was affectionately dubbed, held every amateur world record from 2000m to the hour.

As Britain was unable to send a team to the Games in St Louis that year Shrubb was deprived of the chance of Olympic immortality. Admittedly the 5000m and 10,000m did not enter the programme until 1912 but it is possible that Shrubb would have won the 1500m which went to James Lightbody (USA) in a world best of 4:05.4. As for the 4 miles team race, Shrubb could have been expected to lap the American winner, Arthur Newton (21:17.8).

The Glasgow triumph proved to be Shrubb's last great race as an amateur for after spending several months away touring Australasia he was declared a professional by the AAA in September 1905. He continued to race as a 'pro' for many years without ever quite recapturing the former spark. That's not to say he didn't put up many notable performances, particularly in North America. On one occasion in 1907 he defeated Canadian Billy Sherring, winner of the Olympic marathon of 1906, in a 15 mile race by a margin of six laps – enabling him to make his way back to the dressing room, pick up his camera and return in time to snap his rival finishing. Early in 1908, on an indoor track, he covered 10 miles in 51:33.4, easily defeating a five-man American relay team.

Another time he raced a horse over 10 miles and lost by a mere 15 yards in 52:20. In February 1909 there was huge public interest in a marathon clash at New York's Madison Square Garden (262 laps!) between Shrubb, making his debut at the distance, and Canada's American-Indian Tom Longboat. Shrubb went off much too fast (4:52 first mile) and held an eight-lap lead after 19 miles but later began to limp and at one stage was reduced to a walk. His lead was being whittled down and with just under 2 miles to go Longboat went ahead and Shrubb, having run himself into the ground, was persuaded to drop out.

After living in Canada for ten years, Shrubb served as Oxford University's first professional coach from 1920 to 1927 and in 1928 he returned to Canada for good. The AAA made a pleasant, if somewhat belated, gesture by reinstating him in his 74th year and five years later, in 1958, he donned vest and shorts once more to run the last leg of a relay celebrating the centenary of the Canadian town he lived in. He died there, aged 84.

Not least of Shrubb's legacies to future generations of runners was his dedication towards training, which was much more demanding than that of his predecessors. As he relates in his book *Running and Cross-Country*: "I have never trained but in one fashion, and that is to rise at 7 am and after going through ten minutes free exercise dress quickly and get out of doors for a brisk 2 miles walk before breakfast, going about four and a half miles per hour pace. After breakfast, and sufficient time for digestion, I run 4-5 miles on the track. This distance is increased to 8 miles once or twice each week. Lunch at 1pm and back to the track at 3pm, taking 3 miles continuous run the first week each afternoon, 8 to 10 miles the second week, and 2 miles fast continuous runs daily the third week. Thereafter, vary the afternoon runs at top speed from 2 miles to 4, 5, 6, 8 and 10 miles steady runs."

His warmup consisted of jogging 880 yards wearing heavy boots (decades before Emil Zátopek created a stir by training in Army boots) as "it gave me more spring after putting on light racing shoes."

ALBERT HILL

Born 24.3.1889 Tooting (London); died 8.1.1969.
Clubs: Gainsford AC, Polytechnic H

BRITAIN'S ATHLETE OF the 1920 Olympic Games was undoubtedly Albert Hill, who completed the 800m/1500m double – the last to do so until Peter Snell in 1964, and a feat not emulated by any Briton until Kelly Holmes in Athens in 2004.

Hill first made a name for himself as a cross country and long distance track runner – he won the AAA 4 miles title in 1910 – but was to be the first link in a chain of brilliant half milers which graced British athletics between the two world wars.

After serving in France for three years as a wireless operator with the Royal Flying Corps he was 30 years of age by the time he was able to resume his athletics career, but he quickly made his mark by winning the AAA 880 yards and mile double in 1919, equalling Joe Binks' 1902 British mile record of 4:16.8 later in the year. Hill, a chain-smoking railway ticket collector who trained all of twice a week, wanted to go for the Olympic double but after finishing second to Bevil Rudd in the 1920 AAA 880 yards and not contesting the mile he was at first definitely selected only for the 800m.

As he recalled many years later: "I well remember the strong argument I had with Sir Harry Barclay, the secretary of the AAA, when the teams were being selected, for the committee were opposed to my attempting the 800 and 1500m. But I was adamant on tackling the double and in the end Sir Harry bowed to my arguments. Most of the critics, too, were against my decision – the more so because I had been defeated by Bevil Rudd, the Oxford runner and South Africa's representative in the half mile championship that year. Many considered Rudd as the greatest middle distance runner of that era. But when he beat me at Stamford Bridge my leg was still troubling me. Shortly afterwards, with the aid of a bandage above the ankle, it improved 100 per cent and I was determined to show the critics that I was not the has-been they thought I was."

Show them he did. First came the 800m on August 17, and this is what Hill wrote about it: "I considered Rudd my most dangerous opponent. He was a hot favourite to take the 800m, but I had other ideas. Knowing that Earl Eby, the American, always ran a fast first quarter I was determined to move to the front just after the bend, and take the field along at a fast pace. I realised that, whatever the earlier pace, Rudd always made his great effort at the 300 yard mark and he did so this time. Soon, he had a big lead and, entering the home straight with 120 yards to go, was still leading by three to four yards. Everyone expected an easy victory, but I was watching him closely, and noticed his arms beginning to come up high, and his body getting stiff. The stiffer his action became the more I forced myself to relax, arms down, body slightly forward. And turning on full speed, I caught up with him 20 yards out, going on to beat Eby by a yard with Rudd third.

"Of all the contests in my long years on the track, that one stands out as the victory based most satisfyingly on judgment and tactics. It was, moreover, a case of 'all's well that ends well' for about a month before the British team were to leave for Antwerp

I severely strained the shin muscles in my left leg. In spite of medical attention, the injury persisted and two weeks before our departure it was doubtful whether I would be able to make the trip."

As a bonus, Hill's time of 1:53.4 was a British record. Eby was timed at 1:53.6 and Rudd, who turned his ankle when leading in the finishing straight, recorded 1:54.0. Fourth was Hill's 19 year-old team-mate Edgar Mountain, while in seventh place was the Dutchman Adriaan Paulen, who would serve as President of the IAAF from 1976 to 1981.

Two days later Hill lined up for the 1500m final, run in pouring rain on a very heavy cinder track. "My chief opponent," Hill wrote, "was Joie Ray of America, a great little runner, who always made his third lap very fast. Aware of this, I was determined to be with him at the bell, then take him along at a fast pace. But unfortunately Ray was not at his best. In the third lap he lost the kick, and I had the easiest of victories." His time was 4:01.8, with Philip Baker, who sacrificed his own chances by sheltering Hill during the race, runner-up in 4:02.4. *The Times* described Hill's double in these terms: "It was the greatest individual achievement of the Games. He showed himself to be not only one of the greatest of runners, but also a runner of unbeaten courage and a great track tactician to boot."

At 31, Hill remains the oldest man ever to have won an Olympic 800 or 1500m title. His labours weren't over yet, for on August 22 he took part in the final of the 3000m team race, in which he won a silver medal.

The post-script to Hill's career came in 1921. He planned to lower the world mile record (then 4:12.6) to 4:08 by running four laps of 62 seconds each at the AAA Championships, but the pressures of competition and the large size of the field caused an even pace schedule to be thrown to the winds. Leading all the way, with young Henry Stallard at his shoulder, Hill unreeled the first three laps in 59.6, 64.4 and 67.2. Stallard made a sustained challenge over the last furlong but Hill resisted to win in 4:13.8, a full three seconds inside the British record.

Hill, who had himself been trained by Sam Mussabini with advice also from Walter George, later turned to coaching, his most successful pupil being Sydney Wooderson who in 1937 was to succeed in bringing the world mile record to Britain. Hill settled in Canada, where he died at the age of 79.

WILLIE APPLEGARTH

Born 11.5.1890 Guisborough (Yorkshire); died 5.12.1958.
Club: Polytechnic H

WRITING IN 1934, Harold Abrahams stated: "It is, of course, a matter of opinion as to who is the greatest sprinter that this country has ever produced, but if we could line them all up together on the track at their best, I believe that Willie Applegarth would flash past the tape first." That's quite an endorsement of Applegarth's prowess, considering it came from the man who ten years before that article was crowned Britain's first Olympic 100m champion.

Applegarth, who dominated British sprinting immediately before the outbreak of the First World War, was – like Abrahams after him – coached by the legendary Sam Mussabini. Applegarth had been a champion all-rounder at school and in 1910, at the age of 20, he made a promising debut in the AAA Championships by filling third place in the 100 yards behind F.L. Ramsdell (USA) and South Africa's Olympic 100m champion Reggie Walker.

He was less successful the following year, placing only fifth in the 100y, but in 1912 he established himself as the nation's premier sprinter. At the AAA Championships he was second in the 100y, won in 9.8 by South African George Patching who 15 days later was to finish fourth in the Olympic 100m, and in the 220y he took the title in 22.0 with Patching third. Applegarth was eliminated in the Olympic 100m at Stockholm (he was second in his semi-final to the USA's Donald Lippincott with only the winner qualifying) but made amends by gaining a bronze medal in the 200m.

Drawn in the inside lane, Applegarth ran in storming fashion around the turn and entered the straight slightly ahead but he could not sustain the effort and two Americans (Ralph Craig, the newly crowned 100m champion, and Lippincott) surged past. Craig won in 21.7, with Lippincott showing 21.8 and Applegarth, in his eighth race in five days, a valiant 22.0. In between the two individual sprints, Applegarth became the proud possessor of a gold medal in company with David Jacobs, Henry Macintosh and Vic d'Arcy. With Applegarth on the anchor leg, the British quartet won the inaugural Olympic 4x100m relay final by two metres from Sweden in 42.4. The clear-cut favourites, the USA, had been disqualified in the semi-finals.

Applegarth struck his best form of the 1912 season in September when on successive weekends he set English records at 200 yards (19.4) and 220 yards around a turn (21.8). The latter mark equalled the world best set 17 years earlier by John Crum (USA) ... in spite of a strong head wind in the straight and the fact that Applegarth split a shoe during the race. Next year he became the first home athlete to score an AAA sprint double, his times being 10.0 and 21.6 – the furlong time being a new world's best. He was also credited with 14.4 for 150 yards – "a very wonderful performance" according to Abrahams, for whom Applegarth had been a boyhood inspiration. Later in the season he added his name to the English 100 yards record list with a couple of 9.8's.

He enjoyed an even finer double at the 1914 AAA Championships: the 100 in 10.0 and the 220 in 21.2. The furlong mark, around the sharp Stamford Bridge bends, proved to be the greatest achievement of a distinguished career. It stood as the world record for the curved event until 1932 and as the UK best until 1958! "I was in the crowd as a schoolboy of 14 and watched Applegarth that afternoon, " Abrahams recalled many years later. "I can still see that short, well-built figure travelling round the track at an unbelievable speed and running to an easy victory. I can remember trying to imitate his perfect style, but I never with all the hard work I subsequently indulged in, ever anything like approached to his machine-like precision."

At the height of his fame Applegarth turned professional and in no time established himself as 'world champion'. In November 1914 he chalked up a 100 yards victory over the seemingly unbeatable 'Blue Streak' from Australia, Jack Donaldson (credited with a shade inside 9.4 in 1910) in 9.9. As late as 1922 he was credited with 9.75 for 100 yards in a handicap race in Dundee, claimed as a British professional record, but there is no official confirmation of the timing, track measurement or wind conditions. Applegarth settled in the United States in 1922 and died there aged 68 ... still holder of the AAA Championships 220 yards record.

ARNOLD STRODE-JACKSON

Born 5.4.1891 Addlestone (Surrey); died 13.11.1972. Club: Oxford University AC

ALTHOUGH HE RAN only one truly memorable race, and that was nearly a century ago, Arnold Strode-Jackson, CBE, DSO, remains a larger than life figure in British athletics history.

The race of his life was, happily enough, the 1500m at the Stockholm Olympics of 1912. Never having beaten 4:20 for the mile he was given little chance – except by that shrewd judge of athletes, Joe Binks – against the outstanding American trio of Abel Kiviat (world 1500m record holder with 3:55.8), John Paul Jones (holder of the mile record of 4:15.4) and defending champion Mel Sheppard. Indeed, the British squad – wrote Lt-Col F.A.M. Webster in 1929 – "was probably the poorest Olympic team that has ever left these shores, and the last thing we expected was to win a middle-distance event."

"Jackers", as he was known, was practically a novice. He was a rower until, in 1911, his uncle – none other than Clement Jackson, who had set a world best 120y hurdles time of 16.0 back in 1865, was a co-founder of the AAA and was then Oxford University athletics coach – told him: "You'll never win a Blue for rowing. Come down to Iffley Road and I'll make you into a miler." Admittedly his training consisted less of running than of massages, walking and golf, while he was certainly not averse to smoking and drinking, but he did win the mile in 1912 against Cambridge in 4:21.4.

That won him Olympic 1500m selection along with eight other Britons, for in those days countries were not restricted to a maximum of three per event. He had never run in the AAA Championships (nor did he in future years) and it is said that prior to Stockholm he had never competed on a 400m or 440y track or run with the left foot inside. Oxford in those days had a right-handed track of three laps to the mile.

No fewer than seven of the 14 Olympic finalists were Americans and they teamed up to prevent any outsiders from posing a challenge. Webster wrote in his book *Great Moments in Athletics*: "Jackson strove hard to secure an initial lead, but was beaten in the race to the first bend. Thereafter he tried in vain to find any place he could in the moving file of runners. He could not do so and remained on his own and doing the best he could until the chivalrous Cantab, Philip Baker, set an example of unrehearsed pace-making such as may never be seen again. He steered Jackson wide of the living string winding round the track, both travelling yards further than the rest at each lap, until Baker's bolt was shot and Jackson was in a position to make his own supreme effort."

Into the final straight it was Kiviat, Jones and a third American, Norman Taber, almost abreast, with Jackson fourth. Kiviat, the 20 year-old favourite, pulled away slightly only for the Englishman with the long, springy stride to finish with a fantastic spurt which carried him into the lead some 30m from the tape. His winning time was an Olympic and British record of 3:56.8, and in Webster's words: "No one but an outstanding champion could have won in face of the clever but perfectly fair tactics adopted against him." Jackson claimed in the 1960s that Harvard computers worked out that he had run at least 26 yards over distance in that race, which if correct would point to a true 1500m time of around 3:53.

Baker, who placed sixth in Stockholm, went on to gain the Olympic silver medal in Antwerp in 1920. As Philip Noel-Baker, MP, he served as Minister of Fuel and Power in Clement Attlee's Labour Government and in 1959 he was awarded the Nobel Peace Prize for his campaigning for an international arms control treaty.

Jackson ran his final race at the Penn Relays in Philadelphia in April 1914. Serving with the King's Royal Rifle Corps during the First World War he became the youngest brigadier-general in the British Army and was one of only seven officers in that war to be awarded a third bar to the DSO.

He was wounded three times while serving on the Western Front. In 1919 he changed his name to Strode-Jackson and was a member of the British delegation to the Paris Peace Conference before settling in the USA with his American wife in 1921. He became a naturalised US citizen in 1945 but died in his beloved Oxford aged 81.

One of the finest tributes paid him as an athlete came from the USA's Olympic 800m champion Ted Meredith in 1914, who referred to "Jackers" as "the greatest of present-day runners" and "so good that he can defeat any man in the world if he is within 20 yards of him at the last quarter. He has the nerve, the heart and the legs, and he isn't afraid to run himself out."

TOMMY GREEN

Born 30.3.1894 Fareham (Hants); died 29.3.1975.
Clubs: Southampton AAC, Belgrave H

FOLLOWING A NUMBER of incidents in 1924, walking was dropped from the 1928 Olympic programme but, thanks largely to pressure by British officials, a 50 kilometres road event was introduced in 1932. Fittingly, the winner in Los Angeles was a Briton: 38 year-old father of four, Tommy Green, who had to give up several weeks' wages as a railwayman in Eastleigh to make the long trip to California by ship and train.

Affected by tropical weather which caused the tar on the roads to melt, Green's time of 4:50:10 was nearly quarter of an hour slower than his best time when he won the inaugural national championship in 1930 (4:35:36), but what really mattered was that he finished seven minutes ahead of his nearest rival, Janis Dalins of Latvia – a winning margin which has only once been exceeded in the 15 Olympic 50 kilometre races held since.

He remains to this day the oldest man to win that title. At halfway, reached in 2:23:11, Green, Dalins and Italy's Ugo Frigerio (winner of three short distance gold medals at the 1920 and 1924 Games) were level pegging, and they were still together at the three-quarters distance (3:39:55) before Frigerio dropped back. The next to experience a crisis was Green, who fell a minute behind Dalins at one stage before being rejuvenated by cold water being thrown over him and producing a strong finish. Green covered the final quarter of the race faster than any of the preceding segments and that, combined with the stomach cramps which beset Dalins, enabled Green to win by close to a mile. As soon as he could he sent a telegram to his wife back in Hampshire. "I won the gold medal. Very hot. See you all soon, Love Tom."

It was remarkable that Green ever became an athlete, never mind an Olympic champion, for as Ian Buchanan relates in his book *British Olympians* he was unable to walk until he was five because of rickets, at 16 he was invalided out of the Army (which he had joined under-age at 12) with injuries sustained when a horse fell on him, and while serving in France during the First World War he was wounded three times and badly gassed. Despite all that, he lived to one day short of his 81st birthday.

A doctor advised him to take up athletics as a protection against the wartime gas that remained in his lungs. He started as a runner but drifted into walking after assisting a war-blinded friend who was training for the St Dunstan's London-Brighton event. He won his first walking race, from Worthing to Brighton, in 1926, aged 32, and later victories included the London to Brighton classic in 1929, 1930, 1931 and 1933 and the Milan 100 kilometres race in 1930.

He was unable to defend his Olympic title after finishing fourth in the 1936 50 kilometres trial but continued to compete until he was 54.

GUY BUTLER

Born 25.8.1899 Harrow (Middlesex); died 22.2.1981.
Club: Achilles

GUY BUTLER WAS Britain's most bemedalled Olympic athlete of all-time, a distinction shared since 1984 with Seb Coe. He won four Olympic medals as a 400m and 4x400m relay runner in the Games of 1920 and 1924, including a gold in the 1920 relay.

The son of 1889 English rackets champion E.M. Butler and a cousin of Rab Butler, the former Home Secretary, he first made his mark in the 1917 Public Schools Championships when he won the 100 yards (with Harold Abrahams unplaced six yards behind), 440y and long jump – defeating Abrahams by half-an-inch with his final leap. Two years later, before he even received his Blue at Cambridge, he was AAA 440y champion at the age of 19. In addition to his relay gold alongside Cecil Griffiths, Robert Lindsay and John Ainsworth-Davis, he finished second in the 1920 Olympic 400m, won by his great rival from Oxford (and South Africa), Bevil Rudd, 49.6 to 49.9 on a rain-sodden track in Antwerp. There was certainly nothing hollow about the placings, for the cream of the world's quarter-miling talent was present. Frank Shea (USA), a sub-48 sec 400m performer, placed fourth while 440y record holder (at 47.4) Ted Meredith, another American, did not even make the final.

Despite competing with a strained thigh muscle, necessitating the use of a standing start, Butler reached new heights at the Paris Olympics of 1924. After setting an unofficial European record of 48.0 in his semi, he gave it everything in the final. Second to the inspired Eric Liddell (winner in 47.6) for much of the race he eventually finished third in 48.6. Under any other circumstances such a magnificent and plucky feat would have received the attention and acclaim it merited but on this occasion it tended to be overlooked in the excitement surrounding the winner of the race. Butler picked up another bronze in the relay.

Tall, powerfully built and long striding, Butler was an athlete who – as a result of leg injuries and acute nerves – never quite fulfilled his potential. As Harold Abrahams once wrote: "Ill-luck and a rather wayward temperament played their part in robbing him of distinctions which were well within his capabilities, and had he not been so successful when he was so young he might have been very much more so later on."

One of his finest performances came in 1926 when, a week after winning the AAA 220y in a personal best of 21.9, he equalled the listed world record of 30.6 for 300 yards. He ended his active career at the 1928 Olympics, where he was eliminated in the second round of the 200m.

Butler went on to make a valuable contribution to British athletics in other ways. A former schoolmaster, he became a successful coach (he helped guide Alistair McCorquodale to a sensational fourth place in the 1948 Olympic 100m), lectured and wrote widely on the sport, and became Britain's foremost producer of coaching films and loops. He died aged 81.

HAROLD ABRAHAMS

Born 15.12.1899 Bedford; died 14.1.1978.
Clubs: Achilles, London AC

THANKS TO *Chariots of Fire*, an Oscar-winning film released in 1981, certain events at the 1924 Olympics are familiar to millions of people who were born decades later, and the names of Harold Abrahams and Eric Liddell became famous again.

Harold Abrahams

Abrahams, whose Jewish father (né Isaac Klonimus) fled from Russian-occupied Poland to Britain in the 1870s, had been an athlete of unusual ability from an early age. Encouraged by his elder brothers, Adolphe and Sidney (the AAA long jump champion in 1913 and an Olympic competitor in 1906 and 1912), Harold was only ten when he made a successful racing debut at what was then the mecca of British athletics, Stamford Bridge. It was there four years later, in 1914, that he watched his first AAA Championships. "I well remember the thrill," he recalled many years afterwards, "of seeing Willie Applegarth in the inside string [lane] tearing round the bend in the 220y race with his strides following one another with incredible rapidity." That was the occasion of Applegarth's brilliant world record 21.2 clocking which stood as the UK best until 1958.

By 1918 Abrahams was beginning to make himself known to the public; that year he won both the 100y and long jump at the Public Schools Championships. During a short spell in the Army the 19 year-old 2nd Lt. Abrahams had the opportunity of meeting his boyhood hero, the 29 year-old Company Sergeant-Major Applegarth, in an exhibition 100y race in 1919. The younger man, given a start of two yards, won by six in 10.0.

Two months later he went up to study law at Cambridge. He recorded 'evens' (10.0 for 100y) in the 1920 inter-varsity clash and later in the season, at the Antwerp Olympics, he succeeded in winning his 100m heat in 11.0 but was eliminated in the next round. He was even less successful in the long jump, where not surprisingly he failed to reach the final with a leap of 6.05. "My competing at Antwerp was very far from distinguished, in fact quite the reverse, but I benefited enormously from the experience, and I am sure it played a large part in my good fortune at Paris four years later."

The highlight of Abrahams' 1921 season was equalling the world's best time of 7.4 for the rarely contested 75 yards event (the course at Stamford Bridge was, however, found to be eight inches short) but on the same track the following weekend he had no answer to Harry Edward, who beat him in both AAA sprints. His final appearance in the Oxford v Cambridge match in 1923 was a memorable one. He took the 100y in 10.0, 440y in a career best of 50.8 and long jump with an English record of 7.19 to bring his aggregate of victories in the series to an unprecedented eight. His clash with Eric Liddell in the 1923 AAA 100y was awaited with eager anticipation but Abrahams, victim of a septic throat, failed to reach the final which Liddell proceeded to win in a sensational 9.7. Two weeks after the championships, Abrahams ran the fastest furlong of his life: 21.6 along the Wembley straightaway.

Under the direction of the celebrated Polytechnic Harriers coach, Sam Mussabini – the French-Arab who had previously guided Applegarth and Edward (1920 Olympic 100m and 200m bronze medallist) towards their sprinting triumphs – Abrahams trained diligently during the winter of 1923-24 with the Olympics in mind.

He recalls: "I used to train two or three times a week. Sam was 'dead nuts' – that was the expression we used – on the arm action with the arms kept low, bent at the elbows (we used running corks for a good grip), and maintained, which I believe to be absolutely sound, that the action of the arms very largely controls the poise of the body and action of the legs. My training sessions consisted largely of perfecting the start and practising arm action over and over again. No starting blocks in those days, and we took meticulous care with the placing and digging of starting holes and the accurate control of the first few strides. I always carried a piece of string the length of first stride and marked the spot on the track, at which I gazed intently on the word 'set'.

"Our partnership was ideal, because Sam was not an autocrat. We discussed theory for many hours and argued and argued until I knew that his theories were sound – not because of his experience and knowledge, but because my mind was satisfied with his reasons. We paid infinite attention to my length of stride. Speed, of course, is a combination of length of stride multiplied by the rapidity with which a stride is taken. I used to put down pieces of paper on the track at measured distances and endeavour to pick them up with my spikes as I ran. I shall always believe that the vital factor in my running in Paris was that by conscientious training I had managed to shorten my stride an inch or two and get an extra stride into my 100 metres. Then Sam encouraged me to work on a 'drop' finish."

Such assiduity (it was almost unheard of in those days for a sprinter to train three times a week) was to pay off handsomely and an early indication of his dramatic improvement was provided at an inter-club match at Woolwich in June 1924 when he raised his English long jump record to 7.38 (a mark which stood for 32 years) and clocked a downhill, wind-assisted 9.6 100y. The time was equal to the world record but it was never taken too seriously by the man concerned, who knew better than most the fickleness of sprint times. Two weeks later he became the first man to score a double in the AAA 100y (9.9) and long jump (6.92) championships.

And so to Stade Colombes in Paris. "Truthfully," Abrahams has written, "I did not think I had any chance of a gold medal, nor did anyone else. I never really gave it a thought, though my trainer Sam Mussabini sent me a note just before the Games opened saying he thought I would win. But I had no anxieties, which was a godsend."

He was not being unduly pessimistic, merely realistic. Quite apart from the cream of the rest of the world's sprinters, the American opposition was truly formidable. There was the immortal Charles Paddock, the reigning Olympic 100m champion and then the greatest speed merchant the world had known; Jackson Scholz, fourth in the 1920 final and a 10.6 100m performer; Loren Murchison, a finalist in both the 1920 sprints and double American champion in 1923; and promising Chester Bowman, who in later years was to blossom as a 9.6 100-yarder. All Abrahams could point to was a genuine 9.9 100y, equivalent of 10.8 for 100m, whereas Paddock had once been credited with 10.2 for the slightly longer 110y.

The first round posed no difficulty and Abrahams cruised to victory in a sedate 11.0. Any resemblance to the Abrahams of 1920 ended there and then, for in the second round he won through to the semis with a totally unexpected 10.6 ... equalling the Olympic record.

Next day, at 3.15 pm, he settled in his holes (remember, starting blocks were not patented until 1927) for his semi and rose to the set position. "I did a very stupid thing which nearly lost me the race," he reminisced. "I saw a runner on my right move slightly. The pistol went (I thought there might be a recall), I took my mind right off the work in hand, and started badly as the result." Left an estimated yard-and-a-half down in a field that included Paddock and Bowman, a lesser man might have panicked. Instead, Abrahams revealed the physical and mental qualities of a world champion in the making by smoothly making up the lost ground and winning in 10.6! Now, for the first time, he realised he was capable of winning the final and consequently for the next three and three-quarter hours he "felt like a condemned man feels just before going to the scaffold."

The draw for the final, at 7.05 pm, was Paddock, Scholz, Murchison, Abrahams, Bowman and Arthur Porritt. Abrahams went to his mark with Sam Mussabini's parting words installed in his subconscious: "Only think of two things – the report of the pistol and the tape. When you hear the one, just run like hell till you break the other."

Britain's Dr E. Moir got the field away to a perfect start. By the halfway mark Abrahams was showing fractionally ahead of Scholz and Bowman and – in the words of one observer "scudding like some vast bird with outstretched wings, a spectacle positively appalling in its grandeur" – he soared through the tape in that by now famous drop-finish of his two feet clear of Scholz. The time once again was 10.6. Porritt, who would become surgeon to the British royal family and Governor-General of his native New Zealand, finished well to take the bronze medal.

Abrahams always acknowledged the debt he owed Mussabini. "Under his guidance I managed to improve that decisive one per cent, which made all the difference between supreme success and obscurity. In just over ten seconds I had achieved the ambition of a lifetime." In those days far less fuss was made of Olympic champions than is the case today. There was no victory ceremony, no national anthem, no presentation of medals. His gold medal arrived by post some weeks after the event!

Understandably there had to be a reaction following Abrahams' rags-to-riches transformation to become Europe's first Olympic 100m champion and in the 200m, though he did well even to reach the final (he clocked a personal best of 21.9 in a semi-final), he was never in the hunt and trailed home a weary last in 22.3. Scholz was the winner in 21.6, followed by Paddock and Liddell. An eventful week in Paris was completed for Abrahams by a silver medal in the 4x100m relay along with Walter Rangeley, Lancelot Royle and William Nichol. The team finished in 41.2, only two metres behind the Americans' world record equalling 41.0, after having themselves established a short-lived world record of 42.0 in a heat.

When in May 1925 he seriously damaged his leg while long jumping, bringing his active career to a sudden end, he went on to make an enormous contribution to the sport in other ways. A barrister by profession (he was called to the Bar in 1924 and practised until 1940) and secretary of the National Parks Commission from 1950 to 1963, he brought to the councils of the sport a clear, probing, analytical mind which quickly took him into high office.

He was a member of AAA general committee from the age of 26 and was treasurer of the British Amateur Athletic Board from 1948 to 1968, BAAB chairman from 1968 to 1975 and in 1976 he fulfilled another of his life's ambitions by being elected president of the AAA. He was for many years also an influential member of the IAAF, largely responsible for the framing of the rule book and such innovations as Olympic qualifying standards. He was a prolific writer on the sport (athletics correspondent of *The Sunday Times* from 1925 to 1967) and for half a century provided radio commentaries for the BBC. Another field in which he was pre-eminent was as a statistician. He was a co-founder of the ATFS (Association of Track & Field Statisticians) and the first president of the British offshoot, NUTS (National Union of Track Statisticians). He died at the age of 78.

ERIC LIDDELL

Born 16.1.1902 Tientsin (China); died 21.2.1945. Club: Edinburgh University AC

MORE THAN 80 years after the event, Eric Liddell's triumph in the 1924 Olympic 400m – one of the twin themes of the film *Chariots of Fire* – remains a remarkable story. If ever a man was inspired by the supreme test of Olympic competition, that man was Liddell.

The son of a Scottish missionary, Liddell was the first of our "greats" to be born in the 20th century. At the age of five he was brought from China to Britain for the first time and in 1920 he enrolled as a divinity student at Edinburgh University. The following year, aged 19 and in his first season of competition, he landed his first Scottish sprint titles, impressing one writer on the *Glasgow Herald* to such an extent that he predicted Liddell "is going to be a British champion ere long, and he might even blossom into an Olympic hero."

Liddell made little progress as a runner in 1922, in which year he gained the first of his Scottish rugby 'caps' on the wing, but the next season he established himself as one of the fleetest sprinters in British history. In Edinburgh he was timed at 21.6 for 220y on a grass straightaway, a Scottish native record (despite his having been born in China) which would stand for 37 years, and he duplicated that clocking – this time around a turn at Stamford Bridge – when finishing some five yards ahead of Harold Abrahams in a semi-final at the AAA Championships. Next day he really made his mark on the sprint scene as he won his 100y heat in 10.0, semi in 9.8 to equal the British record and final in 9.7, followed by another 21.6 when winning the 220y. That 9.7 (the official watches read 9.67, 9.65 and 9.65) was a time which, unless one counts McDonald Bailey, was not bettered by a British athlete until Peter Radford's 9.6 in 1958 and was just a tenth shy of the world record.

It was received in some quarters with scepticism, but everything was according to the rules and the time was officially ratified. Liddell was immediately hailed as Britain's great hope for the 1924 Olympic 100m crown and it came as a blow, therefore, when he announced that he would not contest that event in Paris as the heats were to be a run on a Sunday. He decided instead to aim for the 200m and 400m; contrary to the film's storyline this was no last minute switch.

Eric Liddell

His first truly international class quarter-mile race was the AAA championship on 21 June 1924, which he proceeded to win in the personal best equalling but frankly commonplace time of 49.6. "People may shout their heads off about his appalling style," wrote his great sprint rival Harold Abrahams of Liddell the quarter-miler. "Well, let them. He gets there." Be that as it may, his chances of winning through against the cluster of Olympic entrants credited with times in the 48 sec region seemed remote.

That Liddell was in the form of his life at just the right moment was made evident when on July 9 he gained the bronze medal in the Olympic 200m in 21.9 behind the USA's Jackson Scholz and Charles Paddock, with the newly crowned 100m champion Abrahams sixth and last. It was their second and final race against each other, with Liddell coming out on top each time.

But still the world remained unsuspecting. On July 10 Liddell cruised through his first round 400m heat in 50.2 and later in the day finished second in his quarter-final in 49.3 to Holland's Adriaan Paulen, who many years later would become President of the IAAF. Next day Liddell caused a minor sensation by taking the second semi-final in 48.2, only 0.4 slower than the Olympic record set by Horatio Fitch (USA) in the first semi. Six men lined up for the final a few hours afterwards with Liddell drawn in the dreaded outside lane – a particular disadvantage for a relative novice at the event – but he made light of this handicap as he sportingly shook hands with his rivals prior to the start.

At the crack of the pistol Liddell sprinted away like a man possessed; moving at a pace altogether unprecedented for a 400m race he flashed past the halfway mark in an unheard of 22.2, some 4m clear of team-mate Guy Butler. Liddell's head was thrown back, his arms all over the place, his knee drive exaggerated ... the experts shook their heads knowingly; they were watching a classic example of a sprinter misjudging his effort. It was inevitable that he would 'blow up' in the finishing straight if not earlier.

Any other man would have done so but the inspired 22 year-old Scot was in the process of making history. Somehow he summoned up hidden reserves of stamina and, incredibly, even managed to increase his lead in the final stages. At the tape he had no less than 0.8 sec to spare over Fitch, with Butler a close third.

The time was almost as sensational as the manner of his victory ... 47.6 or only a fifth outside the best time on record. In fact Liddell's time, absurdly, was officially ratified as a world record because, reasoned the IAAF, Ted Meredith's 47.4 was made over 440 yards (2.34m further) and not 400 metres! As a European and UK best, Liddell's mark stood for a dozen years and it represented a gain of some 1.7 sec over his pre-Olympic fastest. To be scrupulously fair, it must be pointed out that the Stade Colombes track at the time of the Games measured 500m round, an advantage of perhaps 0.2 compared to a two-turn 400m circuit.

A few days later Liddell bowed out from the international scene with another glorious run, returning an estimated 47.6 for his 440y leg in the British Empire v USA match in London. He took over for the final stage of the mile relay six or seven metres down on Fitch and won by a stride. Next season was his last, for after gaining a splendid treble at the 1925 Scottish Championships (10.0, 22.2, 49.2) he joined his father as a missionary in China. There he ran 400m in 49.1 in 1929 (there are rumours that he clocked 47.8 somewhere in the Far East) and it was there, the land of his birth, that the Rev. Eric Liddell, an ordained minister of the Scottish Congregational Church, died of a brain haemorrhage during internment in a Japanese prison camp just months before the end of the war. He was only 43.

DOUGLAS LOWE

Born 7.8.1902 Manchester; died 30.3.1981.
Clubs: Achilles, London AC

AT THE TIME Albert Hill was creating his piece of Olympic history by winning an 800m/1500m double in 1920, Douglas Lowe was just 18 and the reigning Public Schools half mile champion in 2:06.8. Yet, four years later he would succeed Hill as Olympic 800m champion and another four years after that would become the first man to win a second Olympic gold medal at the distance.

Lowe went up to Cambridge in the autumn of 1921 and in no time was making his mark in university sport. Not only was he awarded his athletics 'Blue' as a freshman but he played outside right in the football team which beat Oxford two-nil. He made his AAA Championships debut in 1922, finishing fifth. Nevertheless, nine days before his 20th birthday, he was picked to run for his country in the first full-scale international match ever held in London. The opponents were France, and Lowe assisted in England's 57-42 victory by filling third place in the 800m behind colleagues Edgar Mountain and Cecil Griffiths.

Lowe made considerable progress in 1923 but there was as yet no indication of the extent to which he would improve the following year. Indeed, he was beaten in two important domestic races in June 1924. At the Kinnaird Trophy he lost to Griffiths and at the AAA Championships he finished behind Hyla (Henry) Stallard with 1:54.8 to the winner's 1:54.6.

Lowe travelled to Paris as second string to Stallard, well aware that his best chance for success rested on a fast pace throughout as his own sprint finish had twice been found wanting in recent weeks. Right from the start of the final Stallard set a swift pace. This suited Lowe perfectly, but as Stallard was quick to point out after the race his intention was to win and not simply draw out his colleague.

With 200m to go Stallard was still ahead with Lowe and Switzerland's Paul Martin closing; 100m left and the hare was caught. This left Lowe and Martin to fight for the gold medal and it was the 21 year-old Englishman, yet to win even his own national title, who proved the stronger and thus reaped the highest honour in athletics. His time of 1:52.4 took a second off Hill's British record, which had also been registered in an Olympic final.

The gallant Stallard also gave his all and was deprived of the bronze medal only in the final stride by Schuyler Enck (USA), both men returning 1:53.0. Happily, he gained a bronze medal in the 1500m two days later, one place ahead of Lowe whose position and time (3:57.0) were remarkable for a novice at that distance. That race was won by Finland's Paavo Nurmi in an Olympic record 3:53.6.

The 1925 season had to be an anti-climax after such heady stuff but Lowe did break Frank Cross's ancient British 880y record of 1:54.6 (set in 1888!) with 1:53.4 in the USA. New heights would be scaled in 1926 ... although Lowe met his match in the person of Dr Otto Peltzer of Germany.

Excitement ran high for their clash at the AAA Championships. Peltzer had covered 800m in 1:52.8, the world's fastest time in 1925, while Lowe had tuned up for the Stamford Bridge duel with a world record 600 yards (then an official world record event) of 1:10.4, passing 440y in a personal best of 49.1, seven days earlier. The event attracted 27,000 spectators and none could have been disappointed, unless on chauvinistic grounds, for both men beat Ted Meredith's world record of 1:52.2. Lowe led at halfway in a sizzling 54.6, repelled Pelzer's persistent challenges along the back straight but found himself unable to counter the German's final sprint for home. Peltzer stormed in three yards ahead in 1:51.6, with Lowe's time untaken but estimated at 1:52.0. Lowe later won at 800m against France in Paris, unpressed, in 1:52.6.

Somewhat belatedly, Lowe captured his first AAA title in 1927. Or rather titles, for two and three-quarter hours after disposing of Griffiths in a 1:54.6 half he came back to win the quarter in a personal best of 48.8.

Lowe's chances of another Olympic success were improved still more at the 1928 AAA Championships, where he produced a throbbing second lap of 55.4 for victory in 1:56.6. As in Paris four years earlier, Lowe ran no faster than necessary in the Olympic preliminaries in Amsterdam and it was to his advantage that whereas he was able to stroll through his semi in a relaxed 1:56.0 (eliminating an ill Peltzer among others) three of his most dangerous rivals – Lloyd Hahn (USA), Phil Edwards (Canada) and Séra Martin (France) – were caught up in a hectic battle which necessitated their running 1:53 or faster.

Lowe, newly qualified as a barrister, got away to a splendid start in the final and was ideally placed all the way. Hahn, who had set a short-lived world record of 1:51.4 earlier in the year, led at 400m in 55.2 with Lowe second (55.6) and Edwards just behind. On the final bend Lowe accelerated clean away to win by a full second in the Olympic and British record time of 1:51.8. Rarely has a runner dominated his rivals so absolutely in an Olympic final; and, make no mistake, they were the world's cream. If one excludes the Interim Games of 1906, Lowe made Olympic history by becoming the first runner to successfully defend a title.

As the official British Olympic Report put it: "To describe Lowe's victory as a wonderful effort is to employ mere words in an attempt to do justice to a performance which, from whatever angle one looks upon it, is unparalleled in the history of Olympic middle-distance running." That was not all. Later in the Games Lowe afforded the world a glimpse of his 400m ability with a 47.6 relay leg, a time faster than Ray Barbuti's winning time in the individual race although it must be conceded that Lowe had the benefit of a flying start.

Lowe's last two races were among his greatest and proved a fitting finale to a glittering career. In the British Empire v USA relays match he took over four yards down on 1500m finalist Ray Conger and left him well behind with an 880y stage run in approximately 1:51 and, in conclusion, he defeated Peltzer in the British record time of 1:51.2 for 800m in Berlin in August 1928. He never raced again but continued to make a valuable contribution to athletics as an administrator, serving as honorary secretary of the AAA from 1931 to 1938. He enjoyed a distinguished legal career; he took silk (QC) in 1964 and became a Recorder (part-time judge) of the Crown Court. He died aged 78.

HAROLD WHITLOCK

Born 16.12.1903 Hendon (Middlesex); died 27.12.1985.
Club: Metropolitan WC

BRITAIN'S NEWLY ESTABLISHED Olympic 50 kilometres walk tradition, originated by Tommy Green, was brilliantly upheld four years later in Berlin in 1936 by Harold Whitlock. Only ninth after 20 kilometres (1:43:36) he moved into third place by the halfway mark, second position at 30 kilometres (2:38:10) and took the lead just before 35 kilometres. A severe case of sickness at 38 kilometres, resulting from drinking a cup of tea, caused Whitlock's lead to shrink but he recovered well to finish almost one and a half minutes clear of Switzerland's Arthur Schwab in 4:30:42.

This was how Whitlock described the race: "My own event only started and finished within the stadium, being conducted on closed roads outside. Every conceivable type of surface made up the course, whether by accident or design I don't know, but it was certainly strange to find a path through woods and parkland included. Last out of the stadium, I began to get through the field by the quarter distance until just after the turn I was third to Jaroslav Stork (Czechoslovakia) and Janis Dalins of Latvia. In another five kilometres Dalins was alongside and sensing his weakness I drove him hard for another five kilometres before going ahead. Victory seemed in sight, but a bout of sickness caused me some concern with the added knowledge that Schwab was closing my lead. Fortunately my recovery soon afterwards allowed me to increase my advantage again, to arrive in the stadium a tired but very proud man, having accomplished what I set out to do three years before – win an Olympic title." This magnificent and always fair competitor completed a rare double by winning the 1938 European title in 4:41:51.

Whitlock's career was as long as it was distinguished. He first came into prominence in 1931 with second place in the national 50 kilometres championship and it was not until 1952 (aged 48!) that he bowed out as an international, placing eleventh in the Olympics in 4:45:13. Between 1933 and 1939 he won the national 50 kilometres title on six occasions with a fastest time of 4:30:38 in 1936. Other honours included a world 30 miles track record of 4:29:31.8 at the White City en route to 50 miles (200 laps of the track!) in 7:44:47.2 and the distinction in 1935 of being the first to walk from London to Brighton in under eight hours, his time of 7:53:50 standing as the record until 1956.

All the long hours of training and competition came during his time off work as a racing car mechanic based at the famous Brooklands circuit. As a coach (he advised Don Thompson, the 1960 Olympic 50 kilometres champion) and official (he was chief judge at those Rome Olympics and was chairman of the IAAF Walk Commission for many years) he remained a prominent figure in race walking circles for the rest of his life, and died aged 82.

His younger brother, Rex, held second place at 35 kilometres in the 1948 Olympic 50 kilometres but was obliged to retire shortly afterwards. He came back in Helsinki in 1952 with an excellent fourth place, four minutes behind the winner.

LORD BURGHLEY

Born 9.2.1905 Stamford (Lincolnshire); died 22.10.1981.
Clubs: Achilles, London AC

LIKE HAROLD ABRAHAMS and Douglas Lowe, Lord Burghley was a product of Cambridge University but unlike them made no impression at the 1924 Olympics. A novice of 19, he was eliminated in his heat of the 110m hurdles. He would eventually set British 120 yards hurdles records of 14.8 in 1927 and 14.5 in 1930, only a tenth of a second outside the world record, but from small beginnings (61.2 for his first 440 yards hurdles in 1924) it was as a 400m hurdler that he became renowned.

Born David George Brownlow Cecil at the ancestral home near Stamford, he was educated at Eton but failed to make his mark on those famous playing fields. Injury prevented his gaining a 'Blue' in his first year at Cambridge but he developed sufficiently as a high hurdler in the summer of 1924 to place fourth in the AAA Championships and qualify for the first of his three Olympic trips as a competitor. Next season afforded a clearer view of his capabilities. After gaining a hurdles double against Oxford with 15.8 for 120 yards and a British record of 24.8 for 220 yards, Harold Abrahams noted: "He has a great future as a hurdler if he continues to train assiduously." That he did, by the relatively undemanding standards of his era, and in 1926 he scored his first major triumph when he won the AAA 440y hurdles title in the British record time of 55.0.

He won again in 1927, his time being 54.2. That was not only a British record but, thanks to the difference in time zones, stood equal to the world record for a few hours – until John Gibson reeled off a remarkable 52.6 for the US title in Nebraska the same afternoon! Earlier in the season Burghley had set a national high hurdles record of 14.8 and the week after the championships he reduced his low (220y) hurdles time to 24.7 to become the first man to hold all three British hurdling records. In 1928 he won the AAA crown in another record time (54.0) and rose splendidly to the occasion three weeks later at the Amsterdam Olympics.

Burghley and his Australian-born British colleague Tom Livingstone-Learmonth, drawn in the outside lanes in the 400m hurdles final, dashed off at a fast pace and led for six flights. Livingstone-Learmonth was unable to hold such speed and faded away to fifth in 54.2 but Burghley, who entered the home straight just ahead of world record holder and defending champion Morgan Taylor and Frank Cuhel, was locked in mortal combat with the American pair. Deliberately chopping his stride in order to make sure of clearing the last hurdle cleanly, Burghley withstood the assault to snap the tape a yard to the good in a British record of 53.4.

It was the first time the USA had failed to win this particular Olympic title and the hero of the hour was carried off the track shoulder high by the three British 800m representatives who were awaiting the start of their semi-finals. The "peerless peer", serving as a lieutenant in the Grenadier Guards at the time, went on to delight the 41,000 crowd at Stamford Bridge for the post-Olympic British Empire v USA match by competing in the 4 x 2 laps steeplechase; hand vaulting the water jump he anchored his team to victory with a 1:58.2 stint.

Burghley was well beaten in the 1929 AAA by his great Italian rival Luigi Facelli but gained revenge in the following year's championships when after a thrilling struggle he prevailed by inches in the British record time of 53.8. He later won at both 120y and 440y hurdles at the inaugural Empire Games in 14.6 and 54.4, while earlier in the season he had clocked 14.5 and an estimated 24.3 for 220y hurdles.

A poor season in 1931 was quickly forgotten as Burghley rounded into top form in defence of his Olympic laurels. Again, in Los Angeles, he displayed his fearsome competitive ability. After placing fifth in the 110m hurdles he cut no less than 1.2 sec from his British 400m hurdles record with 52.2 (52.01 electrically timed) – which was not bettered until 1954 – but such was the standard that even this dazzling time sufficed for 'only' fourth place. The winner in 51.7, in one of the most astonishing breakthroughs in Olympic history, was Bob Tisdall, born of Irish parents in Ceylon and educated at Shrewsbury and Cambridge University. Burghley bowed out from the international stage in the 4x400m relay, contributing a brilliant 46.7 leg for the silver medal winning team.

Incidentally, it was Burghley – not Harold Abrahams, as depicted in *Chariots of Fire* – who in 1927 raced 370 yards around the Great Court of Trinity College, Cambridge within the time it took for the clock to chime midday. Another of the film's distortions was that the aristocratic character based on Burghley would in training clear hurdles with glasses of champagne perched on them. As his daughter, Lady Victoria Leatham, remarked: "He was never one to waste champagne at the best of times. I can't imagine he would have risked the glasses, either." The fact was rather more prosaic than the fiction; he would balance a matchbox on each barrier and try to knock it off with his lead leg without striking the hurdle.

Elected Conservative Member of Parliament for Peterborough from 1931 until in 1943 he was appointed Governor of Bermuda, he became a member of the International Olympic Committee in 1933 and was elected president of the AAA and chairman of the British Olympic Association in 1936. He served as president of the IAAF from 1946 to 1976 and as chairman of the organising committee for the 1948 Olympics he played a vital role in the success of the London Games. He succeeded to the title of Marquess of Exeter in 1956 and died at the age of 76.

MURIEL CORNELL

Born 27.9.1906 Mitcham (Surrey); died 8.3.1996
Club: Mitcham AC

THE 1920S WAS a decade of immense importance in the development of women's athletics, with Britain to the forefront. The first international meeting, in Monte Carlo in 1921, saw British women win six of the ten events; in 1922 the Women's AAA was founded and the 'Women's Olympic Games' – later known as the first World Games following objections by the International Olympic Committee and the IAAF to the use of the word Olympic – were staged in Paris. It was organised as an act of defiance after a demand for women's events to be added to the 1924 Olympic programme (in Paris) was rejected by the IOC. Five nations participated and there were five British victories. The year 1923 saw the first full-scale WAAA Championships, while in Paris Britain defeated France in the first official international match for women.

The novelty of an international meeting at London's Stamford Bridge in 1924 drew 25,000 spectators, yet there was still much male opposition to overcome. Harold Abrahams, the shock winner of the Olympic 100m title that year, wrote: "I do not consider that women are built for really violent exercise of the kind that is the essence of competition. One has only to see them practising to realise how awkward they are on the running track." Nevertheless, women's athletics had come to stay and the jibes and ridicule suffered by the pioneers in their knee length 'shorts' and flapping shirts, were not in vain ... and in time even Abrahams was converted to their cause.

One of the most remarkable performers of that era was Muriel Cornell (née Gunn), who at the age of 19 became a founder member of the ladies' section of Mitcham Athletic Club in 1926. Standing less than 5ft 3in (1.59m), she long jumped 4.65 in her first competition in June that year but progressed so quickly that at the British Games at Stamford Bridge in August she twice exceeded the listed world record with 5.37 and 5.485 (exactly 18ft), although the legendary and tragically short-lived Japanese athlete Kinue Hitomi had jumped 5.75 in June. Later in August, at the Women's World Games in Gothenburg, Muriel jumped beyond 5.50 but, turning to speak to a congratulatory official while she was still in the pit, she made another mark in the sand and her distance was downgraded. Hitomi won with an officially accepted world record 5.50, Muriel clearing 5.44 for second. She ended her season at a club meeting with a European record of 5.57, a distance she equalled at the 1927 British Games and which was ratified as a new world record as Hitomi's 5.75 was never officially accepted. Also that year she won the 100 yards hurdles (sic) as well as long jump in her first WAAA Championships.

In 1928 Hitomi put the world record out of sight with leaps of 5.78 and 5.98 at the Japanese Championships in May but Muriel easily beat her at the WAAA Championships, 5.68 (European record) to 5.36. She also won the 100 yards title. Britain did not send a team to that year's Amsterdam Olympics as the WAAA disapproved of the IAAF's grudging offer of just five events in the first Olympics to offer a women's athletics programme. The long jump was not one of them.

Having married in August 1928, it was Muriel Cornell who set a European record of 5.775 at the WAAA Championships and had a marginal foul of over 6m in a match against Germany, but her best year proved to be 1930. She improved to 5.805 (the first 19ft jump by a European) in June and won against Germany in Birmingham in July with a hitchkick of 5.855, which would remain unsurpassed by a Briton until 1952. At the 3rd Women's World Games in Prague, she again placed second to Hitomi, 5.90w to 5.76w. She also won the long jump and 80m hurdles at the WAAA Championships, having earlier equalled the world record of 12.2. Cornell ranked no 2 in the world in 1931 with 5.77 (the great Hitomi died that year of tuberculosis aged just 23).

In January 1933 she gave birth to a daughter, Lorna (who would herself become WAAA junior long jump champion although her main sport was tennis, twice winning the Wimbledon junior title), but hopes of an international comeback in 1934 were dashed by a severed Achilles tendon. But she contributed to her sport in other ways. She was honorary secretary of the WAAA for 11 years, organising secretary for the Women's World Games and women's events at the Empire Games, both staged in London in 1934, and women's team manager at the 1936 Olympics as well as serving on numerous committees. She died aged 89.

JACK HOLDEN

Born 13.3.1907 Bilston (Staffordshire); died 7.3.2004. Club: Tipton H

BOTH AT THE 1932 and 1936 Olympics, British runners finished second in the marathon through Sam Ferris and Ernie Harper respectively. For the next Games, in London in 1948, Britain's golden hope was Jack Holden, winner of the AAA marathon title in 2:36:45 ahead of Welshman Tom Richards (2:38:03), but he fell victim to the bane of all road runners ... blisters. In order to guard against soreness in a marathon Holden had always pickled his feet in potassium permanganate but this time he overdid it and when blisters developed under the leather-like outer skin he had no alternative but to drop out after 17 miles. He was so distraught that, when interviewed by David Thurlow for *Track Stats* 52 years later, the memory still weighed him down. "I was so disappointed that I had let everybody down. I thought I was going to die, I was so upset about it. I felt really ill."

Holden was not the only poignant figure, for Etienne Gailly of Belgium experienced the mortification of reaching Wembley Stadium first but in such an exhausted state that two men overtook him during the lap of the track. Delfo Cabrera of Argentina won in 2:34:52 with Richards second 16 sec behind. Richards continued in competition for many years, setting a personal best of 2:29:59 in 1954 (at the age of 44), but without ever again featuring prominently on the international scene. It was different in Holden's case. Three years Richards' senior, his greatest moments were still to come.

Within four years of joining Tipton Harriers in 1925 Holden was an English cross country international and during the 1930s he built up the most distinguished record in British cross country history: English champion in 1938 and 1939; International champion in 1933, 1934, 1935 and 1939. He was also a useful track runner – three times AAA 6 miles titlist – though not reckoned to be in world class.

As he was 38 when the Second World War ended, having spent five years as an RAF physical education instructor, it might have been thought that Holden's running days were long over but in 1946, after winning a third English cross country title, he decided to take up marathon running. He made a successful debut by taking the Midland title in 2:46:34 but the selectors overlooked him when picking the team for the European Championships. Just to show them the error of their ways he completed the season with two great runs. He triumphed in the South London Harriers 30 miles road race in 3:02:09 and in a track race over the same distance at the White City (120 laps) he recorded a world's best of 3:00:16.4, his time at the marathon point en route being 2:36:39.4.

Holden – who worked as a groundsman and whose diet included the consumption of 100 eggs a week – gained the first of four consecutive AAA marathon titles in 1947 as he outdistanced Richards by half a mile in 2:33:21, and followed with the fastest '30' on record (2:59:47). His first international success materialised at Enschede in the Netherlands in 1949 but his winning time of 2:20:52 was extremely flattering, the course being only 40k. Nevertheless, it was a brilliant run, worth around 2:29 for the full distance.

His greatest season was 1950 when, aged 43, he proved himself the world's number one marathon runner by winning five races out of five including the British Empire and European Championships. He began in February (while still 42) with the Empire Games in Auckland. He won by over four minutes in 2:32:57, a performance all the more remarkable in that he ran the last nine miles barefoot after discarding his rain-sodden plimsolls ... and was even threatened by a Great Dane a couple of miles from the end. Next came the Midland (2:38:24), Polytechnic (2:33:07) and AAA (personal best of 2:31:04) races, and as a grand finale he seized the European crown in Brussels in 2:32:14. As he was presented to the 19 year-old Prince Baudouin of Belgium this astonishingly durable runner was able to remark: "Glad to meet you, sir. Met your father and grandfather before you!"

Holden made his farewell in 1951. He attained a new level of excellence by winning the Finchley 20 miles road race in a record 1:50:48, a minute and a half ahead of 1948 Olympic 10,000m representative Jim Peters, but in the Windsor to Chiswick race two months later Peters, making a spectacular marathon debut, ran Holden into the ground and set a UK best time of 2:29:24 in the process. Holden displayed his usual aggressiveness; he led by 30 sec at 15 miles but in attempting to stay with Peters over the final few miles he ran himself to a standstill. However, content that British marathon running was in good hands he announced his retirement. Of his 17 marathons he won 14, finished second in one and dropped out of the other two. He outlived all his contemporaries, dying days before his 97th birthday in 2004.

TOM HAMPSON

Born 28.10.1907 Clapham (London); died 4.9.1965.
Club: Achilles

THREE OLYMPIC 800m titles on the trot for Britain. By the law of averages it ought to have been years before the likes of Albert Hill and Douglas Lowe would be seen again in British colours ... but no, along came another supreme champion in the tall, bespectacled person of Tom Hampson.

The son of a middle distance runner with Herne Hill Harriers, Hampson took to athletics with enthusiasm but apart from gaining a standard medal for bettering 2:10 (but only just) for 880y at the 1926 Public Schools Championships he achieved little of distinction until the summer of 1929. While at Oxford he did not even earn a full 'Blue' and in his final year as an undergraduate, 1929, he was a poor last in the inter-varsity match with a time of outside two minutes. Luckily he came in as a reserve for the Oxford and Cambridge tour of the USA and Canada that summer for during the trip he blossomed forth with victories in 1:57.6 and 1:56.0. He never looked back after that.

His newfound authority was evident in 1930 and he made his AAA Championships 880y debut a resoundingly successful one by defeating the redoubtable Séra Martin of France by seven yards in the English native record time of 1:53.2, although this was still well outside Lowe's unofficial figures of 1:52.0 behind Otto Peltzer in 1926. Three days after slamming Martin again in the Britain v France match, Hampson sailed for Canada: destination Hamilton and the first British Empire Games. A series of delays stretched the travelling time to ten days, which was hardly an ideal preparation, but the evening of the 880y final found Hampson in his best form to date. A prodigious finishing sprint carried him to the tape no less than 20 yards clear of the next man in 1:52.4, the fastest time in the world that year.

Hampson retained his AAA crown by a wide margin in 1931 and won his races against France and Italy in slow time; otherwise the season was noteworthy only for a personal best mile time of 4:17.0. He knew what he was about, though, for like Lowe he was a master at timing his peak to coincide with the really important tests – and nothing short of an Olympic title would satisfy him. Accordingly, he planned his training in 1932 with the object of being fit enough to win the AAA title early in July but reserving his very best form for the supreme test in Los Angeles a month later.

Of course, training in those days was very different to more recent times. His typical winter schedule now makes incredulous reading: he did no running at all on Monday, Wednesday and Friday; on Sunday he would walk 5-6 miles or else play 3-4 sets of tennis; on Tuesday and Thursday he would run 3-4 miles at medium pace over roads and paths; and on Saturday he would run 5 miles over the country at 5:30 miling pace or else play soccer or rugby.

A feature of Hampson's racing strategy in 1932 was his remarkable pace judgment. "I was convinced," he once wrote, "having studied some of Professor Hill's researches and knowing the working of the 'oxygen-debt' theory, that the Finnish runners were correct when they maintained that the most economical method of running was to keep as near as possible to an even pace throughout ... I appeared early in the year running largely in miles and I remember the howls of 'Nurmi' when I ran in a club match at Battersea Park with a watch in my hand."

Even without a stopwatch Hampson's ability to run at a pre-determined speed was uncanny. Hampson recalled: "I found that only very rarely did my lap times show a discrepancy of more than two-fifths of a second, which showed that I had mastered the difficult subject of pace which had been my bane two years earlier." Hampson's 880y times included 1:54.4 and he won the AAA title in 1:56.4, finishing second also in the 440y in 50.2.

Hampson wrote: "The intervening period between the middle of July and the beginning of August was of course occupied by the journey to Los Angeles. For a person who had not reached a fairly advanced stage of racing fitness this would have meant a setback of a fortnight. As it was, I was able to regard it as a kind of holiday, and by taking a little exercise of some sort – skipping, trotting or walking on deck, a little PT in the gym, interspersed with visits to the ship's pool which did not altogether please the 'old-timers' – I kept my fitness.

"Three days' break in Toronto enabled us all to regain our land legs, but the worst part of the journey was to come – the five days' train trip across America in the cramped confines of a tourist coach. Even here, however, we were able to stretch our legs with an occasional trot on the station platforms, and five days clear after our arrival in Los Angeles was sufficient to put on the finishing touches."

Hampson ran a perfectly planned and executed race at the Games – a classic example of the merits of even pace – but on the day his supporters must have been swallowing hard at seeing their man some 20m behind the leader, Canada's British Guiana-born Phil Edwards, at the half distance reached in 52.4 after an opening 200m of 24.6! Hampson was having none of this and occupied fifth position in the field of nine in 54.8, dead on schedule for the 1:50 timing that he estimated would be sufficient for victory.

Shortly after the start of the second lap the English schoolmaster began to pick off the men ahead and soon only Edwards was in front. Hampson passed the flagging leader along the back straight but the real race was only just beginning, for another Canadian, Alex Wilson, had been running at his heels all this time and went ahead as the pair reached the final bend. The men were locked in mortal combat all the way to the tape, first one and then the other edging in front, but it was Hampson who prevailed. By a margin of six inches he not only won the gold medal but in the process became the first man to better the elusive 1:50. The time was a magnificent electrically timed 1:49.70, almost a second inside Martin's listed world record and fully two seconds faster than Hampson had ever run before. His lap times: 54.8 and 54.9. From the onlooking American, Ben Eastman, who had recently run an unratified 1:50.0, came this tribute: "He is the greatest middle distance man the world has ever seen."

Hampson ran two relay legs at the Olympics before retiring, and proved himself to be a first-rate quarter-miler – not surprising as he was a 10.1 100y performer. Running the second stage in the 4x400m final he was timed in 47.6 and a silver medal was his reward. He maintained his keen interest in athletics for the rest of his life (he died at 57). He was among the first ten senior honorary AAA coaches to be appointed and was a press steward at the London Olympics of 1948.

DON FINLAY

Born 27.5.1909 Bournemouth; died 18.4.1970.
Clubs: RAF, Milocarian, Surrey AC

TO DESCRIBE Don Finlay as having been merely a remarkable athlete would be to sell him short. He was a remarkable man.

Although the twin peaks of athletic endeavour, an Olympic victory and a world record, eluded him, his career as a high hurdler was unique. Two Olympic medals, victories in the European Championships and Empire Games, and an almost perfect international match record ... that was the considerable sum of his achievements when the War diverted his attentions to more serious affairs in 1939. Yet he returned to competition in 1947, made his third Olympic team, set a British record in 1949 and bowed out of international competition with fourth place in 14.7 at the 1950 Empire Games – as a 40 year-old grandfather. At 42 he was still able to turn in a 14.9 performance!

Finlay emerged as an athlete of promise in 1928 when he won the first of 12 RAF titles in 16.0. Next season he placed third in the AAA final and was selected as reserve against France. As it happened it was as a long jumper in that match that he made his international debut ... finishing sixth and last with the quaint distance of 6.33.

He first bettered 15 sec, hallmark of the top class hurdler in those days, in 1931 when he ran Lord Burghley (14.8) to half a yard in the AAA Championships. Later, against France, he turned the tables in 15.2 for his first international victory. In 1932 Finlay established himself as Europe's no 1 – a state of affairs that continued throughout the 1930s. He won the first of seven consecutive AAA titles and, at the Los Angeles Olympics, surpassed himself by taking the bronze medal in 14.8 behind the Americans George Saling and Percy Beard.

Between 1933 and 1939 he lost only nine races, three of them to the only Briton who ever got the better of him during this period, John Thornton (who was killed during the war). Finlay was almost invariably inside 15 sec – a rare exception being at the 1934 Empire Games when he clocked 15.2 but he won all the same.

It was not until the 1936 Olympics that he managed to dislodge Burghley as British record holder for 110m hurdles. As in LA four years earlier, the supreme challenge of Olympic competition in Berlin drew the best out of Finlay. He won his semi in 14.5, tying the UK best for the slightly shorter 120 yards event, and in the final he burst through spectacularly in the closing stages to move from third to second in 14.4. He finished two yards behind Forrest Towns (USA), who three weeks later was to stagger everyone by hacking the world record down from 14.1 to 13.7.

Finlay's fastest runs came in 1937 but he never received official credit for them. In Paris he recorded 14.2 and in Stockholm 14.1 but both were discounted as European records because of suspected wind assistance. A photo taken at the finish of the Stockholm race, however, shows a flag drooping limply. In that race Finlay beat Sweden's 14.3 performer Haakan Lidman by some seven metres!

He experienced further bad luck in the 1938 AAA Championships when, under the rules then in force, he was credited with 14.4 although the watches registered 14.29, 14.31 and 14.31. However, he did record an official 14.3 when defeating Lidman at the European Championships that year. A foot injury cut short his 1939 season.

During the War, Wing Commander Finlay served his country well as a fighter pilot with 41 Squadron and was decorated with the DFC and the AFC.

He was 38, a silver-haired war hero of high rank in the RAF (he became a Group Captain) when in 1947 he embarked upon possibly the most astonishing comeback in athletics history. He twice clocked 14.6 that year and in 1948 he not only made the Olympic team but was honoured in being selected to pronounce the Olympic Oath at Wembley Stadium on behalf of all the competitors. Unhappily, while leading in his heat he struck the final hurdle and fell. But for that mishap it is not inconceivable that he could have placed as high as fourth in the final, for that position went at 14.6.

Still he was not finished and 1949 proved to be one of his most momentous seasons. He reclaimed the AAA title he had last won 11 years earlier, clocking 14.6 on a flooded track, and won against France in 14.4, the second fastest by a European that year. That race proved a fitting conclusion to his international match career: in 16 races between 1931 and 1949 he won 14 times and was second in the other two behind Burghley and Thornton. What a record.

A few days later, in Glasgow, Finlay achieved perhaps the most startling victory of his entire career: against Dick Attlesey, then a 14.0 performer and third in the US Championships, but destined the following season to set a world record of 13.5. "Of course," wrote American journalist Max Stiles, "such a thing is impossible. It just isn't done by grey, old geezers in their forties." By any normal standards such a feat was impossible – but since when could one judge Don Finlay by normal standards? What a tragedy that following a motor accident a severe spinal injury caused this most active of men to be confined to a wheelchair for the last four years of his life. He was 60 when he died.

SYDNEY WOODERSON

Born 30.8.1914 Camberwell (London).
Club: Blackheath H

ONE OF THE most delightful experiences of my journalistic career occurred in August 1987 when, along with a number of colleagues, I had lunch with one of my all-time heroes, Sydney Wooderson. It was a marvellous idea of Dave Bedford, then chairman of the International Athletes Club, to mark the forthcoming 50th anniversary of Sydney's world mile record by inviting the press to meet the great man.

Wooderson's historic 4:06.4 timing at Motspur Park, Surrey on 28 August 1937 was achieved in a handicap race. He was off scratch, of course; former British record holder Reggie Thomas was off 10 yards and six other runners (including his brother Stanley Wooderson) were given starts of between 60 and 140 yards, thus providing Sydney with a series of targets to aim for.

It was pacing of a sort but, as Seb Coe pointed out, the difference between the paced races of today's international circuit and the handicap events of yesteryear is that in a handicap everyone is trying to win the race. Moreover, if the handicapper has done his job well and all the athletes run close to their normal form, an exciting finish is assured.

Wooderson's aim was merely to break his own British record of 4:10.8 set the previous year shortly before a cracked bone in his ankle ruined his chances in the 1936 Olympic 1500m. "It wasn't billed as a world record attempt ... it just happened," he recalled. "I was amazed." Among the 3000 spectators were two very special milers of earlier eras: 78 year-old Walter George, who as a professional had run a 4:12¾ mile in 1886 (which no Briton bettered until Wooderson ran 4:12.7 in 1935!) and Wooderson's own coach, Albert Hill, the Olympic 800m and 1500m champion in 1920.

Thomas set off at a fast clip, drawing Wooderson with him, and the diminutive Blackheath Harrier was timed at 58.6 for the quarter – way inside the 60/61 envisaged. The half was reached in 2:02.6, the three-quarters in 3:07.2, and a stirring 59.2 last lap enabled Wooderson to lower American Glenn Cunningham's figures by 0.3 to become the first Briton in the 20th century to hold the world mile record. His time at 1500m en route of 3:50.3 was a British best. Wooderson's first three lap times were remarkably similar to those in George's record of 51 years earlier: 58.6, 64.0 and 64.6 as against George's 58¼, 63.5 and 66.0 (3:07 3/4). The huge difference was over the last quarter, run by Wooderson nearly six seconds faster than by athletics' legendary W.G.

Wooderson went on to other triumphs. In 1938, the only year in which he took the event seriously, he set a world half mile record of 1:49.2 (52.6 at halfway), clocking 1:48.4 for 800m en route for another world record in a handicap race staged at Motspur Park. Earlier in the month he had broken Godfrey Brown's British 880y record with 1:50.9 a few days after running a personal best 440y of 49.3 on a poor grass track. Later in the season he lifted the European 1500m title in 3:53.6, covering the final 300m in 43.6. His 1939 campaign, terminated prematurely by a calf injury, included a 4:07.4 mile and a world best three-quarter mile time of 2:59.5 (57.9, 62.1, 59.5). Who knows what he might have achieved in what would have been the Olympic years of 1940 and 1944 had the world not been at war.

Yet, astonishingly, he returned to major competition after the war, running better than ever despite having been dogged by ill health. Indeed, in the summer of 1944 he developed such severe rheumatism that he was in hospital for nearly four months, followed by two months' convalescence, and was told by doctors he could never run again.

They bargained without Wooderson's iron will. Physically frail he might have looked (he was 5ft 6 in or 1.68m tall and weighed 124lb or 56kg) but he was a real fighter. Within six months of leaving hospital he was racing again and amazingly later that same year (1945) he went on to run the fastest mile of his life – a British record of 4:04.2! That race, against Sweden's 4:01.6 ace Arne Andersson in Gothenburg, was the best of his career, Wooderson reckons. "I got through the war without proper training and racing, and yet finished only a couple of yards behind. I was pleased with that." His time en route at 1500m of 3:48.4 was also a British record and his 440y splits were 59.0, 61.5, 62.5 and 61.2.

It was the last major mile race he would run, but he had other worlds to conquer. In 1946 he broke the British 3 miles record in his first serious attempt at the distance with 13:53.2, covering the last lap in what was then considered the phenomenal time of 59.2, and he proceeded to capture the European 5000m title in Oslo in 14:08.6 – slashing a cool 23 sec from the British record and producing the world's second fastest ever time. His estimated 3 miles time was 13:42.0. Among his vanquished rivals was an unknown Czech by the name of Emil Zátopek (5th in 14:25.8) and Belgium's Gaston Reiff (6th in 14:45.8), both of whom would strike gold at the London Olympics two years later.

Even that wasn't quite the end of a glorious career, for in March 1948 Wooderson became English 10 miles cross country champion! Nobody since could claim to have been at one time or another the best runner in the world at 800m, the mile and 5000m, and it was shameful that as Britain's best known and most popular athlete he was not accorded the honour – as he had been led to believe – of carrying the Olympic torch at the opening ceremony of the London Olympics.

Now a retired solicitor, aged 91, Wooderson is glad he is not a modern full-time athlete. "I had it much easier in my day. I would find it very difficult to run as many hard races as they do today. I would have only about three serious races a year – say, the Southern Championships, the AAA Championships and the European Games – with club races in between."

The very thought of the twice a day training which is usual among present day middle distance runners appals him. "Good God, no!" He used to train just five times a week, normally warming up with a run of a couple of miles, doing his 'set piece' (for instance, a three-quarter mile time trial) and jogging another mile or two to warm down. It speaks volumes for his ability that on so little preparation he could run close to 1:48 for 800m and 4:04 for the mile, bearing in mind that there were no synthetic tracks in those days and his racing spikes probably weighed as much as today's road trainers.

The little man in glasses with the long stride and big heart, who inspired such affection from the British public of the 1930s and 1940s, was also the inspiration for many of the great British middle distance runners who came after him, not least Roger Bannister who as an impressionable 16 year-old schoolboy was taken by his father to see the epic Wooderson v Andersson mile clash at the White City in 1945 when 54,000 fans saw their hero run the Swede to four-tenths of a second, 4:08.8-4:09.2.

Wooderson's own source of inspiration was Jack Lovelock, the British-based New Zealander whom he would later rival as the world's premier miler. Between 1934 and

1936 they would meet six times over 1500m or the mile with Wooderson winning four of the races, including the AAA mile in 1936 just a few weeks before the Berlin Olympic 1500m in which Sydney, suffering from an ankle injury, failed to finish his heat and Jack went on to win the final in the world record time of 3:47.8.

Wooderson was one week short of his 32nd birthday when he won the European 5000m title in 1946; the war years coincided with what would have been the most fruitful period of his running career. Had the circumstances been different who's to say that Sydney Wooderson wouldn't have been the world's first sub-four minute miler?

GODFREY BROWN

Born 21.2.1915 Bankura (India); died 4.2.1995.
Clubs: Achilles, Birchfield H

RALPH BROWN (born in 1909) was a successful athlete, winning the AAA 440 yards hurdles title in 1934 and placing third in that year's Empire Games; and so was his sister Audrey (born in 1913), who won a silver medal in the 1936 Olympic 4x100m relay. But the shining star of the family was their younger sibling Godfrey.

He had demonstrated his versatility from the start of his career. Between 1932 and 1934 he not only won the Public Schools 880y title three years running but also took the long jump title in 1933, while at Cambridge he excelled particularly in the 440y, winning that event against Oxford for four consecutive years (1935-1938) as well as successes in the 100y (1937) and 880y (1938).

His great year was 1936, when he met with success at all distances from 100y (he clocked 9.7 on the slightly downhill Fenners track at Cambridge and defeated the redoubtable Arthur Sweeney at the Kinnaird Trophy in 9.9) to the 880y, at which he was Midland champion. Indeed, at the AAA v Cambridge match, he followed up his 9.7 with other victories in the 440y (49.1) and 880y (1:56.0); while at the Kinnaird, the unofficial English inter-club championship, he also took on 1934 Empire Games champion Godfrey Rampling at the quarter for the first time and beat him by inches in 48.3.

Brown, Rampling and Empire Games runner-up Bill Roberts clashed for the first and only time at the 1936 AAA Championships before a White City crowd of 40,000. It was a fine race, although driving rain ruined the times. Roberts went out too fast and cracked in the final straight, with both Brown and Rampling sailing past. Brown won by about 4m in 48.6. The trio reached the 400m semi-final stage in Berlin intact. The first semi saw Roberts safely through in second place in a relatively sedate 48.0 but Brown and Rampling had a tougher task in the other race, for it needed 47.4 to make the final. Brown succeeded with second in 47.3 (clipping 0.3 from Eric Liddell's 1924 UK record) but Rampling was edged out of third place in spite of returning 47.5, the fastest time of his career.

The draw for the final the same day was – from the inside – John Loaring (Canada), Bill Fritz (Canada), Jimmy LuValle (USA), Roberts, Archie Williams

(USA) and Brown. The latter got away very smartly and held the lead at the first bend but, endeavouring to relax, he eased off a shade too much along the back straight. The outcome was that with 150 yards left to run Williams held a lead of 2-3m. Brown strove valiantly to overcome the deficit and all along the finishing straight he was edging closer to the American ... but his mighty efforts resulted in glorious failure. At the tape Williams was still ahead: by seven inches to be precise! The photo finish timing apparatus credited Williams with 46.66 and Brown with 46.68, which makes nonsense of the differential in the official stopwatch times of 46.5 for Williams, 46.7 for Brown. As a European record, Brown's time lasted until 1939; as a British best it survived until 1958. An equally tense Anglo-American struggle ensued for the bronze medal, with Roberts failing by less than a foot to catch LuValle. Both men were given 46.8 (46.84 to 46.87 electrically).

For some strange reason best known to the selectors (over confidence perhaps?), Williams and LuValle were omitted from the USA foursome in the Olympic 4x400m; yet even so the best 400m times of the American team added up to 3:07.2 as against Britain's 3:09.6. Theoretically, then, the USA ought to have won by around 20m ... but fortunately athletic results are not based upon mathematical calculations. Bearing in mind the quality and fighting spirit of the last three runners Britain could win providing the weak link in the chain, Hong Kong-born Freddie Wolff (best time of only 48.6) could stay within reasonable distance of 46.5 performer Harold Cagle on the first leg.

Drawn in the outside lane, Wolff did his difficult job well. True, he took 49.2 for his leg but what mattered was that he finished merely 3-4m down on his American rival. The situation was tailor-made for Rampling (father of acclaimed film actress Charlotte Rampling), always at his best in relays, and with a time of 46.7 he swept Britain into a 3m lead. There was no stopping them now: Roberts (46.4) added another 2m and Brown (46.7) drew right away to snap the tape 15m clear in a superb 3:09.0, second fastest time ever and a European record.

One week afterwards at the White City, Roberts, Rampling and Brown joined forces with Canadian Fritz under the banner of the British Empire to defeat an all-star American team in 3:10.6. It bettered the world record for 4x440y but was unacceptable as the team was a composite one. The race was a thriller all the way and decided only in the last few strides when Brown, who had taken over some metres behind LuValle, came through for victory. His time: an astonishing 45.9!

Brown's successes in 1937 included an exceptional clocking of 19.2 for 200 yards amid the slush and snow of Fenners in February, a barnstorming American tour which yielded British records at 440y (47.7) and 880y (1:52.2), a 47.2 400m in Stockholm and victory at the World University Games. Another significant performance was a 1:51.2 880y (51.0 first 440y!) anchor leg in the mile medley relay against Germany, when he totally outpaced Rudolf Harbig who, two years later, set a phenomenal world 800m record of 1:46.6. In 1938 Brown went through the entire season undefeated and there is little doubt that he was the world's number one. He scored a runaway victory (in 47.4) in the European 400m championship and followed that with wins in Milan

(47.1) and Oslo (46.9). He also ran 47.6 for 440y at the White City, which was a British record but not officially an English one since Brown was born in India. A teacher who became headmaster of Worcester Royal Grammar School from 1950 to 1978, he died at the age of 79.

JIM PETERS

Born 24.10.1918 Homerton (London); died 9.1.1999.
Club: Essex Beagles

JIM PETERS HAD considered retiring after the disappointment of being lapped in the 1948 Olympic 10,000m. At the age of 29 he could look back on a certain measure of success as a track runner – AAA champion at 6 miles in 1946 and 10 miles in 1947 – and although his times were nowhere near world class he had at least achieved his ambition of representing his country.

His coach 'Johnny' Johnston (an Olympic 5000m finalist in 1928) pleaded with him to train for the next Olympic marathon. Peters was reluctant, for he knew the demands that would be made on his time and body, but after continual persuasion from Johnston and such marathon stars of the past as Sam Ferris and Harry Payne he decided, towards the end of 1949, to give it a try. The following May he entered his first long distance road race, the Essex '20', and won it in the moderate time of 1:59:50.

He stayed away from serious competition for the rest of the season and athletics followers could have been pardoned for believing that Peters had retired once and for all. In reality, he was steadily increasing the severity of his training, running (by the then accepted marathon standards) relatively short distances at only slightly under racing speed. The outcome of training every day, which few athletes attempted at that time, was that his weekly mileage was no less than that achieved by more traditional methods ... and the tempo was infinitely faster. In other words, quality had been introduced with no reduction in quantity. By the spring of 1951 Peters was almost ready to shake the road running world.

The first step was the Wigmore '15', which he won in 1:26:55. Later in April he finished second to Jack Holden in the Finchley '20' in 1:52:24. The final tune-up prior to the start of his marathon career was the Essex '20' in May. Here he revealed for the first time his amazing capabilities as he led right from the start to win in the unprecedented time of 1:47:08. No man had ever run the distance that fast and a remeasurement showed the course to be 600 yards short; nevertheless the time was worth about 1:49 for a full 20 miles. The revolution was under way.

It was thus amid much interest and speculation that Peters made his marathon debut in the Polytechnic race from Windsor to Chiswick in June 1951. Good twenty-milers before then had come unstuck over those torturous last 6 miles and 385 yards. Did Peters have what it takes? Jack Holden, for one, was soon to find out. Peters passed the ageing champion before 20 miles, which point he reached in

1:52:05, and stormed away to win by five minutes from another 'first-timer', pre-war 5000m international Stan Cox, in 2:29:24. First to congratulate Peters at the finish was the race referee Harry Payne, whose British record of 2:30:58 set in 1929 had at last been broken. A few weeks later Peters won the AAA title in 2:31:42.

Much faster over the shorter distances than ever before as a result of his enlightened training methods, Peters filled fourth place in the 1952 English cross country championship (he had never previously finished higher than 46th) and represented England. Back on the road he was untouchable, covering the Finchley '20' in 1:49:39 and an accurately measured Essex '20' in 1:48:33. These times were judged phenomenal but it was in the combined AAA/Polytechnic Marathon that he really left the athletics world gasping. The wide difference in courses makes accurate comparison of marathon performances difficult but up until 14 June 1952 the fastest ever recorded was 2:25:39 by Yun Bok Suh of Korea in Boston in 1947. What a sensation, therefore, when Peters snapped the tape in the Polytechnic Stadium, Chiswick, just 2:20:43 after leaving Windsor! Almost as incredible was the time of Cox, another Johnston protégé, in second place (2:21:42). 'Short course' was the first thought of the sceptics but the distance was found to be 260 yards over the standard!

Peters and Cox travelled to Helsinki the following month as favourites for the Olympic gold and silver medals, regardless of the announced intention of Emil Zátopek to contest the marathon as well as the 5000m and 10,000m. Alas, neither was able to finish the race, which the incredible Zátopek won by two and a half minutes in 2:23:04 to complete a treble that may never be emulated. Seemingly carried away by the occasion, Peters opened up a 100m lead while speeding through the first 10k in 31:55. He was caught shortly before 10 miles and just after the halfway mark, while in third place, he developed severe cramp in his left leg. He hobbled gallantly on until eventually collapsing after 19 miles. Meanwhile Cox, suffering from pains all down his left side, had blacked out four miles earlier while in sixth position.

Peters did his best to erase the memory of this blow during a 1953 season of sustained brilliance. He won all four of his marathons: the 'Poly' (142m over distance this time) in a world's best of 2:18:41, the AAA in 2:22:29, the Enschede race in 2:19:22 and the Turku event in another world's fastest of 2:18:35 – a mile and a quarter ahead of Finland's sub-2:20 performer Veikko Karvonen. In addition Peters recorded 29:01.8 for 6 miles for third place on the British all-time list and removed Walter George's 69 year-old English one hour record with 11M 986y on a blazing hot afternoon.

For Peters, 1954 was the important year. The year in which to compensate for Olympic disappointment by winning Commonwealth and European titles. Four marathon races were scheduled. In the first, the Boston classic, he was runner-up to Karvonen in 2:22:40, but in the AAA event over his favourite Windsor to Chiswick route he lowered the world's best yet again with the stupendous time of 2:17:40, with his perpetual shadow Cox second in 2:23:08.

Having just set a personal best 6 miles time of 28:57.8, Peters made his way to

Vancouver for the Commonwealth Games in good spirits. He ran well there for the bronze medal in the 6 miles and all seemed ready for his first major title. The afternoon of the marathon was hot and humid, the long distance runner's nightmare, for even in normal weather the marathon runner sweats profusely and can lose several pounds in bodyweight.

It was obviously prudent to move off at a relatively modest pace in order to guard against the body becoming overheated and dehydrated but Peters, by nature, was a man who refused to compromise. He would not hold himself back and at 20 miles, reached in 1:48, he was a quarter of a mile ahead of Cox with the rest of the field almost literally miles behind.

Disaster struck both men practically simultaneously. Sunstroke caused Cox to run straight into a steel lamp post less than two miles from the stadium, while just a few minutes later the cruel conditions took their toll of Peters. A good quarter of an hour in front of the next survivor, Peters entered the stadium in a groggy manner and proceeded to horrify the crowd (which had thrilled to the greatest mile duel in history, Roger Bannister v John Landy, only minutes earlier) for the next eleven minutes as he repeatedly fell over while attempting to cover the last few hundred yards of track.

The agony came to an end, at least for the spectators, just 200 yards from the mirage of the finishing tape when officials, unable to stand by helplessly any longer, carried him off. Peters, who had intended running in the European Championships 18 days later, never raced again. Indeed he was lucky to stay alive and for the rest of his life (he died at the age of 80) he was afflicted by headaches and giddiness from that ordeal in the sun.

The winner, by the way, was Scotland's Joe McGhee in 2:39:36, but just as the 1908 Olympic marathon will for ever be remembered for the name of the loser, Dorando Pietri, so Vancouver will always be associated with Jim Peters. And, like his Italian predecessor, he was singled out by royalty. He later received a special gold medal from the Duke of Edinburgh, who had watched his agony, inscribed: 'To J. Peters as a token of admiration for a most gallant marathon runner'.

DOROTHY TYLER

Born 14.3.1920 Stockwell (London).
Club: Mitcham AC

THE DISTINCTION OF becoming the first British female athlete to gain an Olympic medal fell to Dorothy Odam who, as the 16 year-old baby of the team in Berlin in 1936 and on her first trip abroad ("I'd never been further than Bognor"), placed second in the high jump. In fact she was unlucky to come away with the silver rather than the gold medal for she cleared the winning height of 1.60 at the first attempt, while Hungary's Ibolya Csák managed it at the second try and Elfriede Kaun of Germany at the third.

Dorothy Tyler

All three failed at 1.62, so under the rule now in effect Dorothy would have been the winner. But in 1936 a jump-off was decreed and Csák – who this time succeeded at 1.62 whereas Dorothy could go no higher than 1.60 – claimed victory. A few days later the IAAF passed a new rule governing ties and, had that been in effect in Berlin, Dorothy would have been hailed as Britain's first women's Olympic champion ... fully 28 years before Mary Rand.

Dorothy had ranked equal fifth in the world in 1935 with 1.60 and jumped higher than anyone else in 1936 with a British record of 1.65 in the Southern Championships. That actually tied the world record but was not ratified. Dorothy topped the 1937 world list too at 1.635 and she was still only 17 when she won the 1938 Empire Games title in Sydney (1.60). The following year she scissored over 1.66 at the Southern Championships in Brentwood for what was eventually ratified as a world record. At the time the listed world record was 1.70 by Dora Ratjen of Germany in 1938, but 'she' turned out to be 'he' (renamed Hermann) and the record was deleted.

There was a change of name also for Dorothy; in 1940 she married Richard Tyler. She served in the Women's Auxiliary Air Force (WAAFs) as a driver and PT instructor from1941 to 1945 and it was not until after the birth of two sons in 1946 and 1947 that she returned to top-flight high jumping.

What a comeback it was. Competing in her native city of London at the 1948 Olympics she again went so tantalisingly close to victory. She was in the lead after clearing 1.66, equalling her British record, at the first try but she needed two attempts at 1.68 while Alice Coachman of the USA succeeded at the first ... and Dorothy had to settle again for silver. That jump of 1.68 (matching her own physical height) ranked her equal first on the world list for 1948 and she was out on her own in 1949 with two clearances at 1.65.

In 1950 she retained the Empire Games title after a gap of 12 years with 1.60 and later that year in the European Championships placed second at 1.63, same height as the winner, her team-mate Sheila Alexander (later Lerwill). Now coached by Arthur Gold, in 1951 she changed her style from the outmoded scissors to the western roll. Despite being short of training after a groin injury and being hampered by a pulled stomach muscle she placed equal seventh at the 1952 Olympics, at the 1954 Commonwealth Games she took the silver medal and at the 1956 Olympics – 20 years after her Berlin debut – she finished equal 12th. That ended her international career but as late as 1961, aged 41, she ranked fifth in Britain at 1.63! She continued in club competition for another two years.

Dorothy was also a fine all-rounder, winning the WAAA long jump and pentathlon titles in 1951, setting a British record in the latter event. Her individual personal bests included 11.8 for 80m hurdles (1950) and 5.73 long jump (1951) with a wind-aided 5.75 (1956), while at the 1950 Empire Games she placed fourth in the javelin (32.84). She later became a coach, official and British team manager as well as taking up golf and these days, at 85, maintains a keen interest in athletics.

ARTHUR WINT

Born 25.5.1920 Manchester (Jamaica); died 20.10.1992.
Club: Polytechnic H

HE WAS JAMAICA'S renaissance man. To have become his nation's first Olympic champion would have been sufficient glory for one lifetime, but Arthur Wint achieved high distinction in other areas too.

He served as an RAF pilot during the war (he attained the rank of Flight Lieutenant), qualified from London's St Bartholomew's Hospital and went on to become a surgeon, and from 1974 to 1978 held Jamaica's most prestigious diplomatic post as High Commissioner to London. A dignified and caring man, he was in every sense an outstanding ambassador for his country.

Although he represented Jamaica in two Olympic Games, Wint was very much part of the British athletics scene in the 1940s and early 1950s, and indeed he ran in the British vest in several matches. There was no more popular victory among the home fans at Wembley Stadium than his unexpected triumph in the 400m.

His international career had begun ten years earlier when, aged 17, he had won the 800m and placed third in the 400m hurdles at the 1938 Central American & Caribbean Games in Panama City. Born of a Jamaican Presbyterian minister (himself a former long jumper of some ability) and a mother of partly Scottish descent, the lanky youngster – who grew to a full height of 1.95m or almost 6ft 5 in with a nine-foot stride to match – was adept at a wide range of physical activities. He won two Jamaican swimming titles and before arriving in Britain as an RAF officer in 1944 he could point to such personal bests as 9.9 for 100y, 48.4 440y (ranking him equal ninth in the world in 1943), 1:56.3 800m, 55.3 440y hurdles, 1.88 high jump using the scissors style and a Jamaican record 7.31 long jump which ranked 30th in the world for 1941.

He began to enliven the British scene once the war was over and in 1946, besides winning AAA titles at 440y and 880y, he made his British international debut, finishing second to Tom White over 880y in a match against France at London's White City which attracted a capacity crowd of nearly 50,000 war-weary, sports-starved fans.

Wint clocked world class times of 47.0 for 400m and 1:50.6 for 800m in Sweden that year, and that 400m mark remained his fastest until the 1948 Olympics where, although recognised as a strong contender for a medal, he was given little chance of beating his fellow Jamaican and former schoolmate Herb McKenley, a man who had set world record figures of 46.0 for 440y (worth 45.7 for 400m) two months earlier.

Whatever hopes Wint might have entertained seemed to be dashed when he streaked to a brilliant but extravagant clocking of 46.3 in his semi ... with the final to follow less than two hours later. But McKenley, who cruised through his race in 47.3, was aware that his friend was in the greatest form of his life (three days earlier Wint had finished second to the USA's Mal Whitfield in the 800m final in a personal best of 1:49.5), attempted to run the legs off him – and committed a fatal error of pace judgement on the heavy cinder track.

At the 200m mark McKenley was seven metres up in 21.4, only 0.3 slower than the winning 200m time at those Games, but he began to tie up when the finishing straight was reached and the 28 year-old University of London medical student (who reached 200m in 22.2) almost reluctantly overtook his desperately flailing opponent 20m from the tape to win in 46.2. He had fleetingly wondered whether to let McKenley win, knowing how much victory would mean to his rival, "but he was decelerating so fast I passed him."

A second gold medal might have come his way in the 4x400m relay but, running the third leg, Wint collapsed with cramp and left the track in tears. It would be a different story four years later.

Together with his fellow Polytechnic Harrier, McDonald Bailey (who hailed from Trinidad), Wint became the greatest crowd-puller in British athletics until the rise of Roger Bannister, Gordon Pirie and Chris Chataway. He was an awe-inspiring apparition when in full flight, his towering height and prodigious lazy-looking stride always drawing gasps of wonder and admiration from spectators, one of whom was this writer who – as a young schoolboy attending his first AAA Championships in 1950 – was so entranced by the sight of Wint in action that he became hooked on the sport for life.

Wint would never run faster than 46.2 for 400m, although he was once clocked at 45.8 in a relay, but at the 1951 AAA Championships he recorded his best ever 880y time of 1:49.6 (equivalent to 1:48.9 for 800m), the fastest in the world that year.

As in London four years earlier, it was the stylish Whitfield who triumphed in the Helsinki Olympic 800m of 1952, returning exactly the same time of 1:49.2 ... and a close second again was Wint who improved on his previous Olympic time by a tenth with 1:49.4.

Three days later history repeated itself as Wint won his 400m semi in 46.3, but in the final later that afternoon it was he, not McKenley this time, who suffered from a suicidally fast start. Equalling his personal best at 200m, the defending champion swept past the halfway mark in 21.7 and paid the penalty by fading to fifth in 47.0. Nevertheless, it was Jamaica's day as George Rhoden (in the outside lane) won from McKenley, each sharing an Olympic record of 45.9.

There was further glory for Jamaica in an epic 4x400m relay. The quartet of Wint (46.8), Les Laing (47.0), McKenley (with a fabulous 44.6, when the world record from blocks stood at 45.8!) and Rhoden (45.5) beat the Americans by less than a metre in a world record shattering 3:03.9 after one of the most enthralling duels in Olympic annals.

Thus Wint closed his Olympic account with two golds and two silvers. A few weeks later he bowed out of international athletics with an emotional lap of honour at a floodlit meeting at the White City. This dignified, multi-talented man died in Jamaica aged 72.

McDONALD BAILEY
Born 8.12.1920 Williamsville (Trinidad).
Club: Polytechnic H

BETWEEN 1946 AND 1953 Emmanuel McDonald Bailey established himself as one of the greatest crowd pleasers in British athletics history. No important meeting was complete without the sight of this tall, slim Polytechnic Harrier in full flight. If any sprinter personified 'poetry in motion' it was McDonald Bailey. His high-level consistency over a long period was astonishing; more often than not running against mediocre opposition on sluggish tracks and in unfavourable weather conditions he turned in dozens of clockings in the range of 9.6-9.8 for 100y and 21.1-21.5 for 220y. In 'Mac' Bailey Britain had the good fortune to possess one of the world's most distinguished sprinters of that era and one wonders what he might have achieved had he been resident in the United States, with the good tracks, weather and competition he would have encountered there. As it was, he almost invariably recorded his greatest times abroad, notably his world record equalling 10.2 for 100m in Belgrade in 1951.

As an 18 year-old, Bailey had made his AAA Championships debut in 1939. Racing on a cinder track for the first time he progressed no further than the heats of the 100y and the semi-finals of the 220y on that occasion, a state of affairs he was to rectify in no uncertain manner in later years. After recording 9.8 and 21.2 in his native Trinidad during the war years, and while still serving in the RAF, Bailey made an indelible impression on the 1946 AAA Championships, the first for seven years, by notching the first sprint double since 1932. He made an outstanding debut for Great Britain by taking the 100y against France in 9.7, a good three yards ahead of Jack Archer, whom he had beaten easily also in the Championships. These convincing victories indicated his standing in Europe, for less than three weeks after the French match Archer captured the European 100m crown in Oslo in 10.6. Bailey, who was ineligible for those Championships, clocked a breathtaking 10.3 in Sweden a few days later – a tenth of a second outside the official world record shared by Americans Jesse Owens and Hal Davis – in defeating Archer by some four metres. It was the fastest time yet by a British qualified sprinter but although none of his marks were ratified as British records several attained European record status.

Bailey enjoyed another devastating season in 1947 and posted marks of the calibre of 9.6 (and a wind-assisted 9.4) for 100y, 10.3 for 100m and 21.2 for 200m. One of his 9.6's came in a heat of the inter-county championships at the White City ("I was not even trying", he claimed) but unfortunately while heading for a sensational time in the final – certainly a 9.5, perhaps even a world record tying 9.4 – he pulled a thigh muscle 20y from the tape while travelling at about 25 mph. Clasping his leg, he hopped the remainder of the distance in agony and anguish ... and still managed to hold on for victory in 10.0!

It was during 1947 that a 21 year-old Coldstream Guard, Lt Alistair McCorquodale, embarked upon his brief and brilliant career and placed fifth in the AAA 100y. That was no indication of what was to follow in 1948. With his considerable raw power properly harnessed, thanks to coaching by former Olympic 400m hero Guy Butler, McCorquodale was a revelation at the Wembley Olympics. Although he had never run faster than 9.9 for 100y or 10.8 for 100m, the burly Scot ran the great American star Barney Ewell (co-holder of the world record of 10.2) to inches in their heat as both were timed in 10.5. He clocked another 10.5 in the second round and both he and Bailey, who was hampered by injury all season, fought their way into the final. McCorquodale then proceeded to thrill the huge crowd by the way he dared to match strides with his famed transatlantic rivals, men who could have given him a five-yard start only a few months earlier. He did not win a medal ... but how close he came. Harrison Dillard (USA) won in 10.3 from Ewell (10.4) and Lloyd La Beach of Panama (10.4) with the inspired Briton fourth in 10.4, equalling Arthur Sweeney's UK record. Later he, together with Archer, Ken Jones and Jack Gregory, gained a silver medal in the relay – and that, more or less, was the end of his track career. He preferred cricket.

As for Bailey (who represented Britain as Trinidad did not have its own Olympic Committee), he finished sixth and last at Wembley in 10.6 and was unfit for the relay, yet when asked in 1950 to single out his most pleasing performance he chose that Olympic 100m final. "Why? Because I had to battle not only against the opposition but against nature, and to reach the final was a just reward. To do this when I was supposedly 'finished' and against mental strain, worry, tension and illness, leaves me extremely gratified."

The 1949 season marked a return to normality, i.e. Bailey 'streets' ahead of all domestic rivals. While in Iceland he recorded spectacular times of 9.5 for 100y and what was adjudged to be a wind assisted 10.2 for 100m although there was no wind gauge in operation and Bailey always thought it to be a genuine performance which would have equalled the world record. He matched his best acceptable time of 10.3 in 1950 as well as breaking through in the longer sprint with 20.9 for 200m. On top of that, he made history by gaining his fourth AAA double ... and would go on to defend both titles successfully for another three years!

Bailey enjoyed his day of days in the Yugoslavia v Britain match in Belgrade in 1951. "Carried by the electrifying urge of the 40,000 crowd", as he put it, he took full advantage of the perfect conditions to equal the world record of 10.2, owned among others by his boyhood hero, Jesse Owens. Next day he tied his personal best (and European record) of 20.9 for 200m. Earlier in the season he was timed at a windy 20.5 over a straight 220y course with Norris McWhirter, later of *Guinness Book of Records* fame, second in 21.5.

Carrying his age lightly, 31 year-old Bailey, whose gazelle like speed and grace had made him a household name in Britain, shaped up as a potential winner of the 1952 Olympic 100m; perhaps also of the 200m for there were few to equal him as a curve runner whereas his starting prowess was relatively ordinary. Largely self-coached and one of the first British sprinters to make use of weight training, Bailey was a stylist of the classic school but it was just his textbook carriage that may have cost him the Olympic

100m crown in Helsinki. Although drawn in one of the worst two lanes, which had been saturated by rainwater dripping from the overlapping grandstand roof, Bailey was on terms with Lindy Remigino (USA) and Herb McKenley (Jamaica) 10m from the finish. But whereas his two rivals lunged for the tape Bailey maintained his upright form, ran through the tape as coaches insist, and lost the race. "It was one of those times," he commented ruefully, "when if I'd stuck out my chest I might have won." As it was, the little known Remigino snatched the verdict by 1/100th of a second from McKenley with Bailey another 3/100ths behind. Officially, all three were credited with a hand timed 10.4. Bailey resolved to win the 200m or bust; in fact he tied up in the straight to finish fourth behind the American trio in 21.0. Nobody questioned the ability of Bailey to have become an Olympic champion; it was his lack of high pressure competition that cost him so dearly.

Bailey wound up his long career in 1953, shortly after gaining his seventh AAA sprint double, in order to turn (briefly) to professional rugby league. His career statistics were astonishing. According to research by Bernard Linley and Ulf Lagerstrom published in *Track Stats*, Bailey lost just nine of his 124 races at 200m/220y and he was unbeaten by a Briton in that event between September 1945 and June 1953. Now in his 85th year, 'Mac' (this writer's first athletics hero, along with Arthur Wint) can take pride from the fact that over half a century later he is still remembered with great affection and admiration by those who marvelled at his speed and consistency.

SHEILA LERWILL

Born 16.8.1928 London.
Clubs: Selsonia Ladies AC, Spartan Ladies AC

SHEILA LERWILL (née Alexander), an international netball player who did not take up athletics until she was 18, occupies a place of importance in the history of women's high jumping on two counts. She held the world record at 1.72 from 1951 to 1954 and, coached by pre-war long jump international George Pallett, was the pioneer among women straddle jumpers.

In his book *Women's Athletics*, published in 1955, Pallett explained that Sheila – then using the scissors style – came under his coaching influence as an Olympic high jump 'possible' for the 1948 Games. Her best then, in 1947, was 1.50. "It was apparent," Pallett wrote, "that while appearing to have no really exceptional spring she was, in general, an attractive athletic proposition. Highly strung, but with a strength of character and self control out of the ordinary, she did not appear likely to be upset by difficulties and she was keen to do well. She was well-built, active and fairly tall – 5ft 7in (1.70m). It was my view that the scissors style of jumping, outmoded and uneconomical for men, was not the best for women, and after consultation with a medical specialist in women's health troubles, I put it to Sheila that, if she changed to the straddle style, at least a British record was a possibility in time, but that as a change would take months to become really effective she might not qualify for the Olympic Games."

She did indeed miss the London Games. Although she progressed in 1948 to 1.57 that ranked her fourth in Britain and she failed to make the team. However, the steady improvement continued with a 1.60 clearance for second to Dorothy Tyler in the 1949 WAAA Championships, and in 1950 – by now more assured with her new technique – she came into her own with victory in the WAAA Championships (1.62), a new British record of 1.69 for second place on the world all-time list and a gold medal (1.63) in poor conditions at the European Championships with Tyler in second place.

The following year was even more notable for Sheila. In March she became Mrs Michael Lerwill and in July she enjoyed her greatest moment at the WAAA Championships at the White City. At her first attempt she succeeded at 1.72 to add a centimetre to the world record which had been held by the astonishingly versatile Dutchwoman Fanny Blankers-Koen (winner of four track event gold medals at the 1948 Olympics) since 1943. Among the small crowd was the author of this book, aged 13 and thrilled to witness his first world record!

Despite suffering from a high temperature, cough and a calf bleeding from a spike scratch, Sheila put up a great fight at the 1952 Olympics in Helsinki. Third-time clearances at 1.63 and 1.65 kept her in contention for the gold medal but South Africa's Esther Brand, a scissors jumper who had briefly held the world record at 1.66 in 1941, had cleared 1.65 at the second attempt and clinched the title by making 1.67.

Sheila's silver medal was the third in a row by a Briton, following Tyler in 1936 and 1948 ... and the sequence would be maintained by Thelma Hopkins in 1956 and Dorothy Shirley in 1960. Alas, the highest placing by a British woman during the last 30 years has been equal 8th by Diana Davies in 1988.

In 1953 Sheila went on to win her third WAAA title and make a number of narrowly unsuccessful world record attempts, ending the year though with a world indoor best of 1.67 in an exhibition at Wembley. In her final season of 1954 she lifted her fourth national title ahead of Tyler and Hopkins and placed fourth in the Commonwealth Games, fifth in the European Championships with both gold medals going to Hopkins.

CHRIS BRASHER

Born 21.8.1928 Georgetown (British Guiana, now Guyana); died 28.2.2003. Club: Achilles

IT IS ONE of the rich ironies of the sport that whereas the first four minute miler Roger Bannister and world 5000m record breaker Chris Chataway never won so much as an Olympic bronze medal between them it was their less exalted training companion, Chris Brasher, who was to become Britain's first Olympic athletics champion since 1936.

Brasher was for years merely a capable but unexceptional flat runner, his only noteworthy success being victory in the World Student Games 5000m in 1951, and it was not until he switched to the steeplechase – an event more suited to his rugged qualities – that he became a world class performer. He made the 1952 Olympic team and in Helsinki improved by over 10 seconds with 9:03.2 in his heat. In the final he pluckily limped home 11th out of 12 after crashing into a barrier on the second lap.

He put his own ambitions on hold for the next two seasons, becoming better known to the public as Bannister's pacemaker and training colleague, and returned to serious steeplechasing in 1955, improving to 8:49.2. That ranked him tenth in the world that year, but he was still only third best in Britain behind John Disley (8:44.2) and Eric Shirley (8:47.6).

Brasher still appeared to be very much the third string at the 1956 AAA Championships where Shirley outsprinted Disley, 8:51.6 to 8:53.4. Brasher finished far behind in 9:02.6 and for a while he was in danger of being omitted from the Olympic team. He later ran Disley (8:46.6) close with a personal best of 8:47.2 to win his ticket.

However, the final test before departure for Melbourne was not a happy one: Brasher tripped headlong into the water early in the race and finished a bedraggled fifth in 9:09.4, Shirley fell heavily and dropped out, and Disley – the winner in 8:57.2 – was short of training following an illness. The first indication that Brasher might fare best of the three came with the exciting news from Australia 15 days before the steeplechase final that he had slashed nearly 13 sec off his fastest 2 miles time with 8:45.6. Reunited with his charismatic coach, Franz Stampfl, Brasher was obviously in the best form of his career.

All three Britons made the ten-man Olympic final and at the bell five runners were still in contention. The order was Semyon Rzhishchin (USSR), Hungarian world record holder Sándor Rozsnyoi, Brasher, Ernst Larsen of Norway and Disley. Shirley, a bundle of nerves, had dropped out of the medal hunt. As the Soviet runner flagged so Rozsnyoi, Brasher and Larsen challenged for the leadership. The Hungarian showed ahead briefly but, four barriers from home, Brasher attacked. Taking his rivals completely by surprise he quickly opened up a gap which stretched to 15m by the finish. Brasher, for so many years little more than an honest plodder, was Olympic champion!

Or was he? The result of the steeplechase, boomed the public address system: "First, Rozsnyoi." Brasher, it transpired, had been disqualified "for interference in the last lap"; more explicitly for obstructing Larsen over the fourth hurdle from home. The Norwegian immediately rallied to Brasher's cause. "Whatever happened," he said, "there was no need for disqualification. Brasher and I both tried to pass Rozsnyoi on the outside together when our elbows touched. It would be shocking to take the gold medal off Brasher." Rozsnyoi also supported Brasher, as did Heinz Laufer, the German who had been promoted to third. "Chris, I do not want my bronze medal like this. If they do not give you the gold medal I will throw my medal back at them." This was sportsmanship at its finest.

An appeal was lodged and, three nerve-racking hours after Brasher snapped the tape, the jury's verdict was announced. "After hearing the evidence of all those concerned, including the two athletes affected, the jury decided unanimously to allow the appeal and Brasher is therefore placed first. The jury consider that Brasher and Larsen came into contact with each other but that it was unintentional and both athletes stated that it did not affect their running." Brasher's time of 8:41.2 was a British and Olympic record. He had covered the final kilometre in a searing 2:47.2. Rozsnyoi was second in 8:43.6, Larsen third in 8:44.0 with Disley sixth in 8:44.6 and Shirley eighth in 8:57.0. After protracted and largely liquid celebrations, Brasher admitted he was more than slightly tipsy when the victory ceremony was held next day!

For Brasher it was a triumphant finale to an otherwise unremarkable career, having never previously won either a national title or an international match event. "Well done the old scrubber" read the telegram he received from his training companions back in London.

Chris Chataway, in Melbourne, said of Brasher: "He is five per cent ability and 95 per cent guts." Bannister wrote of him: "He ran the most perfect race of which he was capable. Brasher, the mountaineer, who was once considered for a Himalayan reconnaisance expedition, had now climbed his own personal Everest."

He never raced again on the track but nearly 25 years after his Olympic triumph Brasher was responsible for another momentous happening when he conceived and masterminded (with Disley as his right-hand man) the London Marathon. Hearing wondrous stories about the New York City Marathon he entered the 1979 edition and was smitten. Writing in *The Observer*, for whom he was athletics correspondent for many years, he began his account: "To believe this story you must believe that the human race be one joyous family, working together, laughing together, achieving the impossible. Last Sunday, in one of the most trouble-stricken cities in the world, 11,532 men and women from 40 countries in the world, assisted by over a million black, white and yellow people, laughed, cheered and suffered during the greatest folk festival the world has seen."

He ended the article by wondering whether London could stage such an inspiring event. The rest is history. Thanks to Brasher's visionary zeal, organisational skills and forceful personality the first London Marathon was held in March 1981 and it eventually superseded New York as the world's biggest, most colourful and classiest marathon.

A huge charity fund raiser each year it is part of the very fabric of London life and for that initiative alone Brasher merited the knighthood he never received.

Renaissance man Brasher was also involved in popularising the sport of orienteering in Britain, and in addition to being a prize-winning journalist and broadcaster (BBC Television's Head of General Features) he was also a most successful businessman. His wife, the former Shirley Bloomer, was ranked no 3 tennis player in the world in 1957 and their daughter Kate was twice British junior tennis champion. He died aged 74.

MAUREEN GARDNER
Born 12.11.1928 Oxford; died 2.9.1974.
Club: Oxford Ladies AC

ONLY MONTHS AFTER the tragically early death of 1964 Olympic 400m hurdles silver medallist John Cooper in the Paris air crash of 1974, Britain prematurely lost another of her most distinguished hurdlers. Maureen Dyson, who as Maureen Gardner was Olympic 80m hurdles silver medallist in 1948, died after a long illness, aged only 45. She was the wife of former AAA Chief National Coach Geoff Dyson.

Maureen, one of the most charming and attractive of women to grace the sport, was a good sprinter before her future husband made her into a great hurdler. She cherished an ambition of becoming a professional ballet dancer but after contracting bronchial pneumonia and pleurisy in 1945 she was told by doctors to put that out of her mind (she was later to run a ballet school, though). During her convalescence, her father happened to take her to the Oxford University track at a time when the newly founded Oxford Ladies AC were holding a training session and that evening Maureen decided to join the club. Within months she was county 100 yards champion. She won the WAAA 100m title in 1946 as a 17 year-old and placed fifth in the European Championships ... from novice to international in a year.

The turning point of her life occurred in February 1947 when Geoff Dyson visited Oxford. After watching her train on the snow-covered track he announced that he was prepared to coach her – but as a hurdler. Five months later she was WAAA 80m hurdles champion in the British record time of 11.5. Maureen became an Olympic medal contender when in June 1948 she clocked a wind-assisted 11.2, as compared to the listed world record of 11.3 although Dutchwoman Fanny Blankers-Koen had registered a legal 11.0 a few days earlier.

At the Wembley Olympics Maureen thrilled the huge crowd and became Britain's best known sportswoman by running Blankers-Koen to inches in the final, sharing the winning time of 11.2 for a British record which stood for six years. Maureen was away to a superb start but ticked the second hurdle which enabled Fanny to draw level and gain the narrowest of advantages which she held to the end. An interesting sidelight on that day was provided by Maureen in an article she wrote for *World Sports* – "I arrived at Wembley by underground train only just in time for the briefest of warm-ups, after fellow passengers had given up their seats to enable me to stretch out on the journey from Baker Street Station!"

Another fascinating insight into this close fought duel came from Blankers-Koen, who ranked that race the most memorable but nerve-racking of her career.

"Never shall I forget the day of the heats. I went to the warm-up track behind Wembley Stadium that morning as the Olympic 100m gold medallist, but nobody could ever have felt less like a champion. My knees trembled. Never had I been so nervous before a race. I went through my warming-up as usual, but my mind was not on it. All the time I was waiting for a glimpse of my rival, Maureen Gardner, whom I had never seen before. She arrived by car, and made a considerable impression on me when I saw that she had brought her own hurdles. An athlete who carries her own hurdles around must really be in the top class, I thought.

"There were no other hurdles available on the training track and because I felt in need of a little practice over the flights before the first heat, I summoned up my courage and asked if I could use hers. We shook hands and I noticed immediately that I was not the only one who was nervous. Both of us were on tenterhooks. Just how good Maureen was I was soon to see. In her semi-final, she scraped a hurdle and lost her balance, but she still managed to achieve third position and a place in the final. My husband was cautious. 'Fanny,' he said, 'no long jumping for you tomorrow. You must concentrate on the hurdles, because this English girl knows her business'".

She certainly did, and the 19 year-old, in only her second season at the event, ran the race of her life. For a while it looked as though she would become the first British woman to win an Olympic athletics title. Blankers-Koen got away to a dreadful start but managed to draw level with Maureen approaching the fifth hurdle. Then disaster loomed up again for the Dutch star. She recalled: "I was going so fast that I went too close to the hurdle, hit it, and lost my balance. What happened after that is just a blurred memory. It was a grim struggle, in which my hurdling style went to pieces. I staggered like a drunkard."

It was close, but by a matter of inches 30 year-old Blankers-Koen had won. "Maureen and I shook hands. It had been a wonderful race and I was proud to have beaten such a brilliant athlete. We left the ground and went to our waiting coaches. My husband was feeling as delighted as I was. 'Well done, Fanny,' he said, 'you aren't too old, after all' – and he left his congratulations at that! But there was Geoff Dyson, giving Maureen a long, long kiss. Ah well ... as somebody standing near said afterwards, 'that's the difference between an engaged couple and a staid old married pair!'"

Maureen and Geoff were married six weeks after the Games to become the most celebrated couple in British athletics. She retired to start a family, but made a successful return to the track in 1950, clocking her fastest hurdles time (a windy 11.1) and winning another silver medal behind Blankers-Koen, this time at the European Championships. News of Maureen's untimely death broke at the start of the 1974 European Championships, shocking all who knew and admired her.

ROGER BANNISTER

Born 23.3.1929 Harrow (Middlesex). Club: Achilles

AS THE WORLD'S first sub-four minute miler, Roger Bannister is arguably the most celebrated name in British athletics history ... and in a way his success can be traced back to one of his predecessors as world mile record holder, Sydney Wooderson. Bannister was 16 when taken by his father to the great August Bank Holiday meeting at the White City in 1945 and the sight of Wooderson battling against Sweden's Arne Andersson made a deep impression on him. "Seeing Wooderson's run that day inspired me with a new interest that has continued ever since," Bannister wrote in his outstanding autobiography, *First Four Minutes*. As Wooderson was coached by 1920 double Olympic champion Albert Hill, whose trainers had included Walter George, there is also a neat link between the man who revolutionised mile running in 1886 and the man who realised the ultimate miling dream in 1954.

On going up to study medicine at Exeter College, Oxford in October 1946, Bannister decided to train seriously for athletics. He made his miling debut in the freshmen's sports that autumn but it was an unspectacular beginning to a momentous career. Uncharacteristically, as it was to turn out, he tried to lead all the way and was beaten in the finishing sprint; his time a mediocre 4:53.

But it was not long before his talent shone through. Although nominally the third string he won the 1947 inter-varsity race the day before his 18th birthday in 4:30.8. He improved to 4:24.6 that season and was invited to become a 'possible' for the following year's Olympic team but he declined the offer as he felt himself unready for such a level of competition. His eyes were already trained upon the 1952 Olympics.

In fact Bannister did make the British Olympic team at Wembley; not as a competitor but as assistant to Evan Hunter, the *chef de mission*. The following year he developed into a miler of international significance. On an Oxford and Cambridge tour of the USA he clocked 4:11.1, the world's fastest by a 20 year-old up to that time. Already people were talking about him as a potential four minute miler.

Examinations in July 1950 left little time for intensive training, so Bannister decided to concentrate on the half mile that season. He followed Arthur Wint home in the AAA Championships and, in his very first international appearance for Britain, finished a splendid third in 1:50.7 in the European Championships 800m final inches behind team-mate John Parlett and French veteran Marcel Hansenne. Just before year's end, in New Zealand, he reduced his best mile time to 4:09.9 with a 57.1 last lap.

The mystique surrounding the lanky, long striding medical student grew throughout 1951. Almost god-like in action he seemed to epitomise the ancient Greek concept of athletic perfection. More to the point, as the Press was eager to exploit, in Bannister Britain possessed a miler capable of becoming the first man to break through the four-minute barrier. A remote figure inclined to recoil from the massive publicity surrounding him, he strictly rationed his appearances at the major meetings. Thus, every race of his at the White City assumed the nature of a special occasion and the crowds flocked through the turnstiles to watch.

Although he ran no faster than 4:07.8 in 1951, Bannister found himself ranked first in the world – the first Briton to achieve that distinction since Wooderson (4:07.4) in 1939. Certainly he was capable of much better, for in April he covered three-quarters of a mile in 2:56.8, only 0.2 sec outside Andersson's world best and nearly 3 sec faster than Wooderson's English record.

Bannister provoked widespread criticism in 1952 by his method of preparation for the only race that mattered to him: the Olympic 1500m final in Helsinki. He decided well in advance not to run any serious mile or 1500m races prior to the

Games, presumably taking it for granted that his 1951 form and obvious potential would automatically win him selection ... an assumption which annoyed his rivals and critics. His only mile race, a 'solo' effort at the inter-hospitals championships, took 4:10.6 but this plus an impressive 1:51.5 victory in the AAA 880y satisfied the selectors.

What was not revealed to the public until after the Games was his astonishing time trial at Motspur Park ten days before the Olympic final. Reeling off the laps in 58.5, 57.5 and 56.9, he covered three-quarters of a mile in a phenomenal 2:52.9. That sort of running suggested he was capable there and then of a mile in well inside four minutes. Like Jack Lovelock 16 years earlier, his unwavering single-mindedness had brought him to a peak at just the right moment.

But fate intervened to deny Bannister the victory that might have been his. At the eleventh hour the Olympic organisers decided to insert a semi-final round in the 1500m. Bannister's hopes were dashed. All his training had been directed towards running a well separated heat and final; now he was obliged to race on three consecutive days. He left for Helsinki a beaten man, psychologically. No longer did he believe in his own invincibility and, being a thoroughbred type of runner heavily dependent upon nervous energy, he could not hope to succeed unless his mind was attuned to victory. In the circumstances his fourth place in the British record time of 3:46.0 was no mean achievement, but that did not prevent several British newspapermen labelling him a flop. The winner in 3:45.2, significantly one of the hardest training middle-distance men of that era, was a rank outsider – Luxembourg's Josy Barthel.

In one sense Bannister's defeat was a blessing in disguise. Had he won he would probably have retired, but in order to compensate for his own personal disappointment he decided to extend his running career for another two years. Although reluctant to admit it publicly, he was intrigued by the very real possibility of becoming the first man to break four minutes. For years the world record of 4:01.3 set by Sweden's Gunder Hägg in 1945 had remained unthreatened. Suddenly, right at the end of 1952, Australia's John Landy – who had been eliminated in Bannister's heat in Helsinki – rocked the athletics world by improving at one stroke from 4:10.0 to 4:02.1! Another serious challenger for the honour arose in the spring of 1953 in the flamboyant person of Wes Santee (USA) who returned 4:02.4. As for Bannister, he launched his own offensive in May 1953 when, assisted by Chris Chataway, he broke Wooderson's British record with a time of 4:03.6.

The following month, amid bizarre circumstances, Bannister travelled even faster. Santee, never reluctant to blow his own trumpet, had announced that he would be breaking four minutes in the American Championships on June 27, so Bannister and two friends, Chris Brasher and Australian Don Macmillan, arranged in secret to try to forestall the young Kansan. Accordingly, taking advantage of the time difference, they set about their task during the lunch break at the Surrey Schools meeting at Motspur Park. Macmillan towed Bannister around the first two laps in 59.6 and 60.1 before falling back but at the bell (3:01.8) Brasher, who had jogged two laps in the time that Bannister had taken to run three, was on hand to act as pacemaker and windshield for the final quarter. That last lap occupied 60.2 and thus Bannister, after passing 1500m in 3:44.8, finished in a magnificent 4:02.0 – 5.6 sec faster than Santee took to win his US title. However, the time never reached the record books as the BAAB rightly considered that the event was not a *bona fide* competition according to the rules. Bannister completed the season with a 4:05.2 win at the AAA Championships, a 4:07.6 anchor leg for Britain's world record breaking 4 x 1 mile relay team and a personal best 880y of 1:50.7.

And so to 1954 and the successful assault on the four minute mile. Bannister and Brasher trained together all winter, with Chataway joining in at weekends; the training, on the advice of Brasher's coach Franz Stampfl, taking the form mainly of fast repetition quarters. The attempt was set for May 6, the occasion being the annual match between Oxford University and the AAA at Iffley Road. The trio had been picked *en bloc* by the AAA and it was agreed that Brasher would lead for two and a half laps, Chataway would take over and maintain a four-minute tempo for as long as possible, and then it would be up to Bannister to complete the job.

Bannister's final three weeks of preparation, as noted by Norris and Ross McWhirter in their wonderful magazine *Athletics World*, went as follows: April 14: three-quarter mile solo time trial in 3:02.0; Apr 15: 880y solo time trial in 1:53.0; Apr 16-19: rock climbing with Brasher in Scotland; Apr 22: 10x440y at average of 58.9 each; Apr 24: three-quarter mile time trial with Chataway in 3:00.0; Apr 26: three-quarter mile in 3:14, 8 min rest, three-quarter mile in 3:08.6; Apr 28: three-quarter mile solo time trial in 2:59.9; Apr 30: 880y time trial in 1:54.0; May 1: easy 4 miles stride, followed by rest until day of race.

The record attempt, which had very nearly been called off owing to a high wind which only died down minutes before the start, was executed with admirable precision. Disregarding Bannister's mid-lap cry of "faster", Brasher covered the opening quarter at just the right speed. He passed the post in 57.4, with Bannister showing 57.5 and Chataway 57.6. The order remained unchanged throughout the second lap; times at the half were Brasher 1:58.0, Bannister 1:58.2, Chataway 1:58.4. As Brasher began to falter so Chataway moved smoothly into the lead as arranged. The plan was working perfectly. The bell clanged with Chataway a yard ahead, 3:00.4 to 3:00.5. Bannister looked full of running but could he muster a last lap of 59.4? With 230 yards to go he accelerated past his gallant pacemaker. The true test had begun.

As Bannister wrote in his eloquent autobiography: "I felt at that moment that it was my chance to do one thing supremely well. I drove on, impelled by a combination of fear and pride. The air I breathed filled me with the spirit of the track where I had run my first race. The noise in my ears was that of the faithful Oxford crowd. Their hope and encouragement gave me greater strength." Running himself to exhaustion, Bannister broke the tape in 3:59.4, having passed the 1500m mark in an unofficial 3:43.0 which equalled the world record.

Bannister had become the most widely publicised athlete in history but such is the ephemeral nature of record breaking that less than two months later he was succeeded as world's fastest miler by Landy who, in Finland, was timed at 3:57.9.

Track fans the world over awaited with bated breath the confrontation of the two fastest milers in history at the Commonwealth Games in Vancouver, Probably no race, before or since, ever attracted such attention; the names of Bannister, the 25 year-old newly qualified doctor from London, and Landy, the 24 year-old schoolmaster from Melbourne, were on everybody's lips.

The race proved to be a classic. Landy, a fluent short-stepping front runner, knew his only chance of winning was to set such a severe pace as to drain off Bannister's legendary finishing powers. He sped through the first quarter in 58.2, five yards ahead of the stately, long striding Bannister (58.8). A second lap of 60.0 enabled Landy to open up a lead of nearly ten yards, 1:58.2 to 1:59.4, but on the crucial third circuit Bannister succeeded in narrowing the gap to a mere yard or two: 2:58.4 against 2:58.7. Throughout the penultimate furlong the situation remained unchanged, then Landy drew slightly further away approaching the final bend. But at that point, in the words of eye witness Ross McWhirter in *Athletics World*, "Bannister raised his tempo – for all the world like a high horse-power car building up the revs – and in he slammed the clutch as he pulled round the Australian. Landy shot a nervous glance over his left and inside shoulder. Panic! Poor John saw nothing. As his head came round all he could see was a white giant on his starboard bow receding in the distance towards the haven of this hell called miling."

Again running himself into a state of collapse, Bannister finished four yards ahead of a much less physically distressed Landy in the British record time of 3:58.8, having covered the laps in 58.8, 60.6, 59.3 and 60.1 with a British 1500m record of 3:42.2 on the way. As Landy (3:59.6) explained: "I had hoped that the pace would be so fast that he would crack. He didn't. When you get a man in that sort of situation and he doesn't crack, you do."

What a supreme competitor Bannister was. Three weeks later, at the European Championships in Berne, he fairly toyed with a talent-laden field to win the 1500m in 3:43.8, the final 200m taking just 25 sec. Bannister, who had completed five seasons without defeat in a mile race, never competed again. In December 1954 he announced his retirement on the grounds that his work as a doctor left him insufficient time to train seriously. He went on to have an illustrious career as a neurologist and was knighted in 1975 for services to medicine.

CHRIS CHATAWAY
Born 31.1.1931 Chelsea (London).
Clubs: Walton AC, Achilles

AMONG THE SPECTATORS in Wembley Stadium for the 1948 Olympics were two lads of 17, born just ten days apart. One was Gordon Pirie, who found his life's inspiration when watching mesmerised as Emil Zátopek methodically killed off his rivals in the 10,000m. The other was Chris Chataway whose imagination was captured by the dramatic 5000m struggle between Gaston Reiff and Zátopek. So different in outlook, background and appearance, they would blossom into two of the world's greatest and most charismatic runners.

Whereas Pirie epitomised the dedicated clubman, Chataway was the archetypal casual public school and Oxbridge athlete. Pirie was dark, tall and lean; Chataway was red-headed, five inches shorter and stocky. Pirie loved to run away from his opposition early in the race; Chataway preferred to sit in and bank on his fiery finish.

Chataway made his debut in national competition at the 1948 Public Schools Championships and finished third in the mile. At the same meeting in 1949 he improved from 4:42.0 to 4:27.2 in second place and maintained the rapid advance in 1950, during his National Service in the Army, when he captured the inter-services mile in 4:15.6 ... with Pirie, of the RAF, third. He attracted much wider notice in 1951. Now an Oxford undergraduate he clocked 4:12.0 for the mile and in his first international race, a 2 miles event at the Whitsun British Games, he missed Jack Emery's British record of 9:03.4 by just 0.4 sec. Later in the month he made a fairly inauspicious 5000m debut in Paris, finishing a distant third in 14:47.8 behind Olympic heroes Reiff and Alain Mimoun. His next major event was the AAA 3 miles but, despite a 57.6 last lap and a time of 14:02.6, the verdict went to Roy Beckett. Pirie was fourth, but had the previous evening won the 6 miles title in the British record time of 29:32.0.

Pirie and Chataway trained for the 1952 Olympics in their own way: Pirie for between two and four hours every day, Chataway for half an hour three or four days a week! The results by both were impressive. Chataway broke Roger Bannister's inter-varsity mile record with 4:10.2, set a British 2 miles mark of 8:55.6 and won the AAA 3 miles in 13:59.6, while Pirie relieved Sydney Wooderson of his national 3 miles record with 13:44.8 and set a British 6 miles record of 28:55.6 in the AAA Championships.

Few seriously expected the young British stars to defeat men like Zátopek, Mimoun and Herbert Schade at the Olympics but, for the first time in many years, there was a possibility of a medal. It was not to be. At the bell in the 5000m final Schade led from Chataway, Mimoun and Zátopek, all in a bunch, with Pirie trailing well behind in fifth spot. With over 200m to go Chataway made an audacious bid for victory. He accelerated into the lead but on the crown of the last bend, just after the other three had swept past, the exhausted Englishman tripped over the raised track kerb and went sprawling. But for the accident he would certainly have been an easy fourth; as it was he finished fifth in 14:18.0. Pirie, unaware of what had happened, pipped him for fourth just before the line. Clocking 57.9 for the last lap, Zátopek won the second of his three gold medals in Helsinki in a time of 14:06.6.

Preoccupied by exams, Chataway did not compete much in 1953, although he improved to 4:08.4 and 8:49.6, but 1954 proved to be a fantastic year for him. In May he played an invaluable training and pacemaking role in Bannister's successful onslaught on the first sub-four minute mile (he was second in a personal best of 4:07.2); in June he only just missed Reiff's world 2 miles record with 8:41.0, the second fastest ever mark, and with a time of 4:04.4 (2:57.5 at three-quarters) helped John Landy to a world mile record of 3:57.9 in Turku. "The record would not have gone if it had not been for Chataway chasing me around the track," the Australian affirmed.

Gunder Hägg's world 3 miles record of 13:32.4 dating from 1942 seemed particularly vulnerable and, sure enough, Chataway clipped off a fifth of a second in the AAA Championships in July ... only to find himself second, with as in 1951 the same time as the winner, on this occasion Freddie Green. The following month Chataway finished two seconds ahead of Green in 13:35.2 to win the Commonwealth Games title in Vancouver, and then finished ahead of Zátopek over 5000m in the European Championships in 14:08.8 ... the only trouble being that Vladimir Kuts – of whom Chataway had never heard – had snapped the tape some 80m ahead in a world record 13:56.6! Chataway and Zátopek, who had set the previous record of 13:57.2 earlier in the season, were so busy eyeing each other that they allowed Kuts to slip clean away. By the time they realised the muscular Ukrainian sailor was not going to crack it was too late to remedy the situation and, somewhat sheepishly, they had to settle for battling out the silver medal.

Revenge, total and sweet, was exacted by Chataway 45 days later during the London v Moscow floodlit meeting at the White City on October 13. The match, which featured the first appearance in London of a Soviet team, generated immense interest and represented the high-water mark of popular support for athletics in Britain. A sell-out crowd of over 40,000 flocked to the stadium and an estimated audience of 15 million watched the proceedings live on TV.

The four-man 5000m race was run at a scorching pace as Kuts tried his utmost to break the spirit and body of his rival. He could have been forgiven for feeling that his sixth lap of 62.4 would have settled the hash of any opponent but Chataway, inspired by the tumultuous roaring of the crowd, stayed with him.

The atmosphere was electric as the bell sounded, with Kuts remaining just a stride ahead. Chataway usually struck with 300y to go and the crowd waited expectantly; nothing happened. It was obvious now that he was being stretched to the very limit in simply sticking to Kuts' hip. Still there was no change as the heroic pair swung into the short finishing straight.

As Norris McWhirter wrote in *Athletics World*: "As if impelled by the roar of the delirious crowd Chataway switched over to the super-human. With sheer savagery he struck late but decisively and with consummate if desperate timing surged past his quarry five tantalising yards before he could claim the asylum of the tape. In a blizzard of flashbulbs Chataway found himself being embraced by Roger Bannister, now not only a friend but a fellow immortal in the history of the track."

The race was the thing [over 50 years later no race has surpassed this one as the most dramatic ever witnessed by the author] but the times also were an occasion for rejoicing. Chataway had sliced no less than five seconds from the world record with 13:51.6 (Kuts 13:51.8) while at the 3 miles post both had clipped Kuts' record of 13:27.4: Kuts with 13:27.0, Chataway with 13:27.1. Such was Chataway's popularity that he, not Bannister, won the inaugural BBC television sports personality of the year award for 1954. Kuts, however, had the last word in terms of world record breaking that year. Ten days after the White City race, in Prague, he beat Zátopek by nearly half a lap over 5000m in 13:51.2.

Chataway returned the compliment in July 1955 by regaining the 3 miles record with 13:23.2 in a race in which he was assisted by new star Derek Ibbotson. Earlier in the season Chataway had become the world's fourth sub-four minute miler when he clocked 3:59.8 behind Hungary's Laszlo Tabori (3:59.0) and just ahead of Brian Hewson (3:59.8) in the first race to feature three men inside what was then still a magical figure. In September 1955 Chataway became Independent [Commercial] Television's first newscaster, later working for BBC's *Panorama*, and although he felt he had a chance of winning the 5000m at the 1956 Olympics he was not able to direct all his attention to preparation. That, with stomach cramp for good measure, caused him to fall away from fourth to 11th place in the last kilometre in Melbourne, his final race.

Like Bannister and Chris Brasher, he proved a high achiever away from the track too: a Member of Parliament from 1959 he became a Minister in the Conservative Government between 1970 and 1974, left politics for a distinguished career as a merchant banker, and while chairman of the Civil Aviation Authority was knighted in 1995 for services to the industry. He has also remained fearsomely fit for his age. While Kuts died aged 48 and Pirie passed away at 60, Chataway – who trained so much less than them in their heyday – was able to run a 5:36 mile when he was 64 and in 2005, aged 74, completed the Great North Run half marathon inside 1:38.

GORDON PIRIE

Born 10.2.1931 Leeds; died 7.12.1991.
Club: South London H

IT WILL BE difficult for anyone much younger than 60 to appreciate the impact Gordon Pirie had on British athletics. He was a megastar of his time, a runner whose appearance in any race would produce a frisson of excitement and anticipation. Among later generations of distance runners perhaps only Dave Bedford came close to matching Pirie's effect on the public. You either loved him or hated him; you certainly couldn't ignore him.

In a more conventional era before the term was coined, Pirie "did his own thing". Inspired by the example of Emil Zátopek he trained like a demon (often covering well over 200 miles a week), he bucked the system by being coached by a foreigner (the demanding German, Waldemar Gerschler), he was continuously at odds with officialdom and the media. When he entered senior competition British distance running standards were at a particularly low ebb, but he had set his sights much higher than merely becoming pre-eminent at home; his consuming ambition was to become the greatest runner in the world, a British Zátopek.

Pirie was born into an athletics-mad family. His father Alick was a Scottish cross country international and Gordon's elder brother Peter was English youths' cross country champion in 1947. Gordon placed third in the AAA junior mile in 1948 but the really significant event for him that year was the Olympic Games. Up in the Wembley stands he fell under the spell of Zátopek, the wondrous Czech runner. As he later reminisced in his autobiography *Running Wild*: "This tremendous dynamo of a man sparked off something inside me and I went home to start on the road to emulate Zátopek. I missed the other days at the Olympics for I was concerned only in running to be a great champion like Zátopek."

Drawing inspiration from a photo of Zátopek pinned to his locker, Pirie punished himself mercilessly in training. Not content merely with covering an unheard of (in Britain anyway) mileage he further tortured himself by running up to eight miles at a time wearing heavy Army boots. He was criticised by many 'experts' who glibly predicted he would burn himself out, but he persevered with his spartan regimen and in 1951 began to reap the rewards. He collected his first British record of 29:32.0 when winning the AAA 6 miles title, aged 20. The following year he improved to 28:55.6 as well as breaking Sydney Wooderson's British 3 miles mark with 13:44.8, but he wasn't yet ready to match strides with his hero. At the 1952 Olympics, where Zátopek won three golds, Pirie placed seventh in the 10,000m and fourth in the 5000m.

The full range of Pirie's talent became apparent in 1953, by which time the tall, crewcut "thin man of athletics" had become one of the major spectator attractions in British sport. At one end of the scale he won the first of three consecutive English cross country titles, at the other he outkicked the flashy American Wes Santee in the inaugural Emsley Carr Mile in 4:06.8 before an ecstatic crowd at the White City. On the track he took part in 32 individual races ranging from 800 to 10,000m, won 27 of them and set world records for 6 miles (28:19.4) and 4x1500m relay, unofficial world bests for 4 miles (18:45.2 and 18:35.6) and 5 miles (23:34.2), and numerous British records including 8:11.0 for 3000m, 13:34.0 for 3 miles, 14:02.6 for 5000m and 29:17.2 for 10,000m. Not since the days of Walter George and Alf Shrubb had Britain seen anything like it.

Never one to beat about the bush, Pirie proclaimed that at the 1954 European Championships he would be ready to run 13:50 for 5000m and 28:50 for 10,000m (the world records stood at 13:58.2 and 29:01.6) and that eventually he would clock 13:40 for the shorter distance, a performance which at the time appeared to be in the realm of science-fiction. However, a cracked bone in his left foot ruined his plans after a promising start when he set personal bests of 1:53.0 for 880y and 4:05.2 for the mile and in the year of Roger Bannister's first four minute mile it was Chris Chataway who took over as Britain's distance running hero as he scored a famous 5000m victory over Vladimir Kuts at a packed White City in a world record 13:51.6.

Pirie bounced back in 1955, defeating Zátopek in three races out of four, setting a personal best of 13:29.8 for 3 miles and recording such diverse performances as a world's best of 6:26.0 for a mile and a half and 22 miles 278 yards in two hours behind Joe Lancaster's world's best of 22 miles 418 yards. But it was in the following year that he translated into reality the sort of times he had previously been ridiculed for suggesting.

Stronger and faster than ever following the introduction of weight training into his preparations, he hacked 25 sec from his previous best to clock a staggering world record of 13:36.8 for 5000m on a rain-sodden track in Bergen in June, producing a 55.0 last lap to finish some 20m ahead of Kuts (13:39.6). But for a lack of foresight by the officials, Pirie would undoubtedly have cracked the world 3 miles record (13:14.2 by Hungary's Sándor Iharos) on the way; as it was he must have clocked somewhere around 13:13. Just three days later, in Trondheim, he equalled Iharos's world 3000m record of 7:55.6 (actually he ran 7:55.5 but times were rounded up to a fifth then) and he completed a momentous week by defeating the East German, Klaus Richtzenhain (destined to win the Olympic silver medal that year in Melbourne), over 1500m in a personal best of 3:43.7.

His next target was Zátopek's 10,000m record of 28:54.2 but a soft track, high wind and lack of opposition conspired against him and, after a 14:20.4 first 5000m, he finished in a British record tying 29:17.2. He later ran personal bests of 4:02.2 for the mile and 8:42.6 for 2 miles and a second trip to Scandinavia in September found him back to his superlative early season form. Taking on the great Hungarian trio of Iharos, Laszlo Tábori and Istvan Rozsávölgyi over 3000m in Malmö he beat the lot in a world record 7:52.8 (actually 7:52.7) – a race Pirie believed to be the best he ever ran. Incidentally, on the morning of the race he did 50 bursts over 100 yards! These were phenomenal performances for the time, but how much faster might he have run had he trained a little less fanatically and eased up for a few days before an important race? "I wish I knew when I was running what I know now," he admitted a couple of years before his death.

Pirie, whose last significant race prior to the Olympics was a personal best 1500m of 3:43.4, went to Melbourne with the intention of returning with two gold medals. Perhaps, had he gone just for the 5000m, he would have become Olympic champion, but he believed that first he could take on Kuts at 10,000m even though the Soviet runner's world record of 28:30.4 was over three-quarters of a minute faster than his own UK record. A less uncompromising athlete might have aimed for a fairly 'safe' silver medal but Pirie, and all credit to him, wanted the gold or nothing. A glance at the result (1st Kuts 28:45.6, 8th Pirie 29:49.6) suggests that Pirie failed utterly, yet the truth is that he came agonisingly close to winning.

It was a searing duel, with the halfway mark being reached in 14:06.8, which was only a fifth of a second slower than Zátopek's Olympic 5000m record! Kuts tortured his rival with a series of bursts and, with just three and a half laps remaining, Pirie finally broke. "I staggered the last three laps at about walking pace," Pirie related. "I was utterly exhausted, like a punch-drunk boxer, but I was still determined to cross the finishing line." Kuts later admitted he was at breaking point himself when he inflicted the burst that finally caused Pirie to crack. Had Pirie been able to respond one more time Kuts would have been the one to give up. Later, in the 5000m, Kuts led throughout to win by some 70m from Pirie (13:50.6) in 13:39.6 with Derek Ibbotson – destined to become world mile record holder next year – third.

Bronze medallist over 5000m in the 1958 European Championships, Pirie once again shaped up as a potential Olympic champion in 1960. He won that year's AAA 6 miles title in a personal best of 28:09.6 and looked tremendous in his last major race before the Games as he won over 5000m in 13:51.6 with a 54.6 last lap. But in Rome, clearly not acclimatised to the intense heat and humidity, he clocked an embarrassing 14:43.6 in his heat, and although he came back with a personal best of 29:15.2 that only sufficed for tenth place in the 10,000m. It was scant consolation when, a fortnight later, Pirie belatedly achieved one of his most nagging ambitions by running a mile in 3:59.9.

Instead of retiring as expected, Pirie decided to continue for one more year – "to ram it down the selectors' throats that they took us to Rome too late". He went out with a flourish, setting a British 3 miles record of 13:16.4 when winning the AAA title, coming close to his world 3000m record with 7:54.8 and posting a personal best of 3:42.5 for 1500m.

Pirie, who had married British 200m and 400m record holder Shirley Hampton in 1956, subsequently turned professional, was British orienteering champion in 1967 and 1968 and became a successful coach, his pupils including Jim Hogan, Mike Wiggs and Anne Smith of Britain and New Zealanders Anne Audain and Alison Roe. Such was the high regard for his achievements that a poll conducted by *Athletics Weekly* in December 1965 to determine its readers' views as to the greatest British athletes of all time resulted in Pirie being voted first with 36% as against 19% by runner-up Roger Bannister. He died of cancer, aged 60.

DEREK IBBOTSON

Born 17.6.1932 Berry Brow, near Huddersfield.
Clubs: Longwood H, South London H

WHEN ROGER BANNISTER made history in the space of 3 min 59.4 sec at Oxford on 6 May 1954 no one, least of all the man himself, could have predicted that his successor as Britain's fastest ever miler would be Derek Ibbotson. Born in a village on the Yorkshire Moors, "Ibbo" – as he was to become affectionately known – had by then established a reputation of being among the country's most promising young distance and cross country runners but had a best mile time of only 4:19.2.

The turning point in the Longwood Harrier's track career was reached shortly before the end of 1954 when he was called up for National Service in the RAF. He found he was able to train more assiduously than in the past and his running benefited correspondingly. Gordon Pirie was attempting the British 2000m record and, as expected, cut out a throbbing pace. All his opponents were dropped ... all that is except for Ibbotson, who near the end of the fourth lap even had the effrontery to take the lead and was timed at the mile post in 4:08.8. This was some 10 sec inside his previous best and there was still another 427 yards to cover! Pirie went on to win in a record 5:09.8 but it was Ibbotson, finishing in a fine 5:12.8, who attracted most attention. The following week he slashed nearly half a minute off his best 3 miles time in winning the inter-county title in 13:34.6, only 8.2 sec away from Vladimir Kuts' world record. One celebrated coach was so impressed that he declared Ibbotson was the strongest runner he had ever seen and predicted he would be the first man to crack 13 minutes. Two days later he finished third in the 6 miles in a world class 28:52.0 and at the AAA Championships he gave a good account of himself in finishing second in the 3 miles to Chris Chataway.

Further evidence of his tremendous stamina was his third place in the 1956 English cross country championship. On the track he continued to make splendid progress, setting a personal best mile time of 4:07.0 and defeating Chataway by inches for his first AAA 3 miles title in 13:32.6. He won against Czechoslovakia in 13:28.2 and two days afterwards – entering the Emsley Carr Mile merely because his fiancée wanted an extra ticket for the post-meeting banquet – he created a sensation by winning in 3:59.4 to become Britain's fourth and the world's ninth four-minute miler with lap times of 59.8, 61.0, 61.8 and 56.8. Admittedly not at his fittest, Ireland's Ron Delany – destined to become Olympic 1500m champion later in the year – finished a distant third in 4:06.4. Ibbotson, however, was selected only for the 5000m in Melbourne and gained the bronze medal in his fastest time of 13:54.4 behind Vladimir Kuts and Gordon Pirie.

Ibbotson was by now one of the most popular figures in the sport, known as the 'Clown Prince of the Track' and 'The Four Minute Smiler' with the fans delighting in his jaunty, swashbuckling manner of running and his infectious sense of fun.

The first of two great days for him that year was 15 June 1957. In the morning his wife Madeline (née Wooller), herself an international half-miler, gave birth to their first child and in Glasgow that afternoon Derek celebrated with a European mile record of 3:58.4 – second only to John Landy's world mark of 3:57.9. It was an exceptional run for it was extremely hot, the track was dusty, he was unpressed over the last 660 yards ... and for good measure he had been spiked early in the race. His lap times were 58.0, 60.3, 61.5 and 58.6. Imagine the sensation, therefore, when Britain's athletics idol was ignominiously eliminated in his mile heat at the AAA Championships on July 12. He arrived at the stadium too late to warm up properly and found himself unable either to win the heat or qualify as one of the six fastest losers. It was a temporary lapse; next day he reassured his public by winning the 3 miles in a British record of 13:20.8.

The highspot of Ibbotson's career took place on the same White City track six days later. Here is my eye witness account of the event published in a booklet entitled *The Ibbotson Story*: "The occasion was the invitation mile race on the first day of the memorable London v New York match. The huge crowd (plus several million television viewers) were treated to one shattering performance after another and by the time the mile came on at 8 pm the spectators were in a high pitch of excitement.

"The line-up was dazzling. There was Ibbotson, holder of the European record at 3:58.4; Stanislav Jungwirth (Czechoslovakia), who only a few days earlier had set an incredible world 1500m record of 3:38.1 [worth around 3:56 for a mile]; Ron Delany (Ireland), the Olympic 1500m champion whose best mile time was 3:59.0; Stefan Lewandowski (Poland), who had run the metric equivalent of about 4:02;

Ken Wood, with a best of 4:00.6; Alan Gordon, a 4:06.2 man; and Mike Blagrove, essentially a half miler but with a 4:07.1 mile to his credit.

"Track and weather conditions were just about as perfect as they can be in England. Straight in front from the gun went diminutive Blagrove, who fairly streaked around the opening bend followed by the ungainly Jungwirth, a zestful looking Ibbotson, and the unorthodox high stepping Delany. The order remained virtually unchanged throughout the first lap which occupied the sensationally short period of 55.3. A second lap of just over a minute followed and Blagrove reached the half mile in 1:55.8, with Jungwirth, Ibbotson and Delany packed close behind.

"Some 150 yards later Blagrove, who had selflessly run himself out, dropped sharply away and Jungwirth shrugged into the lead. The tempo dropped abruptly and the bell tolled for the Czech in exactly three minutes. Ibbotson was half a stride away, and he in turn was followed by Lewandowski, Gordon and Delany, with Wood running comfortably at the rear. A world record was a distinct possibility – but by whom? It was still anybody's race.

"Jungwirth continued plodding along in the van until the beginning of the back straight. Ibbotson made a sudden strike for leadership, dropped back for an instant, and then accelerated strongly past the Czech star. There was still fully 300 yards to go and Ibbotson's move was a bold gamble. But his judgement was not at fault and to tumultuous cheering he strode powerfully around the eighth and final bend and was never seriously challenged in the finishing straight.

"Ibbotson had won the greatest mass mile race so far and moreover his time of 3:57.2 was the fastest yet recorded. It was a complete triumph for the lad from Yorkshire. He had run the distance faster than any other man on earth; he had defeated the most formidable opposition that the world could offer; he had run a perfect tactical race. The full result was: 1, Ibbotson 3:57.2 (world record; British best of 3:41.9 at 1500m); 2, Delany 3:58.8 (Irish record); 3, Jungwirth 3:59.1 (Czech record); 4, Wood 3:59.3 (personal best); 5, Lewandowski 4:00.6 (Polish record); 6, Gordon 4:03.4 (personal best); Blagrove did not finish." Because Blagrove dropped out, one over zealous AAA official (Walter Jewell) tried to block ratification as a record – even though Roger Bannister's paced 3:59.4 had been accepted – but commonsense prevailed.

Bannister was of the opinion that in a more evenly paced race Ibbotson was capable of running 3:55 but the rest of the season proved anti-climactic, even though he beat four minutes again in Finland. Too much racing and travel took their toll and he lost several races he ought to have won. Indeed, Ibbotson was never to recapture his most sparkling form in the seasons that followed but although he never again bettered four minutes his popularity remained undimmed. As late as 1965 he was wildly cheered on to setting a British indoor 2 miles record of 8:42.6.

Incidentally, Ibbotson likes to claim – with a grin on his face – that he, not Bannister, was the first four minute miler. True ... up to a point. In a race at the White City on 3 September 1958, won by Australian Herb Elliott in 3:55.4, Ibbotson finished fourth in 4:00.0, the first such clocking, with Mike Blagrove fifth in the same time!

DEREK JOHNSON

Born 5.1.1933 Chigwell (Essex); died 30.8.2004.
Club: Woodford Green AC

DEREK JOHNSON WAS a brilliant junior who always seemed bound for greatness. He was only 17 when, in 1950, he won the AAA junior 440 yards in 48.8, which ranked him no 4 on the British senior list that year. Following National Service in Egypt, he began medical studies at Oxford in the autumn of 1953. A winter's cross country racing increased his stamina at no cost to his natural speed, and in 1954 the former boy wonder whom many had already written off as 'burned out' emerged from the shadows to become the most exciting half-mile star for many years.

His 47.9 440y at Oxford on May 6 (as Oxford University AC secretary a meeting he helped organise) was understandably overlooked in the turmoil surrounding Roger Bannister's mile that evening but at the inter-county championships a month later he was deservedly acclaimed for his 880y victory in 1:50.2 – a gigantic improvement compared to his previous best of 1:52.9 and a time bettered among British half-milers only by Sydney Wooderson.

Johnson, whose versatility was to astonish the athletics public for several seasons, had found his true event. He once explained his fondness for the half-mile: "I believe it requires all the virtues of the other flat track events – technique, speed, strength and simple decisive tactical ability – plus an unpredictable element of luck, which gives it added spice."

He went on in 1954 to win the Commonwealth Games 880y in Vancouver (1:50.7) ahead of Brian Hewson (1:51.2) and, at the European Championships in Berne, he underlined his British supremacy with a simply magnificent 800m clocking of 1:47.4 – a full second inside Wooderson's UK and former world record. Yet such was the standard of this race that in spite of missing Rudolf Harbig's world record by only 0.8 and finishing within two metres of the Hungarian winner, Lajos Szentgali, his meagre reward was fourth position.

The competition between Johnson and Hewson became more intensive in 1955. Both broke Wooderson's British 880y record of 1:49.2 in the Britain v West Germany match, Johnson winning by 0.2 in 1:48.7; but, 12 days later against Hungary, Hewson took advantage of Johnson's absence to defeat Szentgali in 1:48.6. Midway between these two races Hewson got the better of Johnson in an 880y at Glasgow but the race was won by the American, Tom Courtney.

In the absence of both Johnson and Hewson, the AAA 880y title in 1956 was won by Mike Rawson ahead of Mike Farrell.

As Hewson (who had improved at 800m to 1:47.5) announced his intention of going for the 1500m in Melbourne, Britain's Olympic trio at 800m was Johnson, Rawson and Farrell. Rawson (destined to become European champion in 1958, when Hewson won the 1500m) was narrowly eliminated in the semi-finals, but the other two qualified for the eight-man final.

That final proved to be one of the most thrilling in Olympic annals. The Americans, Courtney and Arnie Sowell, set the pace for the first lap, the positions at the bell, reached, in 52.9 being Sowell (best time of 1:46.7), Courtney (1:46.4), Norway's Audun Boysen (1:45.9), Johnson (1:47.4), the USA's Lon Spurrier (880y world record holder at 1:47.5) and Farrell (1:49.3). Courtney and Sowell entered the finishing straight level with Johnson boxed in behind in fourth place. Suddenly, with 70m to go, a gap appeared between the two Americans ... and, quick as a flash, Johnson darted through into the lead! Sowell could not hold the pace, so it was left to the 1.88m (6ft 2in), 82kg (180lb) Courtney to fight it out with the 1.76m (5ft 9.5in), 66kg (146lb) Englishman. There was absolutely nothing between them until the last 10m, when Courtney's superior strength made itself felt. He snapped the tape first in 1:47.7 while Johnson, surely one of the most heroic losers in athletics history, was timed in 1:47.8. Then followed Boysen, Sowell, Farrell (1:49.2) and Spurrier.

As Johnson was to write in the book *The Road to Rome*: "Tom Courtney was an Olympic champion in the finest sense of the word. He had gathered his deepest resources at a time when many a man would have ceded the race, and had hurled his massive frame past me in the last few strides. I had failed, and failed to achieve the ambition which had meant so much to me. It was a bitter disappointment ... but were I to be given the chance again only to face the same outcome I should have no hesitation in seizing it gratefully, for I believe it is important to take whatever talent we have and to use it to the best of our ability. It is perhaps better to aim at the highest and fail by a fraction than never to aim at all." Courtney revealed: "I had never run myself into such a state. My head was exploding, my stomach ripping and even the tips of my fingers ached. The only thing I could think was if I live I will never run again." Actually, he turned out for the 4x400m relay and won another gold medal!

From the stopwatch point of view Johnson proved even greater in 1957. In finishing second to Courtney in 1:48.5 in the London v New York match he regained the British 880y record and later in the season he lowered his 800m record to 1:46.9 (behind Belgium's world record holder Roger Moens and Courtney) and subsequently 1:46.6 (Courtney winning again).

Johnson took a serious crack at the longer distances in 1959, to such good effect that he topped the UK 1500m rankings with 3:42.9, but shortly afterwards a near-fatal case of tuberculosis forced him to quit athletics competition. The will was still there, though, and after an absence of nearly four years he made a touching and inspiring comeback in 1963, culminating in an 800m time of 1:50.0. As I wrote at the time, "Even if he never runs another race, Derek Johnson has proved when it comes to sheer guts there is not an athlete to surpass him."

That really was the end for Johnson whose fantastic range of performances included 10.0 for 100y, 21.9 for 220y, 47.7 for 440y (but 45.9 in a relay), 1:17.9 for 660y (an indoor world best), 1:46.6 for 800m, 1:48.5 for 880y, 2:20.4 for 1000m, 3:42.9 for 1500m, 4:05.0 for the mile, 9:15.0 for 2 miles, 9:16.8 for the steeplechase, 25.4 for 220y hurdles and 53.7 for 440y hurdles! Well, not quite the end ... for at the age of 50 he covered the London Marathon in 2:55:47. Johnson also made an important contribution to athletics off the track as one of the founders (and later secretary then chairman) of the International Athletes' Club, and was for a time the secretary of the AAA of England. In his last years he bravely battled against leukaemia, eventually succumbing at the age of 71.

DIANE LEATHER

Born 7.1.1933 Streetly (Staffordshire).
Club: Birchfield H

AMONG THE GUESTS of honour at the 50th anniversary celebrations in May 2004 of Roger Bannister's pioneering four minute mile at Oxford was Diane Charles (née Leather). Much to her astonishment as well as delight, it seemed, her name when announced elicited warm applause from the crowd assembled at Iffley Road – most of whom were of "a certain age" and happy to salute another major figure in miling history. Her contribution has not been forgotten. Of course, no one can claim that being the first woman to break five minutes was in any way comparable to becoming the first man to duck under four minutes, but during the infancy of the women's event it was rated a highly significant achievement, coming as it did just 23 days after Bannister's feat.

Diane Leather was a 20 year-old microanalyst chemist when she set her first world record, anchoring a British team to a time of 6:49.0 for the distinctly odd 3x880y relay event in 1953. Later that summer she smashed the world best for the mile (it did not become an official IAAF approved event until 1967), which had stood at 5:08.0, with 5:02.6.

A few weeks later Edith Treybal of Romania ran 5:00.3, a time that Diane reduced to an even more tantalising 5:00.2 early in the 1954 season. Three days after that, at the Midland Championships on May 29 at Birmingham's Perry Barr Stadium, the 1.78m (5ft 10in) tall Birchfield Harrier edged through the barrier with an erratically paced front-running 4:59.6, covering the laps in 68.8, 78.2, 79.3 and 73.3.

It proved a memorable year, for in June she took 2.6 sec off the world 880y record with 2:09.0 when winning the WAAA title; in July she collected another world record plaque when a British team improved to 6:46.0 for the 3x880y relay; and in August she proved her worth internationally by finishing second in the inaugural European 800m championship to the great Soviet runner, Nina Otkalenko, who held the world record of 2:07.3 and had recently broken Diane's 880y mark with 2:08.4. Diane also demonstrated impressive speed for a four-time English cross country champion by clocking 56.6 for 440y, which equalled the world best although considerably inferior to the existing 400m mark of 55.0.

In 1955 Diane made two substantial improvements to the mile record. In May she front-ran 4:50.8 (unofficial world best of 4:30.0 for 1500m en route) with much more even laps of 74.0, 72.5, 71.5 and 72.8, while in September she registered 4:45.0 (world best of 4:22.2 at 1500m) with splits of 71.0, 69.6, 72.2 and 72.2. That time would stand as a world best for seven years and a British best for 11 years. She also set three British 800m records in September (2:08.6, 2:07.7 and 2:06.9) and closed her season with a British 400m record of 56.3.

Clearly she would have been an Olympic medal contender in 1956 at either 800m or 1500m, but neither event was on the programme in Melbourne. Ridiculously, sprinters alone were catered for, the only women's track events being 100m, 200m, 80m hurdles and 4x100m relay! The 800m (staged once before, back in 1928) would return in 1960, but 400m runners had to wait until 1964, 1500m runners until 1972 and long distance runners until 1984 for their chance of Olympic participation.

Diane returned to record breaking in 1957 when, in the finest 800m victory of her career, she won against the USSR at White City in 2:06.8, defeating Yelisaveta Yermolayeva and Otkalenko, world record holder at 2:05.0. She also set unofficial world bests for 1500m with 4:30.0 and 4:29.7 (en route to a 4:50.6 mile), but these were still way outside her 4:22.2 of two years earlier. Another notable achievement was winning the WAAA 880y (2:09.4) and mile (4:55.3) titles on the same afternoon.

For a second time, the tall Midlander with what was once described as "her beautiful, gazelle-like action", struck silver in the European 800m championship. This time, in 1958, she improved her UK record to 2:06.6 in a close finish with Yermolayeva (2:06.3), moving up seven places during the second lap. Married to Peter Charles in July 1959, and by now a teacher, Diane was past her best by 1960 and although she fulfilled an ambition by making the Olympic team she was eliminated in the 800m heats. A mother of four, Diane became a social worker first in London and then in Cornwall, retiring at the age of 70.

DON THOMPSON

Born 20.1.1933 Hillingdon (Middlesex).
Club: Metropolitan WC

FEW ATHLETES PREPARED more thoroughly and imaginatively for an Olympic test than Don Thompson, a small bespectacled London fire insurance clerk. He had learned the hard way at the 1956 Olympics in Melbourne what dehydration and heat exhaustion can do to someone who has not prepared adequately for a 50 kilometres (31 miles) walk in high temperatures. In 90ºF heat he collapsed at 42 kilometres while in fifth place and finished up unconscious in a hospital bed in the Olympic Village. "It was a terrible experience," he reflected 20 years later when interviewed by David Emery for the *Daily Express*. "I was a teetotaler at the time but I realised then just what it was like to feel drunk. The pavement was weaving for miles, then suddenly it just reached up and smacked me on the nose."

Thus acutely aware that the heat and humidity likely to be encountered at the Rome Olympics of 1960 would be a vital factor in determining the result, Thompson set about acclimatising himself. For three months before the Olympics, in addition to his usual gruelling training, he performed exercises on the spot in his tracksuit in an improvised steam room at his parents' house with temperatures hovering around the 100ºF mark. Only much later did he discover that the dizziness he felt was a form of carbon monoxide poisoning as he was using a paraffin heater and boiling kettle and there was no ventilation.

All the discomfort was worth it, for as a result he adapted to Rome's sultry climate without trouble and was able to perform to the best of his ability. He led by a minute at halfway (2:10:30) but was overtaken approaching 35 kilometres by the 40 year-old Swede John Ljunggren, the 1948 champion. At 45 kilometres, with the two men virtually abreast, Ljunggren halted at the drinks station for what Thompson described as "almost a wash and brush up", and the diminutive Briton seized his chance of building up a winning lead. At the finish he was 17 sec clear in 4:25:30, an Olympic record. The sight of Thompson, wearing sun glasses and a French Foreign Legion type head-dress, striding briskly towards the finish in the stadium was one that was not easily forgotten by the British supporters present, particularly as he was his country's only athletics gold medallist in those Games.

His victory was celebrated also by local fans. Known affectionately as *il topolino* ('the little mouse') ever since he won a 100 kilometres race in Milan in 1955, he captured the hearts of everyone in the stadium as he wiggled around the final lap. The glorious tradition established by Tommy Green and Harold Whitlock (Thompson's own adviser) lived on. Modestly, Thompson described his performance as "quite an ordinary one ... which was, however, sufficient for the occasion." He hadn't expected to win; he thought he would have a good race and finish fifth or sixth.

He wasted no time resting upon his laurels. Just ten days afterwards he won the London to Brighton race in 7:37:42 (the sixth of eight consecutive victories in this race), followed up with a UK 50 kilometres track record of 4:17:29.8 in October and finished no less than 25 minutes ahead of Italy's Abdon Pamich (the Rome bronze medallist) in November's Milan 100 kilometres classic.

Thompson, who had set what was considered a phenomenal record of 7:35:12 for the 53 miles 129 yards (86 kilometres) course from London to Brighton in 1957 (an average of over 7mph), had his first experience of a major international title race in 1958 when placing fifth in the European Championships in 4:25:09. At the 1962 edition of those championships he took the bronze medal in 4:29:01. Thompson defended his Olympic title in Tokyo in 1964, but such was the overall standard of the field that although he recorded 4:22:40, nearly three minutes faster than in Rome, he finished no higher than tenth.

During his career he broke the British 50 kilometres record on the road several times. Appropriately, he it was who bettered Whitlock's 1936 figures of 4:30:38 with 4:24:39 in 1956, improving to 4:22:58 later in the season. In 1958 he clocked 4:21:50, progressing considerably to 4:12:19 when winning the RWA title in 1959. Paul Nihill seized the record with his Olympic silver medal winning 4:11:32 in 1964 but the following year Thompson was credited with 4:09:15 when placing fourth in the Lugano Trophy race in Pescara (Italy). There were rumours the course was short but there is no conclusive proof, and no Briton would walk faster until Bob Dobson in 1978.

Don Thompson & Basil Heatley

In 1969 Thompson temporarily gave up walking for road and cross country running (the events in which he started his athletic career), and ran a 2:51 marathon. He became Britain's oldest international when, aged 58, he competed in a French 200 kilometres walk event in 1991.

BASIL HEATLEY

Born 25.12.1933 Kenilworth (Warwickshire).
Club: Coventry Godiva H

BASIL HEATLEY WAS inspired as a 14 year-old by reading (in *Athletics*, the monthly forerunner of *Athletics Weekly*) about the 1948 Olympics and, in particular, Emil Zátopek. Little did he think that one day he would break one of the Czech's world records!

Brought up on a Warwickshire farm, Heatley joined Coventry Godiva Harriers at the end of 1950 and gained his first important success a few months later when he placed third in the English National Youth Cross Country Championship. Five years later, in 1956, he made his marathon debut (winning the Midland title in 2:36:55) but apart from one race in 1957 (retaining the Midland title in 2:32:01) it was not until 1963 that he would again attempt the distance which would prove to be his forte.

Meanwhile, he won the English cross country title – a hugely prestigious achievement in those days – in 1960, 1961 and 1963, and finished first in the International Cross Country Championship (forerunner of the present World Championships) in 1961, winning by a huge 23 sec margin.

A high class track runner with a best time of 28:55.8 for 10,000m, his greatest performance on cinders came in the 1961 AAA 10 miles championship at Hurlingham when he knocked 25 sec off his hero Zátopek's world record with a time of 47:47.0. The mark would last until Mel Batty ran 47:26.8 in the corresponding race in 1964.

His return to the marathon in 1963 was promising. Just a few days before the AAA marathon he clocked his fastest ever 3 miles time of 13:22.8, ranking him second in Britain, and then proceeded to finish second to clubmate Brian Kilby (2:16:45) in 2:19:56. Later that season he placed fourth in Kosice in 2:20:23. That race was won in 2:15:10 by the Essex-based American, Buddy Edelen (holder of the world record with 2:14:28), who commented: "If Heatley put in some long runs and trained for the marathon seriously I'm sure he could run under 2:15."

Well, Heatley did ... and to such effect that he relieved Edelen of the world record in June 1964! Competing in the Polytechnic Marathon on the celebrated Windsor to Chiswick course, he was content to pass 10 miles in 51:05, 45 sec behind the leaders (who included Ron Hill, credited with a world's best 20 miles road time of 1:40:55 two weeks earlier). Heatley passed Hill for the lead shortly before 20 miles (1:42:05 against 1:42:10) and came home 100 yards ahead in

2:13:55. Hill, the UK 6 miles record holder, also bettered the previous record with 2:14:12.

Four months later, in Tokyo, Heatley became the fourth Briton (after Sam Ferris 1932, Ernie Harper 1936 and Tom Richards 1948) to earn an Olympic marathon silver medal. Although outclassed by the incredible Ethiopian Abebe Bikila (who set a world record of 2:12:12), he ran with characteristic determination to prove himself the second best marathon runner in the world. Bothered by stitch for much of the race, Heatley was 12th at halfway ("I was totally in despair, thinking that I had blown it"), eighth at 30km, fifth at 35km and third, 75 sec behind Kokichi Tsuburaya, at 40km. But he finished brilliantly, overtaking his Japanese rival on the stadium lap to the consternation of most of the spectators and ensuring second place by sprinting the final 200m in an extraordinary 32.3 sec. He had no idea at the time that he had run himself into a medal position. Kilby – European and Commonwealth champion in 1962 – placed fourth, his chances having been diminished by a physically draining run-off for the one remaining Olympic team place.

Hill, previously selected alongside Heatley, finished 19th, a victim of the killing early pace. Heatley announced his international retirement after the Games but continued to compete for Godiva for several more years and has remained closely involved with the sport.

KEN MATTHEWS

Born 21.6.1934 Birmingham.
Club: Royal Sutton Coldfield WC

BRITISH WALKERS HAVE been responsible, although regrettably not in recent decades, for many international triumphs – but none has been quite as successful as Ken Matthews. The tall Midlander won four of his five major international tests at 20 kilometres: the European title in 1962 (1:35:54), the first two finals of the Lugano Trophy in 1961 (1:30:54) and 1963 (1:30:10) where he led Britain to victory in what was in effect the world team championship each time, and the Olympic gold medal in Tokyo in 1964. The only blot on his record came at the 1960 Olympics where he was a non-finisher.

Matthews, an electrical maintenance engineer, began his walking career at the age of 18, following in the footsteps of his father Joe, a founder member of the Royal Sutton Coldfield Walking Club and himself a long distance walking participant. It was Joe who coached his son, later on with help from Harold Whitlock.

Ken first attracted attention when, almost unknown, he defeated Britain's 1956 Olympic 20km trio of Stan Vickers, George Coleman and Roland Hardy in a 10 miles race just before the team left for Melbourne. He further boosted his reputation as a giant-killer in 1958 when he beat the newly crowned European champion Vickers over 5 miles.

The following year he captured the first of numerous national titles, began his international career, and set an unofficial world record of 34:26.6 for 5 miles. Lifetime best performances in 1960 of the calibre of 13:09.6 for 2 miles (behind Vickers' 13:02.4 in a great duel at the AAA Championships), 42:35.6 for 10,000m and 1:28:15 for 20km suggested a possible Olympic victory but in Rome he fell victim to a combination of the after effects of 'flu, his own ruthless pace and the searing heat.

The result was that he collapsed and was taken to hospital, echoing Don Thompson's experience in the Olympic 50km four years earlier. Vickers sportingly eased up to help Matthews but his colleague urged him on ... "You go on, my legs are turning to rubber."

Vickers, the 1958 European champion, went on to finish third. As for Matthews, he lost little time in re-establishing himself. Later in the month he set a UK hour record of 8 miles 1018 yards and in another race he reduced his 5 miles world best to 34:21.2, a minute ahead of Vickers and another half minute more in front of Australia's Olympic silver medallist Noel Freeman.

He went on to record an exceptional series of performances at all distances from 2 to 20 miles. Almost unbeatable in domestic events, he won 17 national titles – the AAA 2 miles in 1959 and 1961-1964, AAA 7 miles 1959-1961 and 1963-1964, the Race Walking Association's 10 miles from 1959 to 1964, and the 20 miles in 1962. Between 1964 and 1971 he held every British record from 5 miles to 2 hours, including a world best of 69:40.6 for 10 miles in 1964.

But the crowning glory of his career came in Tokyo where he spreadeagled the best the world could offer to win the Olympic 20km title by more than a minute and a half. As I reported for *Athletics Weekly*: "Judging his pace to perfection, Ken Matthews brought Britain her second gold medal in 24 hours [Mary Rand preceded him] with a 'walkaway' 400 yard victory in the superb time of 1:29:34 [Olympic record].

"He took the lead at about the 3 miles mark and proceeded to draw further and further away from his rivals. His lead grew from 1 sec at 5km (22:19) to 24 sec at 10km (44:23), 53 sec at 15km (66:52) and no less than 1 min 40 sec at the finish. Ken has sometimes been criticised for his extravagant speed in the early stages of his races, but on this occasion his judgement was flawless. The 5km splits were 22:19, 22:04, 22:29 and 22:42 ... marvellously controlled speed walking. Ken received one warning in the early stages but thereafter his style was never in doubt. His only worry was whether, in view of the early speed on a warm (23°C) afternoon, he would last the final 3km. Ken said afterwards that he had put on a few pounds in weight prior to the race and felt the stronger for it."

That walkers were still unfairly regarded as second class citizens in the world of athletics became apparent when Britain's other three gold medallists from Tokyo – Lynn Davies, Mary Rand and Ann Packer – very quickly featured in the Queen's Honours List but it wasn't until 13 years later that, following a campaign organised by the Race Walking Association, Matthews at last received his richly deserved MBE.

THELMA HOPKINS
Born 16.3.1936 Hull.
Clubs: Queen's University, Belfast; Shorts AC

THE FORMIDABLE ACHIEVEMENT of Dorothy Tyler and Sheila Lerwill in setting world high jump records and winning Olympic silver medals was emulated by Thelma Hopkins. Born in Hull but raised in Belfast from the age of nine months and always regarded as a Northern Irish athlete, she – like Tyler before her – flowered early. She was only 16 when she placed third in the 1952 WAAA Championships at 1.625 and fourth in the Helsinki Olympics at 1.58, a competition in which Lerwill finished second and Tyler (who won her first Olympic silver when Thelma was a babe in arms) seventh.

Coached by Franz Stampfl, whose other athletes at the time included Chris Brasher and who helped mastermind the first sub-four minute mile, Thelma won two gold medals in 1954, a double which had always eluded Tyler and Lerwill. She cleared 1.67 at both the Commonwealth Games and European Championships, on the latter occasion coming from behind after Iolanda Balas cleared the Romanian record height of 1.65 at the first attempt, whereas Thelma needed two tries before making the winning height first time. The stork-like Balas would go on two years later to set the first of 14 world records (culminating in 1.91 in 1961) and win two Olympic titles.

For good measure Thelma also struck silver in the Commonwealth Games long jump, an event in which her best was 6.11, just 3cm below the then British record. Indeed, she was such a talented all-rounder that in 1955 she set a British pentathlon record of 4289 in Ballymena ... with a 16 year-old Mary Peters a distant third. She won WAAA titles in the long jump (1955) and 80m hurdles (1957), while at the World Student Games in 1961 she was third in both the hurdles and high jump as well as raising her pentathlon score that year to 4379. It was not until 1964 that she clocked her fastest hurdles time of 11.2. Outside of athletics, she won 40 caps for Ireland as a hockey forward (her sister Moira was an international too) and also represented the Emerald Isle at squash.

But back to high jumping. Her great year was 1956, when she was 20. A dental student at Queen's University, Belfast (she later became a PE teacher), she cleared 1.74 at Belfast's Cherryvale Track to add a centimetre to the world record held by Aleksandra Chudina (USSR) and 2cm to Lerwill's UK record. That stood as a British record for eight years but her reign as world record holder lasted only 70 days before Balas took over. It was anticipated that the Olympic gold medal in Melbourne would go to either Balas or Hopkins, but both were outclassed by the inspired American Mildred McDaniel, who was the only contestant to clear 1.70 and then proceeded to break the world record with 1.76. No fewer than six jumpers made 1.67, with Thelma and the USSR's Mariya Pisareva incurring no failures up to and including that height and tying for the silver medal. Balas placed fifth on countback ... amazingly, she would not lose another competition until June 1967! In 1957 Thelma (later Mrs McClernon) set a modest world indoor best of 1.65 but her glory days were over. Her subsequent best was 1.71 in 1961 and she bowed out after the 1964 season.

ARTHUR ROWE

Born 17.8.1937 Barnsley (Yorkshire); died 13.9.2003.
Club: Doncaster Plant Works AC

FORMERLY A PROMISING full back (he turned down a professional football offer from Rotherham United when he was 17), Arthur Rowe handled a shot for the first time ever while waiting to bat in a cricket match. With his pads on he managed to heave the junior (12lb) implement about 43ft (13.10). It was hardly an epoch-making effort but on the other hand it wasn't bad for someone with no idea of technique. He was taken in hand and won the Yorkshire junior title in 1955. Soon afterwards he met chief national coach Geoff Dyson, who had guided John Savidge to nine British shot records ranging from 14.90 in 1949 to 16.83 in 1954. Dyson told Rowe after seeing him reach 41ft (12.50) with the 16-pounder at the end of their first session together: "You can be Europe's first 60-foot (18.29) shot putter".

Rowe, a fine natural athlete who could run 100 yards in 10.2, worked hard on his strength and technique, and progress came swiftly: 15.72 in 1956, his first British record of 16.94 in 1957. By 1958 the colliery blacksmith was ready to take on the world. He set seven UK records: 17.30 when winning the AAA title, 17.57 for the Commonwealth title in Cardiff, 17.68 at Uxbridge, 17.78 in winning the European title in Stockholm with his final put, 17.81 in Gothenburg and 17.96 at the White City and then again in Paris. Only four Americans stood ahead of him on that year's world list.

Silvano Meconi of Italy beat Rowe to Europe's first 60 footer with a distance of 18.48 in May 1959 (Rowe had reached 18.43 in an exhibition a week earlier) but in August, at White City, Rowe smashed his UK record with 18.29 in the second round and annexed the European record in the fifth round with 18.59, again ranking no 5 in the world (and first non-American) that season.

Judging by a mighty exhibition toss of 19.66 in June 1960 and a new UK record of 18.92 just before the Olympics, Rowe seemed assured of fourth place at the very worst, behind the American trio, but the Rome Games proved to be as monumental a flop for Rowe as they were for Gordon Pirie and all too many others in the British team. There was nothing wrong with his 19.19 training put the day after arriving in the Italian capital but during the succeeding days he was weakened, he claims, by a combination of dysentery and lack of appetite brought on by the considerable heat and humidity. Ten pounds (4.5kg) lighter than when he arrived, Rowe was indeed a pathetic sight in the qualifying competition. All that was needed to make the final was 16.75 but the best he could muster was 16.68.

However, the other two Britons, Mike Lindsay (fifth in the final with 17.80) and Martyn Lucking (eighth at 17.43), rose splendidly to the occasion. The title was won by world record holder Bill Nieder with 19.68, followed by his US team-mates Parry O'Brien (19.11) and Dallas Long (19.01).

So dejected was Rowe that he considered retiring there and then but on reflection he decided to continue, determined to establish himself as the world's number one. Soon after returning from Rome he hit 19.78 in training and, on a bitterly cold and windy October day in East Berlin, amid pouring rain, he lengthened the European record to 19.11.

He carried all before him in 1961; undefeated all season he improved to 19.44 and 19.56. Just one man threw further that year, Long with a best of 19.70, and only one other had ever bettered Rowe's mark ... Nieder with his world record 20.06 in 1960. Rowe was now truly among the greats and, especially after a fantastic training put of 20.15, there was a distinct possibility of his becoming world record holder in 1962 as well as the near-certainty of retaining both Commonwealth and European titles. Unhappily, none of these prizes came his way for in July 1962 – still only 24 – he signed professional Rugby League forms for Oldham. It was a decision he was to regret, for his new career lasted only a few weeks. His official best for the season was 19.49, which ranked him third in the world, while he registered 1cm further in a professional meeting. He continued to compete on the Scottish Highland Games circuit for many years but winning the world caber-tossing title in 1970 hardly compared to the honours he might have accrued had he retained his amateur status. He died aged 66.

JOYCE SMITH

Born 26.10.1937 Stoke Newington (London).
Clubs: Hampstead H, Barnet AC

OTHER ATHLETES MAY have clocked faster times and claimed more titles, but surely there is nothing to compare with Joyce Smith's record of sustained top-class achievement in a career of such prodigious length. She gained her first international badge, as reserve for the England cross country team, in 1956 – and yet in 1980 she was at the height of her powers as the third fastest female marathon runner in history. At the age of 43 she was running better than ever! Joyce has represented Britain at 800m, set UK records at 1500m and come close to reaching the Olympic final, broken a world record and won a European bronze medal in the 3000m, scored great international victories at cross country and marathon running, and totally dominated British road racing.

But it was as a sprinter ("they didn't have any longer events at school") and long jumper that Joyce Byatt began her athletics career. She wasn't bad, either, for one year she was the Hertfordshire county schools long jump champion. Ironically, her career – the longevity of which is now legendary – came close to ending almost before it had even started properly, for she gave up athletics when she left school in 1952. Fortunately, one day in 1954 she wandered over to the local track and joined Hampstead Harriers. She returned to the sprints and long jump but it wasn't long before she discovered her forte lay elsewhere. The turning point came when she was asked to run the half mile in a match, and promptly broke the club record with 2:31.

It wasn't until her then boyfriend, Bryan Smith, started coaching her in the spring of 1958 that her career really took off; in less than a year she was English cross country champion. On the track in 1959 she displayed a penchant for the longer distances, defeating the athlete she most admired, Diane Leather, in a 4:36.6 1500m. Joyce retained her national cross country title in 1960, shortly before becoming Mrs Smith, and challenged unsuccessfully for a place in the team for Rome since the women's 800m was back as an Olympic event for the first time since 1928. In her first run abroad she made an enormous improvement to 2:10.2, well inside the Olympic qualifying standard, but her international match debut proved a disappointing experience ... and turned out to be her last track appearance for Britain for a dozen years!

For several years, dogged by injury, she pottered on happy enough to be just a club runner, but in 1965 she made a successful comeback to top-class competition, winning the WAAA mile title in 4:53.5. At the time she stated that she intended competing "at the most two more track seasons." In fact, following those two seasons she became pregnant and with the birth of Lisa in July 1968 she could have decided that, at 30, her racing career was over.

On the contrary, Joyce couldn't wait to get back into stride and in 1969 she led the Barnet club (Hampstead having been amalgamated) to team victory in the National cross country. Better yet, she finished third in the 1971 International cross country championship, leading the English team to first place. That summer, when Lisa started play school, leaving Joyce with more time to train, she moved up to 3000m and in clocking 9:23.4 to win the WAAA title she smashed the unofficial world's best. At 33 she was a world record holder ... albeit in a then undeveloped event.

The following year, in Cambridge, she ran out the first British winner of the women's International cross country title. It was then that she realised there was the possibility of making the Olympic team at 1500m – although she and Bryan had already booked up to go to Munich on holiday! Her best before that summer was merely 4:25.2 but she improved sensationally to 4:12.8, just 0.1 outside Rita Ridley's UK record, and she not only made the team but was appointed women's captain.

In Munich she distinguished herself by setting a UK record of 4:11.3 in her heat and improving again to 4:09.4 in the semis (covering the final 800m in a personal best of 2:08.4!) but just failing to reach the final. That time would have been a world record at the start of 1972, but the event had moved on ... and so did Joyce.

Later in 1972, the world record having progressed to 8:53.0, she posted the world's second fastest ever 3000m time of 9:05.8 and that was the distance she aimed for in the 1974 European Championships. Two weeks after the world record had been trimmed to 8:52.7 Joyce came close in her *heat* at the WAAA Championships. Covering the first half in an over ambitious 4:22.0 she finished what was in effect a time trial in 8:55.6.

The inaugural European title race went to Nina Holmen of Finland in 8:55.2 with Joyce taking the bronze medal (one month short of her 37th birthday) in 8:57.4 and a fine season was rewarded by her being voted UK woman athlete of the year by the British Athletics Writers' Association.

Following a low-key 1975 Joyce's training was geared to running 4:04 for 1500m at the Montreal Olympics (that was still the longest women's event) but she became pregnant again and Lia was born in August 1976. Although well below her old form she still managed to represent Britain at 3000m in 1978 but as she was no longer enjoying track racing "we thought we would come back and train just for the marathon in 1979." Her real career was just about to start at the age of 41.

Her initial marathon aim was simply to break 2:50, the British best standing at 2:50:54 by Rosemary Cox while the world best was 2:32:30 by Norway's Grete Waitz. Her baptism was the WAAA Championship race at Sandbach in June 1979, and she got off to a flying start by winning, despite errors in pace judgement, in 2:41:37. Her next attempt was the prestigious Avon event in Waldniel, Germany, in September and she won again in 2:36:27, a Commonwealth record and world veterans best which ranked her sixth on the world all-time list. She made it three out of three when in Tokyo in November she scored in 2:37:48.

Every marathon runner eventually has a bad one, and her next race was one to forget. Running in very hot and humid conditions in Miami in January 1980 she virtually blacked out during the final mile and was helped across the line and thus disqualified. She recovered completely in good time for her next marathon, at Sandbach in June, and despite treating it as a training run lowered her Commonwealth record to 2:33:32.

Her main target for the year was the big Avon Marathon in London but a combination of missing training after catching chickenpox and then tearing a calf muscle held her back to seventh in 2:41:22. However, she ended the year on a high in Tokyo in November when she triumphed in 2:30:27, quickest ever in a women-only race. Only Waitz (2:25:42 and 2:27:33) and Patti Catalano (USA) with 2:29:34, all in New York in races against men, had better times. It was a sobering thought that at age 43 she was now faster than Jack Holden, another legendary veteran, ever was.

An even greater race came next: the inaugural London Marathon in March 1981. She hadn't anticipated being in such form, but in the excitement of the event she ran above herself. The spectators were particularly appreciative of the women runners and Joyce, as the first to be sighted, got a tremendous ovation throughout, which helped lift her to new heights. "I got a bit carried away," she said later, as she savoured the news that she had broken through the 2:30 barrier with the glorious figures of 2:29:57, a world veterans best.

In London the following year she ran still faster with 2:29:43, at 44 becoming the oldest athlete ever to set a British record. She reached halfway in a stunning 1:13:39, two minutes clear of New Zealander Lorraine Moller (previously unbeaten in marathons with a best time of 2:29:36), and by the finish was well over a mile clear for her sixth UK marathon record. Although she never bettered 2:32 again, Joyce continued to compete with distinction for several more years, including 11th place (2:32:48) in the inaugural Olympic race in Los Angeles in 1984 ... and she still races, ranking no 1 in Britain in 2004 among the age-65+ group at 800m and 1500m.

RON HILL

Born 21.9.1938 Accrington (Lancashire).
Club: Bolton United H

LIKE SO MANY of his age group, a schoolboy growing up in the immediate post-war years, Ron Hill's athletics inspiration was Alf Tupper, 'The Tough of the Track'. Hill identified closely with this fictitious hero of *The Rover*.

As Hill wrote in part one of his autobiography, *Nearly To The Top*: "Alf was always up against it ... whenever he had a big race coming up something went wrong, there were disasters to avert, emergencies to sort out, usually involving working all night, but he always tried to overcome this and, full of his favourite diet of fish and chips, he would vault over the railings of the track just in time to start the race. Then in a desperate finish he would 'run 'em', the university boys who couldn't stand him, and the foreign athletes.

"It used to bring a smile to my face to think of Alf, walking victoriously away from the track, his holey vest, tattered shorts and running shoes wrapped up in brown paper. Here was a lad (I never thought of him as a man) who, despite all adversities and by his own determination, succeeded." There was a lot of Alf Tupper in Ron Hill's own make-up.

As he progressed through his teens, Hill – himself a Lancashire lad – did well academically. He won a scholarship to the Manchester University Faculty of Technology (after deliberately throwing away a chance of a place at Oxford) but athletically he showed few signs of developing into a world-beating runner. In 1957, his last year as a junior on the track, his best mile time was no faster than 4:53.

His first substantial successes came in cross country and fell running but it was as a marathon runner that, in 1961 (aged 22), he burst into national prominence. Although he had never raced beyond 15 miles on the road before, he entered the Liverpool City Marathon – but only because he couldn't find a more suitable event that day. It may not have been the most positive of reasons for tackling a marathon but the result was a stunning victory in 2:24:22. "Never again" was Hill's immediate reaction, but soon afterwards he picked up a copy of Jim Peters' book *In The Long Run* and he was hooked!

Hill's early marathon running – brilliant though it was on occasion – was all too notable for its inconsistency. He just couldn't do himself justice on the big occasion, largely due to an unquenchable enthusiasm for racing like crazy all over the place. In June 1962 he won the Windsor to Chiswick marathon in 2:21:59 but was drained by the time of his first major international test: the European Championships in Belgrade in September. While Brian Kilby won the gold medal and Alastair Wood placed fourth, Hill dropped out at about 30km.

Having plumbed the depths, as on that occasion, Hill would relish all the more the sweet smell of success in later years, but there were other setbacks to overcome first ... like the 1964 Olympics. He flew to Tokyo as the second fastest marathon runner in history (he ran 2:14:12 behind Basil Heatley's 2:13:55 in the Polytechnic event from Windsor to Chiswick earlier in the year) as well as the third fastest six-miler of all time (27:27.0), but everything went wrong and he wound up, lapped, in 18th place (29:53.0) in the 10,000m and 19th in the marathon (2:25:35) after going too fast early on.

"The first day back at work after Tokyo was very embarrassing," he recalled. "Everyone seemed wary of talking about the Olympic races. It was a subject almost like a death in the family, people wanted to say they were sorry, but didn't like to mention the subject." It was a situation that Paula Radcliffe would find herself in after the Athens Olympics 40 years later.

The 1966 Commonwealth Games (fifth in the 6 miles, lapped by the winner) and European Championships (victim of a stomach disorder, 12th in marathon) brought further anguish ... but the spirit remained unbroken. Dismissing a newspaper story which suggested he was planning to retire, Hill's reaction was "What the hell was there to retire from? I hadn't done anything yet!" Well, only smashing Emil Zátopek's world track records for 15 miles (with 1:12:48.2) and 25km (1:15:22.6) in 1965, a world's road best of 1:40:55 for 20 miles in 1964, a British 6 miles record (27:49.8 winning the 1963 AAA title), an English cross country title in 1964, what was at the time the world's second quickest ever marathon, and so on.

"This latest downfall made me even more determined one day to succeed," he declared, and his sights were set on the Mexico City Olympics of 1968. Stepping up his training he won the English cross country title a second time and finished a close third in the International championship. He felt now he could aim for a medal in the Olympic marathon, regardless of the altitude problem.

Everything was shaping up marvellously; in April he broke Ron Clarke's world 10 miles track record with 47:02.2 and in May he clocked a world's best 20 miles time of 1:36:28 (2:07 marathon pace) ... but, to his chagrin, the selectors did not pick him for the Olympic marathon, just the 10,000m. In the circumstances it was an heroic performance by him to finish seventh, the first man home who had not either lived or trained extensively at high altitude.

That fine run was to prove the turning point in Hill's fortunes in big races. Back in Britain shortly after the Games he reduced his world 10 miles record to 46:44.0 en route to a UK record 20,471m in the hour, and it was during his preparations for the 1969 season that Hill started what he described as "playing around with a special diet". Tests in Sweden, primarily on skiers, had indicated the advantages of using up an athlete's reserves, keeping to a low carbohydrate diet to establish glycogen starvation, and then for two days utilising a high carbohydrate diet – this carbohydrate being converted to glycogen and stored by the muscles to good effect.

Dr Hill (he has a PhD in textile chemistry) brought his scientific mind to bear on the possible application of such a diet to the marathon, and his first tentative trial took place in the week leading up to the Maxol Marathon in Manchester in July 1969. The result was victory in a personal best of 2:13:42 with the Lancashire-born Australian, Derek Clayton, who had recently set a world best of 2:08:34, left almost two minutes behind.

Hill prepared meticulously for the European title race to be staged from Marathon to Athens in September ... to the extent of shaving his legs the morning of the race to give an extra cooling effect and wearing startling new racing gear of string vest and very brief-cut shorts for the same purpose. Belgium's Gaston Roelants built up a huge lead but struggled in the closing stages, enabling Hill to sweep past in the final kilometre for victory in 2:16:48.

The strength of his running late in the race proved that the diet was working and he ended his best year so far with a personal best of 2:11:55 in finishing second to Jerome Drayton of Canada in Fukuoka, Japan.

But 1970 was to prove even more successful, the year in which Hill was to be ranked world's number one. In April he became the first Briton to win the Boston classic, and in the European record time of 2:10:30; while in July he ran the race of his life in the Commonwealth Games in Edinburgh. Pulling away after 8 miles he disposed of Drayton, Clayton and the rest as he zipped through 10 miles in 47:45 and 20 miles in 1:37:30.

He was on course for a time in the 2:08 region, but in the closing stages he played safe by easing off a little. He won by half a mile from defending champion Jim Alder in 2:09:28, at the time a European record, the second fastest performance of all time and easily the best ever in a championship race.

He looked poised to dominate marathon running for the next few years, but it was not to be ... he never again broke 2:12. He described his bronze medal at the 1971 European Championships behind Karel Lismont of Belgium and Trevor Wright as "only marginally better than a kick up the backside" – furious that he had been forced to run in the selection trial only nine weeks earlier.

At the end of the year he asked the BAAB for pre-selection for the 1972 Olympics, but the request fell on deaf ears. He had to qualify through a trial race and in Munich he finished a dejected sixth. His dream of becoming the first Briton to win the Olympic marathon was shattered.

He has continued racing, to this day. In 1979 he set a British veterans best of 2:15:46 and in December 2004 he completed the astonishing record of having run *every single day* for 40 years! Since 1956 he has notched up over 145,000 miles of running and had raced in 87 countries ... and counting.

MARY PETERS

Born 6 July 1939 Halewood (near Liverpool).
Clubs: Ballymena AC, Spartan LAC, Shorts AC

IT WAS NOT until she was 33, after 17 years of pentathlon competition, that Mary Peters 'overnight' became one of the world's great sports stars and a household name throughout the British Isles when in Munich in 1972 she joined the immortals by winning an Olympic title with a world record performance – in the tradition established by Britain's only previous female Olympic champions, Mary Rand and Ann Packer.

Her story is one of perseverance. Overshadowed as a pentathlete by Rand and never quite making world class as a shot putter, her career might well have ended after a disappointing showing at the 1968 Olympics where, hampered by an injured ankle, she placed ninth. She was already 29 and had she quit then she would have been remembered as a very good and big hearted athlete (she placed fourth in the 1964 Games) but not truly the great one she became.

Instead she took off 1969 in order to regain her zest and, competing at her fourth Commonwealth Games, in 1970, she won gold medals in both the shot and pentathlon, representing Northern Ireland. Although born on the outskirts of Liverpool, she had lived in Ulster from the age of 11. Her pentathlon score of 5148 (4515 on the later tables) re-established her among the world's elite after a gap of six years.

Again she passed up competition in 1971 as she prepared for the following year's Olympics, and the indoor season of 1972 saw her transformed as a high jumper. Previously just a competent straddle jumper with a best of 1.67, she emerged as a Fosbury-flopper of close to world class. This dramatic improvement was worth over 100 points in that one event and was the key to her Olympic aspirations.

During the Olympic build-up period she raised the UK record to 4630, which ranked her fifth among the pentathlon contenders, and from the very first event in Munich it was apparent she was in superb form and afraid of nobody. She clocked 13.29 for the 100m hurdles, a UK record on electrical timing; put the shot 16.20, which was only 11cm below her UK record; and ended the first day with an inspired high jump of 1.82 with the predominantly German crowd taking the bouncy blonde with the flashing smile and cheery wave to its collective heart despite the fact that with each successful clearance she was widening her points advantage over West Germany's big hope, the European champion Heide Rosendahl. Mary's overnight score of 2969, the highest ever recorded, gave her a handsome lead over the GDR's world record holder Burglinde Pollak (2872) with Rosendahl only fifth on 2668 ... but with her two strongest events to come.

On the second day Mary went close to her modest personal best of 6.04 with a long jump of 5.98, but Rosendahl – world record holder for the event – cleared a massive 6.83 to narrow the gap considerably. The scores going into the final event, the 200m, were: 1, Peters 3871; 2, Pollak 3824; 3, Rosendahl 3750. Bearing in mind that Mary's personal best for 200m stood at 24.2, compared to 23.1 by Rosendahl and 23.8 by Pollak, it was clear that it was still anybody's title. A duplication of those times would result in Mary finishing with a score of 4790 ahead of Pollak 4781 and Rosendahl 4776. What it amounted to was that Mary would have to finish no more than 1.2 sec behind Rosendahl and 0.4 behind Pollak. It would be the ultimate test of nerve as well as speed.

"My legs went like jelly about 40 yards from home and I had to get those arms going and just drive like hell", she recalled. It was immediately obvious that she had finished close enough to Pollak, as there was not much more than a metre between them at the line. But Rosendahl had finished about ten metres ahead, her time flashing up as 22.96 – a wonderful run into a slight headwind. Hasty consultation of the scoring tables indicated Mary would need 24.18 to win. The suspense was unbearable during the minutes that passed before the other times became available. It was 24.08! Technically, Rosendahl had held the world record for 1.12 sec but Mary had won by 10 points, her final score of 4801 points being a world record for good measure.

She had begun her career as a pentathlete in 1955, aged 16, when she placed third in the Northern Irish Championships with 3253 points, a contest won by her early inspiration, Thelma Hopkins, with a British record score of 4289, with Maeve Kyle second. Three years later she made her Commonwealth Games debut in Cardiff. Undertrained and out of her depth, it's not surprising she didn't exactly set the stadium alight: she placed eighth out of nine in the shot (11.21), equal 10th out of 14 in the high jump (1.47) and also ran on the 4x110y relay team which finished last in the final. She represented Britain for the first time (as a shot putter) in 1961, but it was in 1962 (now coached by Buster McShane) that she made the big leap forward. Her highest pentathlon score had been 3940 in 1961 but she collected her first WAAA pentathlon title with 4190, scored 4420 to win an international event and improved to 4586 for fifth place in the European Championships. At year's end she finished fourth in the Commonwealth Games shot.

The next major test was the inaugural Olympic pentathlon in Tokyo. In May 1964 Mary had claimed her first British record, scoring 4801 for the WAAA title to add 75 points to Mary Rand's 1963 figures. Rand regained the record in June with 4815, but in August Mary struck again with 4823, a score which ranked her fourth on the world all-time list behind three Soviet athletes. Fourth would be her position in Tokyo in October with a score of 4797. Third overnight with Rand fourth, she finished behind Irina Press (world record 5246), Rand (UK record 5035) and Galina Bystrova (4956).

It would be another four years before she returned to that level. In the meantime, as an experiment, she put on nearly three stones (up to 84kg or 185lb) in order to concentrate on the shot. She became British record holder in 1966 with 16.31 but was very disappointed with a silver medal in that year's Commonwealth Games. A further setback came at the 1968 Olympics where a score of 4803 earned only ninth place.

It all started to come good in 1970 and after another deliberate rest in 1971 she began her preparations for Munich. In January 1972 Buster McShane announced his Olympic targets for Mary: 100m hurdles in 13.4 (her best so far was 13.6), 16.76 shot (16.40), 1.78 high jump (1.71, but had only just converted to Fosbury flop), 6.20 long jump (5.73) and 23.9 for 200m (24.5) – a theoretical score of 4844 on the new tables, a fantastic 5480 on the old!

When I interviewed Mary for *Athletics Weekly* a few weeks after her Olympic triumph with the world record score of 4801 (5430 on the old tables), I asked her how she had assessed her Munich chances. "I went for gold; there was nothing else in my mind but gold," she replied. Did she spend an anxious night after her fantastic first day? "I slept very little. I kept thinking what will happen if I sleep in and [team manager] Marea [Hartman] doesn't wake me in time? I was thinking of what I must do in the long jump (Buster predicted I needed 5.94 to keep me in with a chance) ... I was running that 200 so many times in my mind ... and I was going over the high jump bar still – the adrenalin was still flowing. All the time I kept thinking about whether it would be my day tomorrow."

Mary jumped 5.98 to stay in contention for gold. How did she spend her time between that event and the final test, the 200m? "I missed Buster after the long jump and I was upset. I went back to my room, I couldn't even eat. Tears again, nerves, apprehension. As I lay there some of the girls came in and they were saying what are you worrying about, you've got a medal. I said I know, but I want the gold. I wanted it so much [primarily because she wanted her beloved adopted city of Belfast to celebrate something amid all the sectarian strife]. You had told me after the long jump that I needed to run 24.1; I knew I could do it if everything went right but 200 is such a long way round for me."

Tragically, Buster McShane died in a car crash in April 1973, and understandably she never rose to such heights again, but she bade a golden farewell to the Commonwealth Games early in 1974 with a narrow pentathlon victory with 4455. Mary P continued to make valuable contributions to the sport she had graced for so long with her bubbly personality and astounding versatility. She raised a huge amount of money for what became the Mary Peters Track at Queen's University, Belfast (it opened in 1976); she qualified as a senior coach in 1975, was British women's team manager at the 1980 and 1984 Olympics, served a term as president of the British Athletics Federation, and in 2000 was made a Dame for her services to the sport.

PAUL NIHILL

Born 5.9.1939 Colchester (Essex). Club: Surrey WC

IN THE WORLD of walking in the 1960s and 1970s, Paul Nihill was considered something of a phenomenon. Walkers tend to compete over a wider range of distances than their running colleagues, but Nihill's versatility was quite astonishing. Olympic silver medallist over 50 kilometres (31 miles+) in Tokyo in 1964, he was also acknowledged as the fastest – and fairest – of all speed walkers, his achievements including a 6:17.0 mile time in 1970 which broke George Larner's British record which had stood since 1904!

Born of Irish parents, he started out in sport as a boxer, sprinter and hurdler. From 1954 to 1959 he was chiefly a cross country runner (of county standard), but he had to give up running after a knee operation and in 1960 he began training seriously for walking. He won the Irish mile walk title in 1962 and made his British international debut the following year, contributing to team victory in the Lugano Trophy by finishing second to Ken Matthews in the 20 kilometres. It was in that year that he made his debut at 50km (4:51:32), a time he reduced considerably to 4:26:06 in 1963.

Further proof of his ability to perform at his best on the big occasion came in the 1964 Olympics when he pushed the favourite, Italy's Abdon Pamich, all the way and lost by less than 20 sec in the British record time of 4:11:32. Defending Olympic champion Don Thompson placed tenth.

In 1965 Nihill, a London bank clerk, set about gaining a clean sweep of Britain's six national titles. He succeeded in the 2 miles, 7 miles, 10 miles, 20km and 20 miles but, in the final race, the 50km, he 'blew up' and finished fifth. Later in the year, having overtaxed himself mentally and physically, he suffered a breakdown in his health. Further setbacks occurred in 1966 when he was omitted from England's Commonwealth Games team, failed to finish in the national 50km championship and withdrew from the European Championships. He then announced his retirement. Happily, it proved short lived and he returned better than ever.

Except for the Mexico City Olympic 50km, in which he collapsed from heat exhaustion after setting the pace until halfway ("next thing I recall was looking at the roof of the ambulance"), Nihill carried all before him in 1968, winning all four national road titles. The following season he raced away with the European 20km title in Athens. That success was vital for his self-confidence, re-establishing himself as a great championship competitor. His plan was to stay in close touch with the leaders for 15km and then try to break away, and it worked to perfection. Despite the hot and humid conditions he covered the second half of the race in 44:33 to win by 26 sec in 1:30:41. Twelve days earlier, in a training session at Crystal Palace, Nihill had clocked an astonishing 6:06 for a mile walk, some 9 sec faster than the world best. Paced by David Hemery (who of course was running!) and utilising to the full his long four-foot stride, he reeled off the quarters in 92, 94, 89 and 91 sec.

Jaundice prevented his competing in the 1970 Commonwealth Games but he recovered sufficiently to record several fine performances during the year. In 1971, in defence of his European 20km title, he placed a close third. A month before the 1972 Olympics he clocked a world road best of 1:24:50 on the Isle of Man and was justifiably confident of winning the gold medal, but following three weeks of altitude training in St Moritz he could place only sixth (1:28:45) in Munich, where he later finished ninth at 50km. In a letter to *Sportsworld* magazine he expressed his frustration. "It was four years' work down the drain. I really should have won, yet I was well beaten and hardly able to walk afterwards because my legs felt so heavy –

like severe cramp in the thighs. Never in my 17 years walking have I had leg trouble in a 20km except through injury. Obviously, the trouble was due to acclimatisation after returning to sea level." He felt that the lack of knowledge about how, or even whether, to train at altitude also cost Ron Hill the marathon gold medal.

In 1976 he made the 20km team for Montreal to become the first British male athlete to compete in four Olympics. At shorter distances the 'Guv'nor', as he was affectionately known by the walking fraternity, set world track bests of 11:51.2 for 3000m in 1971 and 20:14.2 for 5000m in 1972. By the time he retired from major competition in 1977 he had amassed a record total of 27 national titles between 1963 and 1975 and from December 1967 to June 1970 he sustained only one defeat in 86 races, that dnf in Mexico City. Nihill later returned to running, clocking 76:51 for a half marathon in 1984, aged 44.

PETER RADFORD

Born 20.9.1939 Walsall. Club: Birchfield H

THE DEPARTURE OF McDonald Bailey in 1953, shortly after gaining his seventh AAA sprint double, left a void in British sprinting that was not to be filled satisfactorily for five years. But a wonderful new sprint talent emerged in 1958 ... Peter Radford. A serious kidney disease contracted when he was five confined him to a wheelchair for two years but, like so many other eventual world beaters, this bitter childhood experience equipped him with the grim determination and perseverance that are among the qualities so necessary to excel in sport.

By the age of 14 he was already returning such times as 10.4 for 100y and 24.0 for 220y. The following season (1955) he followed up third place in the Midland Youths 440y championship (54.4) with victory in the English Schools intermediate 100y. In 1956, still only 16, he returned 'evens' (10.0) and in 1957, by now under the influence of AAA National Coach Bill Marlow, he was down to 9.9 and 21.8.

Radford opened his momentous 1958 campaign with a wind-assisted 9.7 and even sceptics, understandably wary of unsubstantiated schoolboy times, were completely won over when he appeared at the important London Athletic Club schools meeting later in April. The surprise of seeing a bearded schoolboy paled in comparison to the sensation he created with his spectacular knee lift as he flashed to victory in 10.0. Obviously this frail looking (1.78m or 5ft 10in, 64kg or 141lb) teenager had an exciting future in store but few were prepared for his rate of progress. On his home track at Aldersley, Wolverhampton in June he became the first British-born athlete to run 100y in an authentic 9.6 and less than an hour later, against the wind, he clocked 21.4 for 220y.

Representing one's country at such a young age can be a testing ordeal but Radford came through with flying colours. He performed splendidly at the Commonwealth Games in Cardiff, placing fourth in the 100y (missing the bronze medal by 1/100th) and assisting England to victory in the relay. A few days later, at the White City, he recovered brilliantly from a poor start to defeat all three Commonwealth medallists in 9.8. Yet better still was to come. He snatched third place in the European 100m final in Stockholm in 10.4, scored the greatest sprint double in British athletics history until then with UK metric record times of 10.3 (10.31 electrical) and 20.8 against France (both were world junior bests), and ended in October with a British 220y record of 21.0 plus a heavily wind-aided 9.4 100y. As a postscript he was credited with a world indoor 50m best of 5.5 in Germany.

He consolidated his position in 1959, although studying for exams caused him to cut down his training. He turned down numerous tempting scholarship offers from American universities but did travel to the USA for his first major competition of the season. Pitted against the 100y co-world record holder (at 9.3), Dave Sime, he flashed into a yard lead at the halfway mark only to lose in a photo finish as both men were timed in a wind-assisted 9.5. The following month he posted two national records in a week: 10.3 (10.33 electrical) for 100m in Paris inches behind dead-heating Jocelyn Delecour of France and Armin Hary of West Germany, and 9.4 for 100y (a European record) on his favourite Aldersley track, although as there was no wind gauge this mark was never ratified.

It was at the furlong, though, that Radford achieved his greatest performance in 1960. The occasion was the Staffordshire Championships at Aldersley, attended by a mere 200 spectators. That Radford was in tremendous form was obvious; he had opened his season with a 10.5/21.0 metric double and in succeeding weeks had registered 9.6 for 100y, 10.4 for 100m, 21.0 for 220y twice (equalling the UK record) and a British 300y best of 30.0, which he later trimmed to 29.9. Conditions at Aldersley were just perfect and, in the absence of any pressure, Radford was ideally relaxed – which is half the battle for a sprinter seeking fast times.

This was the sequence of events on that memorable afternoon: 2.30 – 100y heat in 9.4 (1.7m wind), equalling the European record and only a tenth outside the world record; 3.30 – 100y final in 9.3, the wind blowing at 2.4m/sec as against the maximum allowed for records of 2.0m; 4.30 – 220y heat in 23.2; 5.00 – 220y final in world record (for around a turn) of 20.5. The 20.5 timing also constituted a world record for the fractionally shorter 200m distance. Thus Radford, at the age of 20, became the first British-born sprinter to set a world record since Willie Applegarth in 1914. "The start was perfect," he recalled, "and I picked up speed round the sharp bend. Normally I fade a little going into the straight but this time I felt a new surge of energy and kicked right through to the tape."

Radford never again encountered such a favourable combination of circumstances and subsequently failed to better 20.9 for 200m, but over 100m he came within a metre or so of winning the Olympic gold medal in Rome. Radford's frequently mediocre starting ability let him down when he could least afford it but an incredible burst over the final 30-40m carried him into third place behind Hary (10.2/10.32) and Sime (10.2/10.35) in a UK record equalling 10.3 (10.42). If only he had got away to a decent start ... but athletics history is littered with tantalising hypotheses.

It was, as Radford told Alastair Aitken in an interview many years later, a "race that I not only could, but should have won."

As world record holder, Radford appeared to stand a great chance of winning the 200m but the combination of being slightly jaded after the 100m, his lack of experience of racing top men at this distance and some rather perverse seeding resulted in his being eliminated in the semi-finals (20.9). Later in the Games, Radford joined forces with David Jones, Dave Segal and Nick Whitehead for bronze medals in the relay. Although Radford produced the occasional good mark in later seasons – including in 1963 a share of a world 4x110y relay record of 40.0 alongside Ron Jones, David Jones and Berwyn Jones – he never rose to such heights again.

Following several years in North America, Professor Radford re-emerged on the UK athletics scene during the 1990s and was Executive Chairman of the British Athletics Federation from 1994 to 1997. He also made a name for himself as an athletics historian, writing a well received biography of 19th century long distance walker Captain Barclay in 2001. He is currently Director of Research at Brunel University's Department of Sports Sciences.

ROBBIE BRIGHTWELL

Born 27.10.1939 Rawalpindi (India; now Pakistan).
Club: Birchfield H

CONSCIOUS THAT A best 100 yards time of 9.7 was not fast enough to enable him to reach the heights as a 200m runner, Robbie Brightwell was persuaded to move up a distance in preparation for the 1960 Olympics. "There are," he remarked, "no attractions for quarter-miling as far as I am concerned – just force of circumstances. If I was good enough in the sprints I would sit tight and count my blessings." Reluctant or not, Brightwell lost little time in establishing himself as Britain's fastest ever one-lapper.

After winning the first individual 440y race of his life, in June 1960, in 47.6, he felt that 47 sec represented his limit for the season. He seriously under-rated himself. He finished second (47.0) in the AAA 440y behind India's Commonwealth champion Milkha Singh and in the match against France he recorded 46.5 for 400m. He rose magnificently to the occasion at the Rome Olympics, reducing the UK record to 46.2 in his quarter-final and 46.1 in his semi, failing by inches only to win through to the final. It was quite a performance by a 20 year-old in his first season at the event!

He commenced his 1961 campaign in similarly storming fashion. Running in Moscow he demolished Olympic finalists Manfred Kinder (West Germany) and Milkha Singh in 46.2, and four days later in Helsinki he beat the two leading Americans, Ulis Williams and Adolph Plummer, in 46.6. He was on top of the world ... for 48 hours. Then came stunning news from Oslo: Brightwell's UK 400m record had been lowered to 45.8 by 19 year-old Adrian Metcalfe, whose previous best was 47.3 for 440y! Metcalfe's time was received at first with a

Clockwise from top left: WALTER GEORGE, the world's first great miler; ALF SHRUBB, multi-world record breaker; ARNOLD STRODE-JACKSON, winning 1912 Olympic 1500 metres; ALBERT HILL, gold medallist at 800m and 1500m in 1920 Olympics

Clockwise from top left: GUY BUTLER, four times an Olympic medallist;
HAROLD ABRAHAMS, in 1924 became Europe's first Olympic 100m champion;
DOUGLAS LOWE, Olympic 800m winner in 1924 and 1928;
ERIC LIDDELL, Olympic 400m champion in Paris

Clockwise from top left: HAROLD WHITLOCK, winning 1936 Olympic 50 kilometres walk; LORD BURGHLEY, Olympic 400m hurdles champion in 1928; SYDNEY WOODERSON, world record breaker at 880 yards and mile; TOM HAMPSON, winning the 1932 Olympic 800m with world record

*Clockwise from top left: JIM PETERS, who revolutionised marathon running;
DOROTHY TYLER, Olympic silver medallist in 1936 and 1948; CHRIS BRASHER, en
route to Olympic steeplechase gold in Melbourne; ARTHUR WINT, a giant in every sense*

*A landmark in athletics history as ROGER BANNISTER runs 3:59.4 for the first
sub-four minute mile at Oxford in 1954*

*DEREK IBBOTSON (left), later a world mile record breaker, edges
CHRIS CHATAWAY in 1956 AAA 3 miles on a muddy White City track*

GORDON PIRIE on his way to a world record equalling 7:55.6 for 3000 metres in
Trondheim (Norway) in 1956

Looking like a fugitive from the Foreign Legion, DON THOMPSON becomes the 1960 Olympic 50 kilometres walk champion in Rome

*Another of Britain's most successful walkers was KEN MATTHEWS, winner of the
Olympic 20 kilometres title in Tokyo in 1964*

MARY PETERS, a UK 100 metres hurdles record holder, won the 1972 Olympic pentathlon in Munich in 1972 with a world record score

*MARY RAND was a brilliant all-rounder but her forte was the long jump,
winning the 1964 Olympic title in Tokyo with a world record*

In the penultimate race of her career ANN PACKER beat Maryvonne Dupureur of France to win the 1964 Olympic 800 metres in world record time

LYNN DAVIES found the Welsh-like rainy weather in Tokyo all too familiar and brought off a shock Olympic long jump victory in 1964

A training shot of DAVID HEMERY, who won the 1968 Olympic 400 metres hurdles in Mexico City with a staggering world record of 48.12

BRENDAN FOSTER was a world record breaker at 3000 metres and 2 miles and European 5000 metres champion in 1974

Flamboyant DAVE BEDFORD brought the crowds back to UK athletics with his front running exploits, including a world 10,000 metres record

certain amount of scepticism – after all, he had only broken 48 sec for the first time a few weeks earlier.

The first one-lap clash between these two strapping young men took place in the inaugural match between Britain and the USA at the White City. It was a memorable race, if hardly pleasing to Brightwell who found his 440y time of 46.8 sufficed only for last place. Williams won in 46.3, narrowly ahead of Metcalfe whose 46.4 broke the European and UK records. Plummer, destined two years later to hack the world record down to 44.9, was third in 46.8. Next day Metcalfe became virtually a national hero with a superb 440y relay anchor in 45.3.

This exciting pair tangled on six further occasions in 1961, Metcalfe winning four times. The fastest race was in Dortmund where Metcalfe, in the outside lane, reduced the UK 400m record to 45.7, fastest in the world that season and a world junior best. Brightwell ran a personal best of 45.9 in second place. Metcalfe, described by the noted American coach 'Jumbo' Elliott as possessing "the greatest potential I've ever seen in an athlete of his age", was to be plagued by injury and illness in subsequent seasons and never again ran faster than 46.2 for 400m, and so it was left to Brightwell to maintain Britain's prestige in this event.

Faster than ever he was in his days as a sprint specialist (he cut his 200m time to 20.9), Brightwell enjoyed a magnificent season in 1962. He won the AAA title almost casually in 45.9, worth 45.6 for 400m, for a European record which was only 0.2 sec outside the world record. He ran another 45.9, this time over 400m, in capturing the European title. Actually he misjudged his race, for he ran the first 100m much too fast and was a sitting target in the final stages. Sheer guts enabled him to hold off Kinder, with Metcalfe placing fourth. An attack of dysentery on the eve of the 440y final weakened Brightwell at the Commonwealth Games and he was beaten, though only just, by Jamaica's George Kerr.

A foot injury sustained while making a rare indoor appearance caused him to miss most of the 1963 season but in October he proved himself none the worse for his enforced lay-off by registering 46.2 for 400m. He made it known that 1964 would be his final season and that nothing short of the Olympic 400m title would satisfy him. To that end he trained as perhaps no other quarter-miler had ever trained, often running himself to a state of sickness or even collapse. He believed that the Tokyo victor would be the strongest and not necessarily the fastest man in the field; thus he concentrated on improving his stamina. That he succeeded in this aim was made clear when, early in the season, he defeated Britain's leading half-miler John Boulter in 1:48.1 (worth 1:47.4 for 800m).

However, the hyper-fast 400m times being recorded by his American rivals (Mike Larrabee 44.9, Ulis Williams 45.0, Ollan Cassell 45.6) continued to elude him. His season's best was 'only' 46.0, achieved both in the US Championships (where he was narrowly beaten by Larrabee) and in Warsaw, where he turned the tables on Larrabee but lost the race to Poland's Andrzej Badenski (45.7). Significantly, though, he turned in some tremendous relay performances, most notably 44.7 from a flying start.

Hopes of success were raised again when Brightwell won his Olympic semi on a soggy track in a UK record equalling 45.7, but when it came to the final the inspiration had drained away; Olympic nerves had claimed another victim. Not that he ran badly; indeed he clocked 45.7 again but this time it was mechanical, devoid of passion, and by the time he entered the finishing straight he knew he had lost and there was no fight left. Larrabee won in 45.1, Brightwell was fourth, a failure in his own eyes. That was his last individual race but, happily, he redeemed himself with a truly heroic anchor leg in the relay.

The USA won the first heat in 3:05.3, Trinidad the second in 3:05.0 and Britain the third in a UK record of 3:04.7. An epic final was in prospect. Tim Graham, who had exceeded all expectations by finishing sixth in the 400m final in 46.0, again surpassed himself by running the opening leg in 45.9, a metre ahead of the USA and Trinidad.

Metcalfe, showing a timely return to form after having failed to reach the 400m semis, went hell for leather and built up a lead of 5m over Larrabee. The newly crowned Olympic champion surged past at the beginning of the finishing straight but Metcalfe (45.5) handed over in third place 5m behind the USA but only 2m behind Trinidad. On the third stage 400m hurdles silver medallist John Cooper ran himself out with a magnificent 45.4, yet such was the strident tempo of the race that he actually conceded a place to Jamaica.

Brightwell set out 2-3m behind Wendell Mottley of Trinidad and Kerr of Jamaica, and some 7m in arrears of Henry Carr (USA). Entering the final straight, Carr was out of any possible danger and looking good, but Mottley and Kerr were beginning to buckle.

Now was Brightwell's chance ... and he took it. Striding out to textbook perfection – chest held high, knees well up, arms working powerfully – Brightwell edged up on his two adversaries. He caught Kerr 55m from the tape and took Mottley just 5m from the line in as stirring a finish as one can remember. The crowd rose to Brightwell in admiration for one of the gutsiest performances of the Games. From fourth to second in 50m – the British fighting spirit, so much in evidence in Tokyo, had won through again. The team had run a European record of 3:01.6 (inside the old world record, which the USA lowered to 3:00.7). Splits for that final, pulsating leg: Carr 44.5, Brightwell 44.8, Mottley 45.0.

After the Games, Brightwell married Ann Packer, who followed up her 400m silver medal with a glorious 800m victory in Tokyo. Their son Gary ran a 47.90 400m as an 18 year-old in 1984, while two other sons, Ian and David Brightwell, played professional football for Manchester City.

MARY RAND

Born 10.2.1940 Wells (Somerset).
Club: London Olympiades

"THE GREATEST THING of all would be to do a world record at the Olympics – like Herb Elliott, for instance. That would be wonderful. Needless to say, that's what I would like to do in Tokyo!" Those were the words of Mary Rand when interviewed by the author on 22 September 1964. Twenty-three days later her hopes were translated into deeds in Tokyo's Olympic stadium ... victory, a world long jump record of 6.76, the greatest series of jumps on record, the first Olympic gold medal to be won by a British woman athlete. And that was by no means all, for later in the Games she performed brilliantly also in the pentathlon for a silver medal and second place on the world all-time list with 5035 points, and later still she contributed to the British team's third place in the 4x100m relay to complete a full set of medals.

Mary Bignal, as she was then, first attracted attention while a pupil at Millfield School. She won the 1956 WAAA Intermediate high jump and long jump titles and proved herself at senior level by taking second place in that year's WAAA Championships high jump with the same height as winner Dorothy Tyler and fourth place in the long jump. In 1957, only 17, she entered her first pentathlon and promptly set an English record of 4046; she also made her international debut as a high jumper. Next year she became WAAA high jump champion, took a silver medal in the long jump at the Commonwealth Games and finished seventh in the pentathlon at the European Championships with a UK record score of 4466. It was from that time that John Le Masurier became her coach. In 1959 she produced world class UK records of 6.19 in the long jump and 4679 in the pentathlon.

By the time of the 1960 Olympics she was being talked of as a possible gold medallist in the long jump, having improved to 6.27 at a time when the world record stood at 6.40. Her prospects were enhanced further when in Rome she led the qualifiers with a UK record 6.33, only to wind up ninth in the final later that day with 6.01. The gold medal went at 6.37, the silver at 6.27. The problem was that Mary fouled her first two jumps. Her confidence shattered, she measured out her run-up anew but it was of little avail and she failed to qualify for another three jumps. What went wrong? "Quite honestly I don't think I took it quite seriously enough," she said in our 1964 interview.

"It was the first day of the athletics and there wasn't any atmosphere at all. There were a lot of good girls in it but it was just like a club meeting. Obviously I was nervous – but in a funny sort of way. When I found that I hadn't got into the final six for another three jumps I would have thought I would have broken down and been really upset but actually I felt quite apathetic about the whole thing. It was only later, when I got back to see John, that I just wept. I was still crying when I whipped over to the start of the 80m hurdles to knock my blocks in. And of course I got through to the final, but it didn't make up for it. The hurdles didn't mean that much to me anyway [she placed an unexpectedly high fourth in 11.1]. I should have won a medal in the long jump – no question about it."

She married Olympic sculler Sidney Rand in 1961 and only four months after the birth of their daughter Alison she made a remarkable comeback to earn the bronze medal in the 1962 European long jump championship. She enjoyed a glorious season in 1963, which included a world record (alongside Madeleine Weston, Daphne Arden and Dorothy Hyman) of 45.2 for the 4x110y relay, a 6.44 long jump (the official world record by then was 6.53 by Tatyana Shchelkanova of the USSR), a

British 80m hurdles record of 10.8 and further UK records in the pentathlon of 4712 (with Ann Packer second on 4294) and 4726.

Her *annus mirabilis*, however, was 1964. She hardly put a foot wrong all summer, which began with a 4847 score in the Somerset pentathlon championship back at Millfield School. The downhill track and other irregularities ruled it out as a UK record but it was a great morale booster. In June she claimed back the record she had lost to Mary Peters (4801) three weeks earlier by scoring 4815, with Mary P second on 4492, while in July she not only won the WAAA long jump with UK record leaps of 6.53 and 6.58 (Shchelkanova setting a world record of 6.70 the same day) but also tied the European 100y record of 10.6. She was in fantastic form for her final pre-Olympic appearance, in Portsmouth. Admittedly, the following wind was usually well over the limit, but even allowing for that her series was the finest in history: legal 6.49, 6.70w (+4.0m), 6.48w, 6.58w, 6.63w and 6.58w. The second round jump matched Shchelkanova's world record distance ... and she had some six inches (16cm) to spare on the board!

"If everything went exactly right I could win the long jump and finish first or second in the pentathlon," she predicted. "I think I can do 22 feet (6.70). I'll have to against Shchelkanova."

After leading the qualifiers with an Olympic record of 6.52, the 24 year-old got down to serious business in the final. She opened with a UK record of 6.59 (+ 1.4m wind), consolidated with leaps of 6.56 and 6.57 into the swirling wind, improved to 6.63 (+1.2) and then, in the fifth round, produced an extraordinary jump of 6.76. As John Le Masurier was to write: "Technically it was superb – a fast approach, with the body becoming vertical as she crouched into a powerful take-off. A perfect hitchkick with the feet stretched forward together for landing and just sufficient forward speed remaining to allow her to stand up in the sand." It was a performance ahead of its time, for there was a headwind of 1.6m blowing at the time and the clay runway was rainsoaked. Off a synthetic surface and with that amount of wind in her favour it's possible she would have jumped very close to seven metres – the sort of distance that would not be attained for another dozen years. She completed her series with a 6.61, again into the wind, to become the first British woman athlete ever to win an Olympic title.

Shchelkanova, expected to be her main rival, was well below her best with 6.42 in third place; the silver went instead to the lanky 18 year-old Polish sprinter Irena Kirszenstein, who had only taken up long jumping the previous season and improved in Tokyo from 6.39 to a world junior record of 6.60. Later, as Irena Szewinska, she would make Olympic history herself.

In the pentathlon, which started two days later, Mary again competed brilliantly to become only the second woman ever to exceed 5000 points. She totalled 5035 (10.9 hurdles, 11.05 shot, 1.72 high jump, 6.55 long jump, 24.2 200m) and finished ahead of Irina Press in three of the five events. However, she lost so many points to Press in the shot – no fewer than 384 – that the muscular Soviet athlete ran out the winner 211 points clear with a record breaking score of 5246. Mary Peters, whose own golden moments were still eight years away, placed fourth.

Mary Rand, whose good looks and sunny personality combined with her Olympic triumph made her truly a "golden girl" in Britain, continued to compete for another four seasons but without ever approaching her 1964 form. Subsequently her best long jump was 6.53 indoors in 1966 and her highest pentathlon score was 4785 in 1965. She captured the Commonwealth Games long jump title in 1966 and tried to make the Olympic team in 1968 but was frustrated by injury and retired. Her imposing list of personal bests included 10.6 100y, 11.7 100m, 23.99 & 23.7w 200m, 56.5 440y, 10.8 80m hurdles, 13.4 & 13.3w 100m hurdles, 1.72 high jump, 6.76 long jump, 12.25 shot, 5035 pentathlon. She was also credited with a pioneering 12.22 triple jump in 1959 ("I don't know why it isn't a proper event for women," she remarked in 1964) and even competed in a mile walk race. Divorced from Sidney Rand, she married 1968 Olympic decathlon champion Bill Toomey (USA) in 1969 and gave birth to two more daughters. That marriage was eventually dissolved and in 1992 she wed another American, John Reese. Having lived there for well over 30 years she has become a US citizen but retains her British passport and has never quite lost that Somerset burr.

DOROTHY HYMAN

Born 9.5.1941 Cudworth (Yorkshire).
Clubs: Hickleton Main SC, Dorothy Hyman Track Club

BEFORE SHE HAD celebrated her 24th birthday, Dorothy Hyman was the most bemedalled British athlete up to that time after collecting four gold, four silver and three bronze awards in Olympic, European and Commonwealth Games competition. She also ranked, and continues to be ranked, as the most successful female sprinter ever produced by Britain.

She made her international debut in 1957 at age 16 and the next year she started her medal collection with a gold in the 4x110y relay at the Commonwealth Games in Cardiff when the English team beat the favourites, Australia, in the world record time of 45.3. That was followed later in the season by silver in the European Championships 4x100m. In 1959, now coached by Denis Watts, she established herself as Britain's top speedster by winning the first of four WAAA sprint doubles.

Dorothy excelled herself at the Rome Olympics of 1960. On paper she ranked equal seventh over 100m at 11.6 and 11th at 200m with 23.8, and yet came away with a silver medal in the 100 and bronze in the 200. One of this author's less accurate assessments in his Olympic 100m preview for *Athletics Weekly* was to state that she seemed "to lack the blazing speed necessary to reach the final." In fact she won her quarter-final in 11.6, equalling the UK record she shared with June Paul, Anne Pashley and Heather Young, and then took her semi in 11.5 (11.65 electrical). The only athlete to run faster in the semis was the tall, sleek Wilma Rudolph who tied the world record of 11.3 (11.41) despite a slow start. In the final the American was blown by a 2.8m/sec following wind to an astonishing 11.0 (11.18), winning by two and a half metres from Dorothy, timed in 11.3 (11.43). In the 200m, Dorothy set a British record of 23.7 in her heat and placed third in the final in 24.7 behind Rudolph (24.0) and Germany's Jutta Heine (24.4), the times slowed by unfavourable wind conditions. As she reflected in an interview with the author in 1963: "I think it's an advantage to go with a low ranking, as I did. You've something to fight at and if you lose it doesn't matter anyway. You haven't as many nerves if you're the under-dog and you get more determination to show people that you can do it."

A pulled thigh muscle after taking ballet exercises in the spring of 1961 caused her to miss practically the whole of that season, but it proved a blessing in disguise as it gave her a fresher mental attitude towards the following year and its two major championships and she returned faster than ever.

After equalling the British 100m record of 11.5, she tied the European 100y record of 10.6 and defeated Heine with a UK 220y record of 23.8 (in her sixth race of the day) at the WAAA Championships. Further British records followed at 200m with 23.5 and 23.4, the latter time matching the European record. The European Championships in Belgrade saw Dorothy in scintillating form. First up was the 100m, in which she took the gold medal in 11.3w (+2.3m) with Heine second. Here is what I wrote in *Athletics Weekly* at the time:

"Never have I seen a girl run with such burning determination as Dorothy Hyman did in this final. Dorothy, as we know, is a superb competitor and the more important the occasion the better she runs. Today she reached new heights; she didn't just win, she massacred the pick of Europe's sprint talent. Dorothy said she was in a particularly determined mood for this race. 'I heard them all shouting for Heine and I knew I had to win,' she remarked. No two athletes could be less alike than Hyman and Heine. Their differences extend far beyond the contrast in physique, colouring or even nationality. Jutta has enjoyed an easy life as the daughter of a wealthy industrialist; she has no need to work and has few worries outside of keeping fit for racing. Dorothy, on the other hand, has had to struggle all her life. Dorothy, whose coalminer father died some months ago, is a working girl (she's a tracer for the National Coal Board at Cudworth, near Barnsley) helping to support the rest of her family. Fame has not spoiled the simple charm of the Yorkshire girl who has sacrificed so much in her efforts to become a great sprinter. Modest and reserved off the track, a 'killer' on it, Dorothy is a wonderful example to the young hopefuls who idolise her."

The weather ruined Dorothy's chances of landing the double, for the taller and stronger Heine was far better equipped to push through the 2.3m/sec headwind along the straight in the 200m and won, 23.5 to 23.7. Teamed up with Ann Packer, Daphne Arden and Mary Rand, she completed a set of medals with bronze in the relay.

Dorothy did gain the sprint double at the Commonwealth Games in Perth in November. Her 100y time of 11.2 can be explained by a headwind of 5.8m/sec (in 37°C heat), though she had run a windless 10.7 in her semi, and she went on to take the 220y in a British record equalling 23.8, a great time into a 3m wind. A silver medal followed in the relay.

In 1963 Dorothy was without doubt the world's number one sprinter. She went unbeaten and topped the world list at 100m with two legal marks of 11.3, equalling the European record and only 0.1 outside Rudolph's world record, and 200m with 23.2, a new European record. Neither time was bettered by a British athlete for ten years. She also contributed to a world 4x110y relay record of 45.2, her team-mates being Madeleine Weston, Rand and Arden.

Olympic glory in Tokyo was beckoning but unhappily her prospects for 1964 were dashed by a thigh injury sustained in June. Finishing last over 100m in 12.2 in a match against Holland in September could have done little for her confidence, and in her final appearances before Tokyo she ran no faster than 11.9 for 100m and 24.5 for 220y. However, against all the odds she fought her way to the Olympic 100m final, clocking a season's best of 11.5 in her quarter-final and placing eighth (11.9) in the final. Over 200m she ran 24.0 in her heat but was eliminated in the semis with 23.9w. Her Games weren't over, though, and she anchored a team comprising Janet Simpson, Rand and Arden to bronze medals in 44.0 with Dorothy losing little if anything on her leg to Edith McGuire, the American who had placed second in the 100m.

She retired after the Games to concentrate on coaching, and in 1965 she published an autobiography which, because money was involved, caused her to be barred from international competition when she made a comeback in 1969. But she proved she was still Britain's best by winning the WAAA 200m title in 23.7 and topping the UK 100m year list with 11.5 (11.3w). She was also second fastest at 200m with 23.5. She retired for good early in 1970 after winning the Yorkshire 100m title in a brisk 11.5. In recognition of her services to the sport, both a stadium and an athletics club were named after her.

ANN PACKER

Born 8.3.1942 Moulsford (Oxfordshire).Club: Reading AC

JUST IN TIME, Ann Packer discovered her best event. Whereas Fanny Blankers-Koen began her career at 800m but became a legendary sprinter, hurdler and jumper, Ann started as a sprinter, hurdler and jumper but found fame at 800m. And whereas the Dutchwoman was 30 when she achieved Olympic immortality and continued in serious competition for a further eight years, the British athlete decided to retire immediately after her 1964 Olympic success aged only 22.

She could look back upon an extraordinarily varied career. She won the 100 yards title at the 1959 English Schools Championships, took the WAAA long jump in 1960 (admittedly in Mary Rand's absence) and made her international debut later that season as a long jumper, unexpectedly reached the 200m final at the 1962 European Championships in Belgrade after being controversially selected for the event (adding a bronze medal in the 4x100m relay) and went on to place sixth in the Commonwealth Games 80m hurdles with a silver medal in the relay. In 1963 she moved up to 400m and swiftly burst into world class and finally, in 1964, she took up the 800m – with astonishing results. Her personal bests prior to her final season were 10.9 for 100y (1963), 12.0 & 11.7w for 100m (1960), 24.0 for 200m (1963), 53.3 for 400m (1963), 11.4 for 80m hurdles (1960, 1962 & 1963), 1.60 high jump (1959), 5.92 long jump (1960) and 4294 pentathlon (old tables, 1963).

Despite her early successes it was only from the summer of 1962 that Ann began to take her sport really seriously. As she admitted: "I had just played at athletics until I was selected for Belgrade." A PE teacher by profession and coached by Denis Watts, she realised she would never become a world beater as a sprinter but thanks to training considerably harder that winter she emerged a much stronger athlete in 1963. Her first ever 440y race was unscheduled; there was no sprint race on the programme so she decided to try the quarter and won in 55.9. Her next 440y race took 55.1 and in her 400m debut, in a match against West Germany, she placed second to Joy Grieveson in 54.4.

Bearing in mind her near-novice status, her next 400m was truly remarkable, for in a match against Holland she clocked 53.4, 0.2 behind Grieveson whose time equalled the European record and constituted a new UK record. The pair had another great tussle in the memorable Russia v Britain match in Volgograd, this time Ann winning 53.3-53.4 with the former world record holder Maria Itkina third in 53.7.

During the winter of 1963/64 Ann trained ferociously in the company of her fiancé Robbie Brightwell and the hard man of 400m hurdling, John Cooper. Her Olympic objective was to win the 400m, and to test her enhanced stamina she opened her season with the first 800m race of her life on 6 May 1964, winning in a promising if unsensational 2:11.1. Her second attempt on July 25 was fractionally slower at 2:12.0 for 880y but she won again and a second lap of 63.4 was impressive.

Meanwhile her main event, the 400m, was going well with times of 53.5, 53.4 and 53.7 in August plus her fastest ever 200m of 23.7. Following another 53.5 she lined up for her third two-lap race, at White City on September 11. It was a thriller and although Ann was pipped on the line by schoolgirl Mary Hodson as both were timed in 2:05.3, a UK all-comers record for 800m, it became apparent for the first time that she was a genuine Olympic prospect at this distance and the British team selectors took appropriate action.

The race could not have taken too much out of her, for next day she won the 400m in 53.6 followed 40 minutes later by a 200m victory over WAAA champion Daphne Arden.

Her main aim as she travelled to Tokyo remained the 400m. She ranked second in the world behind European champion Itkina (53.0) and in my *Athletics Weekly* preview I tipped her to win ahead of Australia's 1956 Olympic sprint heroine Betty Cuthbert, stating she "undoubtedly has the ability to clock close to 52 sec on the right day". She came so very close, for after winning her heat in a UK record 53.1

(53.18) and semi-final in a European record 52.7 (52.77) she had to settle for the silver in the inaugural Olympic women's 400m final on October 17 as Cuthbert held her off, 52.0 (52.01) to 52.2 (52.20). Only North Korea's mysterious Sin Kim Dan had ever run faster. It's possible that Ann might have reduced her chances of victory by running faster than necessary in the preliminaries, for Cuthbert sauntered around in 56.0 in her heat and in the semis she conserved further energy with 53.8 in Ann's race.

Whatever, she was dismayed by the result. "I suppose a lot of people would be very happy with a silver medal," she was quoted in *Tales of Gold*. "But I had hoped for the gold and I was favourite for the gold. I just wasn't good enough on the day, and I shall always be disappointed about it."

Ann took a leaf out of Cuthbert's book in the 800m. She was content to place fifth (2:12.6) in a heat won by Frenchwoman Maryvonne Dupureur in 2:04.5. Dupureur ran another fast race (2:04.1) in her semi, while Ann virtually jogged home third in hers in 2:06.0. She was such a novice at the distance that at first she didn't even know where to cut in as the first bend was run in lanes.

Although on paper Ann was the slowest of the eight finalists with her best time of 2:05.3, and most accounts claim she was given no chance of winning, a glance at the forecast in *Athletics Weekly* reveals that Dixie Willis, the Australian who held the official world record of 2:01.2, was picked for first, Packer for second, Dupureur for third and Marise Chamberlain (New Zealand) for fourth. Modesty forbids revealing the identity of the prognosticator in question, but as Willis was ill and never competed in Tokyo his tip to win therefore became Packer.

Of course, Ann wanted to make up for having been beaten in her main event but her strongest motivation as she lined up for the eighth and final 800m race of her life was to win so that she could present a gold medal to her fiancé Robbie as compensation for his own disappointment in the 400m.

Ann ran the race with impeccable judgement even if it was a journey into the unknown. Disregarding the furious early pace, she was sixth at the bell in 59.1, just a couple of strides behind the leader, Dupureur (58.6); she was in third place at 600m (90.7 to Dupureur's 89.8) and second around the final turn. The French runner was still five metres ahead entering the final straight but as she began to flag so Ann's stride lengthened and her spirits soared.

She passed her opponent without encountering any resistance and, with a beatific smile on her face, broke the tape five metres clear, with Chamberlain third. Her time: a world record 2:01.1. "It was so easy, I couldn't believe I had won,' said Ann, who was greeted just beyond the finish line by her beloved and his relay team-mates.

She became Mrs Brightwell shortly after the Games and, explaining her immediate retirement, said "running a home is more important than running races". She and Robbie have three sons; the eldest, Gary, ran a 47.90 400m as an 18 year-old in 1984, while Ian and David Brightwell became professional footballers with Manchester City.

LYNN DAVIES

Born 20.5.1942 Nantymoel, near Bridgend (Wales).
Clubs: Roath H, Cardiff AAC

WELSHMAN LYNN DAVIES, a coalminer's son, was asked towards the end of 1963 about his long jumping ambitions, his personal best at the time being 25' 4" or 7.72. His aim for 1964, he replied, was a jump of 26' 4" (8.03), "which should place me in the final six in Tokyo". His all-time goal was "to win an Olympic medal in Mexico City" in 1968. However, so quickly did he develop in 1964 that he wildly exceeded those aims and – to the world's astonishment – became Olympic champion.

Interviewed by the author in 1966, Davies described his early days as an athlete. "For fun I entered the school sports in 1960 at the age of 18. My first ever long jump was along the side of a rugby field, from an old grass run-up and with hardly any sand in the pit. As I ran down I didn't know which leg I was going to take off on. I eventually took off on my left leg and I did 21' 2" (6.45). After this success I felt I could get somewhere in athletics. I trained seriously for the first time prior to the 1962 season; I did no really specific training for 1961." Davies had improved to 6.73 in 1960 and 7.14 in 1961 but finished last in his first international, Britain 'B' v Switzerland, with 6.72. No one at that stage could have predicted that just three years later he would jump beyond 8 metres and win Olympic gold! He was better at that time at the triple jump, having won the AAA junior title in 1961 and reached 15.43 in July 1962 when his long jump best stood at 7.54, but he was too injury prone in that event and he dropped it.

He continues the story: "The 1962 Commonwealth Games were my first major Games and I went out to Australia really believing I could get a medal without really knowing what was involved. I was thrilled to bits with my series and when I got up to 7.72 (a UK record) I thought I had reached the ultimate! Right up until the final round I was in third place and I could feel the bronze medal in my hand. When Mike Ahey (Ghana) did 8.05 on his last jump, making me fourth, I could have cried. I used the hang technique in Perth, by the way, and my run-up then was 17 strides consisting of 114ft (34m). Now it's 19 strides consisting of 133' 2" (40m).

"I changed to the hitchkick after seeing Igor Ter-Ovanesyan (USSR) in action at the 1962 European Championships [in which Davies placed 11th with 7.33]. I've never been so impressed by anyone long jumping; I was inspired by him at Belgrade. I was standing right by the side of the pit when he did 8.19 and I suddenly saw what it was all about; he gave me a completely new insight into long jumping".

At that stage of his career Davies was still practically a novice. "I knew nothing about the sport," he reflected. "I played soccer with Cardiff City and I'd done some general training but that's all. I felt I wasn't a part of the European Championships, my first full international. On my first jump in the final, which I really had no right to make, I was called by the official, stepped on the runway, got my checkmark down, looked at it, looked at the pit, looked down ... and I still had my warm up shoes on! You can see I was nervous, had no discipline.

"In 1963 I was still experimenting with weight training and was still working on a one-and-a-half hitchkick with the hang technique. It was a very bad year and it was only after Volgograd [when Davies produced a season's best of 7.62 and was beaten by Ter-Ovanesyan by just 3cm] that I began to see what was involved in my preparation. The two-and-a-half hitchkick I use now was working in the winter of 1963. I decided that if I was to improve significantly in Olympic year I would have to double my capacity for work. It was at this time that Ron Pickering, my coach, was most valuable to me in that he helped me to push up my sights in training. He made me believe that I had a right to be competing in the Olympic Games – that's very important."

Stronger and faster (9.5 for 100 yards) than ever before, and technically much more proficient, Davies reached the eight metre mark for the first time in May 1964 and improved the UK record to 8.02 in July. Defending Olympic champion Ralph Boston, who had raised the world record to 8.34 (plus a wind assisted 8.49) at the US Trials, started as favourite, with Ter-Ovanesyan, a previous world record holder at 8.31 and credited in 1964 with 8.18, considered the man most likely to upset Boston. Davies felt he could challenge for the bronze medal.

However, his Olympic challenge came perilously close to being ended in the qualifying round. Needing 7.60 to reach the final, he opened with 7.39 and followed with a foul. All depended on his last attempt ... happily, he jumped 7.78 and the crisis was over.

Conditions for the final later in the day were deplorable: the runway was covered with puddles, the wind blew against the jumpers and the temperature was a chilly 13°C. Not surprisingly the length of the jumps was adversely affected and after four rounds Boston led with 7.88 from Ter-Ovanesyan (7.80) and Davies (7.78). The bronze medal was as good as his but Davies sensed he could win the coveted gold medal. All too accustomed to such weather in his native Wales, he knew he was being unsettled by the damp and dismal conditions to a lesser degree than his opponents. He put his whole body and soul into the fifth jump and, generating a combination of speed, spring, strength and technique that would have spelt 27 feet (8.23) in more reasonable circumstances, he cut the sand at 8.07. Incredibly, in spite of the adverse breeze, the soggy state of the clay runway and the pressure of an Olympic final, he had managed to jump further than ever before while almost everyone else was falling far short of their best.

"When I saw 8.07 go up," he recalled, "I was at the same time tremendously delighted and numb; I couldn't take it all in. Boston reassured me that that jump would be the winner although he had one to go. In the back of my mind I had the feeling he could pull something off and yet at the same time I had a sneaking suspicion that it wouldn't be beaten. The suspense was agony." He could barely dare to look as his rivals took their remaining attempts. Ter-Ovanesyan replied with a fifth-round 7.99 to move into second place, but in the final round Boston – landing heart-stoppingly close to Davies' mark – recaptured second position with 8.03.

Almost 18 months elapsed before Wales' first Olympic champion in an individual event resumed his progression. He admits he became somewhat blasé and lazy in his training in 1965 but the lure of two major championships in 1966 was sufficient motivation for a return to his former dedication. On a tour of South Africa in April he took advantage of the sunshine and high altitude to improve his UK record to 8.13 and 8.18, becoming the third longest jumper in history, and by winning both in Kingston (7.99) and in Budapest (7.98 to beat Ter-Ovanesyan on his last jump) he became the first athlete to complete a hat-trick of gold medals: Olympic, Commonwealth and European.

He created a sensation while training in high altitude Mexico City for the 'Little Olympics' in October 1967 when he cleared 8.42 from take-off to landing (as measured by Mary Rand) – 7cm beyond Boston's world record. In the actual competition, six days later, he registered his season's best of 8.13 but was defeated by Ter-Ovanesyan's record equalling 8.35. The longest legitimate jump of his career came in Berne in June 1968, the measurement being 8.23 or precisely 27 feet – a mark which was to stand as the British record until Chris Tomlinson leapt 8.27 in 2002.

He travelled to Mexico City with high hopes of retaining his Olympic crown, ranking third in the world that year behind Bob Beamon of the USA (8.33) and Ter-Ovanesyan (8.28) although Boston was also a major factor with a windy 8.37 at altitude. In my preview for *Athletics Weekly* I tipped the brilliant but unpredictable Beamon to win ahead of Davies, Ter-Ovanesyan and Boston, commenting: "Beamon is, I feel, the one most likely to have a catastrophic day (i.e. jump below 27ft!) but is equally the one most likely to jump beyond the 28ft (8.53) mark."

Of course, everyone remembers that Beamon blew the competition apart with his phenomenal opening jump of over 29 feet in the final, but few will recall the drama of the qualifying competition the day before. The co-holders of the world record at 8.35, Boston (with an Olympic record of 8.27) and Ter-Ovanesyan, advanced immediately, but both Beamon and Davies fouled twice and faced ignominious elimination. However, they made it at the third try: Beamon with 8.19, Davies with 7.94.

The final proved memorable in terms of yielding a performance (8.90) that, had one not watched it with one's own eyes, would have been dismissed as a misprint or mismeasurement ... but it ruined what had been one of the most keenly anticipated contests of the Games. In effect, before any of the other big guns had stepped on the runway, only the silver and bronze medals were now available and men like Boston, Ter-Ovanesyan and Davies could not get too enthused about that. Davies, in particular, lost all interest in the proceedings. Here he was, ready to defend his title with a jump of 28ft if necessary, and before he had even started along comes a guy who jumps over two feet farther than Davies himself had ever achieved. He ran through on his first attempt, reached 7.94 in the second round and fouled his third jump. As equal eighth Davies was entitled to three more jumps but he didn't take them. East Germany's Klaus Beer, who never had any winning aspirations and thus wasn't psyched out by Beamon's monstrous leap, took silver with 8.19 with Boston (8.16) third and Ter-Ovanesyan (8.12) fourth.

Davies was never quite the same after that chastening experience although he did retain his Commonwealth title in 1970 and by the time he retired following the 1972 season he had jumped 8 metres or further in 22 separate competitions. He served as technical director of Canadian athletics from 1973 to 1976, became British Olympic team manager and, still remarkably youthful-looking in his sixties, is currently President of the governing body, UK Athletics.

DAVID HEMERY

Born 18.7.1944 Cirencester (Gloucestershire).
Club: Ruislip-Northwood (later Hillingdon) AC

THE MEXICO CITY Olympics of 1968 will forever be associated with Bob Beamon's futuristic long jumping exploit, but to British fans those Games were memorable primarily for David Hemery's superlative victory in the 400m hurdles, becoming the first British man since Tom Hampson 36 years earlier to win an Olympic title with a world record performance.

To an unique degree he was a product of both British and American athletics. He began sprinting at prep school in Essex when he was aged nine and three years later he moved with his family to the United States. At high school in Massachusetts he was mainly a half miler (2:03.0 in 1961) but that same season also ran the high hurdles. He returned to Britain in 1962, and came under the coaching influence of 70 year-old Fred Housden, who had been an international high hurdler, long jumper and pole vaulter in the 1920s, and was the man who – in Hemery's words – "taught me how to hurdle." The following year he became AAA Junior 120y hurdles champion and made his debut at 440y hurdles with a less than earth-shattering time of 58.6.

Back in the States he entered Boston University in the autumn of 1964, being fortunate enough to find himself under another excellent coach in Billy Smith. In 1965 he was the second fastest Briton that year at 120y hurdles (14.3) and no 5 at 440y hurdles (52.8), but it was in 1966 that he demonstrated the extent of his potential. During the US indoor season he set European bests of 1:09.8 for 600y and 7.1 for 60y hurdles; outdoors he concentrated on the "highs" to good effect, winning the Commonwealth title and equalling the UK 110m record of 13.9. In one of his rare 440y hurdles races he improved to 51.8. Another fine indoor season followed but a bad hamstring pull caused him to miss practically the entire outdoor campaign in 1967, so he entered Olympic year with a personal best for 400m hurdles (the equivalent of 51.5) that would not have ranked him among the world's top 50 in 1967. However, that injury proved a blessing in disguise for the enforced rest enabled him to undertake a gruelling non-stop 60-week build up for the Games.

In an interview for *Athletics Weekly* I asked him how he rated his chances at 400m hurdles prior to the 1968 season. He replied: "I thought that if I didn't get any injuries I could get under 50 sec and make the team. My coach over there [Billy Smith] always thought I might be able to get under 49." His progression before the

Olympics proved steady rather than dramatic: he set UK records of 50.7 (440y) in April, 50.5 (440y) in May, 49.8 in June, 49.6 in August. On paper he ranked no 4 behind Geoff Vanderstock (world record 48.8/48.94 electrical), Boyd Gittins (49.1/49.27) and Ron Whitney (49.2/49.34) but the Americans' times were altitude assisted. However, I picked Hemery to win in a time of between 48.7 and 49.0, pointing out that in the US collegiate championships in June he had easily beaten Gittins and Vanderstock, and that in a time trial shortly before leaving for Mexico he had negotiated 400m with 11 hurdles (the extra one in lieu of the usual run-in) in 49.8, and carried on to a twelfth! "John Cooper estimated the extra hurdle added half a second to his time, so what with the benefit of high altitude and competition the mind boggles over what Hemery could achieve."

Whitney was fastest in the heats with an extravagant Olympic record of 49.06, while in the semis Italy's Roberto Frinolli was quickest with a European electrically timed record of 49.14 as – in separate races – first John Sherwood and then Hemery clocked the British record time of 49.37.

The line-up for the final was the greatest yet assembled in this event, but Hemery made his opponents look almost ordinary. Drawn in lane six, he blasted from the blocks and in practically no time had made up the stagger on Whitney, in seven. He whizzed along the back straight at breakneck speed, the hurdles hardly disturbing the graceful flow of his stride. He flashed past the 200m mark in an unheard of 23.3 and it became clear that he was either going to win the race by a street or he was going to die a dreadful death in the closing stages.

But it was when the going got toughest that Hemery's prodigious stamina training paid rich dividends. As coach Smith had reminded him: "There are a thousand hills and sand-dunes behind you and there isn't time for the others to catch up." He never flagged and the outcome was that he crossed the finish line at least seven metres clear of Germany's Gerhard Hennige (49.02). The time was a staggering 48.12, smashing the world record by 0.82, and prompting one American track nut to exclaim "that just has to be the greatest performance in track history".

Certainly he had run the sort of race every athlete dreams of ... sheer perfection, and in an Olympic final! Almost unnoticed, as all eyes were on Hemery's triumphal progression, Sherwood (whose long jumping wife Sheila had finished second the previous day) also ran the race of his life as he snatched the bronze medal in 49.03. The last time Britain collected two medals in the same event was the 400m in 1924, and it was appropriate that the medals should be presented by the Marquess of Exeter, who as Lord Burghley won this very title in 1928.

"I had to start out fairly fast because Whitney has a very strong finish and I thought he would be the man to watch at the finish," Hemery explained. "John went out fast in the eighth lane, which helped me. At the sixth hurdle I changed from 13 to 15 strides and from there I had to push, though I tried to relax so I wouldn't tie up in the straight." Such was his tunnel vision during the race that at the finish he wasn't even sure he had won! How surprised was he by the time? "I had heard 48.1 announced but I didn't know if they had made a mistake and meant 49.1. I thought it might have been about 48.9, something like that, because of the wind and the rain. Before the final I thought I might be capable of under 48.8 – perhaps 48.4 on a good day. But the cold and rain may have cost me up to half a second."

Hemery reappeared later in the Games for the 4x400m relay and again excelled himself, clocking 45.1 in the heats and 44.6 in the final. Shortly afterwards he revealed that, having worked so hard and having achieved his goal, he would not run 400m hurdles again. Instead he tackled the decathlon (scoring 6760 on present tables), cut the UK 110m hurdles record to 13.6 and won a silver medal in the European Championships in 1969, while in 1970 he retained the Commonwealth high hurdles title and was hand timed at a flattering 13.4 in Zürich although the electrical time was 13.72.

Having second thoughts, he took 1971 off in a repetition of his preparations of four years earlier and returned to his best event in 1972. His training in Boston that winter was fearsome, covering up to 80 miles a week on the road (including a 10 miles run in 55:25) plus sand dune and hill climbing sessions, but injury held him back to a best of 49.3 prior to the Olympics.

However, in the Munich final he threw caution to the winds. His race strategy was to build up a big lead early and then strive to hold on. Around the final turn Hemery, who flashed through 200m in 22.8, did indeed hold the lead but, running in lane one (a particular disadvantage for an athlete with a right leg lead), Uganda's John Akii-Bua changed gear entering the finishing straight and pulled well away for victory in 47.82, thus eclipsing Hemery's own world record. Ralph Mann (USA) pipped a flagging Hemery on the line for second, 48.51 to 48.52. The Briton's time was comparable to his high-altitude 48.12 in Mexico City and he completed a set of Olympic medals by winning a silver in the 4x400m relay as Martin Reynolds, Alan Pascoe, himself (45.0 after a 44.8 heat) and David Jenkins set a European record of 3:00.46.

Hemery closed his amateur career with a world best for the rarely contested 300m hurdles of 34.6 (that's 46.1 400m pace) and victory in the France v Britain match in 49.30. He remained competitive, clocking 35.8 for 300m hurdles as a professional in 1975 and winning the BBC Superstars title three times.

He later returned to Boston University for seven years as a coach but has lived in Britain since 1983. He served as the first President of UK Athletics for four years from 1998. His younger brother John ran 48.5 for 440y in 1968 and 54.5 for 400m hurdles in 1972, while David's son Adrian (born in 1982) is a British decathlon international with a best score of 7051 in 2005.

ALAN PASCOE

Born 11.10.1947 Portsmouth.
Clubs: Portsmouth AC, Polytechnic H

THE SUPREME HONOURS – a world record, an Olympic title – may have eluded him, but Alan Pascoe's high-level consistency over a very long period was remarkable. Along the way he collected European and Commonwealth gold medals, an Olympic relay silver, 13 AAA titles, 28 sub-50 sec 400m hurdles timings, and the distinction of never having been beaten in that event in international matches. As he was once quoted: "I have lived wonderfully off athletics. Ten years at the top, travelling the world, seeing people and places, knowing moments of achievement few men will ever enjoy. Not at all bad for a round-shouldered asthmatic off a council estate."

Pascoe's wide-ranging involvement with athletics must be unique: world class competitor, British team captain, husband of an international athlete (sprinter Della James), teacher, college PE lecturer, meeting promoter, athletes' representative on the British Board, Sports Council member, TV commentator. In what turned out to be a shrewd and lucrative career move he gave up teaching and lecturing to enter the field of sports promotion and sponsorship and for the past 20 years he has been one of the most influential figures in British athletics as holder of the sport's marketing rights. He is currently chairman of Fast Track, the company which promotes the major televised meetings, and was vice-chairman of London's successful 2012 Olympic bid.

He took up sport on doctor's orders. He suffered from severe attacks of asthma as a youngster and was advised to indulge in plenty of sport as an aid to breathing, but athletics played little part in his life until 1963 when, challenged by a friend who happened to be the school's best hurdler, Pascoe won the race and realised he had found a sport in which he could excel.

Training seriously for the first time, he made a spectacular advance in 1966, setting a UK junior 120y hurdles (39in) record of 14.2, winning his first English Schools title and clocking an outstanding 14.4 over the men's sticks. International representation beckoned, and it was clinched after winning the 1967 AAA indoor 60y hurdles. Outdoors he tied the UK 110m hurdles record of 13.9 (with long-time BBC athletics commentator Stuart Storey clocking 14.1) and made his first attempt at 400m hurdles, clocking a handy 53.6 ... but five seasons were to pass before he made the decision to switch events.

Now coached by George Tymms, Pascoe set his sights for 1968 on reaching the Olympic high hurdles final, but in Mexico City he was beset first by tonsillitis and then by an Achilles tendon problem and although equalling the UK record of 13.9 he was eliminated in his heat. The following year was altogether happier. At the European Indoor Championships he showed for the first time the full extent of his competitive spirit, for despite a sluggish start he came through to win in a UK best of 6.6 for 50m hurdles. Outdoors he lowered the UK record to 13.8, and broke David Hemery's UK 200m hurdles best with 23.0, but when they clashed in a match against Czechoslovakia it was Hemery who prevailed in pouring rain with a Commonwealth record 13.6 against Pascoe's 13.7. Later, at the European Championships, Hemery and Pascoe took silver and bronze behind Italy's Eddy Ottoz. Little went right for Pascoe in 1970, although he did lower his 400m hurdles best to 52.4 and he was credited with a 13.6 in Zürich which was rendered doubtful by the electrical time of 13.99, but 1971 proved to be a fruitful year.

In addition to his hurdling exploits he blossomed forth as a top class sprinter, completing an unique AAA double by taking the 200m in 21.1 against a 2.6m wind as well as the 110m hurdles, and at the European Championships he took the silver medal in the "highs". But the really significant action was to come at the end of the summer. Competing in a 4x400m relay for Polytechnic Harriers, he blasted the anchor in 46.1. Clearly he could now make a mark at 400m hurdles and in his fourth outing at the event he clocked 50.9.

Nevertheless, the high hurdles remained his Olympic goal for 1972; he felt he could be Europe's best and challenge for a medal. In fact the hurdles in Munich was a disaster for him, finishing seventh in his semi, but atonement was to come in the 4x400m relay. His flat form had never been better, having retained the AAA 200m title in 20.9 and run a 45.4 relay leg, and at the Games he clocked 45.3 in the heats and 45.1 in the final in which Martin Reynolds, Hemery, David Jenkins and himself won the silver medals in a European record of 3:00.46. He was at last beginning to realise that 400m hurdles would be his best event, and after clocking 35.4 for 300m hurdles behind Hemery's world best of 34.6, his mind was made up.

He didn't at first set the tracks alight as a 400m hurdler in 1973, improving slightly to 50.6, but in his first international match appearance in the event he broke through to 49.5, followed by further wins in the AAA Championships and European Cup Final. Now it was all systems go for the Commonwealth Games in Christchurch in January 1974, where he ran a good five metres faster than ever before, emerging an assured winner in 48.83 to rank among the world's top ten of all time. Hopes of another success, in the European Championships seven months later, grew steadily dimmer as he experienced one setback after another (bursitis in both legs, strained hamstring, stomach disorder, vitamin deficiency), but he turned up trumps in Rome to snatch victory in 48.82. Another gold medal followed in the relay.

That 1974 campaign earned him second place to Jim Bolding (USA) in the authoritative *Track & Field News* world merit rankings, but 1975 saw Pascoe as undisputed world's number one. It was success, with one pardonable exception, all the way. He opened with a UK all-comers record at Crystal Palace of 49.07 ahead of Olympic champion John Akii-Bua; he defeated the Ugandan again as well as the redoubtable American pair of Bolding and Ralph Mann in Helsinki in 49.28; and in Stockholm overhauled Bolding, with Akii-Bua third, in a personal best of 48.59. Back at Crystal Palace he lowered the all-comers record to 48.90 ahead of Mann and Akii-Bua, but returning after a hamstring injury he sustained his only defeat in Gateshead when both he and Akii-Bua were timed at 49.8. Despite further injuries he won in the European Cup Final (49.00), Zürich (48.69) and Crystal Palace (another all-comers mark of 48.85).

He was shaping up as a genuine gold medal contender for the 1976 Olympics (Ed Moses wasn't even on the radar at this point) but injuries ruined his bid. After a ragged 50.62 win at Crystal Palace early in July, 20 days before the Olympic heats, he admitted that he had lost so much training and racing that "anything beyond the heats in Montreal would be a bonus for me."

In fact, he ran 49.95 to make the final, in which in a do or die effort he matched strides with Moses (who would win in a world record 47.64) for three flights and was still second only a couple of metres down at halfway. But retribution for Pascoe's folly, or bravery, was inevitable and he faded to eighth and last in 51.29.

He was out of luck too in the relay. A consolation medal seemed possible but the team failed to finish in the heats when, on the third leg, Pascoe had the baton knocked out of his hand.

He salvaged something from the season by winning the AAA title and beating Bolding both in Zürich in 49.07 and in Cologne in 48.93, but he was never again to run that fast. He had a best of 49.65 in 1977 and 49.63 in his farewell season of 1978 during which he took the bronze medal at the Commonwealth Games.

BRENDAN FOSTER

Born 12.1.1948 Hebburn (Co Durham; now Tyne & Wear).
Club: Gateshead H

BRENDAN FOSTER, THE man who inspired his home town of Gateshead into becoming the nation's most athletics-mad community, won just about every honour in the sport barring the supreme prize, an OIympic gold medal. Today, some 30 years after his competitive heyday, he remains one of the best known personalities in British athletics thanks to his BBC television commentaries and his brainchild, the Great North Run. Like Alan Pascoe he also gave up teaching to develop into an extremely successful businessman, in his case the sportswear industry. He has been Managing Director of Nova International Ltd since 1987, having previously worked for Nike.

Born a few miles from Newcastle and a member of Gateshead Harriers from the age of 15, he was at first a quarter-miler but was no prodigy as he failed to reach his age group final in the 1963 English Schools Championships. Citing himself as an example he advised newcomers: "Don't be discouraged by lack of success when young. Most of the top athletes weren't outstanding youngsters. It seems like a death wish hanging over your head if you win the English Schools. People start taking notice of you and it's not a good thing at that age."

Encouraged to run cross country (tenth in the 1966 English National Youths) he gradually moved up in distance on the track and ran a 4:07.4 mile in 1967. He lost 1968 through injury and the following year (while reading chemistry at Sussex University) he improved to 3:47.1 for 1500m, but it wasn't until 1970 that he propelled himself onto the national scene. He broke through with 3:42.8 in the England Trials and followed up with the second fastest 2 miles (8:30.8) by a Briton. The Commonwealth Games in Edinburgh served as his international baptism, and he started as he intended to carry on: the bigger the occasion the better he would run. Although ranked only ninth on paper, he finished up with the bronze medal and a personal best of 3:40.6.

He made his 5000m debut early in 1971 in unusual conditions; racing in 34°C weather in Trinidad he finished half a lap behind the great Kip Keino of Kenya in 14:36.0 and it would be another two years before he was prepared to commit himself to that distance. Meanwhile he continued to make progress at 1500m and mile. He became the world's 132nd sub-4 min miler with 3:58.5 and at 1500m he broke 3:40 for the first time with 3:39.4. At the European Championships he finished third in 3:39.2; two major championships, two bronze medals, two personal bests. The following week, in Edinburgh, the other cornerstone of Foster's career – record breaking – was laid. While Belgium's then little known Emiel Puttemans was busy setting a world 2 miles record of 8:17.8, Foster was getting the better of Ian Stewart in a tremendous tussle for second place some 50m behind. His time of 8:24.8 was his first British record.

Coached by the ever cheery Stan Long, Foster started his 1972 track season with a bang. He may have lost to Peter Stewart (UK record of 3:55.3) but he clocked 3:55.9 to become Britain's third quickest ever miler and the fast times were due to his forceful running in the middle two laps of the race. Foster beat Stewart (Ian's elder brother) in their next two encounters, in one of which – a mile in Stockholm – he narrowly beat Finland's Pekka Vasala (3:57.2 for both), the man who would capture the Olympic 1500m title later in the summer! However, the AAA 1500m proved a potential disaster, for whereas Stewart won in a UK record of 3:38.2 Foster finished fourth in 3:39.3. He assumed he had lost his Olympic chance but the selectors instructed him and third-placed John Kirkbride to run off in a match against Finland. Outkicked by Vasala, Foster finished way ahead of Kirkbride to win his ticket to Munich. At the Games he equalled the UK record of 3:38.2 in his semi and went on to place a commendable though for him unsatisfactory fifth in the final (3:39.0).

Realising he would never be a world beater at 1500m, he moved up in 1973. In his first serious test he ran away with the AAA 5000m title in 13:23.8 some 7 sec clear of Olympic bronze medallist Ian Stewart. His return to Crystal Palace was even more notable. On the first day of the Britain v Hungary match he dead-heated with Frank Clement in a 3:38.5 1500m; on the second he joined the esteemed ranks of world record breakers by running 2 miles in 8:13.8 (8:13.68 on electrical timing) to shave 0.2 from Lasse Viren's 1972 mark. That was the day when Foster, a runner's runner well known only to the real athletics fans, was transformed into a national sports hero. Foster was on his own after three and a half laps, reached halfway in 4:05.4 and covered the second mile solo in 4:08.4. Finally and crucially that season he proved his credentials as a racer by winning a tactical European Cup 5000m.

Having already run personal bests in his first three major championships, Foster went one better in his next (the 1974 Commonwealth Games) with UK records in both 1500m and 5000m. Carrying out the appropriate training and building up to a peak effort were vital elements in this ability but equally important was Foster's mental attitude. If anything was certain in athletics it was that Foster would give 100% of himself in a race; there was a dogged streak in his character which ensured that the tougher the going the better he would run.

At the Games in Christchurch in January he lost the fastest 5000m duel up to that time by just a foot or two to Ben Jipcho (13:14.4), himself claiming a British record of 13:14.6 and moving to third on the world all-time list behind Puttemans

(13:13.0) and the Kenyan. Four days later, despite his national record time of 3:37.6, he found himself in seventh place in the most fantastic 1500m race yet seen as Tanzania's Filbert Bayi front ran to a world record 3:32.2 ahead of New Zealander John Walker (3:32.5).

Always a great club man, Foster produced one of his greatest runs in the AAA national road relay championship at Sutton Coldfield in April, covering the 5 miles 900y stage in an astonishing 24:28, representing 26:38 6 miles pace at a time when Ron Clarke's world track record stood at 26:47.0. As the newly appointed Sports & Recreation Manager for Gateshead, his day of days occurred on August 3. He fervently wanted the first meeting on the Tartan track to be a great success – so much so that he even went to the lengths of breaking a world record for the 10,000 ecstatic fans! Fulfilling a life's ambition of making athletics history in his home town he hacked 2.5 sec off Puttemans' highly esteemed 3000m figures with the sparkling time of 7:35.1. The first half, paced by Mike Baxter, took 3:49.0; the second 1500m, running alone, took just 3:46.1, his lap times being 60.1, 60.5, 62.2, 61.2, 60.0, 62.1, 59.9 and 29.1 for the final 200m.

He had proved he could run against the clock, but at the European Championships in Rome he also displayed his uncompromising competitive qualities. Not since the days of Vladimir Kuts had we seen such a talented championship field so completely dominated by one man. Breaking away just before 3000m with a daring 60.2 lap, he was 80m ahead at the bell and but for the sweltering weather would surely have broken Puttemans' world record. No matter, a time of 13:17.2 sufficed to bring him home almost 7 sec clear of Manfred Kuschmann (GDR) with Finland's Olympic hero Viren third.

In 1975 he was again successful in the European Cup 5000m, injecting a murderous mid-race lap of 58.2 (Viren finished a distant fifth), and the year was notable also for a UK 2000m record of 5:03.0 and his first 10,000m race: winning against a crack field in 27:45.4, fastest in the world that year and the quickest ever debut.

His second crack at 10,000m, in 1976, resulted in a win in what was in effect the British Olympic trial (27:53.8) but due to an untimely attack of diarrhoea he was not at his best in the Montreal Olympic final. He finished third (27:54.9) well behind defending champion Viren (27:40.4) and Portugal's Carlos Lopes (27:45.2) to gain Britain's only medal of the Games. "I wanted to go with five laps to go, but when we got there I was hanging on," he reflected ruefully, adding: "Viren is simply the greatest runner there has ever been." Foster went on to set an Olympic record of 13:20.3 in his 5000m heat, finishing fifth in the final (13:26.2) as Viren (13:24.8) completed a fabulous second Olympic double. It wasn't much consolation that Foster easily beat Viren in three post-Olympic races, but he must have been pleased that his speed was still there as in the Emsley Carr Mile he ran 3:57.7 for third behind Dave Moorcroft (3:57.1) and Filbert Bayi (3:57.5) ... with a 19 year-old newcomer named Sebastian Coe seventh in 3:58.4.

Foster achieved one of his greatest ambitions in 1977 by winning the English national 9 miles cross country title and that summer produced two tremendous runs at 10,000m. At the AAA Championships he attacked the recently set world record of 27:30.47 by Samson Kimobwa and reached 5000m in 13:38.9 ("I was floating"), almost 10 sec ahead of the Kenyan's corresponding time and the fastest halfway split then recorded. However, running alone for the last 15 laps in humid conditions caused him to slip behind schedule after 7000m and he finished in 27:45.66. At the end of the season, again at Crystal Palace, Foster defeated one of the finest fields ever assembled in 27:36.62, moving him to third on the all-time list behind Kimobwa (who placed 11th in the race) and the previous world record holder Dave Bedford (27:30.80 in 1973). A merciless second half in 13:39.4 enabled him to win from Kenya's Henry Rono, who would the following year set a world record of 27:22.4.

It was also in 1978 that Foster would run his greatest 10,000m. The occasion was the AAA Championships at Crystal Palace, the conditions were chilly and wet, and Foster led after only four of the 25 laps ... and yet he set a European record of 27:30.3 (13:45.1 + 13:45.2!), which would have been a world record had Rono not got in 12 days earlier.

He went on to lift the Commonwealth title (28:13.7 in hot weather) plus a bronze in the 5000m, but fatigue caught up with him in the European Championships where his time of 27:32.65 sufficed only for fourth. It was a race he felt he could have won had he not gone for the Commonwealth 5000m. Foster broke 28 minutes on one more occasion, clocking 27:41.3 behind Mike McLeod (the first Briton ever to beat him at that distance and at 5000m) in 1979, and he brought his career to an end in 1980. Early in the year he ran his first and only serious marathon, clocking a respectable 2:15:49 in New Zealand ... and never dreaming that one day he would commentate on a woman running the distance faster through the streets of London! His Olympic finale, in Moscow, resulted in his finishing 11th in 28:22.54, let down again as in Montreal by stomach trouble, but he was able to bid farewell to his fans at Crystal Palace and Gateshead on a more appropriate winning note.

LILLIAN BOARD

Born 13.12.1948, Durban (South Africa); died 26.12.1970.
Club: London Olympiades

IN REVIEWING THE athletics career of Lillian Board one must bear in mind that in spite of all her successes there can be little doubt that her greatest triumphs would have been ahead of her. European champion or not, she had barely scratched the surface as an 800m runner. She was by no means at her fittest when she spreadeagled the field in Athens in 1969 in 2:01.4 and in view of her miling exploits early in 1970 it is not unreasonable to assume that Lillian would have achieved her goal of breaking two minutes. It is painful, though, to dwell on what might have happened; let us instead be thankful for all that she did accomplish during her tragically short life.

Lillian, and twin Irene, were born in South Africa, their parents having emigrated there from Manchester soon after the war. The family returned to Britain in 1950

103

and Lillian joined London Olympiades at the age of 12. With her father, George, as coach and clubmate Mary Rand as an inspiration, Lillian became English Schools Junior long jump champion in 1963. She concentrated on the sprints the following season but she did try her first 880y race, finishing wearily in 2:30.8. She improved to 2:20.5 in 1965 but she and her father decided the two lap event could wait and Lillian impressed with a windy 10.9 100y and her best ever legal long jump of 5.80.

It was in 1966, as a 17 year-old, that Lillian was permitted under the rules then in force to tackle 440y for the first time, and it quickly became apparent that she was made for the distance. Early in the year, Mary Rand said of her: "She's going to develop into a great quarter-miler," an opinion endorsed by Denis Watts, who had coached Ann Packer and was now assisting George Board. Her progress was astonishingly rapid, clocking 54.6 for 440y and running a tenth slower for fifth place in the Commonwealth Games.

Her dramatic development was maintained during 1967 and two races that year particularly stood out. In only the third 880y race of her life she produced a strong finish to clock 2:08.7, while in the momentous USA v Commonwealth match in Los Angeles she came from behind to defeat a glittering field in the 400m. On paper she was the slowest in the race at 54.4 for 440y but she unleashed a phenomenal finishing drive to pass Australia's world 440y record holder Judy Pollock a few strides from the tape to register 52.8 for second on the European all-time list behind Ann Packer.

It was a turning point in her career. Previously just a promising young athlete she was now – thanks to that race being televised – a household name. The blonde good looks and bubbly personality endeared her to millions, who from then on began to follow her races with interest. Suddenly she was Britain's new golden girl, freely tipped to become Olympic 400m champion the following year. Lillian herself refused to be carried away by such talk. "I think a silver or a bronze would be fabulous. Even a place in the final sounds great."

She embarked upon the 1968 season stronger, faster and fitter than ever. Her improvement in speed was spectacular, as she cut her best 220y time from 24.6 to 23.7, which meant that in future 400m races she could handle a 24.5 first 200m with a reasonable "preservation time" in hand. Following a 53.5 400m win in Moscow she ran a superb 2:02.0 for 800m in the WAAA Championships, second fastest ever by a Briton to Packer's 2:01.1 ... but she placed second as Vera Nikolic of Yugoslavia broke the world record with 2:00.5. Deciding not to try to emulate Packer, her preparations for the Olympic 400m before leaving for Mexico included a 23.5 200m, 53.0 400m and a share with Anita Neil, Janet Simpson and Maureen Tranter in a world 4x110y relay record of 45.0.

Out there, with the benefit of high altitude, she clocked 23.2 for 200m and an outstanding 36.3 for 300m in time trials. "Lillian has got to go through the first 200m in 24.5 to win," commented Watts. That she did, spot on, in the Olympic final. She ran the third 100m hard to enter the final straight some four metres ahead, and it was only in the final few strides that the unheralded Colette Besson of France edged her way past.

Of course it was frustrating and disappointing for Lillian to come so close to the supreme prize but by any standards hers was a marvellous performance. In only her third season at the event, still aged 19, she had run 52.12 to break Packer's UK record of 52.20, gained the silver medal just 9/100ths behind Besson and moved to no 4 on the world all-time list.

In what was to prove her last full season (1969) she went so well at the shorter distances – including her fastest ever 100m of 11.9 and a solo 52.9 contribution to a world 4x400m relay record of 3:37.6 – that she seriously considered making the 400m rather than 800m her goal at the European Championships in Athens in September. But then she encountered such acute back trouble that all her plans were compromised. For five weeks, including the whole of July, she was unable to race but fortunately the damage was not irreparable.

She came back with a 52.5 relay leg and defeated Besson in a match against France in 53.7. However, the injury affected the nerves in her legs and was more painful the faster she ran, and that made up her mind for her: she would go for the 800m. In her last serious race before Athens she won over that distance in 2:05.1 with a 60.3 last lap.

The European final was a very fast race, which was not particularly in her favour, but she was always up with the leaders, Nikolic and Romania's Ileana Silai (27.0 at 200m, 59.2 at 400m, 90.0 at 600m). But for the strong wind in the finishing straight Nikolic's world record could have been in serious danger. As it was, timing her drive to perfection off the last bend, Lillian strode to victory by eight metres in a championship record of 2:01.4 (2:01.50), ranking her equal seventh on the world all-time list.

With that triumph behind her she could face the relay in a more relaxed frame of mind and in the final she produced the performance for which she is best remembered. On the anchor leg Olympic champion and co-world record holder (at 51.7) Besson seemed to be in an unassailable position at 300m but Lillian, who had passed 200m in 24.2 and then had to ease off, gradually began to pull back her lactic-drowning rival (who had stormed through 200m in 23.6 and 300m in 36.1!) and overtook her in the final stride of one of the most thrilling races anyone ever witnessed. Thanks to earlier brilliant team work by Rosemary Stirling (54.2), Pat Lowe (52.1) and Janet Simpson (52.1), Lillian (52.4) anchored the British team to a world record of 3:30.8.

As a precaution against further back injury, Lillian cut out weight training prior to the 1970 season, building up her stamina instead. In her mile debut in May she clocked a highly respectable 4:55.7. She had been suffering stomach trouble for some time before that race but when, the following weekend, she ran 4:44.6 one felt the ailment could be nothing serious.

A 53.6 400m, her fastest ever early season time, seemed to be the prelude to some explosive 800m performances ... perhaps even the first official sub-2 minute mark. But the condition not only persisted, it grew worse. She looked decidedly laboured when running a 2:07.0 leg for Britain's world record breaking 4x800m team (8:27.0). The following weekend, pale and underweight, she finished third in the WAAA Championships in 2:05.1.

It was her last race. She was in and out of hospital all summer but few outside her immediate family circle realised just how seriously ill she was. Hers was a hopeless case, said top British cancer specialists. As a last resort she was transported to a clinic in Bavaria, but after further intensive treatment the merciful end came on Boxing Day, 13 days after her 22nd birthday. How sad and ironic that it was in Munich – the city in which she had hoped to be crowned Olympic 800m champion – that she died.

Thirty five years later I, along with so many others of my generation, continue to mourn her shockingly early passing. Here is part of what I wrote in tribute to her in the 2 January 1971 issue of *Athletics Weekly*: "It has been my sad duty to write many obituary notices for this magazine but none has caused me so much distress as this one. It still seems unbelievable that Lillian Board, who should have had at least 50 years of life ahead of her, is no longer among us and I feel a sense of deep personal loss that I know will be shared by all readers, whether or not they had the good fortune to have met Lillian.

"Lillian's fame will endure as a result of her wonderful athletics career and her incredibly courageous fight against the illness that was eventually to cut her life so tragically short. Certainly I shall always treasure such magic moments as her thrilling triumphs in Athens and ponder on the bravery of this young woman as she struggled against the unimaginable pain and debilitating effects of her illness. Most of all I shall remember with gratitude Lillian, the friendly and vivacious 'girl next door'.

"Her stunning successes on the track, allied to her very attractive looks and bubbling personality, led to acclaim and publicity of film star proportions to be thrust on Lillian while still a teenager. It could have turned her head, but it most certainly did not. She remained a thoroughly delightful girl: charming, sincere, gracious. A credit to her parents.

"To say that athletics will never be the same again may sound like a cliché, but I mean it. The thought that not only shall we never see that familiar blonde figure pounding round the track again but that she should have been snatched from her family and friends in such a tragic manner leaves me with feelings of indescribable sadness. May her memory and shining example live on for ever."

IAN STEWART

Born 15.1.1949 Handsworth (Birmingham).
Clubs: Birchfield H, Tipton H

FEW ATHLETES WERE so uncompromising in their attitude to racing as Ian Stewart. "First's first and second is nowhere as far as I'm concerned," he stressed. "It's all right saying 'I was second', but suppose they only gave a gold medal at the Olympics and nothing else? See how happy the bloke who came second would be. At Munich in 1972, when I got the bronze, I was terribly disappointed. If you've ever been in a position where all you've ever wanted was a gold medal and you come out with a bronze, it's choking. I'm not a very good sportsman; all I want to do is win races. This country's full of good losers. It's bloody good winners that we want."

Although the very highest honours of an Olympic title or world track record eluded him, Stewart enjoyed his fair share of bloody good victories and even when he didn't win his opponents knew they had been in a race.

Success came early. Coached by Geoff Warr from when he was a 15 year-old, Stewart set his first British age best in 1965 when at 16 he ran 9:12.8 for 2 miles. The following year he landed age-17 bests of 8:55.0 and 13:59.6 for 3 miles, while in 1967 his haul included a European junior 3 miles best of 13:39.8 and a UK age-18 2 miles mark of 8:46.0. In 1968 he went on to break further European junior records: 3000m in 8:01.2, 2 miles in 8:35.6, 3 miles in 13:28.4, 5000m in 13:53.4.

He had only just turned 20 when he set a European indoor 2 miles best of 8:32.2 and landed the 1969 European indoor 3000m title with a UK record of 7:55.4, covering the second half in 3:51.3. Outdoors, he made a sensational leap forward as a miler. From a previous best of 4:06.3, he became Britain's youngest sub-4 min performer with 3:57.3 behind a man who would become one of his keenest 5000m rivals, Ian McCafferty (3:56.8), while in third place Ian's elder brother Peter (3:58.7) also broke four for the first time.

His times at 5000m came down nicely also and he broke 13:40 for the first time in the AAA Championships where once again he ran like the veteran he wasn't with his poise, keen racing brain and physical ability seemingly contradicting his age. He subsequently improved to 13:36.4 behind Dick Taylor's UK record 13:29.0 and tuned up for the European 5000m championship with a UK 1500m record of 3:39.1. In Athens he killed off the opposition with a 56.6 last lap for the gold medal in 13:44.8.

He went from strength to strength in 1970. He won the Emsley Carr Mile in Edinburgh, just pipping brother Peter (both 3:57.4), but the centrepiece of his season was the Commonwealth Games 5000m on the same track the following month. Although very much a Brummie, he opted to represent his father's native country, Scotland, and in front of his 'home' crowd he ran what was probably the finest race of his career.

Indeed, Scottish distance running fans were in heaven at those Games as Lachie Stewart had already scored an upset victory over world record holder Ron Clarke in the 10,000m while the 5000m developed into a battle between two men in the blue vest: McCafferty and Stewart.

It was a fabulous race, the fast times thanks to 10,000m bronze medallist Dick Taylor who led up to 4000m in 10:52.0. Normally such a time would have seen him well clear of any opposition but here there were five men breathing down his neck: the two Scots, Clarke, 1500m champion Kip Keino and Allan Rushmer. With just over 800m to run McCafferty took over but, 450m out, Stewart raced ahead. At the bell (12:27.4) Stewart led by a stride from Keino with McCafferty a further metre behind, while Clarke (world record holder at 13:16.6) was 10m back. Hard pressed by the Kenyan star along the back straight with McCafferty shadowing him, Stewart refused to give way and as the runners hit the finishing straight the already delirious crowd were treated to the sight of Scottish vests in first and second places. The great Keino was beaten.

Now it was a fight to the death between the two Ians. Stewart, who had never ceded the lead since he made his break, was running flat out and yet McCafferty was stealthily gaining on him. For a few seconds it looked as though McCafferty would triumph ... but then, sensing perhaps he could not catch his man before the tape intervened, or maybe lacking Stewart's killer instinct, he slackened off slightly and Stewart was left the winner by four metres: 13:22.8 to 13:23.4. Stewart, who covered the last lap in 55.4 (26.4 final 200m), set a European record and moved to second on the world all-time list with McCafferty third. As no less an authority than Derek Ibbotson enthused: "He's the complete 5000m runner, the greatest Britain has ever produced."

Far from peak fitness due to injury that winter, the 1971 season produced little of note, although brother Peter kept the family flag flying by winning the European indoor 3000m title. But it was all systems go for the Olympic campaign of 1972. He wintered well by placing third in the International Cross Country Championship over 12 kilometres, although he dismissed that as "a bad run" even though he had spiked himself when falling on a stretch of plough.

As ever, winning was all and he was disgusted with his performance in the AAA 5000m, which doubled as the Olympic trial. The important thing was to finish in the first three, which he did in 13:24.2, but he was well beaten by Dave Bedford and McCafferty. Bedford was in amazing form at this meeting, completing a double which Ron Clarke hailed as the greatest in athletics history. On the Friday night he front ran the 5000m in the European record time of 13:17.2, missing Clarke's world record by just 0.6, with McCafferty second in 13:19.8, and next afternoon took the 10,000m in 27:52.4 – a time only he and Clarke had ever bettered.

Following a spell of intensive high altitude training, and without easing down for the race, Stewart set a UK 2 miles record of 8:22.0 in Stockholm, his final pre-Olympic outing ... but far ahead of him, with a world record 8:14.0, was Finland's Lasse Viren. On paper the leading contenders in Munich on 1972 form were Bedford, Viren (13:19.0), McCafferty, the charismatic American, Steve Prefontaine (13:22.8) and Stewart.

However, Bedford's chances evaporated after finishing a distant sixth in the 10,000m, won sensationally by Viren in a world record 27:38.4 after falling over before halfway. In the 5000m final McCafferty and Bedford dropped back to 11th and 12th but Stewart remained in contention as Prefontaine launched a long, fast drive for home four laps out.

At the bell, Viren was slightly ahead of Prefontaine and Mohamed Gammoudi (Tunisia's defending champion), with Stewart as much as 10m down after a heavy knock from the American caused him to lose a lot of ground at a vital moment. Even off the final bend Stewart didn't think he could get back into a medal position, but a dazzling sprint over the final 100m enabled him to get past Prefontaine for third place in 13:27.6 ... not that he was in the least satisfied with a bronze medal. It was the first major track championship he hadn't won. Viren it was who triumphed in 13:26.4 from Gammoudi (13:27.4), having covered the final mile in around 4:03!

Stewart got back to winning ways with a European indoor 2 miles best of 8:28.4 in the USA early in 1973 but the summer season proved a write-off. After finishing second in 13:30.8, fully seven seconds behind new 5000m star Brendan Foster, in the AAA Championships he decided to call it quits for the year. His enthusiasm for racing had drained away, and that applied also to the Commonwealth Games in Christchurch in January 1974 where he could finish only sixth in the 10,000m (in a modest personal best of 28:17.2) and fifth in the 5000m in 13:40.4, nearly half a lap behind the winner.

Disillusioned, he turned to cycle racing that summer. His batteries recharged, he returned to athletics and in March 1975 he scored a momentous double as on successive weekends he lifted the European indoor 3000m in 7:58.6 and the world 12 kilometres cross country title despite an early attack of stitch.

Surprisingly, these were to prove to be the last major international medals of Stewart's career, although he continued to produce high quality runs for several more seasons.

He displayed good speed in 1975 when running a 3:57.4 mile, just a tenth away from his best, and headed the UK 5000m list that year with 13:27.0. In 1976 he set personal bests at 3000m (7:46.8) and 10,000m (28:00.4) but was able to place no higher than seventh in a classic Olympic 5000m (13:27.7), two places behind Foster, with victory going again to Viren (13:24.8).

In 1977, the year he became self coached and switched clubs, he was credited with a world best of 45:13 for an undulating 10 miles on the road ("it's not exceptional", he said modestly), won the UK 10,000m title in 27:51.3 (leading for all but the first three laps), went close to his 5000m best with 13:23.3 and improved further over 10,000m to 27:43.0 but only in sixth place in a race won by Foster in 27:36.6. Stewart made a good start to 1978 by finishing a close second to Bernie Ford in the English cross country championship but that was effectively his last notable race and he retired that summer.

Since then he has coached and from 1994 has been promotions officer for the UK governing body, successfully putting together high class fields for the televised international meetings in Britain.

As previously mentioned, his elder brother Peter was also a top class middle distance runner, his achievements including UK records at 1500m (3:38.22), mile (3:55.3) and 2 miles (8:26.8), while younger sister Mary (later Mrs Cotton) was even more successful. At 1500m she set a world indoor record of 4:08.1 when becoming European indoor champion in 1977 – thus all three siblings won European indoor titles – and was Commonwealth champion in 1978.

GEOFF CAPES

Born 23.8.1949 Holbeach (Lincolnshire).
Clubs: Holbeach AC, Birchfield H, Borough of Enfield H

IN MAY 1966 *Athletics Weekly* featured two promising 16 year-old throwers in the newly instituted 'Spotlight on Youth' section. One was Hungarian-born Joe Bugner, a former English Schools Junior discus champion who would turn professional boxer the following year, controversially defeat Henry Cooper for the British, Commonwealth and European heavyweight titles and go on to fight Mohammed Ali and Joe Frazier. The other was the even more massive Geoff Capes, already almost 1.98m (6ft 6in) tall and weighing in at 230lb (105kg), although he would later fill out to 308lb (140kg). Believe it or not, he was the smallest of five brothers, and in his early days as an athlete he ran a 4:48 mile and raced cross country!

The turning point in Capes' life as well as his athletics career was when he came under the influence of local star Stuart Storey, an international high hurdler. As he told David Cocksedge in an *Athletics Weekly* interview: "I was a right tearaway at that time, and he was probably the only person I'd listen to. Stuart said: 'Right, Geoff, you've got a decision to make now. You either go inside for fighting as you will do if you carry on like this, or you do athletics. And you'll be good at it.' He could see the potential in me at that time when I didn't know myself what I was capable of doing. So we began to work hard and concentrate on the shot."

Capes began setting age records from 16 onwards. In 1968 he threw the men's shot over 17 metres for the first time and the following year made his debut for the national senior team. Police Constable Capes placed fourth in the 1970 Commonwealth Games but his breakthrough year was 1971, when he improved from 17.73 to 19.48, tantalisingly close to the UK record of 19.56 held by his hero, Arthur Rowe. In April 1972 he twice equalled that mark, and in July he smashed it to smithereens. Competing in Helsinki he reached 19.75 in the third round, 19.82 in the fourth and 20.18 in the fifth. That ranked him 11th among those selected for the Olympics, but his motivation that year had been breaking Rowe's record and the inspiration had drained away by the time he got to Munich where he threw what he described as a "pitiful" 18.94 and failed to make the final.

Capes improved upon the Commonwealth record three times in 1973: to 20.27, 20.34 and 20.47; and he also made his mark as a discus thrower with a lifetime best of 58.34. But it was in 1974 that he became one of the world's elite. The year was only six days old when, at a cold and wet Crystal Palace, he raised his record to 20.59 just prior to flying to New Zealand for the Commonwealth Games. A fortnight later, in Timaru, he progressed to 20.64 and at the Games in Christchurch he made sure of the gold medal with his opening effort of 20.74. A fulfilling winter season continued apace as he set a European indoor record of 20.82 at RAF Cosford and lengthened that to 20.95 for victory in the European

Indoor Championships in Gothenburg. For the first time in a major championship against formidable opposition Capes displayed admirable competitive nerve. East Germany's Heinz-Joachim Rothenburg began the contest by breaking Capes' European record with 20.87, but Capes ("I was literally shaking") responded with his opening shot of 20.95 and followed up with 20.90.

Now that Britain had a potential world beater, shot putting was moved centre stage for an international meeting at Crystal Palace in May 1974. Mike Winch, Britain's perennial no 2, had visions of defeating Capes for the first time when he made a huge advance to 20.43 in round 4 ... but the dream lasted only a minute or two as Capes replied with a Commonwealth outdoor record of 20.81. The American world record holder (at 21.82) Al Feuerbach won with 21.12. Just four days later Capes not only beat Feuerbach but extended his record to 20.90 and in June he hit the landmark figure of 21.00 winning against European champion Hartmut Briesenick (GDR). A more important milestone followed in August when he became only the sixth man in the world to reach 70 feet with a put of 21.37. It was all going so well, but at the European Championships in Rome – with everyone throwing far below their best – he had to settle for bronze with 20.21 as Briesenick held on to his title with a modest 20.50. The *Track & Field News* merit rankings rated Capes no 3 in the world.

The 1975 season was one of consolidation rather than progress, although he was world ranked no 1. Capes picked up a silver in the European Indoors and won at the European Cup Final, his best for the season being 20.80. His advance resumed in 1976. Indoors, he set a European record of 20.98 (twice) and regained the European title. Outdoors, he boosted his Olympic hopes with a Commonwealth record of 21.55 on a cold, windy, rainy Gateshead evening, less than a foot behind the world record, but disappointment awaited him at the Montreal Games. Ranked fourth on paper and seemingly in great form with five consecutive puts over 21m in training, he had the third longest throw in the qualifying competition but in the final he admits he "froze" and he could muster only 20.36 for sixth place as the title went unexpectedly to the GDR's young Udo Beyer at 21.05. His despair at missing the opportunity of a lifetime was so intense that in the presence of his coach Stuart Storey he broke down and cried. Later in the summer Capes regained top form with 21.20, but that was no consolation.

It would be another four years, the next Olympic season, before he would improve again. In the meantime he collected several more medals: silver in 1977, bronze in 1978 and silver in 1979 at the European Indoors; gold at the 1978 Commonwealth Games. He should also have taken a medal in the 1978 European Championships but he was prevented from taking part in the final because he didn't have a number on the front of his vest and got involved in a fracas with officials when he protested. His longest throw during that period was 21.30 in 1977 when, before 8000 fans in Spalding, he also lined up for a 200m race against Britain's top distance runner. With Brendan Foster in lane one and Capes – joked announcer Stuart Storey – occupying lanes two, three and four, it was no contest as Capes (more than double his rival's weight!) won easily in 24.9.

It was back to serious business in 1980 and at Cwmbran in May he came up with his longest ever throw. His series: 20.57, 20.85, 21.28, 20.91, 21.68 (a Commonwealth record) and 21.46. Faster and more streamlined than for a long time at 138kg or 304lb, he followed up with marks of 21.50 and 21.35 and went into the Moscow Olympics second on the form chart to world record holder and defending champion Beyer. But a back injury ruined his chances and, going through the motions, he placed fifth with 20.50 as gold went to Vladimir Kiselyov of the USSR at 21.35. Capes went on to become even better known to the general public by twice winning the televised World's Strongest Man title. Both his son Lewis (16.55 in 1991) and daughter Emma (WAAA intermediate champion in 1990) showed youthful promise as shot putters but did not persevere with the event.

DAVE BEDFORD

Born 30.12.1949 Hampstead (London).
Club: Shaftesbury H

A COMBINATION OF flamboyant front-running and a cheeky attitude off the track (not to mention his Mexican bandit appearance and eye-catching red socks) made Dave Bedford the most talked-about British athlete of the early 1970s. He, more than any other individual, was responsible for the return of big crowds to London's major athletics events. His only significant major championship success was winning the International cross country title in 1971, his reputation as one of the world's greatest and most exciting distance runners being based upon his prolific record breaking.

That record breaking started early. Bob Parker, his coach, first spotted him in 1965, when Bedford was 15. "I had seen this gawky, gangly boy running around, all arms and legs, extremely amateurish. I could see immediately that he had that little extra quality which produces champions. I could see it in him from the way he trained with the others, all senior runners, while he was still a boy. He forced himself to try and keep up with them." In 1967 Parker's faith in the youngster began to pay dividends. Already clocking up 100 miles a week in training, some of it while wearing Army boots in the tradition of Emil Zátopek and Gordon Pirie, he set a world under-18 6 miles best of 29:15.8. The following year he ran away with the English Youths cross country title and became AAA Junior 2 miles champion but it was in 1969 that he first really made his mark. He won the International Junior cross country championship by a 21 sec margin and, totally unanticipated, set a UK 10,000m record and world age-19 best of 28:24.4 – clocking a personal best of 14:14.4 at 5000m on the way, followed by a 14:10.0!

Confirmation that here was a very special talent who could simultaneously attract huge admiration from his growing army of fans and mutterings from some traditionalists about being too big for his boots, came at the Southern cross country championships on his home course of Hampstead Heath in February 1970. He made cross country history by winning two titles on the same afternoon. After running

5 miles in the morning, 3 or 4 miles warming up and romping to a 300-yard victory in the senior 9 miles race, he coolly decided to start in the junior 6 miles after a rest of less than 20 minutes and proceeded to win that by an even wider margin! As I wrote at the time: "Silly? Exhibitionist? Pointless? Yes, all that – but wonderful too. Here is a young man of 20 who is so much in love with running, and so talented too, that what might be considered senseless or impossible by anyone else's standards is not necessarily applicable to him. Like Pirie of 20 years ago he is a law unto himself."

Bedford's career was always one of ups and downs. In 1969, following that 10,000m record, his next attempt at the distance resulted in his placing 12th in the AAA Championships and thus he failed to win selection for the European Championships. In 1970, the month after his Southern double, he ran with a back injury and finished 95th in the senior International Championship, and another injury ruined his chances of Commonwealth Games selection, but he bounced back later in the summer with his first AAA 10,000m title and he regained the UK record from Dick Taylor with 28:06.2, ranking him third fastest of all time behind Australia's Ron Clarke and Jürgen Haase of the GDR.

The brilliant streak continued in 1971 as his murderous training schedule of up to 200 miles per week enabled him to front run to a huge victory in the International Cross Country Championship and break Ian Stewart's European 5000m record with a 13:22.2 timing which might have threatened Clarke's world record of 13:16.6 had it not been so viciously windy. Next came another phenomenal run, on a very hot afternoon in Portsmouth, when Bedford – after streaking away with a second lap timed at 59 sec – clocked a European 10,000m record of 27:47.0 on a badly cut-up track, the second fastest in history. He estimated that run would have been worth 27:20 on an all-weather track, a time that would not be achieved until 1984.

Predictably, the bubble had to burst and in his very next race, when attempting the world 5000m record before a sell-out crowd at the AAA Championships and on schedule at least to break 13:20, he was struck down by cramp soon after the 3000m mark. It wasn't the best preparation for his next test, the European 10,000m championship in Helsinki. Bedford led for most of the race but he wasn't in top shape and therefore unable to generate the sort of pace which might have burned off most of his rivals. Consequently he was left for dead on the last lap, which was covered in a fantastic 53.9 by Finland's Juha Vaatainen (once a 10.9 sprinter) as he won a great duel with Haase, 27:52.8 to 27:53.4. Bedford wound up sixth in 28:04.4, which would have tied the European record a month earlier. Before the season was over, though, he had thrilled his adoring Crystal Palace public again – this time in the unfamiliar guise of steeplechaser. The fans gasped at his audacious start (he was 30m clear after two laps), chuckled at his step-on-hurdle technique, roared with delight as he flung up both arms as he took the water jump, and cheered as he outsprinted specialist 'chaser Andy Holden in the UK record time of 8:28.6, only 6.6 sec outside the world record in just his second semi-serious attempt at the event. Bedford would disagree with the term 'outsprinted'; according to him "I only won because I was *jogging* faster than he was."

The Olympic build-up in 1972 saw Bedford in pulsating form. He displayed enhanced speed by setting UK records at 3000m (7:46.4) and 2000m (5:03.16), while at the AAA Championships he completed what Ron Clarke no less described as the greatest ever distance running double. On the Friday evening, he led throughout in the 5000m and, although he was supposed to be running just to secure an Olympic team place, he raced to a European record of 13:17.2 ahead of Ian McCafferty and Ian Stewart, missing Clarke's world mark by just 0.6 sec. Barely 19 hours later he won the 10,000m by a 300m margin in 27:52.4, a time only he and Clarke had ever surpassed. He looked ready for Olympic glory in Munich in one or both events, but yet again there was a downturn in his fortunes on the big occasion. After running extravagantly fast in his heat (27:53.6) although admittedly looking extremely comfortable, Bedford was almost 12 sec slower in the final, finishing sixth after leading through the fastest ever 5000m split of 13:44.0 (although he had hoped to run 13:30!) but dropping out of medal contention at 7000m. Lasse Viren won in a world record 27:38.4 despite a fall on the 12th lap. The 5000m was also a disappointment, for while Viren completed the double in 13:26.4 Bedford trailed home a dejected 12th in 13:43.2.

There was only way to go after that, and in July 1973 – running on his favourite Crystal Palace track – he became the first British athlete to set a world record in an 'Olympic event' in London since Chris Chataway in 1954. Just how distance running had moved on could be gauged from the fact that Bedford covered the second 5000m in the AAA 10,000m in 13:51.4 (0.2 faster than Chataway in his monumental duel with Vladimir Kuts), having run the first 5000m in an unprecedented 13:39.4 – which would have been an Olympic record at that distance prior to Munich. His time of 27:30.8 chopped 7.6 sec from Viren's record. But the jinx struck again and his season ended abruptly a fortnight later with the recurrence of a hamstring injury which had severely restricted his training mileage in preparation for the track campaign ... although his body's enforced rest probably contributed to that world record.

By the time of the Commonwealth Games in New Zealand in January 1974 he felt in such good shape that he was anticipating a time of around 27:10, but he wound up a distant, badly spiked fourth in 28:14.8 after suffering from the roughhouse tactics of the Kenyans. "I lost my cool – and it lost me that race," Bedford admitted. He fared even worse in the 5000m, a listless 11th in 14:18.8. Sadly, that was to prove to be his final major track championship race as leg injuries brought his international career to a premature end.

Asked if he had any regrets when looking back on his racing career, he replied: "The only regret is that injury ultimately forced me out of competition while I was still young and that never gave me the opportunity to learn from my mistakes and then go on to win championships. What I do remember is that my period as an athlete was full of happiness. What a great way to spend your youth ... absolutely brilliant! I have nothing but glowing feelings about that period of my life, in spite of some great disappointments."

Bedford has remained an important and charismatic figure in athletics. He became President of the International Athletes' Club and served as Secretary of the British Athletics Federation and the AAA of England. For several years he has been the hugely successful race director of the Flora London Marathon, putting together fields which are the envy of the world's other leading marathons. His son Tom ran an 8:54.28 steeplechase in 2004.

ALLAN WELLS

Born 3.5.1952 Edinburgh (Scotland).
Club: Edinburgh Southern H

WHO COULD HAVE predicted that the local lad raking the long jump pit at Edinburgh's 1970 Commonwealth Games, enabling him to watch close up his idol Lynn Davies, would – precisely ten years later – become an Olympic champion himself? At the time, Allan Wells was 18 and the reigning Scottish junior triple jump champion.

He made progress primarily as a long jumper, reaching 7.32 in 1972, but was handicapped at that stage of his career by a lack of blazing speed. His best legal 100m mark at the time was a mere 11.1 (a far cry from Lynn Davies' 10.4), and indeed another three seasons were to pass before he so much as broke 11 seconds in authentic conditions. He clocked 10.55 in 1976.

What irony too that at the start of 1978, when Harold Abrahams died, British sprinting was at its lowest ebb for years. The selectors hadn't even bothered to send any 100m men to the Montreal Olympics and the picture wasn't much brighter in 1977, Britain's fastest being Ainsley Bennett at 10.47. Had anyone, at the time of Abrahams' passing, forecast that two years hence in Moscow a Briton would emulate his 1924 Olympic 100m victory, that person would surely have been regarded as crazy! But in July 1978 it became apparent that an exciting new sprint talent had been unearthed in the muscular frame of the 'Flying Scotsman'. In the space of a week Wells – whose previous best was 10.50 – first equalled Peter Radford's 1958 UK 100m record of 10.29 and then reduced it drastically to 10.15 on his home track in Edinburgh.

Wells, who went on that season to win two gold medals (200m and 4x100m relay) and a silver (100m) in the Commonwealth Games, where he was credited with sensational, if wind-aided, times of 10.07 and 20.12, was quite the most unorthodox as well as fleetest sprinter Britain had ever turned out. A product of the Scottish professional running school of training with great importance attached to speedball (a boxer's punchball) work, Wells was unusual also for the fact that he scorned the use of starting blocks. He argued that he could get eight inches (20cm) nearer to the start line without blocks, which could make all the difference in a close race.

As a result of an IAAF rule which made blocks compulsory at the Moscow Olympics (they were fitted with an electronic device to register false starts), Wells had to adapt hastily – but successfully – to them in 1980. Despite injury problems he peaked perfectly for the Games, winning the Scottish titles in 10.05w and 20.11w and defeating Jamaica's Don Quarrie over 200m in a UK record of 20.35.

At the Games he trimmed his UK 100m record to a confidence-boosting 10.11 in the heats. The final, run in less favourable conditions, was one of the closest in Olympic history as Wells (lane 8) and Cuba's Silvio Leonard (lane 1) – drawn the width of the track apart – crossed the line simultaneously. Neither was sure who had won, until the TV action replay suggested what the photo finish was to confirm: that Wells' lunge had won him the race by the narrowest of margins. It was so close that the two men could not be separated even by 1/100th of a second at 10.25. Aged 28, Wells had become the oldest man ever to win this particular title, and the first Scot to lift any athletics gold medal since Eric Liddell's 400m triumph in 1924.

One fancied contender who didn't even make the final was European record holder Pietro Mennea, but the flamboyant Italian's moment of glory was to come in the 200m. Wells ran a scorchingly fast turn in Moscow to enter the straight well clear but Mennea chased after him and forged ahead in the final ten metres to win by 2/100ths. Wells' time of 20.21 was a UK record, but he was furious with himself for failing to complete the double. As he told Simon Turnbull in an *Athletics Weekly* interview: "If I'd run with blinkers on and not kept waiting for Mennea to come back, I think I would have won. I was waiting for him at 50m out. I was looking for him and slowed down ... but I had no chance when he came with only 10m to go. Looking at the video recording of it I see that I reacted slightly which shows that I had something left." There were, of course, no Americans in Moscow because of their boycott, but claims that Wells had won the 100m title by default were literally scotched when shortly after the Games he clocked 10.19 in Cologne, beating the first three finishers from the abortive US trials.

He enjoyed another fine season in 1981. At the European Cup Final he produced arguably the fastest 100m of his life when he recorded 10.17 into an 0.9m wind (his 10.11 in Moscow was with a 1.3m tailwind). He followed that with overall victory in an IAAF "Golden Sprints" contest in Berlin, winning the 200m by a big margin in 20.15w after narrowly losing in 10.15w to France's Herman Panzo in the 100m. Next came the World Cup in Rome where, representing Europe, he took the 100m in 10.20 (with a young American by the name of Carl Lewis, admittedly injured, finishing last) and placed second at 200m. The American magazine *Track & Field News*, which had listed Wells at no 2 at 100m in 1980, accorded him top world ranking at 200m in 1981.

The 1982 season was largely a write off. Possibly overtrained, he ran no quicker than 10.43 and 20.67 all summer and withdrew from the European Championships team rather than risk humiliation – but, refreshed in mind and body, he was back to his best for the Commonwealth Games in Brisbane in October. A powerful finish carried him to victory over up and coming Canadian Ben Johnson in a heavily wind aided 10.02, while in the 200m he dead-heated with Mike McFarlane in 20.43.

He originally had high hopes for the inaugural World Championships in Helsinki in 1983 but his form that season was indifferent and he was downcast to finish fourth in both sprints (10.27/20.52), way behind the American winners Carl Lewis (10.07) and Calvin Smith (20.14). "I'm not physically right. I'm embarrassed to be here, in the condition I'm in. I was trying too hard." In fact he acquitted himself pretty well in the circumstances, missing medals by 3/100ths in the 100 and 1/100th (to Mennea) in the 200. It was some small consolation that shortly afterwards in the European Cup Final he defeated his Italian rival in the 200m. Wells went on to place fifth in Zürich in his equal second best legal time of 10.15, but he would never again generate such speed. A seemingly effortless 10.18 in July 1984 augured promisingly for the following month's Olympics but in Los Angeles his dream of becoming the first man to retain the 100m title came to a premature end when, injured, he finished last in his semi-final.

Following a foot operation he did not compete in 1985, and many assumed that at age 33 he had retired, but he made a remarkable comeback in 1986 with a view to ending his career at the Commonwealth Games in his native Edinburgh. A perpetual battle against injury held him down to just one 100m race, an unimpressive 10.72, and he was dropped from the Scottish team, watching in frustration as Ben Johnson won the 100m in 10.07 well clear of Linford Christie (10.28) and another Canadian, Atlee Mahorn, took the 200m in 20.31w. However, a few days later in Gateshead, Wells – clad in tight black cycling 'shorts' nearly down to his knees, revolutionary athletics gear in those days – shocked all and sundry by winning the 100m in 10.40, with Johnson fourth, and the 200m ahead of Mahorn in 20.76. Swiftly added to the team for the European Championships he finished a respectable fifth in 10.25 (10.22 semi-final), the gold medal going in 10.15 to Christie, who had earlier in the season succeeded Wells as UK record holder with 10.04. Christie paid this tribute: "My thanks to Allan Wells. He opened the way for British sprinters; he showed us the Americans were human."

But Wells wasn't quite ready to accept no 2 ranking among British sprinters, because in his final race of the season he just held off Christie in 10.31 ... the last time for a decade that Christie would lose at the distance to another Briton. In 2005 it was announced that Wells along with Eric Liddell would be the inaugural inductees to the Scottish Athletics Hall of Fame to be housed in Glasgow. Wells' wife and sometime coach, Margot, was herself an international sprinter with a 100m best of 11.50w in 1978.

DAVE MOORCROFT

Born 10.4.1953 Coventry. Club: Coventry Godiva H

DAVE MOORCROFT'S CAREER as a champion track runner spanned 18 years, from 1971 when at age 17 he won the AAA Junior indoor 1500m title to 1989 when he became UK 3000m champion. During that time he was admired not only for his racing successes but also for his modesty, good humour and sporting demeanour. Highlights of that long career included a stunning world record for 5000m, a European 3000m record and Commonwealth titles at 1500m and 5000m. But there were crushing disappointments too; he suffered more than his fair share of debilitating injuries and illnesses, and his dream of winning an Olympic title was never realised. He thus brings to his job as Chief Executive of the governing body, UK Athletics, the insight of an athlete who has experienced first hand the highs, lows, requirements and problems of the sport at club, national and international level.

Nobody paid too much attention in 1973 when Loughborough PE student Moorcroft, recently blooded as a senior British international at 1500m, won a Midland League 5000m race in 14:31.0 ... but it was the first step on a path which would lead nine years later to a world record of 13:00.41, a time still unapproached by any other British runner. Of more immediate significance was the attainment in 1975 of one of his cherished goals: a sub-four minute mile. He cut it fine by running 3:59.9, but that was just the start.

Evidence that Moorcroft possessed impressive stamina for a 1500m specialist was provided early in 1976. A month or so after winning the AAA indoor 1500m title (his first encounter with a youthful Seb Coe, who finished fifth) he was runner-up to Bernie Ford in the English national nine miles cross country championship. Lowering his personal best to 3:39.88 in his semi-final, eliminating Steve Ovett among others, he surpassed himself by reaching the Olympic 1500m final in Montreal, placing seventh in 3:40.94 barely a dozen metres behind gold medallist John Walker. A month later, at Crystal Palace, Moorcroft brought off his biggest win thus far. Not only did he outkick a superb field in the Emsley Carr Mile, headed by world 1500m record holder Filbert Bayi, but he lowered his best time to 3:57.06.

A back injury sustained in New Zealand early in the year caused him to miss the entire summer season of 1977 but he bounced back in 1978 to beat Bayi for the Commonwealth title in 3:35.48, a 3.4 sec improvement over his previous best, the fastest time in the world that year and the second quickest ever by a Briton behind Ovett's 3:34.45 in 1977. By going on to place third in the European Championships 1500m (3:36.70) behind Ovett (3:35.59 with a 24.8 last 200m) and Ireland's Eamonn Coghlan (3:36.57) meant that he was the only British runner to gain an individual medal both in Edmonton and Prague.

Moorcroft continued to flirt with the 5000m, reducing his best to 13:58.4, but in June 1979 – running his first international race at the distance – he won comfortably in 13:30.33, a performance which made Moorcroft think hard about tackling that event in the Moscow Olympics. A month later he came up with a personal best mile time of 3:54.35 in Oslo, but was far from happy as it sufficed only for ninth in a remarkable race won by Coe in the world record time of 3:48.95. Problems with his calves and hamstring were exacerbated by the race, and he decided to bring his season to a premature close.

Personal bests of 13:29.4 and 13:29.1 in New Zealand early in the year persuaded Moorcroft to aim for the Olympic 5000m. Unfortunately, sore calves (later diagnosed as compartment syndrome) continued to plague him and his Olympic hopes received a further setback when he picked up a severe stomach bug in Moscow. "I felt like death out there," he said after surviving his heat, and – totally drained – he found the semi-final "a nightmare from the start." He finished ninth in 13:58.23 and was eliminated. Confirmation that at his best he could have been a medal contender came almost a year later when he reduced his best time to 13:20.51. He was particularly delighted with his performance because the calf problem was still seriously affecting him ("both legs felt as though they were continually clamped in a vice") and he was preparing to undergo surgery. Before then, though, he sped through a 25.5 last 200m to win a hard fought European Cup Final 5000m in 13:43.18. "Now I can consider myself a 5000m runner," he declared.

Free at last from injury and thanks to a great winter's training in New Zealand, Moorcroft experienced his *annus mirabilis* in 1982. Emphasising his new levels of endurance, in April he broke Brendan Foster's highly regarded record for the 5 miles 900 yards long leg in the AAA Road Relay with a time of 24:27 ... and in just his second track race of the summer, on June 26, he displayed unprecedented speed by knocking 5 sec off his best time in recording 3:49.34 behind Americans Steve Scott and Sydney Maree in Oslo's Dream Mile – moving to no 5 on the world all-time list. Clearly he was ready for something special at 5000m and back in Oslo on July 7 for the 20th 5000m race of his career he took aim at Foster's UK record of 13:14.6, knowing that would guarantee him advance selection at that distance in the European Championships later in the summer.

In a classic example of British understatement, the entry in his training diary relating to his Oslo 5000m includes the words "quite pleased." One wonders what he would have had to achieve for the comment "very pleased" to apply! In actual fact, Moorcroft was as shocked as anyone (other than his coach for the past 13 years, John Anderson, who had forecast 13 minutes was on the cards that year) by his phenomenal run at Bislett. In one of the most astonishing performances in the entire history of running, he knocked almost 6 sec off Kenyan Henry Rono's world record with the sensational time of 13:00.41. Such a momentous leap forward might have been a shade more predictable had the race taken the form of those intricately choreographed pacemaking jobs as when Rono (who finished fourth in Oslo) set the previous mark of 13:06.20. On the contrary, Moorcroft – a man who has relied more than most on his finishing speed – was out on his own for the final four kilometres and ended up 20 sec ahead of the next man, Ralph King (USA). Indeed, King – not realising Moorcroft was still in the race, so far ahead was he – thought he had won the race! The kilometre splits were 2:38.0, 2:34.6, 2:37.6, 2:38.5 and 2:31.7.

Four days later I interviewed Moorcroft and asked if he had been nervous approaching the race. "Just the usual: panic stricken, wobbly knees ... my usual approach to races," he smiled. How aware was he of his pace? "I went through four laps in 4:11 and I knew that was okay for Bren's record. The assumption was I would run the first four laps in about 4:12 and slow down to reach eight laps in around 8:28, but I went through in 8:21 [3000m in 7:50.2]. I just kept plugging away, really, and when I got to two laps to go I saw 11 minutes hadn't yet come up. When I got to the bell and it had just turned to 12:01 I knew I had got the world record. For the whole of that last lap, although I was absolutely shattered, I was savouring the fact that I was going to be world record holder." Moorcroft confessed that front running was "so totally out of character for me ... but I felt good, I felt strong, and I enjoyed it. I guess it's an added satisfaction knowing that I did it all on my own."

Buoyed by his new-found status as one of the superstars of the sport, Moorcroft went on to enjoy one brilliant race after another. Ten days after Oslo he was given a hero's welcome at Crystal Palace and rewarded the fans with a thrilling 3000m win over Maree in 7:32.79, breaking Foster's European record and falling only just short of Rono's world record of 7:32.1. The time for his last lap was 54.3. Further personal bests followed at 800m (1:46.64), 1500m (3:33.79) and 2 miles (8:16.75). However, the pressure was taking its toll; he developed an eye infection and swollen glands, and his self confidence began to seep away as the European Championships drew closer. Physically and mentally he was far from his Oslo form and, never feeling at ease, he had unwillingly to settle for third (13:30.42) in the big event of the year, won by West Germany's Thomas Wessinghage in 13:28.90. He did, however, bounce back with victory in the Commonwealth Games (13:33.00). The next target was to have been the World Championships in 1983, but that year was a virtual write-off due to hepatitis and then to a stress fracture in his foot.

Although hampered for much of the year by a pelvic injury, Moorcroft recaptured top form with a 3:50.95 victory in the Oslo Dream Mile in July 1984, but alas the injury returned to ruin his chances in the Olympic 5000m final in Los Angeles. A lesser man would have dropped out, but he was determined to see it through even though it must have been hellish for him as he finished 14th and last in 14:16.61, almost lapped by Morocco's Said Aouita (13:05.59), the man destined to take the world record from Moorcroft in 1985 and lead the way under 13 minutes in 1987.

That gritty showing in LA took its toll and he was never again the same athlete. His fastest 5000m subsequently was 13:29.12 in 1987 and as a swansong he won the inaugural UK 3000m title in 1989 in 7:50.76 and ran a 28:54 10k on the road in 1990. Still that wasn't quite the end of a momentous career, for in 1993, aged 40, he set the still existing outdoor world veterans mile record of 4:02.53!

STEVE JONES

Born 4.8.1955 Ebbw Vale (Wales).
Clubs: Swindon AC, Newport AC

IT WAS AS a 14 year-old Air Training Corps cadet that Steve Jones discovered a modest talent for running but it wasn't until he joined the RAF in 1974 that he had the chance to nurture that gift. A decade later he would blossom forth as the world's fastest marathon runner.

He did not exactly set the world alight on his international debut for Wales, finishing 103rd in the 1977 World Cross Country Championships, half a mile adrift of the winner, but the very next year he placed as high as 11th. On the track his goal that year was to run in the Commonwealth Games at 5000m, a distance he had not yet tackled. He succeeded, but he wasn't yet ready for that level of competition and finished 11th, half a lap behind Kenya's Henry Rono. He progressed to seventh in the 1979 World Cross after having made a valiant attempt to catch Irish winner John Treacy on the last lap. An ankle injury caused him to miss most of the track season but he came back strongly in the autumn with an impressive 10 miles road victory in 46:20 – a pointer to the future.

In 1980 his Olympic ambitions were centred on the steeplechase, but although he improved substantially for a best of 8:32.00 he failed to make the team for Moscow. He did not subsequently pursue the event but it's interesting to note how similar his personal best was to that of East Germany's double Olympic marathon champion Waldemar Cierpinski (8:32.4). His most significant performance of 1980 was a resounding 10,000m debut at the Centenary AAA Championships. Always happiest when out in front, no matter what the standard of opposition, Jones took the lead after 19 laps with Nick Rose at his shoulder and that's how it stayed until Rose went with 200m to go. Jones finished in 28:13.25 and appeared to have found his event, although he later showed a fine turn of speed with a 4:00.6 mile. He improved to 28:00.58 in 1981 but that was only scratching at the surface for in a race against the USSR, which he won in 28:13.67, he was inside world record pace for nearly 4000m.

He expected to go way under 28 minutes in 1982, especially after making great progress at 5000m with a Welsh record of 13:18.6, but it didn't happen and he was outclassed in both the European Championships (7th in 28:22.94) and Commonwealth Games (11th in 29:13.68).

The breakthrough came in 1983 when first he ran 27:59.3 and then a spectacular Welsh record of 27:39.14 after passing halfway in an ambitious 13:41.0. He clocked another fast time (27:47.57) in the heats of the inaugural World Championships in Helsinki but ran an uncharacteristically passive race in the final to place 12th (28:15.03). His finishing speed was found wanting in the European Cup Final (5th in 28:07.03) after being in contention at the bell but six days later in Brussels he astonished everyone with a sprint finish win over Commonwealth champion Gidamis Shahanga of Tanzania in 27:55.38 ... his fourth tough 10,000m race in 19 days.

He ended the year with two tantalising road race performances. As part of his preparation for his marathon debut in Chicago he won a half marathon race in Wales in 61:25, 7 sec inside the world best, but assumed to be on an under-distance course. In Chicago he was up with the leaders until, at 16 miles, he pulled out with a foot injury that had been aggravated when he stepped in a pot hole at halfway. He was so distraught that he offered to hand back the expenses he had been paid by the race organisers.

That injury cost him nearly two months of training but, as so often the case with distance runners, the enforced rest was probably to his advantage and in March 1984 he achieved his highest ever World Cross placing of third behind Carlos Lopes, the Portuguese destined to become Olympic marathon champion that summer, and Tim

Hutchings. It was a pity Jones didn't try for the Olympic marathon team; contesting the 10,000m in Los Angeles he was left far behind in the second half of the race to finish eighth in 28:28.08. But, in October 1984, Jones would meet up again with Lopes – this time over the Chicago marathon course – and life would never be the same again for Corporal Jones.

Athletics at the elite level was now openly professional and the £30,000 prize money he pocketed in Chicago represented about five years of RAF pay as an aircraft technician! It was all very bewildering, as was the impact he made in his first completed marathon. While Lopes and 1983 world champion Rob de Castella fought out a close finish, the 29 year-old Welshman ran out a sensational winner one minute clear in a world's best of 2:08:05, becoming the first European to hold the record since Basil Heatley 20 years earlier. Running in cool, wet and windy conditions, and aiming for around 2:10, he always felt comfortable among the leaders ("I was strolling") and when he made his effort shortly before 20 miles he was surprised no one went with him. In fact it wasn't that unexpected ... he covered the final 10 kilometres in a staggering 29:39, the second half of the race in 63:44.

Despite his new-found fame as a marathon runner, Jones' immediate intention was to run one marathon a year but continue to concentrate on the track with a view to winning a medal in the 1988 Olympic 10,000m. However, the commercial opportunities proved too strong to resist. He collected something like £50,000 for winning the London Marathon in April 1985. The day before, Lopes had relieved him of the world best with 2:07:11 in Rotterdam, but that didn't detract from a great race as Jones was locked in combat with Olympic bronze medallist Charlie Spedding for 23 miles before speeding away to victory by 17 sec in 2:08:16.

In August he set a world half marathon best of 61:14 and in October, back in Chicago, he scored a third brilliant marathon victory, missing the world record by just one second with 2:07:13, a time which remains unapproached as the British record 20 years later. In an incredible display of front running he reached 10 miles in 47:01, halfway in 61:42 and 20 miles in 1:35:22. He was still 23 sec up on Lopes' corresponding time at 40 kilometres and afterwards he said he felt he could have run at least a minute faster had he not run so quick a first half.

Every marathon runner, no matter how great, eventually has a day when it all goes wrong and that happened to Jones in the 1986 European Championships. A UK half marathon best of 60:59 in the Great North Run and a bronze medal in the Commonwealth Games 10,000m (28:02.48) set him up nicely and in Stuttgart he went for broke, opening up a two minute lead before halfway. However, he chose not to take any drinks as the race wore on and he gradually became dehydrated. He was still a minute clear at 30 kilometres but soon afterwards the wheels came off and, although everyone expected him to drop out and save himself for another day, he stubbornly kept on to the finish, 20th in 2:22:12.

In 1987 he finished second in Boston in 2:12:37 but injury kept him out of the World Championships. In 1988 he placed ninth in Boston in 2:14:07 and, after missing Olympic selection, achieved the final outstanding victory of his career by winning in New York by a three minute margin in 2:08:20. By then he had left the RAF to become a full-time athlete and he later moved to the USA. His only marathon in 1989 was New York, where he finished eighth in 2:12:58, and he ran a similar time (2:12:44) to place fourth in the 1990 Commonwealth Games. He had one more marathon win left and that came in Toronto in 1992 when, aged 37, he clocked 2:10:06, the fastest by a Briton for three years. He still races, running a 64:09 half marathon at age 42.

STEVE OVETT

Born 9.10.1955 Brighton. Clubs: Brighton & Hove AC, Phoenix AC, Annan & District AAC

AFTER WINNING THE 1980 Olympic 800m title in Moscow, Steve Ovett could with some justification be considered the greatest competitive athlete Britain had ever produced up until that time, for that success – achieved at the age of 24 – completed a remarkable sequence of major triumphs.

Always tall and strong for his age, Ovett had displayed outstanding promise in his first season with Brighton & Hove AC to register a 400m time of 53.7 in 1969, just 0.1 outside the UK age-13 best. His progress was relentless and exciting: 51.6 and 2:00.0 for 800m at 14 (he also became English Schools under-15 400m champion), 49.8 and a UK age best of 1:55.3 at 15, 48.4 and 1:52.5 at 16 – the same year he finished second in his age group in the English Schools 4 miles cross country championship (with one Sebastian Coe tenth).

That here was a versatile runner physically endowed beyond his years became even more evident in 1973 when, coached by Harry Wilson, he became the world's fastest ever 17 year-old with times of 1:47.5 in his heat and 1:47.3 in the final at the AAA Championships. He followed that up with a British junior mile record of four minutes flat and a dip finish gained him the European Junior 800m title in 1:47.53. In 1974 he sharpened his speed with a 47.5 400m, trimmed his mile best to 3:59.4 and distinguished himself by finishing second in the senior European Championships 800m with a European Junior record of 1:45.8 ... but Ovett's attitude, one of dismay that by being boxed in at the crucial moment when Yugoslavia's Luciano Susanj made his strike for home with 200m to go he lost his own chance of victory, earmarked this young man as a very special breed of athlete.

He included more endurance work in his training the following winter and started 1975 on a high note by romping away with the English Junior 6 miles cross country title by almost 200m. However, it proved a year of consolidation rather than progress as he built up towards the Olympic season. Harry Wilson may not have done him any favours by suggesting, in an interview published in August 1975, that "1:40 in Montreal is not out of the question".

In fact, he was not yet ready at those Olympics to tackle the world's best although it was a great learning experience for him. He did produce a personal best of 1:45.4

123

but, drawn blind in lane eight and too slow into his running, he was never in the hunt and placed a dejected fifth nearly 15m behind the world record of 1:43.5 by Cuba's Alberto Juantorena. He returned to win his 1500m heat in a personal best of 3:37.9 but in his fifth hard race of the Games he ran out of steam in his semi-final.

It was from 1977 onwards that Ovett's trademarks, the unmatched burst of acceleration 200m from the finish and his cheeky waves to the crowd well before the race was over, made him a charismatic and controversial figure known the world over. His first serious track race of 1977, in Jamaica, resulted in a narrow 1500m defeat by Steve Scott (USA) – but that was to prove Ovett's last loss at either 1500m or mile until the 46th race in the sequence, the 1980 Olympic final! During an eventful summer he claimed his first UK senior record (3:54.7 mile), clocked a world class 5000m time of 13:25.0 in only his second race at the distance, played with the field in the European Cup Final 1500m, turned up on impulse for a half marathon and won it in 65:38 ("sheer madness", he admitted), ran an awesome race to obliterate some very classy opposition in the World Cup 1500m with a UK record shattering 3:34.5, and ended the season with a 7:41.3 3000m which made him the second fastest ever Briton at the event.

That World Cup race was a classic. As I reported at the time: "It was in Düsseldorf that Steve Ovett finally graduated from the ranks of the potentially great 1500m runners to one of the world's proven elite. He showed that he really does have all that it takes to become an outstanding champion. We have long known that in a slow race Steve's formidable acceleration and finishing powers could account for practically anybody; what remained to be proved was whether he could handle a good field after a fast early pace. Steve passed this searching test with flying colours. The pace was hot throughout, much faster than anything Steve had previously experienced, and yet he looked and felt as much at ease as in much slower races. When the time came for him to launch his finishing kick it was even more deadly than ever before." His penultimate 100m (timed in 11.8!) destroyed New Zealand's Olympic champion John Walker, who failed to finish. After covering the final 200m in 25.1, Ovett restated his maxim: "I don't run for time, I just run to win."

A further indication of the extraordinary endurance acquired by a man blessed with 47.5 400m speed came in the 1978 inter-counties cross country when Ovett defeated future marathon world record breaker Steve Jones over a snowy, muddy and icy 7.5 miles course and went on to place fourth in the even longer English national championship race. It was a good grounding for the track season. His speed at the end of 1500m or mile races grew even more impressive: 51.6 last 400m in one race, 24.4 final 200m in another – and that included time lost by waving to the crowd, a habit which delighted his fans and infuriated his vanquished rivals.

Meanwhile, Seb Coe had joined the world's elite at 800m, improving his UK record to 1:44.25 (as against Ovett's best of 1:45.4), and everyone assumed that the race for the European 800m title in Prague would be a private British duel with everyone else scrapping for the bronze. As expected, Coe set a fast pace but admitted he got slightly carried away in the excitement of the occasion, for he sped through

200m in 24.3 and 400m in 49.32! It was a fantastic, throbbing, thrilling pace, yet far from ploughing a lonely furrow, with the others waiting for him to crack, Coe was being closely tracked by the East German pair of Olaf Beyer and Andreas Busse as well as by Ovett, whose time of 49.9-50.0 was much faster than anything he had previously experienced. Coe reached 600m in an exceptional 76.2 (1:41.6 800m pace) but Ovett was less than a stride's length down. Entering the final straight Coe was just a metre up on Ovett and 3m ahead of Beyer, and within 30m Ovett had taken the lead for the first time. As Coe fell back, Ovett must have thought the gold was his ... but an inspired Beyer was not done yet. He came storming past Ovett to snatch victory in 1:43.84, a two second improvement, and not far outside Juantorena's world record of 1:43.44. Ovett seized the UK record with 1:44.09 while Coe finished a brave but dejected third in 1:44.76.

Unlike his silver medal of four years previously, Ovett was content with his second place. As he explained to me in an interview for *Athletics Weekly*: "Considering that I never trained for the 800 and I only raced three times in almost two years over 800, to get the silver medal with that sort of background and to break the UK record was really very pleasing."

Four days later Ovett lined up for his main event, the 1500m final, a race which could not have been run in a more ideal manner for him had he stage-managed the whole affair. Sixth in a tightly bunched field at the bell, he launched his kick from 200m out and as so often before was ten metres to the good before anyone began to react. It was all over and covering that final 200m in 24.8 he won unstraining ahead of Eamonn Coghlan and Dave Moorcroft in 3:35.59.

There was more to come before 1978 could be consigned to history. At the same Crystal Palace meeting in which Coe regained the UK 800m record with 1:43.97, Ovett not only defeated multi-world record breaker Henry Rono of Kenya at 2 miles but in the process clipped 0.2 sec from Brendan Foster's outdoor world best with 8:13.5, his second mile taking just 4:04.4. Although he hadn't previously chased records, Ovett knew his late season form was too good to waste and in Oslo he took a crack at John Walker's world mile mark of 3:49.4. The cold, wet and windy conditions destroyed his chances but he still came home in 3:52.8 to reclaim the UK record he had lost earlier in the year to Frank Clement (3:54.2). His momentous season finally came to an end in Tokyo where he won the Golden Mile in 3:55.5.

Asked in the 'AW' interview whether he now had a hunger for the world mile record, Ovett replied: "No, I don't think so. It's just that last year I ran out of opposition; I beat everybody and the only thing I had to go for towards the end of the season was a good time. It was just a last resort and I don't think I've got the appetite for world records. I don't think I ever will have. It seems pointless to me."

All that would change from 1979, for in the space of 41 days Coe set three astonishing world records – 1:42.33 for 800m, 3:48.95 for the mile and 3:32.03 for 1500m – and Ovett suddenly found he was no longer the king of the middle distances in Britain never mind the world. He knew he had to respond and at Crystal Palace he went close to the mile figures with 3:49.57, making him the third man after

Walker and Coe to break 3:50, and a few days later in Brussels he was even closer to the 1500m record with 3:32.11, the second fastest ever.

It was in Oslo on 1 July 1980 that Ovett succeeded in becoming an official world record holder. In a fantastic evening for British athletics, first Coe smashed the world 1000m record with 2:13.40 and then Ovett – wearing his favourite Soviet national team vest – ran a hand timed 3:48.8 (quarters of 55.7, 58.1, 57.2 and 57.8) for the mile with 19 year-old Steve Cram runner-up in 3:53.8. Two weeks later Ovett struck again in Oslo's Bislett Stadium, clocking 3:32.09 for 1500m. Although 6/100ths slower than Coe's 1979 time Ovett received credit for equalling the world record of 3:32.1 as in those days they were ratified to the tenth of a second above.

The stage was set for two momentous clashes against Coe at the Moscow Olympics, the general feeling being that Coe would be too speedy for everybody at 800m (final on July 26) while Ovett, with 45 wins on the trot at 1500m and mile since May 1977, would maintain his winning streak in the 1500m (August 1). In the end each man did take home a gold medal, but in the 'wrong' event!

As I commented in 'AW' at the time: "Some people are never satisfied! British runners fill first and second places in the Olympic 800m, and yet I'm left with a feeling of anti-climax. Steve Ovett ran so physical a race that he can consider himself lucky not to have been disqualified; while Seb Coe chose an Olympic final of all occasions to run the most abysmal tactical race of his career. Instead of the full-blooded battle we had been anticipating so excitedly, the race turned out to be an untidy, ill mannered affair won in the modest time of 1:45.40 (to Coe's 1:45.85). We didn't see the best of either Ovett or Coe. Having got that off my chest, and putting aside my reservations about the manner in which Ovett set about clearing a path for himself, I must congratulate Steve on his victory. After much frenzied pushing and shoving earlier in the race, Steve – the supreme *racer* – got himself in the right place at the right time and when he struck for home early in the finishing straight there was never any doubt as to the outcome. Whereas Coe was left floundering in the cut and thrust of an Olympic final, Ovett was absolutely in his element. He has taken time out to break world records recently, but it's man against man that really motivates Steve." Ovett, by the way, ran the second lap in 50.8 with a final 200m of 24.3.

The rematch over 1500m was even more intriguing now. Surely Ovett, having won his supposedly weaker event, would be unbeatable in his speciality. Yet, with a gold medal already in the bank, would he be as hungry for success as Coe, whose whole reputation as a championship racer as distinct from a great time triallist was now on the line? As Coe said at the time, "I've got to come back and climb the mountain again. I MUST win it".

In terms of fitness and physical ability there was probably little to choose between the two men but, in that 1500m final, it was Coe's stronger will which made the difference. It was no longer – in athletic terms – a matter of life and death for Ovett whether he won; for Coe it was.

Coe, this time, was always in touch with the leaders, well placed to take advantage of the sharp acceleration in pace injected by East Germany's Jürgen Straub 700m from the finish. Straub covered the third lap in a sizzling 54.2, Coe happily tucked away in second place with Ovett third and no jostling as in the 800m. Straub held a four metre lead with 200m to go but Coe and Ovett were gathering themselves for the final strike.

Decisively, it was Coe who got his blow in first, producing a double kick along the finishing straight which carried him over the line three metres clear in 3:38.40, an unremarkable time until you consider he covered the last lap in 52.2 and the final 700m was run at sub-1:47 800m pace! Ovett just could not get past the inspired Straub and had to settle for third in 3:38.99. "I'm proud of my bronze as I am of my gold because I did my best," said Ovett. "I don't bear any grudges against Seb, he was a worthy winner. I just couldn't lift myself after the 800m."

Ovett had one more ace up his sleeve. In Koblenz on August 27 he clarified the 1500m world record situation by running 3:31.36 with the final 400m covered in 53.9.

The public was thirsting for further clashes between the two most charismatic runners in the world, but they had to wait four years until the next Olympics. A combination of commercial factors, injuries and illness conspired to keep them apart, but 1981 was still a thrilling season as they constantly pursued world records. Coe achieved much the higher success rate: he ran 800m in 1:41.73 in Florence on June 10, 1000m in 2:12.18 in Oslo on July 11, mile in 3:48.53 in Zürich on August 19 and 3:47.33 in Brussels on August 28, with Ovett snatching the mile record for just two days with his 3:48.40 (56.6, 57.9, 57.0, 56.9) in Koblenz on August 26. Prior to that Ovett had won mile races in 3:49.25 and 3:49.66, thus owning four of the six fastest ever times before Coe got to work, and the second quickest ever 1500m time of 3:31.57.

Unfortunately, Ovett suffered a dreadful knee injury when he ran into some church railings while training in December and did well to race at all in 1982. He did run a world class 7:43.87 3000m and set a UK 2000m record of 4:57.71, but shortly after running a 1:46.08 800m he tore a hamstring and that was the end of his season. He got back to top form in 1983, a solid winter's training demonstrated by a 28:55 10 kilometres on the road in April (he would run 28:16 in December), but for once his tactical brilliance was absent at the inaugural World Championships, where despite a 51.9 last lap he could finish no higher than fourth (3:42.34) in a race won by Steve Cram in 3:41.59. "It was the worst race of my life ... I ran like a goon," Ovett admitted. With the major prize lost, he set his sights on breaking the world 1500m record. As preparation he won a 3:50.49 mile and clocked his fastest 800m time for four years (1:45.25) but, although spurred on by the news that his world record had just been broken by South African-born Sydney Maree of the USA with 3:31.24, he fell short with 3:32.95 in Koblenz. However, four days later in Rieti, he achieved his goal. Superbly paced by the USA's David Mack (54.17, 1:51.67) and taking over at 1000m to pass 1200m in 2:49.14, Ovett stopped the timer at 3:30.77 and declared that if it hadn't been windy he might have broken the 3:30 barrier.

Ovett travelled to Los Angeles for the 1984 Olympics as defending champion in the 800m and world record holder at 1500m, but his third Games was to prove a traumatic experience. He ran 1:44.81, his best for six years, to scrape into the 800m final but finished last of eight, walking across the line in 1:52.28 ... to be taken away on a stretcher and admitted to hospital suffering from bronchial problems, dehydration and hyperventilation. He ignored medical advice to withdraw from the 1500m, and although visibly a sick man in the heat and smog of LA he battled through to the 1500m final in 3:36.55. That was one miraculous effort too far, for in that final (won by Coe in 3:32.53 with Cram second in 3:33.40) he dropped out on the third lap after experiencing more chest discomfort.

He would never be quite the same athlete again although he had his moments, as when in 1986 he ran his fastest 5000m of 13:20.06 and won the Commonwealth Games title in 13:24.11. He retired from competition in 1991, one year after Coe bowed out. And how did Ovett rate his friend and rival? "I was always aware that Seb was a far better athlete than I was. That's not false modesty, that's the truth. He was a far greater natural talent." Coe returns the compliment: "I think Steve's the greatest runner I ever competed against, probably the most complete athlete I knew."

Ovett, who married hurdler Rachel Waller in 1981, has worked as a TV commentator for many years and now lives in Australia where their daughter Alex clocked the promising 800m time of 2:18.24 at age 14 in 2004.

TESSA SANDERSON

Born 14.3.1956 St Elizabeth (Jamaica). Clubs: Wolverhampton & Bilston AC, Borough of Hounslow AC

HISTORY OF VARIOUS sorts was made in the Los Angeles Coliseum on 6 August 1984 when Tessa Sanderson's opening throw of 69.56 – an Olympic javelin record – remained unsurpassed throughout the rest of the competition and the 28 year-old from Leeds by way of Jamaica and the West Midlands was crowned champion. She thus became the first Briton, male or female, ever to win an Olympic throwing title and the first Afro-Caribbean woman athlete to gain an Olympic gold medal in British colours. She would take her place in Olympic annals as the athlete who cried for joy atop the victory rostrum in LA four years after weeping in frustration and disappointment when failing to qualify for the final in Moscow in which, at worst, she was expected to place second. Tessa's story is of a multi-talented athlete who, beset by so many injury problems, could easily have faded from the scene before realising her true potential, but who persevered during the dark days, fought back and finally captured the biggest prize of all. As her then coach Wilf Paish testified at the time of her Olympic triumph: "the tenacity and toughness of the girl has to be believed."

Jamaica, an island with a great Olympic tradition in sprinting and 400m running since 1948, was where Theresa Ione Sanderson was born. From the age of one she was brought up by her grandmother in Jamaica while her parents sought work in Britain, and it wasn't until she was eight that Tessa joined them near Wolverhampton. She was first spotted as an athlete of unusual potential at the age of 13 by John Moogan, who became her coach for several years. At 15 (1971) she collected her first national javelin title, at the WAAA Intermediate Championships, but was already displaying great versatility for in her age group as well as ranking no 1 in the javelin she was second nationally in the pentathlon, fourth in the long jump, fifth in the 400m and hurdles, eighth in the 100m. She had her first taste of international competition at the 1973 European Junior Championships, placing a disappointing 12th, but she ended that year on a high note by setting a UK age-17 best of 51.34 which qualified her for the Commonwealth Games early in 1974. With four of her throws ruled fouls (one of which was so close to winning her the silver medal) she wound up fifth in her senior international debut.

During the summer of 1974 she became UK Junior record holder with 55.04, and it seemed just a matter of time before she eclipsed Sue Platt's long standing British senior record of 55.60. She did it in 1976 (56.14), which clinched her Olympic place, and she more than justified her selection for Montreal by qualifying for the final with another UK record of 57.18. At 20 the youngest finalist, she acquitted herself honourably to place tenth with 57.00 and she progressed slightly to 57.20 after the Games. Observers felt that she might well progress to the magical 60m mark in 1977 ... but no one surely could have foreseen that in the space of a single season she would improve by precisely ten metres, go close to the world record and defeat the seemingly invincible East German double Olympic champion Ruth Fuchs!

It was also in 1977 that Tessa's all-round talents were developed a stage further. She represented Britain indoors at 60m hurdles and placed third in the inaugural UK 400m hurdles championship in 60.46. The day after the latter race she broke through the 60m barrier (60.24), a British record she extended to 64.42 in Germany. That was also her first Commonwealth record and shot her up to fifth place on the world all-time list.

The metamorphosis of Tessa Sanderson, from promising youngster to a world beater, was completed in Dublin. The occasion was a European Cup Semi-Final and the result of the javelin shook the world of athletics. Fuchs, world record holder at 69.12 and who led the 1977 world rankings with 67.66, threw a not inconsiderable 64.46 ... but was well beaten by Tessa's astonishing 67.20 which moved her to no 2 on the world all-time list. A fit of pique helped produce this massive breakthrough. She explained: "I brought my own javelins from Britain but they took them away and wouldn't let me use them. I had to use the ones they supplied. After my first throw (60.34) I was so mad I went right to the back of the banking and made my record throw." Subsequently, in the European Cup Final, Fuchs won by 68.92 to 62.36 and in the first ever World Cup the East German won with 62.36 with Tessa third (60.30), one place ahead of the USA's Kate Schmidt who shortly afterwards threw the world record distance of 69.32.

Although more consistent than in the previous season, Tessa threw a best of 'only' 64.00 in 1978, although for the second year running she was merit ranked no 2 in the world behind Fuchs. Hot favourite for the Commonwealth title, she duly won that gold medal by a margin of almost seven metres with 61.34, but was no match for Fuchs – who set a European record of 69.16 – in the European Championships. Without much of an interval between Edmonton and Prague, Tessa was delighted to throw 62.40 for the silver, becoming the first British woman thrower ever to win a European medal.

Interviewed for *Athletics Weekly* by David Cocksedge, Tessa left no doubt about her attitude towards performance enhancing drugs. "When it comes to anabolic steroids and drug taking I just switch off. I know I'll never take them, and that's all I need to know. It's just not worth it; because it's a sport after all. Steroids can be very dangerous for women, and I feel I'm a woman first and an athlete second. I compete against girls I know are taking steroids and whatever, and it does get me down a bit, but there's no way I'd ever risk my health to throw further."

In 1979, now coached by Paish, Tessa threw 65.34, was ranked fourth in the world and had every reason to believe she could challenge for a medal at the following year's Moscow Olympics. Her status was enhanced in June 1980 when she extended her Commonwealth record to 69.70 which would have been a world record had Fuchs not thrown 69.96 a few weeks earlier. The Games, though, proved to be a nightmare. She appeared to suffer from something akin to stagefright as she attempted to qualify for the final, which would normally have been a formality. The usually confident, composed Tessa was nowhere to be seen. In her place was a hesitant, uncertain athlete. Her first throw dipped into the turf at a mere 48.76; the second and third didn't travel much farther and were fouls anyway. Her Olympic bid was over before it had even really started. Four years of sweat and tears had gone down the drain. Maria Colon of Cuba took the title with a throw of 68.40.

Tessa put the Olympics firmly behind her in 1981, when she not only reclaimed second place on the world javelin rankings but also emerged as Britain's finest female all-rounder. She was particularly suited to the new heptathlon with all those lovely points to be gained in the sixth of the seven events and in her second try she set a Commonwealth record of 5906 in appalling weather conditions, a score she later improved to 6110 which was boosted by a throw of 64.64. She also finished a close second in the WAAA 100m hurdles in 13.46. Her javelin went well too, as she threw her second best of 68.86.

By javelin throwers' standards Tessa had been fairly fortunate in the matter of injuries but her luck ran out early in 1982, a year in which she had set her heart on throwing beyond 70m and capturing a European/Commonwealth double. A heavy fall during an indoor relay ruptured her Achilles tendon and broke the bone in her throwing elbow, leaving her on crutches for four months. She had only one competition, at the end of the summer. Hobbling up to the line, she threw 66 metres! That missed season saw the world record raised to 74.20 by Sofia Sakorafa of Greece and for the first time since 1973 someone other than Tessa topped the UK year list as Fatima Whitbread, five years her junior, had improved to 66.98.

Fatima beat her for the first time in 19 meetings since 1977 at the 1983 UK Championships, and that was just the spur Tessa needed. The following weekend she produced her first 70m throw – a Commonwealth record of 70.82. Later that month she threw 73.58, elevating her to third on the world all-time list behind the new world record holder, Finland's Tiina Lillak (74.76) and Sakorafa. But at the inaugural World Championships in Helsinki it was Fatima who posed the main challenge to the local heroine with a bombshell of an opener (69.14). The gold medal was hers, until Lillak snatched it away with her final effort of 70.82. Tessa placed fourth with 64.76, "a good result" in her estimation as she was still suffering the effects of that indoor injury and a few days later she underwent further surgery on both legs.

Early season results in 1984 were vastly encouraging. She threw 68.58 in May while in June she won the Olympic trial with 67.02, followed by a 68.88. She was going well, but so too was Fatima who had upped her best to 71.86 in April although she had since had an internal operation. Their paths crossed twice in July, Fatima winning both times, but Tessa was satisfied with her final pre-Olympic test in Potsdam. She threw 67.92, well beaten by the East German duo of Petra Felke (74.24) and Antje Kempe (71.56), but because of the Soviet bloc boycott of the Games they would not be among her opponents in Los Angeles.

What happened in that Olympic final fulfilled all of Tessa's dreams. She was the one who unleashed a tremendous opening throw of 69.56 and, unlike Fatima in Helsinki, that initial throw held up as the winner. Lillak, hampered by an ankle injury, came rather too close for comfort in the second round with 69.00 but after she had to withdraw the only credible challenger was Fatima, whose best on the day proved to be 67.14 for the bronze medal. Thanks to the coaching input of three men – Brian Newman (weights), Wilf Paish (technical side of throwing) and Hungary's 1976 Olympic javelin champion Miklós Németh (help with technique and conditioning) – she had become Britain's first female Olympic champion since Mary Peters 12 years earlier.

Although Tessa continued to compete at the highest level for many more years, she was usually outshone by Fatima. Their rivalry became acrimonious at times but, as Tessa put it: "It's nice when we're out there battling it out together. We would never, ever, be the best of friends but we're damn big rivals in athletics and that's the way I like it to be." In 1985 Tessa threw 71.18; Fatima threw 72.98. At the 1986 Commonwealth Games Tessa scored a deeply satisfying victory over Fatima, with a season's best of 69.80 to 68.54, but injury kept her out of the European Championships which Fatima won with 76.32 after setting a fantastic world record of 77.44 in the qualifying round. Tessa lost further ground in 1987, for while Fatima won the world title with another massive throw of 76.54 Tessa had to settle for fourth at 67.54.

In 1988 Tessa reclaimed top spot on the UK list with 71.70 but at the Seoul Olympics Fatima took the silver medal (70.32) well behind Felke's 74.68 while Tessa relived her Moscow experience by failing to reach the final ... not surprising as she was carrying a serious Achilles tendon injury. It was a much happier story for Tessa in the 1990 Commonwealth Games as she won easily with 65.72, and at the 1991 European Cup she defeated Felke (now world record holder at exactly 80 metres!) for the first time with a throw of 65.18. She rated it the second most satisfying performance of her career, after the Olympic win, "because I was really so unfit mentally and physically".

She closed her remarkable career in 1992, aged 36. Apart from topping the UK list by a seven metre margin with 64.88 (Fatima had already retired) she became the first British athlete to compete in a fifth Olympic Games – placing a meritorious fourth in Barcelona (63.58) – and ended on a suitably high note by winning at the World Cup in Havana. Awarded the MBE in 1985, OBE in 1998 and CBE in 2004, Tessa has been Vice-Chairman of Sport England since 1999.

SEBASTIAN COE

Born 29.9.1956 Chiswick (London).
Clubs: Hallamshire H, Haringey AC

WHO IS THE greatest ever British athlete? All the possible claimants are included in this book, but – in this observer's opinion – two men stand above all others. One is Daley Thompson, the other is Seb Coe. If pressed hard to nominate one supreme champion/record breaker that vote would go to the rather more lightly built half of the duo who – bizarrely for such a diverse pair of athletes – had almost identical personal bests for 400m: 46.86 for Thompson, 46.87 for Coe.

Another curiosity is that Coe should have been that fast at 400m (and he was once timed at 45.5 from virtually a standing start in a relay) and such a legendary performer at 800m. All the signs from the early stages of his career were that he would develop into a longer distance runner. Yorkshire Colts cross country champion at 14 (when he weighed just 41kg or 90lb), AAA Youth 1500m and English Schools Intermediate 3000m champion at 16, his future looked to be mapped out.

But, after taking the bronze medal in the 1975 European Junior 1500m and with best times of 1:53.8 (800m), 3:45.2 (1500m) and 8:14.8 (3000m) to his name, he and his father/coach Peter Coe came to a momentous decision. If Seb was to approach his limits as a 1500m runner and above his basic speed had to be improved drastically.

Coe Senior would later remark: "At 14 I knew he was good. At 16 I felt a strange kind of certainty that if I was patient I had a world beater." As Seb revealed in his book *Running Free* (written with David Miller): "The partnership with my father has worked because I like the guy. I would like him even if he were not my father. He can be a bit brutal, certainly, but he has been right so often. When I was only 13 he drew up a projection of progress for me to 1980 with an optimum 1500m time of 3:30, and that at a time when I had achieved only 4:31.8 and the world record was still Herb Elliott's 3:35.6 in the Rome Olympic final. So often over the years he's had more faith in me than I have had in myself."

Coe's emphasis on speed began to bear fruit in 1976 as in quick succession he improved his 800m time to 1:53.0, 1:50.7 and a startling front-running 1:47.7. As a miler he first attracted widespread attention when in a star-studded race in very windy conditions at Gateshead he opened up a huge lead, being 40m ahead of the newly crowned Olympic 1500m champion John Walker at one stage. On the third lap Dave Moorcroft realised Coe was capable of stealing the race and set off in pursuit and at the bell the pair of them were still 25m ahead of the New Zealander. Walker, world record holder at 3:49.4, produced an astounding finish to win in 3:59.9 from Moorcroft (4:00.4) with Coe third in 4:01.7. Eight days later, in the Emsley Carr Mile at Crystal Palace, Coe tried again to run away from a world class field. More than 10m clear at halfway in 1:59.4 he eventually wound up seventh but he fought hard to the finish to record 3:58.35. Back at Gateshead on 14 September 1976, still aged 19, he finished second over a mile to New Zealander Rod Dixon in 4:01.5, the significance of that race being it was the last time he would lose at a mile or 1500m (excluding heats) until June 1983. Indeed he would remain undefeated at a mile for seven years.

It was during the 1977 indoor season that Coe established himself as an international 800m star, lifting the European title in, appropriately, San Sebastian in 1:46.5 (1:46.54), just 0.1 sec away from the world indoor best. Fears that because of his slight build (1.76m or 5ft 9in, 58kg or 129lb) he would be at risk in the hurly-burly of indoor racing proved groundless as he sped away from any possible trouble from the start and led all the way.

An Achilles tendon injury delayed the start of his outdoor season but he came on strong during late summer. In the Emsley Carr Mile at Crystal Palace, Coe bided his time on this occasion and demonstrated he had a kick to be respected, edging ahead of Filbert Bayi, Tanzania's world 1500m record holder, 30m from the finish to win in a personal best of 3:57.67. In his final appearance of the season he ran Mike Boit of Kenya to a metre or so over 800m, clocking a UK record of 1:44.95, the fastest by a European that year.

The decision was taken that he would concentrate on the 800m during 1978 and he signalled that he was peaking just right with a super run in Brussels a fortnight before the European Championships, lowering his UK record to 1:44.25 after passing 400m in 50.6. He and Ovett made an impressive showing in the preliminaries in Prague, and the stage was set for an epic showdown in the final. It would be the first time their paths would cross in competition since the 1972 English Schools cross country championship for Intermediates when Ovett was runner-up to Kirk Dumpleton in 21:42 and Coe – a year younger – placed tenth in 22:05.

The race was indeed a memorable one as Coe attempted to run the legs off his pursuers. He swept through the first 200m in 24.3 and reached 400m in an heroic but suicidal 49.32. He had misjudged it; planning for a time of between 50.0 and 50.5 which he believed would enable him to finish in close to 1:43, he had been carried away by the excitement of the occasion.

He went by 600m in 76.2 and was still in the lead entering the final straight but by then he was a spent force and powerless to prevent first Ovett and then Olaf Beyer of the GDR going past. He finished a bitterly disappointed third in 1:44.76 while Ovett took the UK record with 1:44.09 behind the previously unconsidered Beyer (1:43.84). Not that Ovett held it for long, as off a 51.0 first lap, Coe ran 1:43.97 at Crystal Palace.

The 1979 season proved to be a magical one for Coe. That he was wintering well was shown when he took the national indoor 3000m title in 7:59.8. The stamina was there, even though he averaged only 50 miles a week in training, but could he improve his speed more to effect further progress at 800m? A 46.3 400m relay leg in May provided the answer. Another aspect of the intelligent way Coe approached his running was his use of relatively unimportant races to experiment. He knew he could run a first lap in close to 50 sec and flourish, and the Prague experience had taught him that the law of diminishing returns begins to operate if one is too ambitious.

Now was the time to test the effectiveness of a fast second lap, and in one slow race he even managed to generate a 50.3 last 400m. The remarkable change of pace he achieved along the finishing straight when winning the 800m (1:46.63) in the European Cup semi-final in Malmö hinted at great things to come, but no one – not even Coe himself – was prepared for the first of his Oslo explosions just four days later.

When Alberto Juantorena, in his first year at the event, won the 1976 Olympic 800m in Montreal with a world record of 1:43.50 everyone thought that here was the man to revolutionise two-lap running. And yet, for all his speed (44.26 400m) and power, the Cuban succeeded only in clipping another tenth off the record. Instead it was the slight figure of Coe who went down in history as the athlete who, like Germany's Rudolf Harbig in 1939 and New Zealand's Peter Snell in 1962, pushed back the frontiers of 800m performance.

In the 17 years since Snell ran 1:44.3 the world record had advanced by just 0.9 sec ... until on 5 July 1979 Coe chopped 1.11 sec off Juantorena's mark with a phenomenal 1:42.33, becoming the first Briton to set a world record in this event since Sydney Wooderson in 1938. Paced through 400m in 50.6, he ran a tremendous third 200m to reach 600m in 75.4 and completed the second lap in 51.8. His race plan had been to run 50.0-50.2 followed by a 53.0 for a time in the 1:43.0-1:43.2 region, so he was as shocked as everyone else.

At Crystal Palace for the AAA Championships on July 14 Coe was the first British finisher in the 400m in a lifetime best of 46.87 and then it was back to Oslo and another earth-shattering exploit on July 17. This time, competing in the IAAF's Dubai Golden Mile, he broke Walker's world record of 3:49.4 with a time of 3:48.95, thus becoming the first man since Snell to own simultaneously the world records for 800m and mile. En route he broke the European 1500m record with 3:32.8 and thus smashed Ovett's UK records of 3:34.45 and 3:52.8.

Coe entered the race as the slowest man in the glittering field for his best mile time was 3:57.67 and he had run only two mile and no 1500m races in almost three years. Totally at ease despite his paucity of big race experience at the distance, Coe was fourth at 440y in 57.8, third at 880y in 1:55.3 and overtook Steve Scott (USA) shortly before the three-quarter mark reached in 2:53.4. As he strode elegantly through a final quarter in 55.6 (1:53.7 for the second half) the 20,000 spectators in the Bislett Stadium rose to him. He commented later: "When I was so far ahead I honestly thought I had misjudged things and a big kicker would come up on me before the tape. When I looked back twice in the final straight it was fear, it was panic, not pain, that I was feeling. I certainly wasn't in the slightest distress at the finish. I was astonished when told I had broken the world record."

He hadn't finished yet, for on August 5 in Turin he won the 800m at the European Cup Final in 1:47.3 (24.4 last 200m) plus a 45.5 relay leg, and in Zürich on August 15 he collected his third world record in the space of 41 days. By running 1500m in 3:32.03 (ratified as 3:32.1) he broke Filbert Bayi's mark of 3:32.2 (3:32.16) and became the first Briton officially to hold this record. Kenya's Kip Koskei set too fast a tempo for the first lap (54.25) but Coe felt bound to stay with him and thus his time was a potentially suicidal 54.3 (25.9 at 200m)! With Koskei flagging on the second lap Coe was obliged to forge ahead some 40m before the 800m reached in 1:53.2 (58.9 lap), nearly 20m up on Boit. Instead of permitting himself a slight respite on the third lap Coe zipped round in 56.3 to pass 1200m in 2:49.5 and his final 400m took 56.9. "It was the only time I've ever gone consciously for a record," he stated. "As a piece of pace running it was pretty diabolical, but I suppose the final time is all that counts." That Coe could produce such times became less surprising when one learned that one of his training sessions involved 5 x 800m in 1:52 apiece with 90 sec recovery between each – followed by a sixth in 1:49.5!

At the end of 1979 I travelled to Loughborough University, from where he had graduated that year with a B.Sc honours degree in economics and social history, to conduct a lengthy interview for *Athletics Weekly*. Among the topics discussed were his plans for the Moscow Olympics. At that stage he hadn't decided if he would run more than one event. "I'm an inexperienced 1500 man," he cautioned. "Before this year I hadn't run 1500 since 1976 and I've run only one mile a year. In a way it's rather false to build up a big thing about the 1500."

Although the whole world was thirsting for a series of races between Coe and Ovett, commercial considerations dictated that any clash would have to be postponed until the Olympics. The anticipation mounted after both men set world records in Oslo on 1 July 1980. Despite being coaxed into too fast an early pace in the 1000m race (Coe's first ever) by another over enthusiastic hare, Coe (51.0 at 400m) flashed past 800m in 1:45.2 and held on grimly for a time of 2:13.40, breaking the record of 2:13.9 by Rick Wohlhuter of the USA. Coe set off for his lap of honour as holder of four world records, but before an hour had elapsed he had to settle for three again as Ovett trimmed the mile record to 3:48.8. Two weeks later, again in Oslo, Ovett equalled Coe's 1500m record of 3:32.1 (then ratified to 1/10th of a second) although he was actually fractionally slower with 3:32.09 to Coe's 3:32.03.

The feeling, at least in Britain, was that the Olympic 800m and 1500m would take the form of two private duels between Coe (considered a near certainty for the 800) and Ovett (expected to extend his three year win streak at 1500). In fact, although each won the 'wrong' event, both men left Moscow as meritorious Olympic champions. Ovett struck first, running with characteristic flair and aggression to take the 800 in 1:45.40 while Coe, seemingly suffering from a form of stagefright and unable to concentrate on the task in hand, ran a tactically poor race and although he managed to take second place in 1:45.85 he was disgusted with his performance.

In our interview the previous winter, Coe had replied to a question about whether winning an Olympic gold medal was a consuming ambition with "It's not a consuming ambition. It's important. I go to Moscow fully committed. If I lose I'll be pretty choked for a couple of days, but life does go on." In Moscow, his perspective changed after the 800m setback. "I've got to come back and climb the mountain again. The 1500 was going to be a hard event, anyway, but now it's going to be the big race of my life. I *must* win it."

Learning from his mistakes in the 800m, Coe ran a perfect race. At no time, from the shuffling beginning to the flat-out sprint finish, was he ever outside the first two places and he was always well poised either to launch his own strike or cover anyone else's. Instead of the hesitant near-novice of the 800 final here was a man in complete control. He shadowed Jürgen Straub through the first two slow laps in 61.6 and 2:04.9, at which point the tough East German – a former world class steeplechaser – in effect began his run for home in the hope that a sustained drive might just take the sting out of the British pair.

That burst of speed was a godsend to Coe who was happy to follow in the knowledge that as the previously closely clustered pack behind him fell back the chances of his being bumped or boxed were being minimised. He was having a clear run. Ovett lurked ominously in third place as the runners passed the 1200m mark: Straub 2:59.1 (54.2 for the lap!), Coe 2:59.5, Ovett 2:59.7. Straub went faster still but rounding the final turn Coe, with Ovett at his heels, closed up for the kill. Both gathered themselves for one last lung-searing effort but it was Coe who got in first. Turning into the straight Coe drew level with Straub and then with another burst of acceleration 80m out, the 'double kick' of which we had heard whispers, he was away and winging to everlasting glory. For once Ovett ("I just couldn't lift myself after the 800m") failed to summon his normally explosive finish and was unable to pass the determined Straub for second place.

The overall winning time may have been an ordinary 3:38.40 but Coe had zipped around the final lap in 52.2! As Peter Coe remarked: "You've seen an athlete come back from the grave. He's got all the guts in the world. You can do all the training, all the routines and all the schedules, but it is those famous words in the last analysis – it's all about character. I really gave him stick about the 800m but he just came straight back and that makes the man."

Coe had one more notable race in 1980, trouncing a glittering 1500m field in Zürich in a near world record 3:32.19, and then it was on to another *annus mirabilis*. He began 1981 on a high note indoors, clocking a 3000m personal best of 7:55.2 and setting a world indoor 800m record of 1:46.0. Outdoors, in his first international race of the season he ran 1:44.06, eliciting the understatement: "I would be willing to admit now I'm in fairly good condition." Seven days later, in Florence on June 10, he reduced his world record to a staggering 1:41.73. That was the time as ratified by the IAAF as determined by analysis of three photo-cells positioned at three heights at the finish as the photo-finish equipment failed to function properly.

On hand timing it would have been 1:41.6. Billy Konchellah of Kenya, later to become a double world champion at 800m, was the hare and Coe tucked in behind with splits of 24.6 and 49.9. Coe went on to reach 600m in 75.0 and only in the last 30m did he begin to tie up. He was now 1.71 sec faster than the next best of all-time (Juantorena), an amazing margin, and that world record would stand for 16 years.

He set a personal best of 3:31.95 for 1500m in Stockholm on July 7 and in Oslo four days later he achieved another long-lasting world record. Paced through 400m in 51.3 and reaching 800m in 1:44.6, he improved his 1000m figures to 2:12.18, unbeaten for 18 years. There was still more to come, for in Zürich on August 19 he broke Ovett's world mile record with 3:48.53; his quarter mile splits were 56.2, 1:53.6 and 2:51.68 with a 1500m time of 3:33.27.

Seven days later Ovett regained the record with 3:48.40 but just two days after that, in Brussels, Coe struck back. Paced by Tom Byers (USA), Coe was towed through 440y in 55.3 and 880y in 1:53.3. Some 130m before the bell Coe slipped ahead, chased by Boit, to reach the three-quarters in 2:51.9 (0.4 slower than Ovett in his 3:48.40) and produced a great finish to cover the last quarter in 55.5 and a time of 3:47.33 (3:32.94 at 1500m). Despite having now broken the world mile record in his last three outings at the distance plus an Olympic gold medal and former world record at 1500m, Coe maintained: "I still don't feel I am primarily a 1500/mile runner." His target for 1982 would be the European 800m and he wanted to experiment with a sub-49 first lap in a bid to break 1:40.

The world awaited agog as plans were laid for a series of three races (3000m, 800m, mile) between Coe and Ovett in 1982, as well as probable clashes in the European Championships and possibly Commonwealth Games, but none of it came to pass as injuries and illness kept them apart. Coe did contribute a 1:44.01 solo anchor leg (49.1 at 400m) to ensure a still standing world record of 7:03.89 for the 4x800m relay (Peter Elliott, Garry Cook and Steve Cram were the other team members) but, suffering from what transpired to be glandular fever, he was overhauled in the finishing straight at the European Championships to finish second to the unheralded Hans-Peter Ferner of West Germany in 1:46.68.

His troubles appeared to be over in 1983 after world indoor records at 800m (1:44.91) and 1000m (2:18.58). In June he clocked the world's fastest time for two years of 1:43.80 but again illness took its toll and, debilitated by glandular toxoplasmosis which led to a number of defeats, he withdrew from the inaugural World Championships on medical advice.

Although he wasn't able to get back into full training until mid-March, Coe ran 1:45.2 as early as May 1984 but he suffered a setback in the AAA Championships in June when, hampered by an injury but obliged to demonstrate fitness to the Olympic selectors, he was beaten by Peter Elliott in a slow 1500m – his first defeat by a Briton at the distance for eight years. Controversially, Coe was picked for the Los Angeles 1500m at the expense of Elliott (both were named for the 800m) ... but he would have the last laugh over those who doubted his ability to come up with the goods again in the cauldron of Olympic competition. Coe was back on course five days later when he won in Oslo in 1:43.84 but his only other race before the Games was a low-key 3:54.6 mile victory.

In Moscow Coe had been devastated to finish second in the 800m but in Los Angeles he was content with his silver medal. After the trials and tribulations of the previous two seasons he was satisfied to run 1:43.64 behind Brazil's Joaquim Cruz (1:43.00), acknowledging that "I was beaten by a guy who was younger and stronger; he is a supreme champion worthy of an Olympic crown". A severely dehydrated Ovett trailed home last in the final and was whisked to hospital.

Astonishingly, Ovett fought his way into the 1500m final alongside Coe and world champion Steve Cram, but hopes of a British 1-2-3 ended when he dropped out while in fourth place on the third lap of a pulsating race. In becoming the only Briton to gain four individual Olympic medals and the first man ever to retain a quadrennial Olympic 1500m title, Coe ran a flawless race.

This time he was indebted to Scott, who uncharacteristically swept ahead as early as 500m and ensured the race would be a good honest one with victory going to the strongest. That Coe should emerge as the most durable and inspired as well as the fleetest should have come as no great surprise to those who recalled the events of Moscow; he may look frail but he has immense physical resources at his command. This may have been his seventh race in eight days but his time of 3:32.53 smashed the Olympic record and was barely half a second outside his fastest.

At 400m he was third in 58.94, at 800m he was second to Scott in 1:56.92 and at 1200m he was level with José Abascal of Spain in 2:53.21 with Cram next (2:53.55). Coe made his move with 200m to go, neatly slipping between Cram (whose own strike he pre-empted) and Abascal. Completing his last lap in 53.25, he won by six metres from Cram and rated this victory as even more satisfying than Moscow's.

"I've worked very hard. This year has been as much a mental comeback as anything, and it's a bit of a dream come true. This time last year I had just come out of hospital and didn't run from July to Christmas." Coe had one more race in 1984, in Zürich, and won in his fastest time (3:32.39) since 1981.

We weren't to know it at the time, and he would go on to clock his best ever time in 1986, but Coe's reign as the world's foremost 1500m/mile runner ended in 1985. That was the year Cram took over with world records of 3:29.67 and 3:46.32, beating Coe (3:49.22) for the first time in the latter race. Even at 800m Coe (1:43.07 behind Cruz) was only second fastest in Britain to Cram (1:42.88), but his fortunes improved in 1986 when at last he nailed a major title at the distance by winning the European championship in 1:44.50 followed by Tom McKean and Cram.

"It's very special; I don't think I've ever run a race which was so tactically perfect," he enthused. Three days later, though, Cram's 50.91 final 400m proved too much for him in the 1500m final, 3:41.09 to 3:41.67. It was in Rieti a week afterwards that Coe finally met his father's 3:30 target drawn up when Seb was 13. Passing 1200m in 2:48.10 he finished in 3:29.77 for equal third on the world all-time list behind Morocco's Said Aouita (3:29.46) and Cram (3:29.67).

By now, aged 29, Coe was already Vice-Chairman of the Sports Council and on his way to a still developing career in sports administration. He maintained ambitions on the track, including a third Olympics in 1988 for which he controversially failed to be selected and a serious move up to 5000m which never materialised (he had run 14:06.2 in 1980), but had to content himself with the occasional glimpse of what had been. He ran 1:43.93 in 1988, and topped the UK year lists for one last time in 1989 with 1:43.38 and 3:34.05, but his glorious international career came to a rather poignant end at the Commonwealth Games in February 1990 when he placed sixth in 1:47.24, weakened by a respiratory infection.

There was one postscript: he ran 2:56:20 in the 1991 London Marathon and still, 14 years later, he looks fearsomely fit. A Conservative MP from 1992 to 1997 (he was a government whip during the last two years of that term) and subsequently William Hague's private secretary, he was created a life peer, Baron Coe of Ranmore in the county of Surrey, in 2000. A former President of the AAA of England, and a member of the IAAF Council, he won immense public acclaim by leading London's successful 2012 Olympic bid.

KEITH CONNOR

Born 16.9.1957, Anguilla. Clubs: Windsor Slough & Eton AC, Wolverhampton & Bilston AC

JONATHAN EDWARDS IS obviously the greatest of all British triple jumpers but he wasn't the first to attain the highest world class standards. Fred Alsop placed fourth in the 1964 Olympics with a UK record leap of 16.46, only 12cm behind the silver medal winning mark, while Keith Connor became European and Commonwealth champion and record holder, Olympic bronze medallist and world indoor record holder at the discipline.

Connor was aged six when he came to Britain from the West Indies. He was brought up in Slough and was just a so-so sprinter until he tried the triple jump. In his first year, as a 16 year-old, he improved literally by leaps and bounds all season, finishing up by winning the England Schools Intermediate title with a leap of 14.25. Coached by his schoolmaster Ted King, he progressed to 14.78 in 1975 while the following year he was second ranked in Britain to Aston Moore with 15.95, a UK age-18 best. In 1977 he became briefly co-holder of the UK indoor best with 16.02 and outdoors took over the nation's top spot with 16.33.

If 1977 was Connor's year of international apprenticeship, 1978 marked the start of his emergence as a master of his craft. Indoors at Cosford he jumped 16.54 to exceed the UK record (set outdoors) of 16.52 by Aston Moore, while in Milan he reached 16.53 for the silver medal at the European Indoor Championships. Only 20, he handled his first international championship with a sense of purpose and flair which augured well for the future and his medal was the first by a British triple jumper at European level. He felt that 17 metres was within range by 1980 but in fact he reached that standard only months later at the Commonwealth Games in

Edmonton. In the second round he jumped 16.76 to relieve Moore of the UK record of 16.68 he had set earlier in the season and later in the competition he sealed victory with two massive wind-aided jumps of 17.21 (+2.4m) and 17.17 (+2.6m). The latter effort was even more impressive considering that Moore (third with 16.69) was sure that his rival's toe wasn't even on the board, losing him at least 20cm. The European Championships soon afterwards saw Connor in third place with 16.64 at the halfway mark but an injury caused him to retire before the end of the contest and he slipped back to sixth.

Another turning point in Connor's career occurred later in the year when he enrolled as a student at the University of Texas at El Paso. He improved his speed, running a windy 10.69 100m, but a badly bruised right heel severely restricted his triple jumping in 1979 and it wasn't until Olympic year – having followed his American coach Ted McLaughlin to Southern Methodist University in Dallas – that he really made his mark. The big jump came early, in Melbourne in January. Up against Australia's Ian Campbell, who in the second round set a Commonwealth record of 17.09, Connor opened with a UK record of 16.90 and after four fouls closed with a barrier-breaking legal effort of 17.16. That jump remained the best non-windy mark in the world that year prior to the Moscow Olympic final which Jaak Uudmae (USSR) won at 17.35 with Connor, who pulled a hamstring a fortnight before the Games, a commendable fourth at 16.87. He would have needed 17.22 for a sniff of a medal.

A development of vital importance to Connor's future occurred that year. He was reunited with Ted King, who took an appointment under Ted McLaughlin as jumps coach at SMU, a move which made the Dallas set-up just perfect for Connor. Not only was he receiving a good education but he now had his own personal coach as well as all the superb facilities on campus. The university had its own all-weather track and magnificently equipped weights room – a far cry from the situation in Slough where he would have to spend hours a day on buses just to get to and from decent training facilities. Connor's tremendous talent might have flowered in a British environment; in the States there was never any doubt about it just provided he could stay healthy.

He did indeed remain blessedly free of injury during his build-up for the 1981 indoor season, and the results were sensational. A few weeks after raising the UK indoor record to 17.08 and improving considerably as a long jumper with 7.71 behind a world indoor best of 8.49 by Carl Lewis, Connor not only won the prestigious US national collegiate (NCAA) title but set a world indoor best of 17.31 in the process. Adding to the merit of the performance was that it came off a runway of less than 100 feet (30m) instead of Connor's customary 130ft (40m) approach and that the pit was so small that he had to forego full leg extension at the completion of the jump for fear of hitting a barrier at the end of the sand.

"I got a real good hop," he explained. "I thought I could go around 55ft 10in (17.02) because of the short runway, but when your adrenalin is flowing anything can happen." Outdoors that year it didn't quite happen; his best mark was 17.02 when finishing fourth in the US Championships and he was bronze medallist with 16.88 in the World Student Games.

Everything clicked into place in 1982 when Connor became undisputed world's number one. He won all five major championships he contested and had nine separate competitions over the world class benchmark of 17m. The average of his ten best results was 17.27. The first big jump came in New York in February when with a leap of 17.04 he became only the second Briton (after long jumper Mary Rand in 1965) to win an American indoor title, his beaten rivals including Willie Banks who had only the previous week broken Connor's world indoor best with 17.41. He went on to add the NCAA indoor title with 16.84 but did much better at the outdoor collegiate summit in June in Provo, Utah (at 1387m altitude) where he broke every record in the book except for the world mark with a massive jump of 17.57 in windless conditions. That smashed his own Commonwealth record and the great Viktor Saneyev's European record of 17.44 set in 1972; the only man ahead of him in the history of the event was Brazil's Joao Carlos de Oliveira with 17.89 at the much higher altitude of Mexico City in 1975. It stood as the UK record until Jonathan Edwards surpassed it (with a vengeance!) in 1995.

Just four days later and some 5000 miles away, at London's Crystal Palace, Connor was the star turn of an international meeting. Having whipped the fans into a frenzy of excitement and appreciation, Willie Banks – a charismatic showman who introduced rhythmic clapping and did so much to popularise triple jumping for the spectators – presented them with the first 17m jump ever witnessed in Britain, only for Connor to steal his thunder just a few minutes later with a leap of 17.30, best ever by a Briton at or near sea level. He was just 1cm short of that in Athens when capturing the European title, but it was a case of 'you ain't seen nothing yet' for at the Commonwealth Games in Brisbane a month later he not only retained his title but produced two monster jumps of 17.72 (+ 3.8m) and 17.81 (+4.6m). Admittedly they were heavily wind aided but the only longer jump in history, de Oliveira's 17.89, was equally advantaged by the thin air of Mexico City, while the legal sea level best at the time was Banks' 17.56. Although one cannot gauge exactly the effect on distance either of rarefied air or wind assistance (Connor hazarded a guess that high altitude might be worth 20-30cm) it is entirely possible that Connor's two great jumps represented the event's highest achievement up to that date.

Anti-climax was to follow in 1983. In the States he jumped a windy 17.48 and retained the NCAA crown with 17.26 ahead of two men who would develop into Olympic champions, Al Joyner and Mike Conley, but an Achilles tendon injury ruined his European campaign. Admitting he just couldn't "put it together", he failed even to qualify for the final at the inaugural World Championships in Helsinki, reaching just 16.18.

The title went to Poland's Zdzislaw Hoffman at 17.42. A year later, at the Olympics, Connor's career drew to a close in a somewhat downbeat fashion. He salvaged an otherwise mediocre season by producing his longest jump of the summer (16.87) and finishing third in Los Angeles, the first Briton – other than Irishman

Tim Ahearne in 1908 – to earn an Olympic medal in this discipline, but he was hardly enthused. "I'm disappointed because I thought I could win," he said. "It was a very dull competition; there wasn't any excitement out there [Joyner 17.26w won from Conley 17.18]. I probably won't compete any more. I've had enough."

He did indeed retire, just before his 27th birthday, his achievements inspiring a new generation of British triple jumpers among whom was 18 year-old Jonathan Edwards who in that same summer of 1984 took his first small step towards greatness by becoming English Schools champion. Foiled in his ambition of landing a full-time coaching job in Britain, Connor first returned to the USA and then settled in Australia where he was for some years director of coaching for the national team.

DALEY THOMPSON

Born 30.7.1958 Notting Hill (London).
Clubs: Haywards Heath Harriers, Essex Beagles

WHEN IT COMES to assessing the most successful British athlete of all time there is only one genuine rival to Seb Coe ... Francis Morgan Thompson, known to all as Daley. Why Daley? As his Nigerian father (his mother was Scottish) was named Frank, and Francis had an elder brother called Franklin, Thompson Sr decided to avoid confusion by giving Francis a Nigerian name, Ayodele. That in turn was short-ened to Dele, pronounced Daley, and it's stuck ever since.

Like Coe, Thompson won two Olympic gold medals and set world records but although he didn't push performances into a new realm in the Coe manner he did achieve a momentous win streak of 12 decathlons over a six-year period, during which he collected world, European and Commonwealth titles as well as his two Olympic triumphs. Until injury brought him down to the level of a mere mortal he was not only unbeatable but could never even consider being defeated. His rivals, most notably West Germany's giant Jürgen Hingsen, with whom he traded world records, were continually psyched out by a man whose mental resolve matched his immense physical skills.

He was always highly competitive. His brother recalled that sport was life and death to Daley, even as a young kid growing up in Notting Hill. When at the tender age of seven he was packed off to boarding school in Sussex he found himself in an environment which, apart from providing education and discipline, offered an outlet for his sporting prowess and aggressive drive. He made his mark as a footballer (he would have trials as a youngster with Fulham and Chelsea) as well as an athlete and, to keep him usefully occupied in the evenings, he was introduced by his headmaster to the local athletic club, Haywards Heath Harriers. He began competing in 1973, aged 14, and it was soon evident that he was a natural all-rounder. Success came quickly and he finished fourth in the English Schools Intermediate 200m the follow-ing summer. Shortly afterwards, having by then left school and returned to London, he had a lucky break when he was spotted by Essex Beagles coach Bob Mortimer.

Within months of joining the club he had won his first national title (1975 AAA Junior 60m indoors) and in June of that year – still a mere 16 – he took part in and won the first decathlon of his career, amassing the remarkable total of 6523 when rescored on the tables currently used.

Such was his rapid development that barely a year after that precocious start he was, at 18, British senior record holder. He ended 1975 with a UK junior record of 6941 and in 1976, now coached primarily by Bruce Longden, he progressed to 7517 and 7748, in the meantime making a promising showing in the Montreal Olympics where – placing 18th with 7330 – he impressed the all-American gold medallist and world record smasher Bruce Jenner as a likely successor to himself.

Over those next four years Thompson gradually approached, and then surpassed, Jenner's score of 8634. In 1977 he set world junior records of 8056 and 8082 and became European Junior champion; in 1978, before his 20th birthday, he boosted his Commonwealth record to 8226 and a few days after leaving the teenage ranks he piled up the monumental score of 8470 to win the Commonwealth title in Edmonton. Using electrical timing that was the third highest total ever but it couldn't be ratified because of excessive wind assistance in the long jump where he achieved the spectacular distance of 8.11.

Three weeks later he produced a valid record of 8258 in the European Championships in Prague, but Thompson was distraught. Never mind the score, he had finished second and that had never entered his mind, particularly after his main rival, European record holder Guido Kratschmer of West Germany, had injured himself in the first event and took no further part. Nearly 300 points up on Aleksandr Grebenyuk after the first day the title appeared to be in the bag but a mini-disaster in the hurdles cost him many points and by vaulting only 4.20 as against his then personal best of 4.90 he opened the door to his Soviet opponent. What rankled was that he had failed to perform to his own high standards. As he related to American writer Skip Rozin in his 1984 book *Daley Thompson: The Subject Is Winning*, "It was a great shock. I didn't think it could happen, but it did. I felt so bad. I couldn't shake that feeling of failure. It was like I'd died, but nobody's buried me." An over-reaction perhaps, but he resolved never to repeat the experience. He knew he was the best all-rounder in the world and he would prove it. And, from 1980 onwards, he did just that to the extent of becoming the greatest ever competitor in the ten-event test.

Sometimes spending up to eight hours a day training to perfect the diverse skills required of the decathlon, Thompson was one of a new breed of full-time athlete, unable due to training demands to contemplate a job and therefore existing on officially channelled sponsorship money. Later the sport would become totally professional at the elite level. As what would prove to be a momentous 1980 season dawned, Thompson could point to the following superb collection of personal bests: 100m – 10.45 & 10.36w, long jump – 7.93 & 8.11w, shot – 14.82 & 15.45 indoors, high jump – 2.07, 400m – 47.30, 110m hurdles – 14.39, discus – 45.22, pole vault – 5.00, javelin – 62.00, 1500m – 4:20.3.

He realised his ambition of becoming world record holder in Götzis (Austria) in May 1980. Like Jenner in Montreal, Thompson was pushed to new heights by Kratschmer while third place went to Hingsen. He led throughout the first day with marks of 10.55, 7.72, 14.46, 2.11 (pb) and 48.04. "At this point I didn't think the world record was on," he admitted. He knew that he would need to score over 200 points more than he had ever done before on the second day to get that record. He started on a high note in the hurdles with 14.37 (pb), lost ground with a moderate discus throw of 42.98 but finished strongly with 4.90, 65.38 (a big pb) and 4:25.49 (pushing really hard with a 46 sec final 300m) for a score of 8648. "I wasn't expecting the world record, but I was in good enough shape to do it", he explained. "I look at it this way, whatever decathlon you go to: if you're in 8800 points shape you'll score 8600. I thought I was in 8600 shape, so I thought I'd score 8400, but fortunately it went well for me. I was lucky."

Thompson's reign as world record holder lasted all of four weeks for Kratschmer struck back with a score of 8667. He would have been the main rival for the Olympic title in Moscow the following month but, frustratingly, the West Germans had joined the American boycott of those Games. As Thompson remarked at the time: "I feel sorry for the Americans. They're meant to be the greatest democracy in the world and no one gets a choice there. I'm sorry, too, for Kratschmer; he's as sick as a pig."

An athlete can only beat who's there and Thompson was unstoppable in Moscow. He built up an enormous lead on the first day with performances of 10.62, a legal pb of 8.00 into the wind, a decathlon best of 15.18, 2.08 and 48.01 in a swirling wind. Hopes of regaining the world record fizzled out because of the weather on the second day. It poured in the morning and he ran the hurdles cautiously for a time of 14.47. He was held down to 42.24 in the discus due to a slippery circle and greasy implements. The policy was safety first and after vaulting 4.70 and throwing the javelin 64.16 he would have needed to run a pb 4:17.2 1500m for the record. Understandably, instead of risking blowing up in pursuit of such a time he settled for a steady run at the back, taking 4:39.9 for a score of 8522. Four days before his 22nd birthday, Daley Thompson had fulfilled his destiny; he was Olympic decathlon champion.

During a low-key 1981 season he continued to improve in various events, registering a 10.32w 100m, 5.20 vault, 15.32 shot and 47.44 discus. Indoors, early in 1982, he high jumped 2.14. All was in place for an amazing summer of competition.

First stop was the annual May decathlon fest in Götzis and there he not only comfortably disposed of the challenge of Hingsen (8541) but seized the world record with 8730. Only a back strain sustained in the second event, the long jump, and unfavourable rainy weather on the second day prevented a much higher score. As he remarked: "I'm not as good as I could be. I can improve all round and the 9000 points barrier is possible." His first day score was the highest yet achieved, a massive 4675 made up of 10.50, 7.95, 15.31, 2.08 and a brilliant pb 46.86 in which he covered the first 200m in 21.6! On day two he registered 14.31 (pb), 44.34, 4.90, 60.52 and 4:30.55.

Again, Thompson was able to bask in the title of world record holder for only a short period, as in August Hingsen scored 8723 ... and to add to his woes, after badly injuring himself when a pole broke in a club match Thompson was struggling to regain peak fitness in time for the big showdown at the European Championships in Athens in September.

Thompson drew first blood with his 10.51 100m and drew further away with a 7.80 long jump, so after two events on the scoring tables then in use he was already 171 points clear. Hingsen, on paper much the better shot putter, clawed back only a few points as Thompson produced an outdoor pb of 15.44, and as American decathlon guru Frank Zarnowski declared: "at 12.44 on the first day, it's all over". Most present were inclined to agree but there was a big turnaround in the high jump where Thompson cleared only 2.03 to the German's 2.15 before a 47.11 400m enabled Thompson to lead by 114 points at the end of the day. On the tables now used, his score was 4584, 91 fewer than during his earlier world record. On the second day, though, Thompson couldn't put a foot wrong. He ran 14.39, spun the discus 45.48, vaulted 5.00, threw the javelin 63.56 and – needing a 4:26.4 1500m to break the world record – ran a gutsy 4:23.71 (63.5 last 400m) for a total of 8774 with Hingsen scoring 8530. That made Thompson the first man in any event to hold Olympic, European and Commonwealth titles as well as the world record.

Although immensely popular with the public, Thompson was often involved in controversy and, like Steve Ovett (who once famously described the decathlon, in order to provoke his team-mate, as nine Mickey Mouse events plus the 1500m!), refused to talk to most sections of the British press. That feud intensified when his decision to decline the honour of carrying the England flag at the opening ceremony of the Commonwealth Games in Brisbane later in 1982 became headline news. Single minded in his approach to competition, he felt he could not risk standing around in the heat for several hours. Had the conditions been conducive he would have chased his world record but right from the start the elements were against him and he contented himself with a routine 8424 score, good enough to win by some 400 points.

The big target for 1983 was the inaugural World Championships which, unlike the boycotted 1980 and 1984 Olympics, would bring together all of the world's best athletes. As in the previous year injury played havoc with Thompson's preparations and again Hingsen took the world record away with a score of 8825. But in Helsinki as in Athens there could be only one winner. Not that victory was a foregone conclusion; he was putting himself on the line in facing up to a gruelling contest with a superbly trained and in-form Hingsen, while he himself could not possibly have been at his very best after struggling to recover in time from injury. Actually, it was touch and go right up to the last moment whether he would take part.

Having made the decision to compete, he knew he had to strike a psychological blow by piling up the points in his strong early events. That he did, and the opposition never quite recovered. Look at it from Hingsen's perspective: he's the world record holder, he's been showing the best form of his life in recent competitions, and all he's heard about Thompson in recent weeks has been negative ... striving to regain fitness after a groin strain which in turn followed a back injury, uncertain even whether he's going to compete in Helsinki. Hingsen naturally feels confident, the glint of that gold medal already in his mind's eye. In reality, though, he has built a false sense of security. For Thompson does show up, and in the first event, the 100m, shows no sign of any physical problems as he races to a 10.60 clocking, over three metres clear of Hingsen. That's a blow to Hingsen, but he can console himself with the thought that the long jump is next and that he's cleared 8.00 this year while his rival can point to only 7.63. Conditions are unfavourable – it's cool and raining – and Hingsen is pleased with his opening leap of 7.75, all the more so when Thompson fouls. But his sense of well-being vanishes in the second round when he fouls and Thompson comes through with 7.88. Instead of closing the gap, Hingsen finds himself further behind. Don't panic, thinks Hingsen. The shot is next and he's put over 16m whereas Thompson has yet to reach 15.50, but with 15.66 to 15.35 he gains only a few points. Thank goodness, he feels, that it's time for the high jump. As a 2.18 performer he can count on pulling back a good number of points. At least he thought he could, but an attack of cramp holds him down to a mere 2.00, while Thompson (2.03) widens his advantage. The only bright spot of Hingsen's first day – and likewise Thompson's only faltering moment – comes in a rain-soaked 400m. Thompson's less than desired state of fitness lets him down and he fades to 48.12 with Hingsen ahead of him in 48.08, a fine run for him but all that effort gains him precisely one point. At the end of the first day Thompson leads by 120 points; on today's tables the scores would have been 4527 to 4407.

If Hingsen starts the second day thoroughly demoralised, Thompson – although elated by his solid lead – is equally worried as he confronts the hurdles as because of his injuries he hadn't been able to train for the event. His fears prove groundless for he runs close to his pb with 14.37 inches behind Hingsen and relinquishes just one point from his lead. That potential crisis safely behind him, Thompson picks up bonus points in the discus, throwing 44.46 whereas Hingsen is way down on his normal standard with 43.30. The German's only hope now is that Thompson will bomb out in the vault. No chance! Hingsen matches his pb of 4.90 but Thompson succeeds in clearing 5.10, equalling his best ever in a decathlon. Thompson's awesome competitive drive can be seen also in the javelin. After two rounds he trails by a huge margin, 60.44 to Hingsen's lifetime best of 67.42, but with his final attempt he unleashes a throw of 65.24 despite increasing pain from his groin injury. Thus, as the curtain rises on the final act of the drama, the 1500m, Thompson leads by 162 points. Hingsen runs bravely but finishes only 8 sec ahead of Thompson (4:29.72), who totals 8714 as against 8599. As Hingsen sportingly remarked: "I came to win, but in the end I'm satisfied with my silver medal because Daley is truly the greatest among us, for he has no weaknesses."

That was even more apparent at the 1984 Olympics, which would prove to be the supreme moment of his wondrous career. He spent most of the year preparing in California, sprinting to his fastest 100m times of 10.36 and 10.26w and achieving shot and discus bests of 16.10 and 47.68, but he was disappointed by an abortive attempt on

ALLAN WELLS became the second Briton (56 years after Harold Abrahams) to win the Olympic 100 metres title, in Moscow, 1980

DAVE MOORCROFT created a sensation in Oslo in 1982 when he smashed the world 5000 metres record with 13:00.41

Pictured here in the 1984 Olympics, STEVE OVETT won the 800 metres gold medal ahead of Sebastian Coe at the 1980 Games in Moscow

*The first Briton ever to win an Olympic throwing title (javelin in Los Angeles, 1984),
TESSA SANDERSON competed in five Olympics*

SEBASTIAN COE at the 1984 Olympics where (as in Moscow) he finished second at 800 metres and triumphed over 1500 metres

DALEY THOMPSON was in typically brilliant form at the 1984 Olympics where he retained his decathlon title with a world record score

Britain's most successful sprinter ever, LINFORD CHRISTIE was world 100 metres champion in 1991 and the next year took Olympic gold

STEVE CRAM wins the 1983 world 1500 metres title in Helsinki ahead of Morocco's Saïd Aouita (549). In 1985 he cracked the 3:30 barrier

FATIMA WHITBREAD won the 1986 European javelin title, after setting a world record of 77.44m, and became world champion in 1987

*LIZ McCOLGAN on her way to the world 10,000 metres title in Tokyo in 1991,
pursued by a young Ethiopian by the name of Derartu Tulu*

JONATHAN EDWARDS at the 1995 European Cup where he shocked everyone, himself included, with a windy 18.43m triple jump

The only woman to complete the 'grand slam' of titles – Olympic, world, Commonwealth and European – hurdler SALLY GUNNELL

COLIN JACKSON, here competing in the 1993 World Championships where he set the current world 110 metres hurdles record of 12.91

An exuberant KELLY HOLMES captures her second Olympic title in Athens, taking the 1500 metres ahead of Russia's Tatyana Tomashova

The shot was one of DENISE LEWIS'S strongest events at the Sydney Olympics of 2000, paving the way to her heptathlon victory

PAULA RADCLIFFE en route to her amazing world marathon record of 2:15:25 in London, 2003 – faster than any British man ran that year!

the world record in Los Angeles in May. His first day score was his lowest for years and although he rallied to reach 7938 after nine events (including a pb 14.26 hurdles) and an average run in the 1500m would have brought his score to around 8500 he decided to save precious energy and therefore recovery and training time by pulling out.

His next decathlon, in the huge Los Angeles Coliseum in August, was an altogether different affair. Thompson had an Olympic title to defend and he was simply unbeatable. For Hingsen it was a case of hope over experience, They had clashed six times since 1977, it was 6-0 in Thompson's favour and any belief that Hingsen could this time turn the tables disappeared very quickly when Thompson blazed to his fastest ever legal 100m in a decathlon with 10.44 into a 1m/sec wind, followed by a wind-free pb long jump of 8.01 to open up a devastating lead of 164 points. The shot (Thompson 15.72, his best in a decathlon) brought little comfort to Hingsen although he did make inroads in the high jump where Thompson cleared 2.03. However, a superb 46.97 400m enabled Thompson to end the day 114 points clear of the towering German with a world's best halfway score of 4633 (4677 on the revised tables now in use).

Significantly faster than his rival at the hurdles, Hingsen failed to gain more than a few points (14.29 to 14.34) but he must have felt that his luck was about to change. He threw the discus a lifetime best of 50.82 whereas Thompson managed only a feeble 37.90 and 41.42. If he couldn't improve upon that with his final attempt then Hingsen would sail into a 68 point lead and strike an immense psychological blow. It was just the sort of challenge that Thompson relished. He threw 46.56, close to his best, and the crisis was over even if his lead had been narrowed to 32 points. There was no stopping Daley now. He easily outvaulted his rival with 5.00 and threw the javelin nearly five metres farther with 65.24, so that after nine events his score was a colossal 8241 to 8032 by Hingsen whose world record looked doomed. In fact, Thompson was happy to use the 1500m (4:35.00) as a protracted lap of honour instead of hurting himself in pursuit of the record and finished on 8797, one point short of the record, with Hingsen scoring a meritorious 8673. However, in a bizarre twist, Thompson's hurdles time was later corrected from 14.34 to 14.33, the extra point enabling him to tie the world record. Even that wasn't the end of the story for when the new IAAF scoring tables came into effect in April 1985 Hingsen's 8798 converted to 8832 but Thompson's 8798 to 8847 and so he became sole world record holder. Poor Hingsen never could beat him!

Thompson's only notable mark in the non-championship year of 1985 was a discus pb of 48.62, but the following year he was ready to renew his attack on the 9000 barrier. When I interviewed him in May 1986 he felt that he hadn't "yet achieved enough to justify the talent I've got." He was still motivated by the prospect of a third Olympic decathlon title, and when questioned over what he saw as possible marks for him in the ten events, he reeled off low 10.20's for 100m, 8.20-8.30 long jump, 16.50 shot, 2.16 high jump, 46.1 400m, 13.80 hurdles (despite being so immobile that he confessed he couldn't touch his toes!), 51m discus, 5.40-5.50 vault, 70m javelin, sub-4:20 1500m.

He never did achieve any of those ambitious targets but he did chalk up three more great decathlon victories in 1986. He scored 8667 (4505 first day) in Arles and 8663 (4602 first day) in the Commonwealth Games in Edinburgh, his first decathlon in Britain since he was 17. That included a decathlon pb 100m of 10.37 and an absolute hurdles best of 14.22. In non-decathlon competition that year he also broke new ground with a 5.25 vault and 49.10 discus throw.

The big contest, of course, was the confrontation with Hingsen in the European Championships to be held on his home soil in Stuttgart. "I know there will be 80,000 people or whatever in the stadium all wanting him to win, but that's the biggest motivation I could possibly have. I really cannot wait to set foot on that track knowing I'm the most hated person there." His opinion of Hingsen: "I have the highest regard for him. He really is a great athlete and I don't know if I would have the perseverance that he's got. I'd be really browned off by now. Just look at him. How could anyone who's 6ft 7in and looks as good as him be beaten all the time by a little, short, squat, ugly guy!"

Thompson couldn't have enjoyed a finer start. He streaked to his best 100m time of 10.26, fastest ever in a decathlon, and was immediately 142 points up on Hingsen. However, after the long jump (7.72), shot (decathlon best of 15.73) and high jump (2.00) he found himself in the novel situation of being in third place. Clearly he had to run a swashbuckling 400m to win back the lead overnight. That he proceeded to do, although it was his legs rather than his swash which were buckling in the finishing straight after he had run the first 300m a little too enthusiastically. Still, he held on to clock 47.02 and a first day score of 4617 and a slim advantage over Hingsen (4589).

After a largely sleepless night, Thompson knew he would have to produce the greatest second day of his life to win. He thrived on such challenges and in the hurdles he smashed his pb with 14.04 for an 88 point lead. However, he was below par in the discus (43.38) and Hingsen recaptured the lead, 6335 to 6320, with the other German threat Siggy Wentz still close on 6266. The decisive event was the pole vault and Thompson caused the hearts of his followers to flutter. In difficult, rainy conditions he chose to come in at 4.70 and promptly soared under the bar. All was well at the second attempt and he went on to clear 5.10 as against 4.90 for Wentz and a disastrous 4.60 for Hingsen.

Thus, after eight events, Thompson led with 7261 to 7146 by Wentz and 7125 by Hingsen. Thompson threw the javelin 62.78 to concede a few points and with the 1500m to come the scores were Thompson 8041, Wentz 7964, Hingsen 7929. Knowing he would have to run hard for a change, Thompson clocked his fastest for four years with 4:26.16. He finished with 8811, Hingsen 8730, Wentz 8676. "A different story but the same ending," he quipped.

Who could have foreseen then that Thompson, unchallenged as the greatest ever all-round athlete, would never win another decathlon? Sadly, injuries brought him down to earth. Third after the first day at the 1987 World Championships in Rome and still believing he could win, he finished ninth with his lowest score (8124) in a completed decathlon since he was a junior as the title passed to the GDR's Torsten

Voss with 8680. Thompson, who could have dropped out before the finish, won many new admirers for sticking it out as an also-ran and his graciousness in defeat.

He still hoped to make history with a third Olympic decathlon gold in Seoul in 1988; he failed ... but how heroically he tried, winning plaudits for his courage and tenacity in the face of mounting adversity. The Thompson of old would have destroyed this field, weakened as it was by the withdrawal of the injured Wentz and the sensational disqualification of Hingsen for three false starts in the 100m, but he was handicapped before the competition even started by a thigh injury sustained in training a week earlier. At halfway Christian Schenk (GDR) led with 4470, followed by Christian Plaziat (France) 4375 and Thompson 4332. He was still third after seven events but the gods were not with him in the vault where he might have expected to gain points. His pole snapped at his first attempt at his opening height of 4.70, a terrifying experience at the best of times. Yet, despite the shock and pain (he aggravated his leg injury and hurt his shoulder), he resisted any temptation to quit.

In an incredibly gutsy display he went on to clear 4.90 but effectively lost further ground. Off a limp-up rather than a run-up, he threw a miraculous 64.04 for a pb with the new specification javelin and was back in third place, but with his left thigh encased in a bandage he could run no faster than 4:45.11 for 1500m and he wound up fourth with 8306, the title transferring to Schenk with a modest score of 8488.

That effectively was the end of the road, for although he lined up for four more decathlons between 1989 and 1991 the accumulation of injuries took a savage toll and he did not complete any of them. Still, when he retired he was still world record holder (Dan O'Brien of USA scored 8891 in 1992) and a true legend of the sport.

KRISS AKABUSI

Born 28.11.1958 Paddington (London).
Clubs: Southampton & Eastleigh AC, Team Solent

KEZIE UCHE CHUKWU Duru Akabusi (that's his full name), an English born and bred prince from the Ibo tribe in Nigeria, can thank the British Army for his development as a top-class athlete. He joined up when he was 16 and at 18 ran 49.1 for 400m. By the time he was 22, by then a sergeant stationed in Germany as a PT instructor, his fastest stood at 48.0 and his athletic ambitions were limited to being Army or Inter-Services champion. The turning point came in 1983, at age 24. He still hadn't broken 48 sec so someone suggested he try 400m hurdles. He clocked 55.0. "I won the race but it was terrible," he recalled. "I ran and I stuttered, I ran and I stuttered. The funny thing is that the following week I ran the sprints in 10.7 and 21.6, a massive improvement on my basic speed, and then at the UK Championships I ran 46.85 in second place and I thought to myself 'forget the hurdles'. I was on my way as a 400m runner."

It was no coincidence that his substantial improvement came soon after he began being trained by Mike Smith. By then posted close to Southampton, he flourished on the hard work undertaken by a group the star of which was Todd Bennett and by the end of 1983 his personal best stood at 46.10 and he was a British international. A year later he was the proud possessor of an Olympic silver medal. After whittling down his best to 45.85 to earn his place in the team for Los Angeles he improved in the heats and quarter-finals to 45.64 and 45.43 – ranking him second to David Jenkins on the UK all-time list – before being eliminated in the semis with 45.69. But his moment of glory came later in the 4x400m relay in which he, Garry Cook, Todd Bennett and Phil Brown ran their hearts out for themselves, for each other and for their country to finish a mere ten metres behind an all-star American team. In the process they cracked the European and Commonwealth records with a time of 2:59.13. Following a season of consolidation in 1985, during which he clocked an impressive 800m time of 1:48.2, he won further relay medals in 1986, striking gold with England at the Commonwealth Games and Britain at the European Championships.

His switch to 400m hurdles in 1987 was a self-protective move. He had run 45.65 for 400m in 1986 but that had ranked him only sixth in Britain and he realised he might lose his place in the national team. As he put it in a 1991 interview: "I thought I wouldn't ever again run faster than about 45.5. I just didn't have the basic speed; at the time my best 200 was 21.4. I thought to myself: 'You're a carthorse, Kriss. You're just a 45.5 man and in the future that's not going to be good enough to make the relay team'. I knew that in the 400m hurdles I could be one, two or three in the British team and that's why I decided to have a go."

Mike Smith introduced him to Mike Whittingham, a coach who had run a 50.58 400m hurdles only a few years earlier, and Akabusi proved to be a quick learner, finding also that his basic speed was enhanced as a result of all the bounding, hurdling and plyometric work involved. His rate of progress in 1987 was astounding: he opened promisingly with 50.16 in mid-May and a week later he dead-heated for the UK title in 49.56. He peaked at just the right time, clocking 48.64 in his semi-final at the World Championships in Rome (for third on the UK all-time list behind David Hemery and Alan Pascoe) and placing seventh in the final in 48.74. Even more satisfying was his performance in the 4x400m where he sped around the second lap in 44.60 and, with the help of Derek Redmond, Roger Black and Phil Brown, took home a silver medal in the European record time of 2:58.86.

His Army career was going well also, promoted to Warrant Officer at 29, and great things were expected on the track in 1988, particularly after winning the AAA 400m title in 44.93, achieving his long-held ambition of breaking 45. But his hurdles times stagnated, albeit at a high level. He ran 48.67 and 48.89 in the run-up to the Seoul Olympics, where he finished sixth in 48.69. The picture didn't change much in 1989. He won the opening event at the European Cup in Gateshead in 48.95, inspiring the British men's team to their first victory in this contest, and improved his personal best slightly to 48.59 in a late season race, but he had to wait until 1990 for the major breakthrough.

The year started well with victory in the Commonwealth Games in January in 48.89 and after equalling his best of 48.59 he advanced to 48.34 and then 47.92 to win the European title in Split. In true Hemery style he pulverised the opposition and the time, breaking Hemery's UK (and former world) record of 48.12, was a bonus which sent him into a frenzy of excitement which added to his reputation of being among the most extrovert of athletes. His infectious laugh had already become a legendary feature of British athletics. Three days later came another gold medal as the British relay squad of Paul Sanders, Akabusi (44.8), 200m champion John Regis and Black triumphed in a European record of 2:58.22.

Akabusi's knack of always being in top form for the biggest occasions continued at the 1991 World Championships in Tokyo. Ranked fourth on paper, he came up with the fastest runs of his life, lowering his British record to 47.91 when winning his semi and 47.86 for the bronze medal – a mistake at the final hurdle possibly costing him the silver. Samuel Matete of Zambia won in 47.64 ahead of Jamaica's Winthrop Graham (47.74), with Kevin Young (USA) – who would create a sensation at the Olympics next year – fourth.

There could not have been a more rousing finale to those magnificent World Championships than the 4x400m relay. It was a mind-blowing, excruciating, joyous race for the British camp ... for the Americans it was just mind-blowing and excruciating. The heats provided an indication of the epic to come. The US foursome won their heat in 2:59.55 but the British set down their marker when they took theirs in 2:59.49 with Akabusi contributing a 44.2 anchor. In the final, the individual silver medallist Black, chosen controversially to run the first leg, clocked a swift 44.7 but his lead over the USA's Andrew Valmon (44.9) was less substantial than hoped. On the second leg, despite an excellent 44.0 by Redmond, it looked as though the British plan had misfired, for Quincy Watts, who came up with one of the fastest splits on record (43.4), built up a lead of almost four metres. Next to go was Regis, who after a disappointing display in the 200m needed a great run not only for the sake of the team but for his own self esteem. He produced a gallant 44.22 split, gaining valuable ground on Danny Everett (44.31), but even so Akabusi took over a daunting three metres behind the newly crowned world champion Antonio Pettigrew. It was to prove his finest and proudest moment. For him, a hurdler, to anchor the squad was a very special honour and it brought out all his tenacity and competitiveness, as Pettigrew found to his cost. Akabusi closed the gap, swung out to challenge the American and miraculously found the very last ounce of speed and strength to edge past some four strides from the line. His split was 44.59 to Pettigrew's 44.93 and the British team had won a famous victory by 4/100ths in 2:57.53, a European and Commonwealth record. It was the greatest GB triumph in this event since the Americans were upset in the 1936 Olympics.

The 1992 Olympics in Barcelona proved a fitting climax to his career at the age of 33. Once more he hit his peak at just the right time. Again ranked fourth on the season's form with a best of 48.26, he won his semi in 48.01 and in the final he trimmed his British record to 47.82 behind Kevin Young's phenomenal world record of 46.78 and 47.66 by Winthrop Graham. Akabusi now owned the five fastest ever times by a Briton ... and that's still the case all these years later. There was one more medal to come, a bronze in the relay with Akabusi clocking 45.1 on the third leg. In 1993 he bowed out to pursue a career in television, the top man in Britain (at 48.73) for the seventh year running.

LINFORD CHRISTIE

Born 2.4.1960 St Andrews (Jamaica).
Clubs: London Irish AC, Thames Valley Harriers

HE HAD TWO predecessors as Olympic champion in Harold Abrahams (1924) and Allan Wells (1980), but there is no disputing that Linford Christie – the 1992 gold medallist – was the most successful of all British 100m runners. In addition to his Barcelona victory he won the 1991 world title in a European record of 9.87 which at the time was just 1/100th outside Carl Lewis's world record, he captured several European and Commonwealth titles and was consistent at the highest world level over a lengthy period. The only shadow over an otherwise brilliant career is that he, alone among the 78 all-time greats featured in this book, failed a drugs test. Twice, in fact. The first time was at the 1988 Olympics in Seoul when the level of pseudoephedrine in his sample was just over the acceptable limit. His explanation was accepted and he was cleared on that occasion, but at the very end of his career – when he was 38 and primarily a coach – he was suspended by the IAAF for a doping offence involving the prohibited steroid nandrolone.

Yet Christie always spoke out strongly against the use of drugs. Early in 1985 he commented: "More and more athletes are being caught and what they don't realise is that not only are they damaging their sport but their own health. So many people have made the top on natural ability and hard work before steroids; why not now? Can those athletes who are not caught ever feel good knowing that they are cheating themselves?" Later he argued that athletes caught using such aids should not only be banned from athletics for life but be imprisoned. Interviewed in 2005 for the *Observer Sports Monthly* he stated: "The fact is I can sleep at night. I love all my kids dearly and I can swear on their lives that I would never and have never taken anything to enhance my performance. That's all I can say."

Christie was brought to Britain at the age of seven and grew up just a stone's throw from the former home of British athletics, White City Stadium – where he ran in a primary schools meeting. He started his club athletics career as a long and triple jumper for London Irish AC and in his first year of sprinting (1977) ran 10.9 for 100m and 23.2 for 200m.

He first attracted attention in 1979 when he placed second in the English Schools 200m and his best times as a junior, that year, were 10.7 and 21.89. Coached by Ron Roddan at West London Stadium (which in 1993 would be renamed after Christie), he was on his way. Not that his progress was meteoric. He still played around with other events, claiming to have triple jumped 14.25 in 1979 and run 400m in 47.3 and 400m hurdles in 55.9 in 1980, and for a long while he was not the most dedicated of trainers. He switched clubs to Thames Valley Harriers in 1982 to afford a higher level of competition but, following the 1984 season, Roddan gave him an ultimatum on the lines of: "either work seriously or don't waste my time". That was the turning point. In 1985 we had the first glimmer of something special to come when he clocked a wind assisted 10.20 in Finland, while in domestic races (where his best was a legal 10.42) his exceptional speed over the last 50m was noted.

It was as a 200m runner, though, that he first made his mark on the international scene at the 1986 European Indoor Championships in Madrid. Although he hoped to reach the final, Christie entertained no hopes of beating the formidable indoor specialist Aleksandr Yevgenyev but, early in the finishing straight, the Russian showed signs of faltering and that was just the incentive Christie needed. He powered past to win in 21.10, his fastest yet indoors or out. That gave him all the self confidence in the world, confirmed to him that hard training did make the difference, and that summer he made the huge leap into top world class.

He set the ball rolling with a pair of personal bests (10.33 and 20.79) in Oslo and then came the sensational breakthrough to 10.04 with a 1.8m tailwind back in Madrid. Helped by the 640m altitude of the Spanish capital, Christie had smashed Allan Wells' UK record of 10.11 ... and even coach Roddan found it difficult to believe when Christie phoned him with the news. That instant elevation to the world elite also had sweet financial implications, for suddenly he found himself 50 times more valuable! Instead of the £100 per race he had been paid previously to compete in televised British meetings he was now eligible for £5000.

After winning the 100m in 10.22 he had hopes of becoming the first Briton to complete a AAA sprint double since McDonald Bailey over 30 years earlier but he weakened in the closing stages of the 200m and despite a personal best of 20.51 he finished third behind John Regis and Todd Bennett. Ranked second on paper to Ben Johnson, the formbook held true at the Commonwealth Games in Edinburgh with the Canadian winning in 10.07 by a two-metre-plus margin over Christie (10.28), the first Englishman to win a medal in the short sprint since Cyril Holmes won the 100 yards title back in 1938. Christie clutched his leg as he finished and the hamstring injury kept him out of the 200m and 4x100m relay. The European Championships in Stuttgart proved more fruitful. He became the first Briton in 40 years to become 100m champion, clocking 10.15. Running on "dead legs" he narrowly missed making the 200m final but anchored Britain to bronze medals in the relay. It had been an amazing season of transformation for Christie, even if in his final race he was narrowly beaten by Wells. He wouldn't lose again to a Briton in a 100m final for ten years!

Following a sprint double in the 1987 European Cup and a personal best 20.48 200m in Oslo, he shaved the UK record to 10.03 (1.7m wind) in Budapest. At the World Championships in Rome the 100m final was simply sensational as Johnson flashed to a 9.83 clocking, a full tenth inside the world record, with Carl Lewis (USA) second in 9.93. Jamaica's Ray Stewart finished third in 10.08 with Christie fourth in 10.14. Later, following his disqualification at the 1988 Olympics, Johnson's 1987 world title and world record would be disallowed retrospectively and so Christie was eventually awarded the bronze medal.

He began 1988 with a bang. At the European Indoor Championships in Budapest he let rip with a 6.55 semi to take 3/100ths off his recently set UK 60m record and in the final he overcame an appalling start to prevail in 6.57. Next day he cruised to a 20.79 200m semi but, inhibited by having to run in lane 3 in the final, he lacked his usual panache and finished third in 20.83.

As the Olympics approached, Christie completed that coveted AAA Championships double and in fine style with times of 10.15 and a personal best 20.46 into headwinds, but his penultimate race before the Games underlined the monumental task ahead. In Zürich he ran 10.07 and yet wound up fifth as Lewis won in 9.93 from fellow American Calvin Smith (9.97) and Johnson (10.00). The Seoul Olympic final proved an unforgettable race, mainly for the wrong reasons, as Johnson – first over the line in a literally unbelievable 9.79 – was chucked out of the Games in disgrace when the drug tests were analysed. That left Lewis as Olympic champion in 9.92 (+1.1m wind), which was eventually ratified as a new world record, while Christie set a European and UK record of 9.97 in second place just ahead of Smith (9.99). He was understandably elated. "I just followed Carl all the way and managed to stay relaxed for about 99 metres. My dream was to run under 10 seconds." But dreams would turn to nightmares shortly afterwards.

In the meantime, amid rumours that another 100m runner had failed a drugs test, he had the 200m to run. Again he ran above himself, clocking 20.33 in his semi and a UK record of 20.09 for fourth in the final, won by Joe DeLoach (USA) in 19.75. Then came the bombshell. It was Christie's sample, showing a level of pseudoephedrine just over the acceptable limit, which was under question. Christie claimed that was as a result of drinking ginseng tea, which can contain pseudoephedrine as an additive, and on a majority decision of the IOC Medical Commission he was given "the benefit of the doubt" in the words of Prince Alexandre de Merode, the chairman. Had the verdict gone the other way Christie would have lost his medal and been banned for three months. "I've been to hell and back", he said after learning that he had been cleared and could run in the relay where he gave vent to his feelings by anchoring the team to UK records of 38.52 in the semis and 38.28 in the final where, with Elliot Bunney, Regis and Mike McFarlane, he won another silver medal.

A fine indoor double in Stuttgart in February 1989 (UK record of 6.52 plus 20.65) augured well but a toe injury kept him out of the European and World Indoor Championships and the training time lost meant that he had a relatively subdued summer. There was one late season highlight: winning at the World Cup in Barcelona ahead of US champion Leroy Burrell in an eased-off 10.10. That set him up well for the Commonwealth Games in Auckland early in 1990 and yet again he rose to the big occasion. After winning his semi in a legal 10.02 he stormed to victory in a windy 9.93 (+3.9m). Another gold followed in the relay, but that wasn't it for the winter as he went on to win the European indoor 60m in 6.56 in Glasgow, followed by a European record equalling 6.51 in Athens, just 1/100th away from the world record. The main target for the summer was to retain the European 100m crown and that was accomplished in Split with a just wind-assisted time of 10.00, followed by third place in the 200m (20.33) and second in the relay in a Commonwealth record of 37.98.

All those medals notwithstanding, Christie could still not be regarded as the world's no 1 at 100m... and he was frustrated again in 1991. During the winter he picked up his first world record – a share with Darren Braithwaite, Ade Mafe and Regis in an indoor 4x200m record of 1:22.11 – and two silver medals in the World Indoor Championships, but the big prize eluded him even though he ran faster than ever before at the World Championships in Tokyo. The standard on what was regarded as the world's quickest track was fantastic. In a quarter-final Lewis ran a heavily wind-blown 9.80 (+4.3m) ahead of Christie's 9.90, with Namibia's Frank Fredericks taking another heat in 9.89w. Lewis took the first semi in 9.93, world record holder (at 9.90) Leroy Burrell the second in 9.94 in front of fellow American Dennis Mitchell (9.99) and Christie (9.99).

The stage was set for the greatest sprint race in history with all of the world's best not only present but in top form, and after a thrilling battle the first two broke the world record with Christie smashing his European record but without a medal to show for it! Quickest to react to the gun was Mitchell; too quick in fact. No false start was called, but it transpired that the starter was not plugged into the Seiko false start detector which emits an acoustic signal, audible to the starter, whenever the reaction time is less than 0.100 sec. The apparatus revealed Mitchell's reaction time to be 0.090 ... in other words he was allowed to get away with a flier. As Mitchell was to finish third just 1/100th ahead of Christie that was to prove crucial. Lewis charged to victory in 9.86 (+1.2m wind) to smash the world record. Burrell was also inside his old figures with 9.88, Mitchell was credited with 9.91 and Christie ran 9.92, gaining sole ownership of the Commonwealth record in the process. Barely two months earlier that 9.92 would have constituted a world record. Christie ran out of steam in his 200m semi but came away with a bronze medal in the relay.

For so long the "almost man" of world sprinting, Christie finally became "*the man*" in 1992. He displayed impressive form in Rome in June, winning the 100m easily in 10.11 and clocking his second fastest 200m time of 20.25 inches behind Frank Fredericks of Namibia and Michael Johnson (USA). A further boost to his Olympic chances came when, while Lewis was failing to make the US team in either sprint, he shone in the AAA Championships. He took the 100m in 10.09 and finished a close second to European champion Regis (20.27) in 20.29. He improved to 10.07 in Lausanne, although losing narrowly to Nigeria's Olapade Adeniken, and scored a victory over 100m (his 20th in 21 races that season) in his final pre-Olympic outing in Gateshead.

A week before the Games I asked Christie for his assessment. "I think I've got as good a chance as anybody else," he replied. "It's a wide open field and there's no outstanding favourite as such. This has been my most consistent year. I'm bigger, I'm stronger and I believe I'm faster. I feel that if I need to run faster than 9.92 to win in Barcelona I can do it." In fact, he didn't need to run quite that quickly to win the blue riband event of the Olympics.

The capacity crowd was hushed as the eight men settled in their blocks. At the third time of asking they were away ... and Christie got a beauty of a start. For once Christie found himself on level terms with his main rivals almost from the outset. By 60m, which he reached in 6.48 (as against 6.43 in Tokyo), he was clear and sprinting towards gold and glory. He crossed the line upright in 9.96 (+0.5m wind) as his well beaten rivals lunged desperately for the other spoils. It was at the time the second fastest mark of his career but by any other criterion it was the race of his life. Fredericks took the silver medal 6/100ths behind, Mitchell the bronze.

After so narrowly failing to win a medal in the previous year's World Championships, Christie had considered taking his leave of the sport but, as he said after his Olympic victory, "I'm just glad I didn't retire then. That's the best decision I've ever made. This is something that Ron and I have been working for over the last 10 to 12 years". Christie made Olympic history by displacing Wells as the oldest man to win the 100m crown, at 32, although the rest of his Games proved an anti-climax. He failed to make the 200m final with 20.38 and a fumbled changeover kept the British relay team out of the medals. Christie lost a few post-Olympic 100m races, not that it mattered, but was back on song for the late season World Cup in Havana, winning the 100m, placing second in the 200m and captaining the British men's team to a brilliant second place overall behind Africa and ahead of Europe, the Americas and the USA.

Christie remained the global no 1 in 1993. A much-hyped clash with Lewis in Gateshead proved no contest as Christie won in 10.08; he also finished ahead of him in Zürich (10.03) but on that occasion the race went to Burrell in 10.02. However, the only event which mattered was the World Championships in Stuttgart and there he reached, at 33, what proved to be a lifetime peak. Not only did he win by a clear margin over the US trio of Andre Cason (9.92), Mitchell (9.99) and Lewis (10.02) but his European and Commonwealth record time of 9.87 could be considered the greatest ever 100m performance up to that time as the wind of 0.3m was appreciably less than that behind the only faster legal mark: Lewis's 9.86 (1.2m). Third at 30m, second at 60m (in 6.45), he drew level with Cason at 80m and had at least half a metre to spare at the finish. A second European record fell in the relay where, along with Colin Jackson, Tony Jarrett and Regis, he anchored the team to second place in 37.77, the fastest ever non-winning time.

Few sprinters have reigned as the world's no 1 for three seasons but Christie succeeded in doing so in 1994 even though Burrell set a world record of 9.85 while Christie's best was 9.91. A European indoor 60m record of 6.48 was encouraging and outdoors he posted no fewer than 14 legal and two windy marks inside 10.10. Blown along by a 3.7m wind he ran the fastest ever time in Britain of 9.91 at the AAA Championships in Sheffield, and went on to win his four most important races of the season: the European title in Helsinki (10.14), an all-star Zürich confrontation where his 10.05 in pouring rain and into a 1.4m wind was an astounding piece of sprinting (Burrell placed seventh in 10.39), the Commonwealth Games final in Victoria (Canada) in 9.91 (+1.9m) and the World Cup at Crystal Palace in 10.21.

Christie enjoyed a fantastic indoor double in Liévin (France) in February 1995, setting a European 60m record of 6.47 followed an hour later by a world record breaking 20.25 200m – the first world record by a British sprinter since Peter Radford in 1960. Could he remain the top man, at age 35, for a fourth year? The answer was not quite. Although he continued to run below 10.10 virtually at will, he had to settle for no 2 on the world rankings to Canada's Donovan Bailey who claimed the fastest time of the year at 9.91 and took the world title in 9.97. As usual Christie was a massive points scorer in the European Cup with a swift 10.05/20.11 double and the world's fastest ever 150m time of 14.74, albeit heavily wind assisted, augured well for the World Championships, particularly as he comfortably beat Bailey. But a hamstring injury put paid to his chances of retaining the title in Gothenburg and he did well to place sixth in 10.12. Ten days later he showed his true form by beating Bailey in Zürich in 10.03 against a 1.9m wind. The season ended with his two fastest times of the year: 10.00 in Tokyo (his fifth win in nine races against Bailey) and an altitude assisted 9.97 in Johannesburg.

It all started to unravel in 1996, for while Bailey went on to win the Olympic title in a world record 9.84 Christie ran no faster than 10.03 (not bad, all the same, for a man of 36!) and experienced a disastrous Games in Atlanta. His Olympic build-up went well. He returned to Madrid, the city of his first major international successes, to score another twinkling European Cup double in 10.04 (a Cup record) and 20.25w. It was his seventh consecutive 100m victory in that competition and with four also at 200m his total of 11 European Cup wins was a record. He went on to beat Bailey in Nuremberg (10.06-10.09), picked up a record eighth AAA title in 10.04 and clocked times of 10.03 and 10.04 in the Olympic preliminaries. However, in the final he – of all people – was disqualified for two false starts. He refused at first to accept the decision and the race was delayed for several minutes while he argued unavailingly with officials. But the evidence was there – an illegal reaction time of 0.086 – and he had to go. Eliminated in the quarter-finals of the 200m and not a participant in the relay, his Olympic career came to a sorry end. He bounced back in Zürich with a close third in 10.06 (-1.4m wind) behind Mitchell (10.04) and Bailey (10.06), but in Sheffield he finished behind Ian Mackie for his first 100m defeat by a Briton since 1986.

It wasn't quite the end, though, for in 1997 he ran a brisk 6.51 indoor 60m, while outdoors he brought his tally of legal marks inside 10.10 to a staggering 54 and extended his sequence as no 1 in Peter Matthews' UK rankings to 12 years, the best in any other event being ten by shot putter Geoff Capes. For one last time he shone at the European Cup, winning the 100m in a record equalling 10.04, his quickest of the year, and deadheating for first in the 200m in 20.56. That would be his final appearance for the British team and it took to 55 the number of individual wins he had chalked up in international matches (10 at 60m, 28 at 100m, 17 at 200m). In all, he gained 23 major international championship medals, ten of them gold in individual events.

That was it, so we thought, but now that he had become a successful coach (most notably of Darren Campbell who in 1998 succeeded him as European champion in 10.04) he couldn't resist showing the new generation he was still up for it and in August 1998 he set a world age-38 best of 10.38. It was a pity he didn't leave it there, for early in 1999 he had a few indoor races in Germany and Sweden, clocking 6.57, but in August it was revealed that he had tested positive at the Dortmund meeting in February where he had run 6.59 and 21.02.

The news came as a bombshell to the British public for whom he was a sporting icon. His sample produced an adverse finding of metabolites of the prohibited steroid nandrolone. Christie stated: "I am completely innocent of any wrongdoing and any case against me will be vigorously defended." In September the UK Athletics Disciplinary Committee unanimously decided to lift his suspension (although he had by now retired from competition anyway) and cleared him of all charges, concluding that it could not be proven beyond reasonable doubt that the substance present in Christie's sample was derived from a prohibited substance. However, the ultimate authority – the IAAF – referred the case to its independent Arbitration Panel, which in August 2000 decided that UK Athletics had reached an erroneous conclusion and that Christie had committed a doping offence and was suspended for two years. It was a sad conclusion to a momentous career.

KATHY COOK

Born 3.5.1960 Winchester.
Clubs: Reading AC, Wolverhampton & Bilston AC

DURING ALMOST A decade of international sprinting, Kathy Cook (née Smallwood) amassed 23 championship medals, a total surpassed only by Colin Jackson and matched by Linford Christie, and was so far ahead of her time that, more than 20 years later, she still holds the British records for 100m, 200m and 400m.

Tall (1.80m or 5ft 11in) and willowy, she began her athletic life as a high jumper with a best of 1.63 at 15. By that time, though, she was concentrating on the sprints. Having joined Reading AC and finding there was no high jump coaching available at the club she gravitated to the sprint group coached by former sprint star Jim Spooner. Her breakthrough came in 1977 when she progressed from 12.0 to 11.71 for 100m and from 24.46 to 23.22 for 200m, a UK junior record. That was the year she commenced her medal collection – three bronzes at the European Junior Championships – and, of ultimate significance, she ran her first 400m race in 56.0.

Kathy (short for Kathryn) reduced that UK junior record to 22.99 when winning her semi at the 1978 Commonwealth Games in Edmonton, having earlier clocked a windy 22.73, and thought she was ready to take her first gold medal at the age of 18. In fact she wound up fifth – one of the rare occasions on which she failed to do herself justice. "I feel I got into the frame of mind that I had done well to make the final, that I had done better than I had been expected to do. I think the pressure and my inexperience got to me ... I went through the motions." She did strike gold in the 4x100m relay, though.

Next year, assisted by the high altitude, she gained her first UK senior record, clocking 22.70 for second to Marita Koch (GDR) in the World Student Games in Mexico City. Also at those Games she was silver medallist in the 100m in her best time of 11.27 (down from 11.64) and, still playing with the event, improved to 54.5 for 400m that season.

The 1980 Olympics in Moscow came a little too early in her career but she acquitted herself well by setting a personal best of 11.24 in her 100m quarter-final and placing sixth in the final (11.28), while over 200m she finished one position higher in her best time of 22.61 despite entering the finishing straight in eighth and last place. That was a characteristic piece of running at that stage of her development. As she explained: "In the 100 I try hard all the way, but in the 200 I just seem to coast the bend and leave the work to the straight ... I don't know if it's psychological or not." She ended the Games on a high note as she, Heather Hunte, Bev Goddard and Sonia Lannaman took bronze medals in the relay with a Commonwealth record of 42.43. Shortly after the Games, back at Crystal Palace, Kathy – her long tresses snipped off – celebrated her new look with a UK 200m record of 22.31, finishing a metre clear of Jamaica's Olympic bronze medallist Merlene Ottey. Incidentally, her younger sister Maria Smallwood ranked seventh in Britain that year at the long jump with a leap of 6.26.

At the 1981 World Student Games Kathy collected her first individual gold medal, winning the 200m in 22.78, but there was better to come for at the World Cup in Rome – for which she had been a reserve – she produced an astonishing run in the 100m, clocking 11.10 and splitting two legends: Evelyn Ashford (USA) and Marlies Göhr (GDR). That was a curious race for Kathy. Usually she took quite a while to get those long legs moving at full speed and gained on everybody in the closing stages. Not on this occasion. "I ran a superb 80," she reflected without false modesty. "Normally I come through like a train in the last 20 but I wasn't able to in that race. If only I had been able to put my usual last 20 on the end of that race ..."

Shortly afterwards, Kathy ran her first serious 400m at the celebrated Coke Meeting at Crystal Palace. Starting the race with a personal best standing at 54.3 from the previous year, she clocked a notable 51.08 – just 0.20 outside the UK record – behind Jarmila Kratochvilová, the Czech who would later become a world record breaker at this event and 800m. "I've never been so nervous," she recalled. Her apprehension was a mixture of fear of the distance ("I knew I was going to have to suffer and I didn't really know how I was going to run it") and a secret dread that she would 'blow up' and humiliate herself in a race which would be watched by millions of television viewers. She actually performed splendidly, even if she did collapse in a heap at the finish and vowed "never again"! "It was agony," she said.

Kathy never did get to enjoy racing the full lap, and preferred to concentrate on the 200m. One couldn't blame her, for her results at 200m continued to progress brilliantly. Her finest run thus far came at the 1982 European Championships in Athens, where she finished less than a metre down on Olympic champion Bärbel Wöckel (GDR) to take the silver medal in the Commonwealth record time of 22.13. It was a wise choice of event, as it turned out, for she would not have finished as high as second in the 400m, a fantastic race which saw Koch win in a world record 48.16 with Kratochvilová runner-up in 48.85. Actually, Kathy had planned to race 400m for the first time in a championship at the much lower-level Commonwealth Games – and indeed she set a Commonwealth record of 50.46 a week after Athens – but some lack of communication resulted in her not being selected for that event in Brisbane ... a race won in windy conditions in 51.26 by Australia's Raelene Boyle. Kathy had to content herself with a very close second in the 200m, clocking a windy 22.21 behind Ottey's 22.19.

The end of 1982 was notable also for the fact that she married Garry Cook, who had that year joined with Peter Elliott, Steve Cram and Seb Coe to set the still exist-ing world 4x800m relay record of 7:03.89 and retired with personal bests of 46.0 for 400m and 1:44.55 for 800m. Like Kathy, he won several major relay medals (but at 4x400m), including gold at the 1982 Commonwealth Games and silver at the 1984 Olympics. They had met at the 1978 Commonwealth Games.

Not having gained the hoped for championship experience at 400m, she opted for the 200m at the inaugural 1983 World Championships in Helsinki and once again excelled herself by filling third place in 22.37 behind Koch and Ottey. She shone brightly also at the Los Angeles Olympics the following year. Admittedly, the absence of the East Europeans devalued her events and it's extremely unlikely she would have come away with third place in the 400m and fourth in the 200m had all the stars been there – but by her own standards she reached the greatest form of her life on the most important occasion of her career, and you can only test yourself against those who show up.

She broke the Commonwealth record in the 400m with 49.43 behind the American pair of Valerie Brisco-Hooks and Chandra Cheeseborough, and fol-lowed up with a UK record of 22.10 – just 1/100th away from the bronze – behind Brisco-Hooks, Florence Griffith (later to metamorphose into Flo-Jo) and Ottey. "I can't complain," she said. "I ran my best ever in the best 200 field I've ever been in." Another Olympic bronze came her way in the relay.

Kathy, who set a world best of 35.46 for 300m in 1984, never ran as well again after 1984. Injuries and a certain lack of motivation took their toll and subsequently her best times were 11.54, 22.87 and 51.36 in 1985, although she still managed to collect another four medals at the 1986 Commonwealth Games. Astonishingly, every year from 1977 to 1986 (except for 1985 when nothing was on offer) she acquired at least one championship relay medal. At the time of her retirement in 1987 she remarked: "I've no regrets. Although people have said I might have trained harder, I've always given my best. At the end of the day I am happy with what I've achieved." So too were the fans who had followed the illustrious career of this most modest and endearing of athletes.

STEVE CRAM

Born 14.10.1960 Gateshead. Club: Jarrow & Hebburn AC

IT'S NOT OFTEN that the most precocious of athletic talents go on to fulfil all their bright promise as senior athletes. Steve Cram was an exception: he first achieved a national reputation as a 16 year-old in 1977, a year later he was running for England in the Commonwealth Games, and he just kept on improving. That huge stride of his carried him to triumph after triumph, including a fabulous hat-trick of 1500m titles – European, Commonwealth and World – and a silver medal behind Seb Coe in the Olympics. And there was more, for in 1985 he made sure of an honoured place in the history of athletic performance by becoming the first to crack 3:30 for 1500m, followed by new records at the mile and 2000m.

Born of a Geordie father and German mother, he was first spotted as a 400m runner with potential as an 11 year-old by Jimmy Hedley (who would remain his coach for his entire career) and he joined Jarrow & Hebburn AC in 1972 – his heroes being local stars Jim Alder and Brendan Foster. At 14 he placed fourth in the English Schools Junior 1500m; the following year (1976) as an Intermediate he finished fifth in the 3000m. His best times that season were promising but unexceptional at 1:59.7 for 800m, 4:07.2 for 1500m and 8:52.8 for 3000m.

The first big leap forward occurred in 1977 when he set a UK age-16 1500m best of 3:47.7. It was no flash in the pan, for in June 1978 he broke Steve Ovett's UK age-17 best by 2.2 sec when clocking 3:42.7 in the Durham Schools Championships. Yet even that astonishing run hardly prepared us for his exploit in the Emsley Carr Mile at Crystal Palace three weeks later. In his first ever mile race he finished fourth in 3:57.43 to take 1.6 sec off Jim Ryun's world best by a 17 year-old! That won him selection for the Commonwealth Games in Edmonton, and although he was eliminated in his heat he was not disgraced by his time of 3:44.8.

On his return from Canada, he lowered his 1500m best to 3:40.09, scoring a rare victory over his great but ill-starred contemporary, Graham Williamson, but in 1979 the Scot was clearly the superior (beating Cram by a yawning margin in the AAA Junior Championships) and Cram went for the 3000m rather than the 1500m in the European Junior Championships. He duly won that title in 8:05.2, covering the second half in just 3:55, and shortly afterwards he smashed his best 800m time of 1:53.5 with 1:48.5. He ended the year with a best mile time of 3:57.03 behind Ovett.

The obvious target for 1980 was to make the Moscow Olympic team. With Coe and Ovett pre-selected and Dave Moorcroft opting for the 5000m, it was really between Cram and Williamson for that third spot. When Cram fell over in the trial, while Williamson finished second to Moorcroft, it looked all over for him ... until he turned in a personal best 1500m of 3:37.3 four days later. The selectors decided to hold fire until a head-to-head between Cram and Williamson could be staged. Cram, meanwhile, ran Ovett to two metres with a world teenage best of 3:35.52, before clinching the issue by finishing ahead of Williamson, 3:53.8 (personal best) to 3:56.4, in an Oslo mile which was even more notable for the fact that Ovett won in a world record 3:48.8.

An awestruck Cram did well enough to reach the final in Moscow, placing eighth (3:41.98) in that dramatic race won by Coe in 3:38.40. Later in the season he reduced his world teenage best to 3:34.74 in Zürich, placing fifth in a race won by Coe in 3:32.19, and he finished eighth in the IAAF Golden Mile at Crystal Palace in 3:55.71, victory going to Ovett in 3:52.84. It was in races such as these that the blond youngster was learning his trade, free from the pressures placed on Coe and Ovett.

Feeling that he could never generate the leg speed of those two, Cram expected in time to move up to 5000m and his over-distance ability became apparent in 1981, his final year as an 'apprentice', when in June he ran a 67:28 half marathon in the Great North Run. His 800m speed was becoming quite impressive, though, for in September he ran 1:46.29. In between, he lowered his 3000m time to 7:47.82, won the AAA 1500m title and broke 3:50 for the mile for the first time with 3:49.95 behind Coe's world record breaking 3:48.53 in Zürich. He was running marvellous times for an athlete of his age, but he was still a supporting player rather than a star. It was all good experience, and in 1982 Cram came into his own. It's possible he would have been number one anyway in view of his constant progress, but injury and/or ill-ness ruled Coe and Ovett out of the two big 1500m championships that season, and Cram capitalised on their absence. The only significant race he lost was to Sydney Maree (USA) over a mile in Cork and even then he set a personal best of 3:49.90.

The run which demonstrated he had moved up a class came four days after Cork when he front ran to the world's fastest 800m time that year with 1:44.45. For a man whose under-distance speed had previously seemed inadequate that was the performance which finally convinced him that he was ready to take on anyone at 1500m.

Cram was now being heralded as a prospective 1500m world record breaker, a belief reinforced by his best win yet – in Zürich – where he led for the entire last lap to beat a starry field in a personal best of 3:33.66. His last race before the European Championships was for the British team which smashed the world record for the 4x800m relay; he produced a sizzling 1:44.54 on the third leg, his 50.5 first lap being perilously close to his quickest ever 400m time of 49.1!

He showed himself to be a quick-witted racer with his win in the European 1500m in Athens. His victory was achieved the hard way; after a long run for home 600m out. He might have preferred to have gone at the bell but he took advantage of the momentary confusion when the luckless Williamson fell by accelerating hard. Running the third lap in a stunning 55.4, he opened up a 20m advantage. A man of lesser nerve might have crumbled as he saw (on the giant TV screen) his lead dwindling but Cram raised enough of a gallop in the finishing straight to win by four metres in 3:36.49. He went on to collect a second gold at the Commonwealth Games in 3:42.37, clocking a spectacular 50.9 last lap.

Although Cram was destined to win the world title in August 1983, the path to Helsinki was strewn with obstacles. Towards the end of 1982 he first sprained an ankle and then experienced shin trouble. After that the winter went well until, in April, he sustained groin and foot injuries when he tripped over a kerb during a run. He insisted on running in a road race a few days later and aggravated the injury. As a consequence he was reduced to occasional jogging for several weeks and, in late May, just as he was starting to build up the mileage he suffered a calf injury which halted his progress yet again. Not until mid-June was he able to get back to twice a day training – only for disaster to strike one more time. He sprained an ankle when stepping on a discarded Coke can, and another two weeks of valuable training time were lost.

The situation was beginning to look hopeless in terms of being in peak condition for Helsinki. However, his racing comeback began in July and a 3:35.68 win in Nice plus the AAA title restored confidence and he won his final test over 800m, beating an admittedly ailing Coe for the first time in 1:45.03. The speed was back ... but could he handle three races in three days after all the training he had lost? The answer was emphatically in the affirmative. He won his heat in 3:40.17, semi in 3:35.77 and the final in 3:41.59 ahead of Steve Scott (USA), Saïd Aouita of Morocco and Ovett, covering the last 800m in 1:49.0 and the ultimate 400m in 52.0.

Coe was not in Helsinki, but there could be no devaluing Cram's victory, for he beat a dazzling array of runners fair and square. Tipped off by Brendan Foster, he was ready for Aouita's break 500m from home, responded and took the lead with just under 200m to go to become the inaugural world champion in the event. The pre-race assessment of 1976 Olympic champion John Walker proved uncannily accurate: "The man with the best head out of all of us is Cram. He's a tough young guy who just goes out and does his own thing, supremely confident and unconcerned about others. If he's in front with 100 metres to go, God help the rest of us."

Cram was now just getting into stride. He won the European Cup 1500m and for the second year running claimed the year's fastest 800m time with 1:43.61. He reduced his 1500m best to 3:31.66 – just 0.3 outside Ovett's world record – when winning in Brussels, and he made a gallant if unsuccessful bid to break Ovett's world 2 miles best with a time of 8:14.93 (7:43.1 at 3000m). Five days after running a solo 3:33.06 in dreadful conditions in Norway he notched up one of the most satisfying victories of his career. In a fondly remembered, dramatic head-to-head mile at the Coke meeting he launched his drive for home some 350m out and fought off Ovett's challenge to score in 3:52.56.

'Crammy' was pre-selected with Ovett for the Los Angeles Olympics of 1984 ... but again his preparations were hampered. A knee injury marred a training/racing trip 'down under' early in 1984, and he wound up an embarrassing ninth (3:44.18) in a New Zealand 1500m race but was in fine form for his first serious race in mid-June when he ran 2:15.98 for 1000m. The following week he won the AAA 800m title in 1:46.84 but as he eased up approaching the finish he felt a sharp pain in his calf. It was three weeks before he felt able to race again and that turned out to be a disaster as – running now with an ankle injury – he faded from first to last in a 1000m race (2:23.01). In his final pre-Olympic race he was second to Williamson over 1000m, clocking 2:17.58. It was hardly the ideal build-up towards his forthcoming battle with Coe, Ovett etc.

On the eve of leaving for LA he ran a 1500m time trial in 3:39.8 in dreadful conditions. It wasn't a marvellous time but it gave his confidence a timely boost. At the Olympics he impressed with a semi-final win in his season's best of 3:36.30, which in the final he cut to 3:33.40. It was a magnificent effort in the circumstances, but it wasn't enough to beat a fabulous run by Coe in retaining his title in 3:32.53. Cram was just preparing to launch his strike with 200m to go when Coe pre-empted him. "I am satisfied," said Cram. "I couldn't have done anything else. Seb was brilliant on the day. It was so fast. I just didn't have the legs at the end. It was a strong man's race and Seb was the man."

Cram was full of running after the Games. Too quick an early pace (54.5/1:50.9) may have cost him the chance of beating Ovett's 1500m world record of 3:30.77 in Budapest (3:33.13). He set off even faster (54.1 at 400m) in Brussels to finish in 3:34.08, and followed that with a personal best mile of 3:49.65 in Koblenz. Following a successful Far East tour, during which he clocked a 47.6 400m relay leg, he enjoyed his best ever cross country season in 1985, winning the Northern title.

That summer of 1985, despite continuing calf problems, he put together one of the greatest series of races in middle distance history. On June 27 in Oslo he ran the third quickest ever 1500m with 3:31.34 and 19 days later in Nice he achieved immortality by becoming the first to duck under 3:30. In perfect conditions the race got off to a very swift start as Babacar Niang of Senegal raced through 200m in 26.86 and 400m in 54.36 with Cram heading the non-pacemakers in 27.5 and 55.5. The second lap was much slower as a flagging Niang reached 800m in 1:53.68, dropped out and was replaced as hare by Sudan's Omer Khalifa. Cram followed in 1:53.9. Khalifa raised the pace to such effect that by 1000m (2:21.89 to Cram's 2:22.0) the time was ahead of Ovett's schedule. Khalifa reached the bell in 2:36.18 with Cram on 2:36.3. A last lap of under 54.5 was needed by Cram for the record. "I knew we were on a fast time and I just decided to go for it from the bell," he said.

That early strike won him the race for as he strode past the 1200m mark in 2:49.66 he was at least six metres clear of Spain's José Luis González and Aouita, the Olympic 5000m champion. Realising his mistake, the Moroccan tore into second place and set about reducing the deficit. However, as Cram was winging along the back straight at 13.13 100m pace he gained nothing. Cram was still 5-6 metres up entering the final straight, but from then on Aouita closed with every stride. Unaware, until the last few metres, of what was happening behind him Cram sailed on serenely as Aouita pulled out all the stops in frenzied pursuit. At the line just 4/100ths separated them. Cram had run his last lap in 53.4 for a time of 3:29.67, Aouita around 52.7 for an African record of 3:29.71. Cram had broken the world record by the biggest margin since Jim Ryun in 1967.

That was just the start of a record blitz. In Oslo on July 27 Aouita opted for the

5000m, clipping 1/100th from Dave Moorcroft's world mark with 13:00.40, and barely had the excitement subsided than the runners were out for the Dream Mile. James Mays (USA) was the appointed hare and he cut out a good pace with 56.01 at 440y and 1:53.82 at 880y. After a cautious start (57.5/1:54.9) Cram was always in a good position but Coe ran with alarming lethargy in the early stages and had to run a very swift second quarter to get up to fifth place at halfway. However, the third quarter, with Mike Hillardt of Australia up front, was so slow at 59.32 (2:53.14) that Coe was able to close up behind Cram (2:53.3), who at that stage thought the chance of a world record had gone. Cram accelerated at the bell, with Coe in pursuit, but when Cram fairly exploded around the final bends even Coe had no answer – not surprising since Cram covered that last 200m in 25.39! The final quarter took him 53.0 and his time of 3:46.32 (3:32.29 at 1500m) took 1.01 sec from Coe's record. Coe himself was passed just before the 1500m mark by González, who went on to finish in a Spanish record of 3:47.79 with Coe (3:49.22) next.

When Coe broke three world records in the space of 41 days in 1979 we doubted whether we would ever see the like again. Well, Cram surpassed that by setting three world records in just 19 days. In Budapest on August 4 he broke John Walker's 2000m mark (hand timed 4:51.4) with 4:51.39. Paced first by Mays and then by Britain's Rob Harrison, Cram passed 400m in around 59.0 and 800m in 1:56.1 before running the second half of the race solo. He reached 1200m in 2:54.58 and 1600m in 3:53.95 (estimated 3:55.4 at the mile) prior to a last lap of 57.47. "It was very tough, and no wonder the record has stood for so long [nine years]. You have to run a world class mile pace and then a lap further."

But for cold, windy weather back in Gateshead on August 9 he might have made it four world records in 24 days. Although Coe's greatly admired record of 2:12.18 (set in near perfect conditions in Oslo) survived – indeed, right through to 1999 – Cram's 2:12.85 was probably intrinsically the greater performance. To attempt such a brilliant record (Coe considered it his best) in such abysmal conditions appeared to be a doomed enterprise, but Cram decided to have a go. His plan was to hit 800m in about 1:45 (Coe had run 1:44.6) and rely on his strength to see him through a 27 sec last 200m. A capacity crowd cheered on the local hero and if human warmth could only have cancelled out the cold and wind the 'Jarrow Arrow' would surely have scored another bullseye.

The pacemaking, by Mays, was spot on with Cram towed through in 25.7 and 51.8. At 600m (78.84) Cram took over and went for it, reaching 800m in 1:44.94. He now required a final 200m of 27.23, but it was too much to ask with the wind in his face along what must have seemed like an endless finishing straight. His final time was the second fastest ever and even today he ranks third on the world all-time list. He completed a momentous season with a slow European Cup 1500m win notable only for the speed of his last 200m (24.7) and a scintillating 800m victory over Brazil's Olympic champion Joaquim Cruz in Zürich in a personal best of 1:42.88, making him the fourth fastest ever at the distance – not bad for someone who never considered himself to be an 800m runner!

Although he would never again run as fast as he did in 1985, Cram continued as a major force in world middle distance running for several more seasons. He was particularly effective in 1986, during which he lost only one race at 800m and went undefeated at 1500m or mile. Faulty pacemaking ruined any chance of challenging his world mile record in Oslo; nonetheless he clocked 3:48.31 for the world's quickest time that year. With a 1:43.62 800m victory in Nice also under his belt, Cram went to the Commonwealth Games in Edinburgh in confident mood and came away with two gold medals.

Unfortunately, Coe had to withdraw from the 800m final on medical grounds and thus the world may have been deprived of a great duel, but the race still proved memorable as Cram pulverised the opposition in 1:43.22, covering the last 200m in 25.0 as Tom McKean (1:44.80) overtook Peter Elliott (1:45.42) for second. In the 1500m Cram simply toyed with the opposition in a ludicrously slow race (3:50.87); chasing after a determined John Gladwin he covered the penultimate 200m, mainly against a strong wind, in 24.9 and completed the final lap in 51.3.

Cram had hopes of completing a similar double at the European Championships in Stuttgart but had to settle for gold and bronze. He ran 1:44.88 in the 800m behind Coe (1:44.50 with a final 200m of 24.7) and McKean (1:44.61) on a red letter day for British running, and revenge over Coe was exacted three days later in a disappointingly pedestrian 1500m, 3:41.09 (50.8 last lap) to 3:41.67.

In his next race, in Brussels, Cram took aim at the world 1500m record, which had passed to Aouita with 3:29.46 in August 1985. He had wanted to race the Moroccan, but Aouita opted instead to attack Cram's 2000m figures, and both chalked up near misses. Aouita ran 4:51.98 and Cram 3:30.15, the second fastest of his career. He was ahead of Aouita's schedule at 1200m with 2:48.73 but the record slipped away in the closing stages. Two days later, in Rieti, Cram posted his second fastest 800m time (and the world's quickest of 1986) with 1:43.19 while Coe produced his best ever 1500m time of 3:29.77. All three were present at Crystal Palace but, all too typically of the international circuit, each went his own way. Coe took the 800m in 1:44.28 and Aouita the 2 miles in 8:14.81 while Cram won the mile in 3:49.49.

Cram's world supremacy came to an end in 1987, a year which saw Aouita break Cram's 2000m record with 4:50.81, crash through the 13 minute barrier at 5000m and top the world year lists at 1500m (3:30.69) and mile (3:46.76). Cram's self assurance was dented after he was outkicked (despite a 50.2 last lap!) in the European Cup 1500m by González, his first defeat at the distance since the 1984 Olympics, and although he chalked up two good wins in Oslo (3:50.08 mile and 3:32.93 1500m a month apart) and another in Zürich (3:31.43 well ahead of González), he was destined for the biggest disappointment of his career thus far at the World Championships in Rome. After a very slow first kilometre it looked like a confident move by Cram when he went with 450m to go.

At first all seemed well, although ominously Abdi Bile of Somalia was quick to respond, and he covered the 200m stretch from 1000m to 1200m in a sizzling

25.41. Cram continued to dig in, more despairingly, but Bile not only refused to be shaken off but passed Cram on the last bend, followed by González. Bile went on to win convincingly in 3:36.80, having covered the final 800m in 1:46.6, but – quite uncharacteristically – Cram ("there was nothing there") gave up. Although still third midway along the straight he slowed up dramatically and finished up jogging over the line eighth in 3:41.19.

The 1988 season was a tantalising one; several fine runs enabled him to be ranked as the world's no 1 1500m/mile runner for a fifth time but, even more disappointingly than his showing in Rome, he finished out of the medals at the Seoul Olympics. He ran a 3:48.85 mile in Oslo (the year's quickest) and won the AAA 800m in 1:44.16; he ran faster still (1:43.42) finishing third in Zürich and in his final pre-Olympic 1500m, in Brussels, he posted the world's fastest time of the year with 3:30.95. It was shaping up so well until a calf strain caused him to drop out of a 1000m race, and in the Olympic 800m he was way below form, eliminated in the quarter finals in 1:46.47. However, the main item of business was the 1500m and what with the controversial non-selection of Coe, the withdrawal before the Games of an injured Bile and the scratching of Aouita at the semi-final stage due to hamstring trouble, the race was seemingly made for Cram. Alas, he was not in the best of health and the supreme prize – the only honour to elude him – again slipped from his grasp. The unheralded Peter Rono of Kenya struck gold in 3:35.96 ahead of Elliott (3:36.15) with a deeply frustrated Cram fourth in 3:36.24.

For the rest of his career (1994 was his final season) Cram struggled unavailingly to recapture the old magic. He broke new ground by winning the 1989 UK 5000m title in 13:28.58 but never again would he better 1:46, 3:33 or 3:51. In 1992 he clocked 28:46 for 10k on the road (ten years earlier he ran 28:23) and a 65:33 half marathon, while in 1998 he recorded 2:38:15 in the London Marathon and even took part in ultra-distance races. He has retained a high profile as the BBC's lead commentator on athletics and as chairman of the English Institute of Sport.

FATIMA WHITBREAD

Born 3.3.1961 Stoke Newington (London).
Club: Thurrock H

THE FIRST TIME Margaret Whitbread laid eyes on the 13 year-old who would eventually become her adopted daughter she whispered to club coach George Holroyd: "This girl is going to be the greatest javelin thrower the world has seen." It took 12 years for that seemingly far-fetched prophecy to come to pass ... 12 years of blood, sweat and tears, culminating in two fantastic throws at the 1986 European Championships in Stuttgart which made all the hard work, sacrifices and setbacks totally worthwhile.

There had been many times over the years when fate appeared to be blighting all of Fatima Whitbread's efforts to become the best in the world, for rarely was she absolutely free of injury or illness. Perhaps it was nature's way of telling her that a price must be paid for the tremendous demands she made on her body. That fearsome training regime made her one of the strongest women in Britain, yet one of the fastest too. She was timed at 11.9 for 100m in training and clocked 24.38 for 200m in competition. Remarkably, despite all the occasions when she had to endure the frustration of missing competitions because of injury, she improved every single season for 12 years, from a best of 34.94 as a 14 year-old in 1975 through to a phenomenal world record 77.44 in 1986.

The motivation to throw the javelin had originated in the classroom. "We were read an interesting story about a Greek goddess, Atalanta, who could throw a spear farther than any man could fire an arrow," she recalls. "By sheer coincidence the following lesson was PE and we were introduced to the javelin. I enjoyed both lessons and when I arrived home I asked my mum to let me go training with her." Margaret Whitbread, a prominent coach and former international javelin thrower herself (best of 45.18 in 1959), was only too happy to oblige and thus was born an athletic partnership which would in time make history.

It was in 1977 that Fatima first met in competition her inspiration – and later bitter rival – Tessa Sanderson. Tessa (21), who had just carried the UK record beyond 60m, won with 57.76 while Fatima (16) placed an unnoticed seventh with 42.88. Fatima went on that summer to become English Schools and WAAA Intermediate champion and a British junior international. While Fatima matured and developed her strength and skill, Tessa would win all 18 of their confontations up to and including 1981. However, Fatima never lost hope that one day she would be able to turn the tables, and having one of the world's greatest throwers as a perpetual target in domestic, never mind international, competition was just the incentive she needed.

Gradually the gap between them narrowed and in 1979, the year she made her mark by becoming the first British thrower to win a European Junior title (with a UK junior record of 58.02), she finished just 2.40m behind Tessa in a match against West Germany. She even managed, at the 1980 Olympics, to throw farther than Tessa ... but as they were competing in separate pools and both failed to qualify for the final ("my rubbish beat her rubbish", as Fatima put it) it might be better to draw a discreet veil over that result. It was in 1981 that Fatima broke into world class. She increased her personal best (60.14 in 1980) to 60.54 and then 62.82 and later got her closest yet to Tessa (64.18 against 65.28). She took her first UK and WAAA senior titles, improved to 65.82 and notched up her first international match victories.

The watershed in Fatima's career was the 1982 season. For the first time Tessa was not around (out injured) and thus Fatima's took over the mantle of Britain's no 1. She edged her personal best out to 66.98, defeated Cuba's Olympic champion Maria Colon and in a high class European Championship final in Athens was close to her best with 65.10 in eighth place. A similar throw would have won her the Commonwealth title in Brisbane a month later, but elbow and shoulder problems held her down to a disappointing 58.86 and she had to make do with the bronze medal.

When Tessa returned to the fray in 1983, Fatima was in no mood to revert to her traditional role as British second string. An early season 66.72 in Cyprus (her natural parents were Cypriot) set her up nicely, and at the UK Championships she finally defeated Tessa at the 19th attempt. Her euphoria was short lived, for the following weekend Tessa broke through the 70m barrier with a Commonwealth record of 70.82. Not that Fatima disgraced herself; she fought hard, raising her best to 67.46. In a later contest Tessa threatened the world record with 73.58, although again Fatima responded with a personal best of 68.36. The following weekend, in a small local meeting, Fatima progressed to 69.54, but an attack of tonsillitis nearly cost her the chance of competing in the big event of the year, the inaugural World Championships in the javelin throwers' Mecca of Helsinki.

She was so ill the week before the Championships that her doctor advised her to withdraw, but having put in so much hard work in preparation she refused to back out. She survived a crisis in the preliminary round, making it to the final only as the 12th and last qualifier with 60.96 on her third attempt (the Finnish favourite Tiina Lillak led with 69.16), but with that near disaster behind her she approached the final with excited anticipation.

Every thrower likes to seize the psychological advantage by getting in a big throw ahead of the opposition, and it fell to Fatima to achieve that in the final. She let rip with her opening throw. It was a beauty, the crowd of javelin connoisseurs watching mesmerised as it sailed on and on, finally dipping earthwards just short of the 70m line. A roar of approval erupted from the stands, repeated when the distance of 69.14 flashed on the indicator board. Fatima was in seventh heaven. Maybe not quite the best throw of her life, but what a time to unload a potential winner! What's more, she had been able to take her throw in a relaxed manner – a luxury now denied the opposition. Lillak started with 67.34, Sanderson 64.76, but nothing much else of significance occurred until the fifth round when Lillak threw 67.46 and Greece's European champion Anna Verouli supplanted Tessa as bronze medallist with 65.72. That was still the situation as Lillak, world record holder with 74.76, picked up her javelin for the final time. A wave of sound accompanied her as she made her approach run, building to a crescendo as the spear left her hand. The crowd willed a winning throw, and they got it ... 70.82. It was an emotional moment, one's joy at sharing the Finns' elation tempered by the realisation of how shattering a blow that must have been to Fatima. Of course, second place was a fantastic performance, but it was a tough way to lose after practically feeling that gold medal around her neck for so long. The last British thrower to win a global medal was hammer thrower Malcolm Nokes as long ago as the 1924 Olympics. Fatima completed her momentous season with victory in the European Cup with 69.04 to become the first British woman to win a field event in that competition.

On the basis of her performance in Helsinki, Fatima was pre-selected for the 1984 Olympics and thus free to prepare for Los Angeles as she wished. Much to her disgust, Tessa was not accorded the same privilege and perhaps it was her feeling of 'I'll show them' that was the crucial factor in her Olympic triumph. For

Fatima, though, 1984 was a disappointing season. True, she did produce a monster throw of 71.86 but that came in her first meeting of the season, a low-key affair in Cyprus.

She later underwent an operation for the removal of a growth on her womb and subsequently she developed fibroids and was haemorrhaging. It might have been prudent to have abandoned the season, but this was Olympic year and she was determined to see it through.

Disregarding medical and parental advice she went ahead and in mid-July she twice defeated Tessa with marks of over 67m, but she was fighting a losing battle against her physical problems. Just two days prior to flying out to LA she had another operation on her womb. In the circumstances her bronze medal (67.14) barely a fortnight later was a remarkable effort, but that takes nothing away from the magnificent display by Tessa whose first round 69.56 stood up as the winner. It was a proud moment for British javelin throwing with two women on the rostrum, although it should be remembered that three potential medallists were absent due to the Eastern bloc's boycott.

Restored to full vigour, Fatima ranked second globally in 1985 to Petra Felke, who had succeeded Lillak as world record holder with 75.40. Twice Fatima pushed up her personal best: to 72.12 and 72.98. In between she won all five clashes with Tessa and even gave Felke a fright in the European Cup when she threw 71.90 before the East German responded with 73.20. In all, Fatima topped 70m in six different meetings and that year she averaged 70.53 for her ten best marks, but in 1986 the figure was a staggering 72.79 as she bettered 70m in 12 separate competitions. Her consistency was amazing and even on the two occasions she was defeated that season she threw the not inconsiderable distances of 68.54 and 69.40.

She had made no secret of her desire to score a grand slam of javelin titles – Commonwealth, European, World, Olympic – and all appeared to be proceeding smoothly towards the winning of the first, and logically least difficult, gold medal in Edinburgh. She won UK and WAAA titles, comfortably beat Tessa in two domestic contests, and scored fine victories also in Belfast, Oslo and Nice.

What wasn't generally known was that her teenage brother had been taken seriously ill and that, apart from the worry that had caused, the time spent visiting him each day in hospital had thrown out Fatima's normal training routine. Although everything seemed to be going her way, she was in fact on a knife-edge emotionally and all her feelings surfaced at the Commonwealth Games. It was a competition she believed she could not lose, but when Tessa popped out a 69.80 throw in the fifth round and Fatima was unable to respond (best of 68.54 for the silver medal) it was too much for her to handle and she broke down.

Deserved plaudits for Tessa, who was prevented by injury from competing again that summer ... but there was greater glory ahead for Fatima. She showed character by immediately bouncing back after the Edinburgh debacle, producing her longest throw thus far in major competition with 72.26 in the UK v Commonwealth match five days later, and the first of her two red letter days occurred on August 28. The venue was an almost deserted Neckarstadion in Stuttgart, the time 9.19 am, the occasion the qualifying round of the European Championships. Wham! The spear flew out to the undreamed of distance of 77.44 – over two metres beyond Felke's world record. She thus became the first British thrower in history to break a world record, in the process claiming the UK record for the first time. Although nearly four and a half metres ahead of her previous best the throw was no fluke, for next day in the final – despite nursing a shoulder injury – she took the lead in the fourth round with 72.68 to Felke's second round 72.00. The East German improved to 72.52 with her final throw but the gold by then was Fatima's. She still had one more attempt and with the pressure off she was able to relax ... and the implement sailed out to 76.32, the second longest throw in history.

Fatima's fabulous form continued throughout 1987. She won 16 of her 17 contests, losing just once to Tessa, she again had 12 competitions beyond 70m and her ten best average rose to a remarkable 73.85. She threw 75.62 at the UK Championships and 76.34 ahead of Felke (72.68) in Oslo, but later Felke reclaimed the world record with 78.90.

Fatima commented: "It's just the right motivation I'm looking for. The important thing is Rome [World Championships], and I think it will need a throw of 75/76m to win." She was a good judge. In the fourth round she overtook Felke (71.76 in second round) with 73.16 and on her fifth attempt she settled the issue with 76.64, her second and the world's third longest ever throw ... and that despite suffering extreme pain in her shoulder and arm throughout the contest. Once again the by now famous 'Whitbread Wiggle' was in evidence as she celebrated her success before the TV cameras.

However, continued shoulder problems, together with hamstring and heel injuries not to mention glandular fever, an abscess and a mouth infection, conspired to turn 1988 into what Fatima described as "a nightmare". She did notch up a record eighth consecutive UK title, throwing 70.10, but she had only one other competition over 70m – although, fortunately, that was the Olympics in Seoul. Felke was by now in a class of her own, having boosted her world record to exactly 80 metres, and she duly lifted the gold medal with a throw of 74.68 but in the circumstances Fatima's 70.32 for the silver medal was a near miraculous achievement.

That, effectively, was the end of her international career. She felt in the form of her life in May 1989 when she opened with 72.26 in a local meeting but on her second throw she ruptured a small muscle that slots into her shoulder, surgery was required and her season was over before it had even started.

She was still selected for the Commonwealth Games but after finishing fourth in a warm-up meeting in Sydney in January 1990 with a mere 54.14 she withdrew from the team. She returned for the UK Championships in June, but that was even more of a disaster; she could finish only third with 51.50 and injured herself again. That was her final competitive appearance. She married former British Athletics Promotions Officer Andy Norman in 1997 and gave birth to a son but in 2005 it was reported she was seeking a divorce.

PETER ELLIOTT

Born 9.10.1962 Rawmarsh (Rotherham).
Club: Rotherham H

HE MAY NOT have won global titles or set individual world records like Seb Coe, Steve Ovett and Steve Cram, but Peter Elliott – who endeared himself to the British public with his no-nonsense attitude to racing – went closer than anyone since to attaining the very pinnacle of middle distance endeavour. He was also among the last athletes to hold down a manual job while training and racing at world class level.

He was something of an infant prodigy. He scored his first important win at 14 in the Northern Boys cross country championship and later that year (1977) became English Schools Junior 800m champion. The following season he set a UK age-15 best of 1:52.1 and in 1979 he carried all before him in his age group, winning the English Schools Intermediate and AAA Youth titles and clocking 1:50.7 for a UK age-16 best. The 1980 season was notable for his victory in the English National Youth cross country, while on the track he raced against Seb Coe for the first time, placing sixth in 1:51.3 as Coe won the Northern title in a blistering 1:44.7.

This combination of cross country and 800m success as a youngster was unusual. When, in an interview in *Athletics Today* in 1991, I asked if his career had mirrored Coe's in that instead of moving straight to 1500m he had first concentrated on building speed over 800m, he replied: "That's right. There can't be many people who have won English Schools titles at 800m and cross country. Two years ago Brendan Foster told me I had been running the wrong event, 800m, for years. Maybe, but at least by serving an apprenticeship at 800m I believe it made me a better athlete at 1500m and the mile. If I had stepped up to the 1500m earlier in my career maybe I would have been running 5000 and 10,000m by now, and believe me I would much rather run three and three-quarter laps than twelve and a half!"

Coached by Wilf Paish, the man who guided Tessa Sanderson to Olympic gold in 1984, he improved substantially in 1981 to 1:47.35 for fourth in the European Junior Championships. Having previously reduced his quickest time to 1:46.76, he scored a glorious victory in the 1982 AAA 800m in 1:45.61, breaking Ovett's UK teenage best of 1:45.77 from 1974. It takes nerve to lead all the way in a major championship against rivals with more impressive credentials than yourself, but he never relinquished the lead and even succeeded in kicking away at the end.

It was to prove a season of contrasting fortunes for Elliott. He was bitterly disappointed when the England selectors failed to pick him for the Commonwealth Games and at the same time he incurred an injury. Disillusioned and confused, he went on holiday to Spain at the time of the British Board's European Championships 800m trial – only to discover on his return that not only had he been chosen for Athens but that he was due to run the first leg in a 4x800m world record relay attempt! Still heavily suntanned and way below peak fitness, he began struggling after 600m. With strain, pain and frustration written all over his face, he handed over 10m behind the 'B' team's Rob Harrison in 1:49.14. Happily, Garry Cook (1:46.20), Cram (1:44.54) and Coe (1:44.01) made up the lost time and the British team's 7:03.89 remains the world record to this day.

Elliott withdrew from the team for Athens but didn't have long to wait for his chance of a European medal. In March 1983 he struck silver at the European Indoor Championships and that set him up well for a breakthrough that summer into world class. He improved to 1:45.49 winning the UK title and to 1:44.98 when finishing third in Oslo, a race won by Coe in 1:43.80. At this stage of his career making the final of the first World Championships in Helsinki would have been a meritorious achievement, but Elliott ran his finest race to date by finishing fourth in 1:44.87. That it was such a quick race, with West Germany's Willi Wülbeck the winner in 1:43.65, was down to Elliott and Joaquim Cruz of Brazil. Both noted front runners, they waged a tremendous duel. Cruz blazed the first 200m in 24.4 with Elliott ahead at 400m in 50.58. Along the back straight Elliott fought like a tiger to hold off Cruz but at 600m the Brazilian drew level with Wülbeck a menacing third. In the final straight, as the two pacesetters tired, the German turned on the power. Dutchman Rob Druppers came through from fourth to second in the final few strides, while Cruz held on for third. Later in the month, in Oslo, Elliott moved to third on the UK all-time list with 1:43.98 behind Cram's 1:43.61, becoming at 20 the world's youngest sub-1:44 performer.

It was in January 1984 that Elliott began racing seriously at 1500m, winning a race in New Zealand in 3:38.13, followed two days later by 3:58.54 in his first ever mile. At around this time, in an *Athletics Weekly* interview conducted by Nigel Whitefield, Elliott offered an illuminating insight into his lifestyle as a world class athlete who was also a joiner employed by British Steel. "I feel much happier at work because although it gets pretty hard as a joiner rolling around in muck all the time it does hammer home your priorities. Athletics is very important to me but it's not everything; it could all be finished tomorrow if you get an unlucky break. There's no time to get bored when you're doing a 7.30am-4pm shift and trying to fit in two or three training sessions as well." Fans of the fictitious athletics hero Alf Tupper were regarding Elliott as the new 'tough of the track'.

He duly won his 800m place in the Olympic team, winning the British trial in 1:45.72, and announced he would be challenging Coe in the AAA 1500m with a view to doubling in Los Angeles. As a stepping stone he won the Emsley Carr Mile in 3:55.71, and then came the drama of that AAA 1500m. As Cram and Ovett had already been selected, there was only one place to fill and the AAA championship was widely regarded – although not officially designated – as a run-off for that final spot.

When Coe kicked past at the start of the final straight it looked all over but Elliott never lost heart and, as Coe ran out of steam in the closing stages, he inched past to snatch victory in 3:39.66 to become the first Briton to beat Coe at this distance for eight years. Nonetheless, the selectors controversially opted for Coe to defend his Olympic crown. As I editorialised at the time: "One's sympathy must go out to Elliott, who won in such splendid fashion, and it is easy to understand his indignation at being passed over by the selectors for this event. However, taking the overall picture, the right man was picked."

The following week Elliott reduced his best to 3:36.97, but in the end it was all academic. Coe ran sublimely to defend his title with an Olympic record 3:32.53, while Elliott – who ran a season's best of 1:45.49 in the second round – had to scratch from the 800m semis because of a stress fracture of the foot.

Another stress fracture and a torn calf muscle effectively put paid to his 1985 season and it wasn't until the summer of 1986 that Elliott returned to top class racing. Over a mile in Gateshead he finished far behind world record holder Cram in 3:54.22 but at least had the satisfaction of deposing the legendary Herb (3:54.5) as the fastest ever miler by the name of Elliott! Another personal best followed at 1500m (3:35.62) while, dropping down to 800m, he picked up the bronze medal at the Commonwealth Games in Edinburgh with 1:45.42 behind Cram (1:43.22) and Tom McKean (1:44.80). Such was the strength of UK 800m running at that time that Elliott couldn't make the team for the European Championships which saw a British medal sweep by Coe, McKean and Cram.

Elliott ran supremely well to capture the silver medal at 800m in the 1987 World Championships. Although he hadn't run faster than 1:45.15 all season prior to Rome, an early season knee injury restricting his preparations, he clocked 1:43.41 in the final behind Kenyan Billy Konchellah (1:43.06). It was a fast race throughout, just as Elliott liked it. José Luis Barbosa of Brazil took the first lap in 50.59 with Elliott third, and into the finishing straight it was Konchellah, Barbosa and Elliott. Digging hard into his final resources, Elliott snatched second place in a time which made him the third quickest Briton ever behind Coe and Cram. He also made excellent progress at 1500m and in Rieti he pressed the great Moroccan, Saïd Aouita, clocking 3:33.23 to move to fourth on the UK all-time list behind Cram, Coe and Ovett. His season ended well with a 2000m time of 4:52.82, a mark bettered only by Cram among British athletes.

Previously so injury-prone, Elliott succeeded in going from January to September 1988 without missing a day's training, and his results reflected that. Now coached by Kim McDonald, a highly successful athletes' agent who was himself a 4:02.1 miler in 1983, he set UK indoor records for 1500m (3:37.9) and mile (3:53.70), but they were small beer compared to his outdoor exploits. In Oslo he ran Cram (3:48.85) close with a mile time of 3:49.20, making him Britain's fourth quickest ever, while in Brussels he lowered his 1500m time to 3:32.94 again behind Cram (3:30.95).

Unfortunately, neither Cram nor Elliott was in top form at the Seoul Olympics, although from Elliott's results you would not have realised he was running with a newly sustained groin injury necessitating daily pain-killing cortisone injections. In the 800m he entered the finishing straight second to defending champion Cruz but a medal slipped through his fingers as Kenya's unheralded Paul Ereng came through in 1:43.45 ahead of Cruz (1:43.90) and the ever remarkable Aouita (1:44.06). Elliott placed fourth in 1:44.12. However, a coveted Olympic medal did come his way in the 1500m. The early pace was slow until Kenya's Peter Rono began to stretch the field with a 56.38 third lap. With 200m to go he held a two metre lead over Elliott and that margin remained substantially unaltered until the line, the last 300m taking 39.27 and the final 400m 52.8. In the finishing straight Jens-Peter Herold (GDR) momentarily crept past Elliott on the inside but Elliott counter-attacked to make sure of the silver (3:36.15) behind Rono's 3:35.96.

The 1989 season proved low-key following another stress fracture but he was in superb form early in 1990, even contemplating an attack on Aouita's world 1500m record of 3:29.46 at the Commonwealth Games in Auckland after a spectacular training session when he ran 1200m in 2:45.9 followed, after a four minute rest, by a 38.2 300m. The windy conditions brought him down to earth but he still impressed greatly, clocking a 53.04 last lap for a winning time of 3:33.39. Six days and many time zones later he set UK indoor records of 3:36.13 for 1500m and 3:52.02 for the mile in New Jersey and a memorable February ended in Seville where he smashed the world indoor 1500m record with 3:34.21. Soon afterwards he took the decision to quit work as a joiner and become a full-time athlete.

"I couldn't believe I had run that quick" was his reaction after returning to Seville in May and winning over 800m in 1:42.97, becoming only the sixth man (third Briton after Coe and Cram) to break 1:43. He truly believed he was now ready to threaten the world records at 1500m and mile but, again, injury ruined his plans. A damaged calf muscle interrupted his season and he did well to clock 3:49.76 in Oslo's Dream Mile, being overtaken by an inspired American Joe Falcon (3:49.31) 40m from the finish, with Jens-Peter Herold (GDR) third. That was encouraging but then he lost further training time because of a chest infection and a knee injury.

Nevertheless, Elliott started as favourite to lift the European 1500m title in Split, but it wasn't to be. He was knocked over in his heat, sustaining spike wounds to the shin and shoulder plus a swollen wrist. That appeared to be that, but the Jury of Appeal added him to the final although he hadn't asked to be reinstated. As Elliott wrote in a column for *Athletics Today*: "I didn't sleep well because of the pain. Not only that, I was hardly in the right frame of mind to run, especially after I was jeered and booed by athletes and the crowd. I mean it wasn't my fault that I got in because of a rule. So I was in a no win situation, on a hiding to nothing. There was no way mentally I was ready to run." At one point on the last lap Cram and Elliott were first and second but in the end they virtually dead-heated for fourth place, Elliott finishing 1/100th ahead in 3:39.07 as the title went to Herold in 3:38.25.

Two late season races in which he was again followed home by Cram underlined Elliott's true quality. Running locally at Sheffield's new Don Valley Stadium he set a UK all-comers record of 3:32.69, while the following week he was timed at 3:47.83 in New York's slightly downhill Fifth Avenue road mile to become the first man to win the event for a third time. What a roller coaster 1990 had been. He had a Commonwealth title, the world's quickest 800m and second fastest 1500m time of the year ... but just think what might have been achieved that summer but for those setbacks.

The 1991 campaign was equally frustrating although it started so well. He became UK champion in his first attempt at 3000m (8:07.51) and gained a satisfying victory over Herold in the European Cup 1500m in a pedestrian 3:43.39 but with his fastest ever last lap of 51.12. As he remarked: "People used to think I was just a front runner without a kick, but we've been working on this kick since 1988." In July he scored a brilliant win in Oslo's Dream Mile in his second fastest time of 3:49.46 but Elliott never even got to the start line for the World Championships in Tokyo. He flew home because of a recurrent Achilles tendon problem and watched on TV as Morceli produced a 51.55 last lap to win by a street in 3:32.84. Elliott had recovered in time to confront Morceli in Brussels later in September and although he lost he finished much closer than anyone had in Tokyo with 3:32.94 to the Algerian's 3:32.38. Two days later he brought his track season to a close with an Emsley Carr Mile victory in 3:52.10. That effectively was his swansong for he raced only twice early in the 1992 season before withdrawing from the Olympic team with a knee injury. He always intended to return but further injuries conspired to make his retirement permanent. Later he helped coach fellow Yorkshireman John Mayock to record a faster 1500m time (3:31.86) than he himself ever accomplished.

LIZ McCOLGAN

Born 24.5.1964, Dundee (Scotland).
Club: Dundee Hawkhill H

WHEN LIZ MCCOLGAN ground down the opposition to win the world 10,000m title in Tokyo in 1991, Brendan Foster described it as "the greatest performance by a male or female British athlete in the history of long distance running." That judgement is still valid as far as track racing is concerned. Others may have broken world records and Paula Radcliffe has since run much faster but the fact remains that no other Briton has won a global title at 5000m or 10,000m. That run in Tokyo proved to be the summit of her career, but she made several other ascents to the upper slopes of athletic greatness, including an Olympic silver medal, a world half marathon championship, two Commonwealth titles, a world indoor record, world bests on the road and marathon victories in London and New York.

Liz Lynch didn't exactly set the world alight as a youngster. The skinny girl from a run-down Dundee housing estate had best times of 4:25.9 for 1500m and 9:34.5 for 3000m as a junior, but finishing an otherwise unremarkable 71st in the 1982 World Cross Country Championship in Rome was to prove of special significance. A recruiting scout for a junior college in Idaho had taken note of her and later in the year she was offered an athletic scholarship. A home-loving 18 year-old, her initial reaction was 'no way' but her coach, Harry Bennett, had recognised her potential (he predicted she could develop into one of the world's greatest 10,000m runners) and urged her to take advantage of the offer. Bennett, together with Liz's family and clubmates, chipped in to raise the airfare and other expenses and in February 1983 she flew west. Everything at Ricks College was totally unlike anything she had previously experienced – the weather (too cold in winter, too hot in summer), the 5000ft altitude, college life – but once she had settled down, her running thrived, and as a bonus she met fellow-student/athlete Peter McColgan, a promising steeplechaser from Northern Ireland whom she would marry in 1987.

Liz's results at junior college level were so good that she began to attract attention from more prestigious educational establishments and she transferred to the University of Alabama. In 1985 she shattered her personal bests with times of 4:15.20 for 1500m and 9:03.80 for 3000m and at the end of the summer she ran her first 10,000m, the initial step in fulfilling the prophecy of Harry Bennett who, tragically, had died of a heart attack aged 51. Her time was a Scottish record of 33:19.14, placing fourth in the World Student Games in Kobe, Japan.

Her big moment on the American scene came at the 1986 National Collegiate (NCAA) Indoor Championships when she won the mile and placed second over 3000m, but her college career was to end abruptly. She had been receiving prize money from road race events which, although channelled into a trust fund, was strictly against NCAA rules and she was declared ineligible. The transgression did not infringe Liz's status in terms of British and international competition, and she came home to further her career.

Her first big domestic victory came at the 1986 UK Championships where, in windy conditions, she led all the way to reduce her Scottish record to 32:59.59. She then exhibited impressive speed to improve her best 3000m time to another Scottish record of 8:46.53, so her international breakthrough at the Commonwealth Games in Edinburgh was not a total surprise. The first women's 10,000m to be staged at a major Games proved to be a memorable race, particularly for the Scottish fans who were treated to the sight of Liz racing away from New Zealand's Anne Audain over the last couple of laps and scoring a brilliant victory in the Commonwealth record time of 31:41.42. Tired mentally and physically a month later, at the European Championships in Stuttgart, she came down to earth when, after placing 12th in the 3000m final, she was lapped by the great Ingrid Kristiansen of Norway (30:23.25) in the 10,000m and found that her time of 31:49.46 sufficed only for seventh place.

There was still much to do to close that gap but John Anderson – who had guided Dave Moorcroft to the world 5000m record in 1982 and was now coaching Liz – understood the priorities. "If you are going to be the best in the world at 10,000m, you have to be damn near the best at 5000m, and not far off top British standard for 800m/1500m. You can't hide from the faster athletes these days, not even at 10,000m."

Liz made a momentous start to 1987. Within the space of two weeks she scored two highly lucrative 10k road victories, registering 31:58 ahead of Kristiansen in Bali and 31:07 in Orlando – the latter claimed as a world best on a loop course. She finished ahead of Kristiansen again in the World Cross Country Championship in Warsaw after an enthralling display of front running ... although the title went to the unheralded Annette Sergent of France who sprinted past the flailing Scot 120m from the line. During the summer that emphasis on speed led to a dramatic improvement in Liz's times. Her 800m came down to 2:05.9, the 1500m to a remarkable 4:01.38 which made her the fifth fastest ever Briton. At 3000m and 5000m she was a winner in Nice (8:39.85) and Oslo (15:01.08) respectively, moving to fourth and second (to Zola Budd) on the UK all-time lists. The focal point of the season was the 10,000m at the World Championships in Rome and there, despite her feet being severely blistered from the qualifying heat, she smashed the Commonwealth record with 31:19.82 in fifth place. Kristiansen won as she pleased in 31:05.85 but, although the gap was closing, Liz was devastated at losing a race she believed she could have won.

A week after her wedding in October 1987, as part of a racing honeymoon, Liz McColgan won a 10k road event in Idaho in 31:13, while in Orlando in February 1988 she was timed at 30:59 to lower her world best on a loop course. Even that did not satisfy her. She felt she was still just scratching the surface of her talent and believed not only that she was capable of close to 30 minutes for 10,000m but that a sub-2:20 marathon was on the cards, and this at a time when the world best was Kristiansen's 2:21:06. That could wait, though; first she wanted to become Olympic 10,000m champion, if not in 1988 then in 1992.

That Olympic crown started to look more realistic when, in Oslo in July 1988, she not only improved her Commonwealth record to 31:06.99 (reaching halfway in 15:19.2) but became the first woman to beat Kristiansen at the distance. She completed her Olympic racing build-up with a fine 5000m victory over Kristiansen at the IAAF Grand Prix Final in Berlin (15:03.29). However, the Seoul 10,000m, expected to be virtually a private duel, departed from the script. Kristiansen impressed with an inaugural Olympic record of 31:44.69 in her heat, but had to drop out of the final before 3000m with a foot injury. With 13 laps to go Liz took the lead, intent on burning off the opposition. With her body stooped, elbows working furiously, she ploughed on remorselessly and with a kilometre left only one woman – the USSR's former world record holder Olga Bondarenko – remained in contention. When Liz surged, she surged; when Liz eased so did she. Bondarenko was perfectly content to follow the Scot's every move, biding her time. It was with precisely 200m to go that Bondarenko launched her own bid. In a flash it was all over. In the space of that final half lap she drew 20m clear to win in 31:05.21 with Liz a gallant second in 31:08.44. "Next time it will definitely be gold," she declared.

She was as good as her word, for she did indeed strike gold in the next global 10,000m championship, but that was three years away in Tokyo. There were other remarkable happenings on the way, and none more bizarre than at the 1989 World Indoor Championships in Budapest. She ran first in the 3000m where with a fantastic piece of front running she knocked 5 sec off Zola Budd's world indoor record with 8:34.80, and still got beaten. She deserved a kinder fate, although all credit to Holland's Elly Van Hulst for staying with the ferocious pace before kicking to victory in 8:33.82. That would have been a good day's work for any other athlete, but Liz then made her way to an ambulance outside the stadium, breathed in pure oxygen while she changed her kit, and jogged back in time for the start of the 1500m just 13 minutes later! Amazingly, she clocked 4:10.16 in sixth place. One week later, in Orlando, she settled all arguments as to the world's fastest road 10k time by clocking 30:38, breaking not only her own loop course best of 30:59 but Kristiansen's 30:46 on a point to point course and 30:39 in a relay.

She looked all set for an extraordinary season but various off-the-track matters got in the way and it proved a low-key summer. That, however, increased her appetite for the Commonwealth Games in Auckland in January 1990 and there she followed up a distant third place in the 3000m (8:47.66) with a tactically uncharacteristic victory in the 10,000m. Determined for once not to lead until near the end, she allowed the race to become a dawdle with halfway reached in 16:39. Taking charge with about a kilometre remaining, Liz covered the second half in 15:44 (2:56.70 final kilometre) to retain the title in 32:23.56.

That would be her last race for the year, for on November 25 she gave birth to daughter Eilish ... who is already a more precocious runner than Liz was at her age and who in 2004, aged 13, ran 2:12.65 for 800m, 4:36.70 for 1500m and 10:17.88 for 3000m. With her father, Peter, the Northern Irish steeplechase record holder with 8:27.93 in 1991 perhaps that is the event which will prove her best. Liz, who trained through to the eighth month of her pregnancy, was back on the roads just 11 days after the birth despite experiencing acute pain from the stitches, her sights set first on the world 10,000m title in Tokyo in August 1991 and subsequently on her first marathon.

The other major event of 1990 was a less than amicable split between Liz and her coach John Anderson in August but her racing comeback early in 1991 – with husband Peter now advising her – went smoothly. Astonishingly, just 119 days after giving birth, she finished third to Lynn Jennings (USA) and Derartu Tulu (Ethiopia) in the World Cross Country Championship. A British half marathon best of 69:15 in May was another step forward but it wasn't until she smashed her Commonwealth 10,000m record with 30:57.07 in Hengelo in June that she was convinced she was on course for her target. On her own after six laps, she moved to second on the world all-time list. She won a 3000m in Nice in an outdoor personal best of 8:38.23, was almost as fast (8:39.27) when outkicked by fellow Scot Yvonne Murray in Edinburgh, and completed her preparation with victory in Zürich in 8:43.77.

Everything came together brilliantly in Tokyo, where she front ran her way to a famous victory in 31:14.31 for the first global track title by a British woman since Ann Packer in 1964. It was Liz at her uncompromising best. In hot and humid conditions she flung down the gauntlet right from the start with an opening kilometre of 3:02.95 and gradually the field of 25 fell by the wayside. Before halfway (15:34.15) even such formidable rivals as Kristiansen and Jennings were out of contention, while European champion Yelena Romanova (USSR) had dropped out. Just one athlete doggedly held on, 20 year-old Derartu Tulu who was then on the threshold of one of the most successful careers in distance running history. With 3000m to go the Ethiopian briefly got past Liz in order to slow it down and make it a sprint finish, but the canny Scot was having none of that and eventually Tulu faded to eighth place.

Just a couple of months later Liz lined up for the New York Marathon. The previous weekend she had sharpened up with a world 5k road best of 14:57 in Chicago and on the day she swept to victory in 2:27:32, at that time easily the fastest ever debut marathon. "Today was all about winning," she said. "I was not concerned at all about times. Today I was in shape to run sub-2:24." Ultimately she believed herself capable of breaking 2:20, but would not move up seriously to the marathon until she had fulfilled her 10,000m potential ... and by that she meant winning the 1992 Olympic title and breaking Kristiansen's world record of 30:13.74.

She made a terrific start to Olympic year by winning the Tokyo Half Marathon in a world best of 67:11 and setting a world indoor 5000m record of 15:03.17 in Birmingham ... with an 18 year-old Paula Radcliffe finishing fourth almost two laps behind in 16:16.77. Their paths crossed again a month later at the World Cross Country Championships in a snowy Boston. This time the glory went to Paula, winner of the Junior title, whereas an out of sorts Liz suffered her worst ever international race, placing 41st over a minute behind the winner Jennings.

Only the Olympics mattered that year, but it was not to be Liz's day in Barcelona. Her race plan was to average 72 sec per lap and run away with the gold medal in a world record time of 30 minutes. The trouble was that only her first lap was on schedule and her halfway time of 15:35.9 was not fast enough to damage her main rivals. After 6000m she fell out of contention as Elana Meyer and Tulu broke clear, the Ethiopian running out the winner in an African record of 31:06.02 and afterwards running a highly symbolic lap of honour together with runner-up Meyer, a white South African. Liz struggled to finish fifth in 31:26.11. "It was just a bad race, I couldn't breathe very well," Liz explained. In fact medical tests revealed she had been suffering from anaemia for the past six months but, after taking iron tablets, she regained top form to become world half marathon champion by covering the Great North Run course from Newcastle to South Shields in 68:53. Three weeks later, in her native Dundee, she was timed at 68:42 and in November she wrapped up a rollercoaster of a year with her second marathon victory, taking the Tokyo race by nearly half a mile in 2:27:38 with Russia's newly crowned Olympic champion Valentina Yegorova finishing fourth.

Various injuries to the knee, back, hamstring and toe took an increasing toll for the remainder of her career. After placing third in the 1993 London Marathon in 2:29:37 she was effectively out of competition for nearly two years. In 1995, her first track season for three years, she did at last break 15 minutes for 5000m with 14:59.56, but by then Radcliffe and Murray were running faster. At 10,000m a time of 31:40.14 placed sixth in the World Championships. Her two marathons proved a disappointment with fifth in London (2:31:14) and seventh in Tokyo (2:30:32), but in 1996 she achieved her last important victory, taking the London classic in 2:27:54. That was followed by 16th place in the Atlanta Olympics (2:34:30) and third in Tokyo (2:30:50). Within a few strides of the line it looked as though she would prevail again in the 1997 London Marathon, but Kenya's Joyce Chepchumba nipped past to win in 2:26:51 with Liz running her fastest ever time of 2:26:52. A race best forgotten was her 14th place in Tokyo in 2:35:45 but she bounced back one more time in 1998 when clocking 2:26:54 as runner-up in London to Ireland's Catherina McKiernan (2:26:26).

In between business activities, giving birth to three sons and carrying out her duties as Chairman of Scottish Athletics, not to mention recurring injuries, she continued to race spasmodically, clocking 56:12 for 10 miles in 2003 and, in her 40th year (2004), winning Scottish titles at cross country and indoor 3000m (9:31.11)!

ROGER BLACK

Born 31.3.1966 Portsmouth.
Clubs: Southampton & Eastleigh AC, Team Solent

RARELY HAS ANYONE made such an immediate impact on British athletics as Roger Black. As an 18 year-old in 1984 he had run 47.7 for 400m and his best competitive performance was finishing fourth in the English Schools 200m. He had enjoyed more success as a rugby winger, getting as far as an England under-16 trial. However, towards the end of 1984 he switched clubs from Fareham to Southampton & Eastleigh, joined Mike Smith's coaching group, began training seriously alongside the likes of Todd Bennett and Kriss Akabusi (who nicknamed him Bambi as his legs would invariably buckle at the end of a race) ... and seemingly in no time had developed into one of the world's most exciting 400m talents.

Indoors in 1985, such a novice he had never used starting blocks before, he set a British junior best of 47.24 and became a senior international, suffering a baptism of fire in his first major championship – the European Indoor – when he was forced off the track in his semi-final. At that stage there was a huge gulf separating himself and Bennett, who took the European gold medal in a world indoor best of 45.56, but statistically Black was breathing down his neck that summer for whereas Bennett improved his personal best to 45.35 Black made a quantum jump to 45.36. He hit that peak at the European Junior Championships in Cottbus where he won by almost a second and his time broke David Jenkins' UK junior record of 45.45 set when winning the European senior title in 1971. A second gold followed in the 4x400m relay.

The son of a doctor, Black embarked upon his medical studies at Southampton University in the autumn of 1985 but quickly realised he had made a mistake. He knew he had a special gift for running and would forever regret it if he did not pursue it as a career. As he wrote in his autobiography *How Long's The Course?*, "I was faced with a choice. I could spend the next five years reading medicine ... or I could become a full-time athlete, train three or four hours a day, spend three months out of every year in sunny California, run for my country in the Olympic Games, have fame and a degree of wealth and, more importantly, have 10,000 women screaming at me whenever I walked out into an athletics stadium. Tricky one!" Tall and blessed with film star looks, Black was widely known as 'Sex on Legs', and during an amazing 1986 season became one Britain's most successful as well as recognisable sporting stars.

The key to his improvement at 400m was the speed he could now generate. Previously no quicker than 21.6 for 200m he ran a scorching 20.63, while at 300m he broke Todd Bennett's UK best with 32.08. At the AAA Championships he ran Australia's Darren Clark (44.94) close with a personal best of 45.16 and at the Commonwealth Games in Edinburgh he easily got the better of him, again raising his game when it mattered most. From lane six, he never gave Clark, out in lane eight, a chance to get on terms. He made up the stagger by soon after the 200m mark and hit the straight with a big lead. Previously Black had been vulnerable in the closing stages, but on this occasion he fought a winning battle against lactic acid as well as Clark and maintained his exuberant stride to the finish for victory in 45.57 in extremely windy conditions.

Having become the first Briton to win this title since Bill Roberts in 1938, and going on to win another gold in the relay, Black lowered his best to 45.00 in Zürich (in seventh place!) and then came up trumps again in the European Championships in Stuttgart. He and Thomas Schönlebe waged a tremendous duel, so close (4/100ths between them) that it wasn't until the East German came over to congratulate him that he realised he had won. His time of 44.59 broke Derek Redmond's UK record and was the second fastest ever by a European. Two days later he teamed up with Redmond, his training partner Akabusi and Brian Whittle (minus a shoe!) to win the relay in 2:59.84 with an anchor leg of 43.95.

Six championship races, six gold medals, and still only 20. It couldn't go on like that and the ups and downs of life as a top athlete began to make themselves felt in 1987. In a dip finish Schönlebe pipped him, 44.96 to 44.99, in the European Cup, but Black never thereafter ran quicker than 45.58 that year as both his running and his confidence suffered as a result of persistent hip and leg injuries. He finished fourth (third Briton) in the AAA Championships in 45.92 and although selected for the World Championships in Rome he opted just for a place in the relay team. The individual title went to Schönlebe in a European record of 44.33 with Redmond fifth after breaking Black's UK record with 44.50 in his semi, while in the relay the team of Redmond, Akabusi, Black (44.81) and Phil Brown took the silver medals behind the USA in a European and Commonwealth record of 2:58.86. The injuries got worse and extended to a stress fracture of the right foot. The entire 1988 season was wiped out and he watched the Seoul Olympics on crutches with his foot in plaster following surgery. It wasn't until September 1989 that he was able to race again, clocking 46.2 in windy conditions in Jersey. The man who had helped most to get him back was international 400m hurdler Mike Whittingham, who now also trained Kriss Akabusi, and Black parted company from Mike Smith to switch to his coaching.

That low-key Jersey race, after two years in the wilderness, was a turning point. Had it gone badly, Black would probably have retired. As it was he was fired up again. He ran 45.56 in New Zealand in January 1990 as a warm-up for the Commonwealth

Games where he would run just the relay but the England team never got through the heats due to disqualification. The European Championships in Split proved a much happier affair. By now stronger (1:51.2 800m) and speedier (20.60 200m) than ever, he was the first to admit he misjudged his pace, was struggling at the finish and his time of 45.08 was slower than anticipated, but retaining the title was so sweet after those bleak times. He had a close call against arch-rival Schönlebe (45.13), his smile of relief at the finish saying it all. Another victory followed in the relay where Paul Sanders, 400m hurdles champion Akabusi, 200m champion John Regis and Black (43.96) clocked 2:58.22 for a European and Commonwealth record. Note that all bar Regis were members of the Team Solent club.

The following year would be even more memorable. Early season times of 10.57 for 100m, 20.60 for 200m and 76.2 for 600m were encouraging and he achieved the rare feat of opening his 400m campaign with 44.79 and breaking 45 sec in his next three races too. In fact he would better 45 sec no fewer than 11 times in 1991, but one of the rare occasions he didn't was at Crystal Palace where he ran 45.14 for second in his first encounter with the American who would dominate both this event and the 200m for so many years ... Michael Johnson (44.86). Black completed his racing build-up for the World Championships in Tokyo with victories in Malmö (44.71 ahead of the USA's Antonio Pettigrew 44.88) and Gateshead (45.09). Yet again he hit top form when required as he won his semi in 44.64 and clocked 44.62 in the final. He went out a little too fast, leading through 200m in 21.15 and 300m in a personal best of 32.06 and was passed 15m from the line by Pettigrew (44.57). Revenge came in the relay, where Black – normally the anchorman – instead ran the first leg. He played his part by giving the team the lead with a 44.7 stint and in an immensely exciting race Redmond (44.0), Regis (44.22) and Akabusi (44.59) combined to beat the Americans in the European and Commonwealth record time of 2:57.53. That wasn't quite all for 1991 as Black ended his season with a win in the Grand Prix Final in 44.97.

The 1992 season started promisingly with a UK title win on a windy day in 44.84 and what was probably his finest ever 200m, 20.65 into a 1.5m sec wind for third place in the AAA Championships. Worryingly, his form dipped after that, running no faster than 45.15 as a right hamstring problem held him back, and the Olympics would be a low point in his career. True, he went close to his personal best with 44.72 but that gave him only fifth place in his semi (won by the USA's Quincy Watts in an Olympic record 43.71 with David Grindley fourth in a UK record 44.47) ... and he was out. Watts proceeded to win the final in 43.50 with Grindley (19) sixth in 44.75. The relay offered some consolation in the form of a bronze medal (2:59.73) but the team was not only outclassed by the Americans, who set a world record of 2:55.74, but unexpectedly pipped by Cuba. Black was timed at 44.9 for the first leg.

Having worked so hard to get back to world class athletics after missing 1988/89 it was all the more distressing that after a couple of poor early season races in 1993 he was diagnosed as having the debilitating Epstein Barr virus, a form of glandular fever which left him perpetually tired and depressed. That kept him out of competition for practically a year, but he made a tremendous comeback to win the 1994 AAA title in 44.94, followed by a European Cup victory in 45.08. His relative lack of training caught up with him in the European Championships with heats and semis to be run, and he had to settle for second place (45.20) to team-mate Du'aine Ladejo (45.09), but in the relay he was back to his glorious best with a 43.94 third leg which ensured victory for Britain in 2:59.13. Later in the month he clocked 44.78, fastest of the year by a European.

"Full of frustration" was how Black described 1995, a season hampered by pains in the back of his left knee. "Somehow I managed to equal my personal best [from 1986] of 44.59 that year in Lausanne. I don't know how I did it, I was in absolute agony after the race." He knew he could not do himself justice at the World Championships in Gothenburg but, despite being in pain, he fought his way to the final and placed seventh in 45.28. The winner, by a huge margin, was the fabulous Michael Johnson (undefeated at 400m since 1988) in a near world record 43.39.

Black deserved a change of fortune and 1996 saw the realisation of his ambitions. Personal best sprint times of 10.48 for 100m and 20.56 for 200m in California in early May were a morale booster, and in June he won the AAA title in Birmingham in 44.39, thus regaining the UK record. However, the US Olympic 400m trial in Atlanta a few days later underlined the magnitude of Black's task in seeking a medal as Johnson (43.44) was followed home by world record holder Butch Reynolds (43.91) and Alvin Harrison (44.09). Johnson clashed with Black in Lausanne. The outcome was never in doubt, with Johnson clocking 43.66, but Black was not over-awed and took second place in a strong field in 44.37, improving his UK record and falling just 4/100ths short of Schönlebe's European record.

The Olympics saw Black at the apex of his career. Considered a likely bronze medallist behind Johnson and Reynolds, he excelled himself when on successive days he won his heat in 45.28, quarter-final in 44.72 and semi-final in 44.69, and then ran 44.41 in the final for the silver medal behind the untouchable Johnson (Olympic record 43.49), Reynolds pulling up with a hamstring injury in his semi. Black's was the first British Olympic medal in this event since Godfrey Brown in 1936, and he was absolutely delighted with it. He had been realistic enough to know that only if Johnson totally misjudged his race could the American be beaten, so instead he concentrated on running his own race to the best of his ability. As he wrote in his autobiography: "As I crossed the line, peace was what I found. After a career which had switchbacked between triumph and disaster for ten dizzying years, I had an Olympic medal. It was silver. It felt like gold – because it testified to a race which I had run to perfection, something I had been striving for since first setting foot on a track." In fact, Black left Atlanta with two silver medals, for in the relay the British squad of Iwan Thomas (44.92), Jamie Baulch (44.19), Mark Richardson (43.62) and Black (43.87) set a European and Commonwealth record of 2:56.60 to finish second to the USA (2:55.99).

Having fulfilled his aspirations in Atlanta, the rest of Black's career proved something of an anti-climax. A virus affected his running in 1997 and he never broke 45, while his final season in 1998 ended in frustration. A fantastic AAA championship was won by UK record holder (at 44.36) Thomas in 44.50 ahead of Richardson (44.62), Solomon Wariso (down from 45.70 to 44.68) and Black (44.71) ... but, to his chagrin, the selectors picked the internationally untested Wariso over himself for the European Championships. The British Grand Prix meeting in Sheffield was to have been one of Black's final stepping stones on the way to bidding for an unprecedented third European 400m title. Instead, as a result of a bewildering selectorial decision, he used the occasion to take leave of his doting public and received a standing ovation after finishing third to Richardson and Thomas, the latter going on to keep the European title in British hands in 44.52. Black has since carved out a career as a TV presenter and corporate motivational speaker.

JONATHAN EDWARDS

Born 10.5.1966 Westminster (London).
Club: Gateshead H

DIAGNOSED AS SUFFERING from the energy-sapping Epstein Barr virus following an increasingly lacklustre 1994 season, Jonathan Edwards could have been tempted to retire. He was 28, had been triple jumping for 13-years and as far as he knew he might have reached his limits anyway. It had been a good if not entirely fulfilling career, the highlights of which had included two Commonwealth Games silver medals, a splendid World Cup victory and a bronze medal in the World Championships. Among British triple jumpers he ranked second of all-time behind Keith Connor with a best of 17.44, a distance which placed him equal 36th on the world all-time list.

Fortunately, he decided to persevere. Echoing the sentiments of 1924 Olympic 400m hero Eric Liddell (of *Chariots of Fire* fame) he felt that as a committed Christian – the son of a vicar – it was his duty to develop to the full his God-given talent, even if his special gift was merely jumping a long way into a sandpit. His objective for 1995 was simply to rebuild his strength and confidence, and hopefully get back into international competition. No one, least of all himself, ever imagined that he was destined to take the art of triple jumping into a new era. His metamorphosis from just another world-class jumper to a trail blazer bordered on the miraculous.

Only a modest sprinter and long jumper as a kid, Edwards quickly found out that the triple jump suited him best and he made rapid progress: 12.75 in 1982, 13.84 in 1983 and 14.87 in 1984, in which year he won the English Schools title with a heavily wind assisted 15.01. He inched forward with 15.09 in 1985, his last year as a junior, and broke through early in 1986 with 16.05 to take the British Universities title representing Durham where he was reading physics. Towards the end of that year he began to be advised by national coach Carl Johnson and he continued to progress steadily if unspectacularly: 16.35 in 1987, 16.74 in 1988. Despite missing the selection trials because they were held on a Sunday, he made the Olympic team but his showing in Seoul hardly indicated that here was a future gold medallist as he placed 23rd in the qualifying round with 15.88.

Edwards, now working as a scientific officer in a Newcastle hospital's cyto-genetics laboratory, continued to avoid Sunday competition on religious grounds for the next four years. That caused him to miss a number of important events, most notably the memorable 1989 European Cup Final at his home stadium of Gateshead and the 1991 World Championships, but nevertheless his career proceeded promisingly. In 1989 he first exceeded the world class benchmark of 17 metres with 17.07w in Vigo and he later returned to Spain to place third in the IAAF World Cup in Barcelona with a legal 17.28 to move to third on the UK all-time list. That installed him as favourite for the Commonwealth Games title in Auckland in February 1990 but, as he confessed, "I was beaten by somebody I'd never heard of." He thought he had the event sewn up when he reached a windy 16.93 in the fourth round, but an inspired Marios Hadjiandreou of Cyprus topped that by 2cm in the fifth.

After deciding to work only part-time in order to spend more time on athletics his jumping took on a new impetus as in 1991 he progressed to 17.36 and then 17.43. Frustratingly for him and his supporters, he had to skip the World Championships, the title going to Kenny Harrison (USA) with 17.78, but for the first time he felt he could challenge the world's best. "I think I can get close to 18 metres on the right day," he ventured at a time when the world record stood at 17.97 by the event's showman, Willie Banks (USA).

To his relief and delight he was able to set his sights on the 1992 Olympics as the qualifying round was scheduled for a Saturday with the final two days later. The build-up went well; he jumped 17.26 in June and 17.22 in July, but the Games in Barcelona proved even more devastating than those of four years earlier. Expected to be in the running for a place in the first six, he could muster only an abysmal 15.76 in the qualifying competition to place 35th. While Linford Christie was dancing around celebrating his 100m triumph, Edwards was in tears.

Once he had come to terms with his immense disappointment, Edwards set about salvaging something from the season. There was one other big target – the World Cup in Havana – and there he showed his true worth with a winning jump of 17.34, good enough to have earned fourth place in Barcelona although still far behind the massive and only just wind assisted 18.17 achieved by Mike Conley (USA) when winning the Olympic crown.

It was at this time, after much soul searching, that Edwards decided he would in future compete on Sundays. He reasoned that he could best honour God by giving full rein to the undoubted but as yet unfulfilled talent he possessed as an athlete. In his first Sunday competition he jumped 17.27 for second place in the 1993 European Cup, followed five days later by a wind assisted 17.70 in Edinburgh, while at the World Championships in Stuttgart he produced a legal personal best of 17.44 for the bronze medal behind Conley (17.86) and Russia's Leonid Voloshin (17.65). That excellent result led to Edwards becoming a fully-fledged professional athlete but after an admirable victory at the 1994 AAA Championships (17.39) he began to feel increasingly lethargic and his form disintegrated. He wound up a dejected sixth (16.85) in the European Championships and in the circumstances was fairly pleased to take a silver medal in the Commonwealth Games (17.00), just 3cm behind team-mate Julian Golley. Medical tests supplied the answer to what was wrong; he was suffering from the debilitating Epstein Barr virus and rest was required.

He approached 1995 cautiously, not quite sure what to expect ... least of all that he was on the brink of becoming world record holder and champion! The season started well enough as he added a centimetre to Connor's UK record with 17.58 at Loughborough, and it just kept getting better. Two weeks later, at the European Cup in Lille on June 25, he created a sensation. News of his wind assisted jumps of 18.43 (+2.4m) and 18.39 (+3.7m) reverberated around the world with many followers of the sport initially wondering whether they were reading misprints for the rather more likely 17.43 and 17.39. As Malcolm Folley put it in his biography *A Time To Jump*, "Edwards had just gone from being Clark Kent to Superman without visibly visiting a phone booth."

That 18.43, the first 60ft clearance and comprising a hop of 6.50, step of 5.60 and jump of 6.33, was no fluke result, though. During the series he had a legal effort of 17.72 for another British record, and in his next competition – on home ground at Gateshead – he registered a windy 18.03 and an officially accepted 17.74. That was followed by 17.69 at Crystal Palace and on July 18 he succeeded Banks as world record holder with 17.98 in Salamanca with its friendly 800m altitude. He opened with 17.39 and then bounced his way to 17.98 with the wind gauge registering 1.8m. He thus became the first Briton (as distinct from Irishman) to set a world triple jump record ... but he wasn't entirely satisfied. "Technically the jump was not good." In his next competitions he recorded 18.08w in Sheffield and 17.58w at altitude in Sestriere, and then it was time for the World Championships in Gothenburg where he would carve a permanent niche for himself in athletics' Hall of Fame.

The date was August 7, and his first attempt in the final brought the crowd to its feet with a massive world record shattering jump of 18.16 (+1.3m) which was as aesthetically pleasing as it was athletically imposing. Quick and deceptively strong for a man of slim build, Edwards was a joy to watch in action as following an 18-stride approach run he skimmed smoothly from one phase to another in stark contrast to the crash-bang-wallop style of many of his rivals. The individual components of the 18.16 were 6.12, 5.19 and 6.85. One round later he made further history as, with plenty of room on the board, he cut the sand at 18.29 (+1.3m), causing even Americans to gasp in wonder as that translated to the world's first authentic 60-foot jump. He hopped 6.05, stepped 5.22 and jumped a phenomenal 7.05. He thus became the first triple jumper ever to set two world records back to back. Not surprisingly, Edwards totally demoralised the rest of the world's elite. Although world indoor champion Brian Wellman from Bermuda did reach a highly respectable 17.62w the winning margin of 67cm – over two feet – was the widest at Olympic or World Championship level since 1896.

The bemused Edwards was unable to pinpoint the reason for the extraordinary progress which had made him the Bob Beamon of triple jumping. His coaching team now comprised Norman Anderson (weights and gym work) and Peter Stanley (technical) as Carl Johnson's role diminished, he was faster and stronger than ever and his new arm action modelled after Mike Conley's helped his balance and thrust, but none of those factors fully explained a stunning five per cent improvement. Perhaps Wellman got it right when he said the key was Edwards' maintenance of high speed throughout all three phases. Others have tried to reproduce that flowing velocity but no one has yet approached Edwards' distances.

Edwards finished up winning all 14 of his competitions in 1995, including a late season 18.00 at Crystal Palace, and scooped just about every award going, notably being voted the IAAF's male athlete and the BBC Sports Personality of the year. The downside after such an *annus mirabilis* was that everyone was already hanging the Olympic gold medal around his neck, a huge burden for any athlete. It was a no-win situation: if he triumphed in Atlanta it would only be a confirmation of the obvious, while anything short of victory would be deemed a failure.

The 1996 campaign started well with a personal best 100m of 10.48 in Florida, followed by a morale boosting win (17.59w) at a meeting held to inaugurate Atlanta's Olympic Stadium. He continued to keep a clean sheet right up to the Games, his season's best of 17.82 topping the world list although ominously the frequently injured Kenny Harrison had won the US trial – his first contest for 16 months – with a windy 18.01. After qualifying for the final with 17.58, his best legal mark for five years, Harrison opened up with an Olympic and American record of 17.99. Edwards, by contrast, was encountering a crisis. He fouled his first two trials, only to produce 17.13 and a reprieve at the third attempt. The real action came in round four. Edwards moved into second position with 17.88 but Harrison completed the round with a timely 18.09, the third longest legal jump in history after Edwards' two world record efforts in Gothenburg. The pressure now was on Edwards but his last two attempts, although way beyond 18m, were fouls and his 22-win streak came to an end. His 17.88 still ranks as easily the longest ever non-winning performance.

Edwards beat Harrison by a big margin in their next five encounters – in Zürich, Gateshead, Brussels, Berlin and the IAAF Grand Prix Final in Milan – but Harrison nailed him in their final encounter of the year in Tokyo. Usually the Olympic champion earns top spot in Olympic year, but the American magazine *Track & Field News* ranked Edwards no 1 and the *Athletics International* panel came up with a tie. Harrison, a year older than Edwards, would never again be in contention for the top world ranking, but Edwards would continue at the highest level for many more years in pursuit of his Olympic dream.

The 1997 season proved frustrating. Edwards was intent on retaining the world title in Athens but in June, in the process of pulling off a fine European Cup victory with 17.74, he incurred bruising to his left heel which would play havoc for the rest of the summer. At the World Championships, Yoelbi Quesada opened with 17.60 and a Cuban record of 17.85 (best in the world that year) and Edwards had his hands full staving off another Cuban, Aliecer Urrutia, for second place, 17.69 to 17.64.

He was not happy; indeed he was in tears afterwards. Echoing the sentiments of Ian Stewart, he remarked: "Silver's better than nothing but not much."

Edwards won only five of his ten contests in 1997 but the following year saw him back on top by a wide margin. Needing a short-term goal following the summer's disappointments, he elected to compete indoors for the first time since 1994 and smashed Keith Connor's UK indoor record with 17.64 in Birmingham, leaving Quesada trailing at 17.20.

A fortnight later he captured the European indoor title with 17.43. Outdoors, he came up with his longest jump (18.01) since his world record. It happened in Oslo, in the first of the IAAF's newly created Golden League meetings. It was timely, too, as Russia's Denis Kapustin led 17.65-17.46 until Edwards' final effort. A subsequent victory in Rome (17.60) suggested Edwards could be in line for the million dollar jackpot to be shared by athletes who could win at all seven Golden League events but, hampered by a sore ankle, he fouled three times in Monaco and that dream was over. Just four days later he won in Zürich (17.75) and he followed that by lifting the European title in Budapest with 17.99, a massive 54cm clear of defending champion Kapustin.

He underwent arthroscopic surgery on his troublesome ankle the following month but it didn't solve all his injury problems and 1999 proved a disappointing year. Although he was world ranked no 1 by *Athletics International* in a subdued season for triple jumping he never jumped farther than 17.52 (other than a windy 17.71) and, by his standards, the World Championships in Seville were a write-off as he placed third (17.48) behind Charles Friedek of Germany (17.59) and Bulgaria's Rostislav Dimitrov (17.49). "I couldn't envisage not winning," he said. "It was a complete disaster."

Now aged 34, a virtual geriatric in triple jumping terms, Edwards embarked upon his fourth and final Olympic campaign. At least this time it was not being assumed that he had only to turn up in Sydney to be awarded the gold medal and he welcomed the pressure being less acute than prior to Atlanta. He travelled 'down under' top of the world list for 2000 with 17.62. and there in Sydney he fulfilled his destiny to become easily the oldest ever Olympic champion in this most physically demanding of disciplines.

He went ahead in the second round with 17.37, to which Kapustin responded with 17.46, but with his third jump Edwards leapt to 17.71, the world's longest of the year and the winning distance although some way short of his unavailing 17.88 behind Harrison in Atlanta. That's how it stayed until the final round when Quesada knocked Britain's Larry Achike (17.29) out of the medals with 17.37, only to be deposed himself by Cuban team-mate Yoel García's last gasp silver medal winning 17.47. With Achike finishing fifth and Phillips Idowu sixth (17.08) this was Britain's best ever showing in an Olympic field event. Unremarked among the non-qualifiers was a gangling 20 year-old Swede, Christian Olsson, the reigning European junior *high* jump champion. He would swiftly develop into Edwards' main rival for the remainder of the Briton's career and succeed him as Olympic champion.

Olsson improved from 16.97 to 17.49 in 2001 and did beat him twice but Edwards won all 15 of his other outdoor competitions, including four against Olsson and notably the all-important World Championships in Edmonton, Alberta. Edwards (17.26) had placed second to Italy's inspired Paolo Camossi (17.32) at the World Indoor Championships in Lisbon but was in much better form in Canada.

He had a scare, though, in the qualifying competition. He was in deep trouble after wasting his first jump and reaching only 16.51 on his second for 16th overall. One last try ... the Edwards magic returned and he bounced out to 17.46 to lead the qualifiers. In the final he opened with a modest 16.84 and after a tantalising second attempt (landing at about 18m from the most minuscule of fouls) he was in fourth place with Olsson the leader at 17.47. His third jump, though, was an Edwards special of 17.92, his and the world's longest for three years. At 35 he was world champion again.

Edwards topped the world merit rankings for the seventh time in 2002, although Olsson was now breathing down his neck. The score was 5-4 in Edwards' favour but although both Olsson (17.53) and Friedek (17.33) finished ahead of Edwards (17.32) in the European Championships, the grand master of triple jumping did enough elsewhere to merit the no 1 spot.

Whereas Olsson's best all year was 17.64, Edwards jumped 17.75 in Paris and 17.78 in Stockholm, and came up with the world's leading mark of 17.86 (with Idowu a marvellous second at 17.68) when winning at the Commonwealth Games. For 11 days Edwards claimed the distinction of holding Olympic, World, Commonwealth and European titles simultaneously. He then lost the European crown but there was some consolation when he ended the season with victory in the World Cup, the contest in which he had first displayed true world class form 13 years earlier.

The curtain came down in 2003, by which time he was spending more time as a BBC television presenter than on athletics training. He placed fourth in the World Indoor Championships (17.19), the title going to the now super-consistent Olsson at 17.70, and took part in just four outdoor meetings. The first of those, in Gateshead, produced a remarkable result in that Edwards made his best ever non-windy debut to a season with 17.61 (a world age-37 best!) behind Olsson's windy 17.92 and legal 17.74. But it was downhill after that with third places in Stockholm (17.14) and London (17.19), being stretchered off on the latter occasion after twisting his ankle.

That could have been the end, but he returned in time for the World Championships in Paris. The sixth best qualifier with 16.94, his final competition proved to be a melancholy farewell.

While Olsson sewed it up with his opening leap of 17.72, Edwards collapsed going into the jump phase on his first attempt and his second (16.31) was a very tentative effort. Deciding he wasn't sufficiently fired up to challenge for a medal (bronze went at 17.26), he passed up his third attempt and thus finished 12th and last. A fabulous career was over ... but that world record remains unapproached after a decade.

JOHN REGIS

Born: 13.10.1966 Lewisham (London).
Clubs: Herne Hill H, Belgrave H

THE SON OF the champion bodybuilder of St Lucia, the immensely powerful physique of John Regis made him the most recognisable of sprinters. He was also one of the most versatile of speed merchants, his achievements including the distinction of being the only man to win four medals in a single European Championships, a world indoor 200m title and so very nearly an outdoor one, a European low altitude 200m best, a World Championships gold medal at 4x400m relay and one of the fastest 200m hurdles times on record.

Regis started off, however, as a triple jumper, reaching 14.28 as a 15 year-old in 1982 when winning the European Catholic Schools title in Spain. A certain Jonathan Edwards, who was five months older, did no better than 12.75 that season! As a first year junior in 1984 Regis ran a promising 21.31 for 200m and made a momentous decision. Until then, football had been his main sport. A cousin of England centre forward Cyrille Regis, he had played at Charlton, Newcastle and Arsenal as a schoolboy and was on the Gunners' books, but decided for a year at least to concentrate on athletics.

It was during that year (1985) that he really started to make an impression and he put football behind him. He dead-heated with Linford Christie for the UK 200m title, improved his 200m time to 20.78, and at the European Junior Championships in Cottbus he gained a bronze medal in the 100m in his best legal time of 10.51 and anchored Britain to victory and a UK junior record of 39.80 in the relay.

By 1986, still a teenager, he was ready to mix it with the best seniors; indeed he became the fastest European at 200m that summer when winning the AAA title in 20.41. That made him the third quickest Briton of all time behind Allan Wells (20.21) and Todd Bennett (20.36) and he had high hopes for the two major championships to follow. However, he placed a listless eighth in the Commonwealth Games (21.08w) and as a consequence failed to make the team for the European Championships. A feeling that his preparation had been wrong led to a change of coaches and he left Eric Bennett to join John Isaacs' group at Haringey.

He prospered under the new set-up and enjoyed an excellent winter season in 1987. He improved upon the UK indoor record three times, climaxing with 20.54 for the bronze medal in the European Indoor Championships, a race won in a world record 20.36 by Bruno Marie-Rose of France. Significantly, too, he ran his first 400m relay leg in an England v USA match at Cosford ... and he was a revelation. He was timed at 45.6, great running indoors – but it hurt!

Outdoors, despite losing nearly eight weeks of full training after injuring an ankle playing badminton, he won the AAA title in the UK all-comers and English record time of 20.25. "I can't believe it," he gasped. "But I hope I can run faster still in Rome." He did, for at the World Championships he not only broke Wells' UK record with 20.18 (into an 0.4m wind) but he very nearly stole the title. Running his best ever bend despite being drawn in lane two, he was in the lead with ten metres to go ... at which point he admits he panicked, allowing Calvin Smith (USA) and Gilles Quenéhervé of France to edge past and share a time of 20.16. The only other Briton ever to have got so close to winning a global 200m title was Wells when he finished 2/100ths behind Pietro Mennea at the 1980 Olympics.

Regis himself now loomed up as a potential Olympic medallist at the 1988 Games in Seoul and his build up went well with a personal best 100m of 10.31, a 20.32 200m and a time of 46.57 in his individual 400m debut. But the Games proved to be an acute disappointment.

"I was useless," he admitted. "I had trained harder than I believed was possible and had failed to do myself justice." Expecting a recall that never materialised, he was left in his heat of the 100m, and was eliminated at the semi-final stage of the 200m with 20.69. To rub salt into the wound, arch-rival Christie broke Regis's UK 200m record with 20.09. However, consolation followed in the relay where Regis and Christie, along with Elliot Bunney and Mike McFarlane, set a UK record of 38.28 to finish second to the USSR's 38.19, the closest to a British win in this event since 1912.

Finishing second to team-mate Ade Mafe in the 1989 European Indoor Championships, 20.92-21.00, was a reasonable result but his moment of glory came in Budapest where he left Mafe over three metres behind to win Britain's first ever World Indoor Championships gold medal in 20.54, equalling his UK indoor record. Regis had his moments outdoors that summer but his fastest time of the year was a somewhat disappointing 20.35.

Much more rewarding was Regis' outdoor campaign in 1990. It started early at the Commonwealth Games in Auckland in January where after a legal personal best of 10.25 in his semi he placed seventh in the 100m (10.22w), finished second to clubmate Marcus Adam (20.10w) over 200m in 20.16w, and played his part in England's 4x100m victory (38.67). Better was to come seven months later in Split, for he ended up with four medals – the most any man has ever won in a single edition of the European Championships.

After a personal best of 10.20 in his 100m semi he took the bronze in the final in an only just wind-aided 10.07 (+2.2m/sec), gold going to Christie in 10.00. Two days later he ran his fastest 200m time of 20.16 in his semi, prior to winning the final by a two metre margin in 20.11 (nil wind), and then contributed to Britain's UK record 4x100m mark of 37.98 along with Darren Braithwaite, Adam and Christie in second place to France's world record breaking 37.79. His ninth race provided a golden finale when, as Britain's 'secret weapon', he simply ran out of his socks in the 4x400m. Following legs of 45.9 by Paul Sanders and 44.4 by 400m hurdles champion Kriss Akabusi, Regis thought he might be capable of something in the mid-44's on the third stage. Instead he blasted through the first 200m in 20.5 or faster and held on heroically to be electrically timed at 43.93! Individual 400m champion Roger Black completed the job with a 43.96 stint, enabling the team to win by a 20m

John Regis

margin in a European record of 2:58.22. *Athletics Today* ranked Regis as no 3 in the world at 200m, behind Michael Johnson (USA) and Brazil's Robson da Silva.

Although he went very close to his best time with a 20.12 victory in Lausanne and clocked an intrinsically superior 20.16 into a 1.1m wind for third place in Zürich behind Michael Johnson and Frank Fredericks of Namibia, Regis wound up sixth in the world merit rankings for 1991. He was dragged down by his failure to make the final in the World Championships in Tokyo, placing a disappointing fifth in his semi in 20.52 while Johnson (20.01) and Fredericks (20.34) went one-two in the final.

Much earlier in the summer Regis had equalled the previous European best of 22.79 for 200m hurdles, behind Colin Jackson (world best of 22.63) and Nigel Walker (22.77), and set a European 300m best of 31.99. Fortunately for Regis in Tokyo there were two relays to contest and he returned home a hero. In the 4x100m he took a bronze medal (38.09) but his golden moment came some 80 minutes later in the 4x400m.

Roger Black handed over in the lead after the first leg (44.7) but despite running 44.0, Derek Redmond, up against an amazing 43.4 split by Quincy Watts, passed the baton to Regis nearly four metres adrift of the Americans. He needed to produce something special, not just for the team but for himself, and he came up with the goods, clocking 44.22 to gain valuable ground on Danny Everett. Even so, Akabusi took over a daunting three metres behind world champion Antonio Pettigrew but with a beautifully judged 44.59 split he clinched a famous victory for Britain in the European and Commonwealth record time of 2:57.53.

Regis eventually split from Isaacs and began working with Mike Whittingham (speed endurance) and Mike McFarlane (technique and speed). The new set-up led to Regis running his best times for 200m, 300m and 400m, but he fell short of expectations in the 1992 Olympic 200m final.

There were some excellent results on the way; he beat Christie, 20.27 to 20.29 into a 1.5m wind, at the Olympic Trials; he improved the European and Commonwealth 300m record to 31.67; and in Barcelona he clocked 20.16 in his quarter final and equalled Christie's UK record of 20.09 in his semi. In the final, though, he slumped to 20.55 for sixth place, far behind the 20.01 by American winner Mike Marsh.

The 4x100m (fourth in 38.08) brought further frustration but the 4x400m at least yielded a bronze medal with Regis, on the anchor leg for the first time, record-ing 45.0. A few days later he was tempted to run an individual 400m, reducing his personal best to 45.87 in windy conditions.

Regis might have worried that he had lost the knack of rising to the big occasion at 200m, but in 1993 he reached new heights. Early season races indicated he was stronger and fleeter than ever, for he set personal bests both at 400m (45.48) and 100m (10.15). He had always believed that when he got his time down to around 10.15 he would be ready to break 20 sec for 200m, and at the World Championships in Stuttgart he was proved right.

He ran 20.16 in his semi and in the final, as in Rome six years earlier, he found himself in the lead approaching the finish. He had led at the 100m mark in a tremendous 10.28 ahead of Carl Lewis (10.31) and knew he had the measure of him in the straight ... but Fredericks, only fourth at halfway in 10.39, was in the process of delivering one of his spectacular finishes and edged past for victory by a metre in the African record time of 19.85.

Regis, timed at a world best of 14.93 at 150m, clung on to second place and with his brilliant 19.94 (+0.3m wind) not only smashed the UK record but became the swiftest ever European at 'sea level'. Another silver came Regis' way in the 4x100m where Colin Jackson, Tony Jarrett, himself and Christie broke the European record with 37.77 behind the USA.

Regis, merit ranked second in the world to Fredericks in 1993, dropped back to third (behind Johnson and Fredericks) in 1994, which would prove to be his last season at such an exalted level. An early highlight, in California in April, was a 200m relay leg timed in 19.1, the fastest on record, against 19.4 by Carl Lewis. Even that was overshadowed by his exploit in Sestriere high up in the Italian Alps at the end of July when, aided by the 2050m altitude and a friendly 1.8m/sec wind, he set a UK record (although never ratified) of 19.87 – the world's fastest that year – ahead of 19.97 by Fredericks.

He followed that two days later with another splendid performance in Monte Carlo, registering 20.01 behind Johnson's 19.94. with Fredericks fourth. An Achilles tendon injury prevented Regis defending his European title and although he returned in time to run 20.25 in the Commonwealth Games he was no match for Fredericks' 19.97. He did, however, beat him in the last big event of the season, the World Cup, in 20.45 from the inside lane.

He enjoyed another good win over Fredericks in Nice with his best time of 1995 (20.26) but finished a distant seventh (20.67) in the World Championships as the incomparable Johnson won in 19.79 ahead of Fredericks (20.12). The decline continued in 1996; his best sea level time was 20.47 and he failed to reach the Atlanta Olympic final in which Johnson ran his phenomenal 19.32. Injury ruled out practically the entire 1997 season, but he made a decent comeback in 1998 to clock 20.40 for the bronze medal at the Commonwealth Games behind England team-mate Julian Golding (20.18) and Welshman Christian Malcolm (20.29). In 1999 he missed his indoor personal best by only 2/100ths with 20.50 but wasn't able to approach that form again and he switched his attention to the management side of the sport.

SALLY GUNNELL

Born: 29.7.1966 Chigwell (Essex).
Club: Essex Ladies AC

ANN PACKER STARTED off as a hurdler, long jumper and pentathlete before eventually achieving immortality as Olympic 800m champion, and Sally Gunnell likewise competed in a wide variety of events before finding her forte, the 400m hurdles, in which she became Olympic and world champion and world record holder. Young athletes and their coaches don't always know what event will ultimately be their best and drawing upon her own experience Sally has said: "I would advise youngsters to try as many events as possible – I even used to run cross country – and don't decide to specialise until later on in life."

It was touch and go whether Sally took up athletics seriously at all. At school she was equally into gymnastics and it was only when a friend plumped for athletics that she decided to follow suit. At the age of 11 she joined Essex Ladies and it was as a long jumper that she achieved her early successes: she was WAAA and English Schools Junior champion in 1980 and the WAAA Intermediate winner the following year. In 1982 she contested her first heptathlon, her score of 4771 incorporating such personal bests as a 5.84 long jump, 25.5 200m and 15.0 100m hurdles. Her development under the guidance of Bruce Longden, who had coached Daley Thompson to Olympic gold, was swift and in 1983 she produced an impressive array of marks: 24.56 200m, 2:16.99 800m, 13.71 100m hurdles, 1.67 high jump, 6.08 long jump and 5564 heptathlon, a British age-16 best.

Her final season at heptathlon was 1984. She improved to 5680, an age-17 best which came close to winning her Olympic selection, but by then the 100m hurdles was emerging as her strongest event. She set a UK junior record of 13.30 when finishing second to Shirley Strong (destined to become Olympic silver medallist later that summer) in the WAAA Championships, a time that ranked her as the fastest junior in the world, but she missed her chance of qualifying for Los Angeles as she was not invited to the Olympic Trials.

Two years later she was crowned Commonwealth champion. Much faster on the flat than ever before with wind aided sprint times of 11.79 and 23.38 to her name she won the title in Edinburgh with a personal best of 13.29. She improved that to 13.11 prior to the European Championships but her time of 13.22 in Stuttgart placed her only sixth in her first round heat and the title went to Bulgaria's Yordanka Donkova in 12.38.

Her target in 1987 was to break 13 sec and she came so close. On three occasions she was clocked at 13.01, making her the second fastest Briton of all time behind Strong (12.87 in 1983). However, there was still a chasm between her standards and those of the very top performers. At the World Championships she went out in the semis with 13.06 while another Bulgarian, world record holder (at 12.25) Ginka Zagorcheva, took the gold medal in 12.34. Bruce Longden was realistic enough to know that gap could never be fully bridged and persuaded her to try a low-key 400m hurdles race in June 1987, and although she hadn't trained or practised for it ("I mucked up every hurdle," she confessed) she won in 59.9.

As Sally told me in an interview for *Athletics Today* two years later: "I thought at the time it was a bit strange going out and doing that event, but I suppose Bruce had ideas then but was waiting for the right time to switch events. I think he wanted me to reach my peak first at 100m hurdles; he wanted me to get that before making the change as I was still young and there was plenty of time left." A 51.9 400m relay leg that season was another pointer to the future.

Sally enjoyed the best of all possible worlds in 1988. Not only was her potential at the sprint hurdles pretty well fulfilled (she thought 12.78-12.80 would be her limit) but in her first serious season at the event she became a top class 400m hurdler. Never having raced 400m from blocks before, she made a brilliant start to the year during the indoor season. She began with 53.80 and progressed to 53.28, 52.81 and 52.22 before breaking Verona Elder's UK record with 51.77 for fourth place in the European Indoor Championships. Outdoors in June she was unlucky to lose what would have been a UK record 12.86 100m hurdles time as the wind was 2.1m/sec and lowered her 400m hurdles best to 57.5 and 56.47.

In July she clocked her fastest ever mark of 12.80 (+3.3m wind, though) while in August her results included three British records: 55.40, 12.82 (0.8m wind) and 55.00. Her results at the Seoul Olympics in September confirmed the wisdom of doubling up: she went out in the semis of the shorter race in 13.13 (Donkova taking the title in 12.38) but set another UK record of 54.48 in her 400m hurdles semi and went faster still in the final with 54.03, fighting her way from seventh to fifth in the finishing straight. Debbie Flintoff-King, the Australian who won in an Olympic and Commonwealth record time of 53.17, said of Gunnell: "She is going to be a danger in the future. To do what she has done so quickly is great." Sally wasn't finished yet, and in the 4x400m relay she produced a 51.04 anchor leg as Britain finished sixth.

The 1989 season began promisingly when Sally won the European Indoor 400m title in 52.04 but her chances of lifting the World Indoor title a fortnight later evaporated when she drew the inside lane and she finished sixth and last in 52.60. Although she didn't approach her UK record (her best was 54.64), Sally finished second in the European Cup and third in the World Cup and moved up the world merit rankings that summer. Fifth in 1988, she was rated third behind Sandra Farmer-Patrick (USA) and Petra Krug (GDR).

The Commonwealth Games in Auckland early in 1990 saw Sally come away with two golds and a silver. She won her speciality event in 55.38, ahead of Flintoff-King, kept her hand in as a sprint hurdler by finishing second (13.12) to Kay Morley of Wales (12.91), whose sister Sue was UK 400m hurdles record holder before Sally, and ran third leg for the victorious England 4x400m relay team. The summer campaign proved a disappointment, though; she never ran faster than 55.35 and wound up a stuttering sixth in the European Championships (55.45) although she did obtain a bronze medal in the relay (UK record 3:24.78). Her world ranking in the hurdles was tenth ... but her apprenticeship was now at an end and the glory years were just about to commence.

Evidence of her improved endurance came during the indoor season when she ran 800m in 2:08.36, and early in the outdoor season she ran an impressive 51.11 for 400m to rank fifth on the UK all-time list. She was also still a sprint hurdler to reckon with, even though that event was merely a diversion by now, and she won the WAAA title in 13.02, her fastest for three years. Clearly something special at

400m hurdles was imminent and within the space of four days she twice broke her UK record with splendid victories in Monte Carlo (53.78) and Zürich (53.62).

She travelled to Tokyo for the World Championships as a likely medallist, a possible winner, and came so very close to snatching the title. The chubby and unpredictable European champion, Tatyana Ledovskaya, chose this occasion to run the race of her life. She held a lead of several metres entering the finishing straight and although Sally closed considerably – and might have won had she not momentarily lost concentration and stuttered before the final barrier – the Belarussian scraped home by 5/100ths in 53.11, the second fastest time ever behind the world record of 52.86 by Marina Styepanova (USSR) set in 1986. Sally's time of 53.16 was the third quickest ever and broke Flintoff-King's Commonwealth record.

"I was a bit worried about going off too fast because I knew if I had gone with her I could easily have blown up," Sally explained. "I wanted to run my own race, which I did and all that went wrong was the last hurdle." Able to hurdle efficiently off either leg, she had run fifteens to the sixth hurdle, sixteens to the eighth barrier and seventeens home.

She translated her exceptional form to the relay. She was timed at a spectacular 49.6 for her anchor leg in the heats and travelled even faster in the final with 49.46 on the third leg (23.5 at 200m!). She improved the team's position from fourth to third but eventually Britain placed fourth in a UK record 3:22.01. A further boost to her morale came at the end of the year when *Athletics Today* ranked her no 1 in the world.

The build-up towards the Barcelona Olympics of 1992 did not go as smoothly as hoped. The flamboyant tutu-clad Farmer-Patrick beat her in Stockholm (54.59-54.64) and Lille (54.88-55.20) and it wasn't until after she had won in London in a season's best of 54.40 that she felt everything was clicking nicely into place. She went to Barcelona as third fastest of the year behind Farmer-Patrick (53.62) and former world record holder Margarita Ponomaryova (54.03). Here is how Sally described her thrilling Olympic experience when interviewed by me for *Athletics Today* a few weeks later:

"I had a certain amount of confidence beforehand, and was talking about medals, but as I went through the heats and semis that's when I realised I could win. I was lucky; I had the easier semi for sure, had a good run [53.78] and was given the best lane [three with Farmer-Patrick in four] for the final. I was really quite calm for the final. I was quite surprised; I thought I would be a nervous wreck. The race that I ran was one of the races that I had been running in my mind, so it just went to plan. I ran fifteens to hurdle six, changed down at seven and then sixteens home. It was the first time I had ever managed that.

"I remember going down the back straight thinking 'okay, I haven't lost too much on Sandra, I'm in a good position.' Then my next thought was coming off the eighth hurdle, being level almost and realising that a lot of people had said to me that if I could be up there at the eighth hurdle it was mine on the way home. That gave me a lot of positive thought and I just concentrated so hard down the home straight. I ran very conservatively at the beginning just to keep my energy for the last part of the race. So many people went off so fast and that's why, apart from Sandra [53.69] and I [53.23], the times were very slow. They all hammered it out.

"I really stretched for the last hurdle. Last year I had a negative thought at that stage, but this time I was so determined and had run it so often in my mind that I was going to get there. I was still running scared, waiting for Sandra to come up, but I was just as determined that she wasn't going to be able to. Technically, it was my best race. All the way around that lap of honour I just couldn't believe I had done it. It was like being in a dream world."

To add to her gold medal she picked up a bronze in the relay (3:24.23) where after good work by Phylis Smith, Sandra Douglas and Jenny Stoute she anchored the squad with a 50.4 split. And, as if all that was not enough excitement for one year, Sally was married two months later on a Florida beach to Jon Bigg, a 1:48.40 800m runner she had met on a junior international trip to Australia in 1985.

As Olympic champion her life was transformed, her new commitments including television work (initially standing in for Sue Barker as a presenter on Sky Sports and in recent years best known as a trackside interviewer for the BBC). But she was not one to rest on her laurels and in 1993 she created further history by becoming world record holder.

The season went perfectly. Her flat speed was never better, ranking third in Britain at 200m with 23.30 and top at 300m (36.44) and 400m (51.29 plus 49.8 relay anchor), while in a rare outing at 100m hurdles she captured yet another national title in 13.08. At 400m hurdles she went undefeated up to and including the World Championships in Stuttgart. She clocked 53.73 in the European Cup in Rome, 53.86 in Lausanne and 53.52 in Zürich. In Stuttgart she prevailed after a titanic battle with Farmer-Patrick, the Jamaican-born American.

Here is how she described the race in her autobiography, *Running Tall*: "I came off the eighth hurdle and Sandra was in the lead, but I knew I could get her! I closed up on her a bit as we went over the ninth, and closed up a bit more on the tenth. Sandra was still slightly in the lead as we hit the ground – she's always fast on the flat, the hurdling is the weakest part of her race – but I was looking straight ahead, knowing she was there but not knowing how close she was or anything at all ... and then I was just going and going and going for the line. It was like a slow-motion film again, going for the line. I dived forward, thrusting my chest out. I crossed the line, and I didn't know whether I had won or not."

Analysis of the splits at each hurdle show that Farmer-Patrick was 0.04 ahead at the ninth, 0.08 at the tenth, but victory went to Sally, 52.74 to 52.79, with both inside the world record. And once again there was another medal to come in the relay, where Sally ran 49.90 on the anchor leg for third place in 3:23.41. She was voted woman athlete of the year in the poll conducted by the International Athletic Foundation.

More honours came her way in 1994. She lost only once in her speciality, finishing second to her future successor as world champion and record holder Kim Batten in Nice, 53.72-53.91, but she beat the American in all four of their other encounters for a fourth consecutive no 1 world ranking.

Two days later she won the flat 400m in a match against the USA in a personal best of 51.04 and followed up with 53.51 (to Batten's 54.22) in the Goodwill Games, gold medal triumphs in both the European Championships (winning by a huge 1.35 sec margin in her season's best of 53.33) and Commonwealth Games (54.51), and the World Cup (54.80). She thus joined Daley Thompson and Linford Christie as the only athletes to complete the grand slam of titles: Olympic, World, European and Commonwealth. She was busy in relays, too. She clocked her fastest ever split of 49.45 for fourth place in the Europeans (3:24.14) and anchored England and Britain to victory in the Commonwealth Games and World Cup respectively.

She wasn't to know it at the time, for at 28 she felt she could still improve, but her medal winning days were now at an end. Foot injuries restricted her to just two 400m flat races in 1995 and although in 1996 she ran 54.65 to win the AAA hurdles title followed by a 51.45 400m she pulled up injured in Lausanne and broke down again in her Olympic semi-final in Atlanta.

The title passed to Jamaica's Deon Hemmings, runner-up to Sally in the Commonwealth Games, in 52.82 with Batten (world record holder at 52.61) second in 53.08. Sally's final season of 1997 was also thwarted by injury. She added to her outstanding European Cup record with a win in 54.57, her best for three years, and ran slightly faster (54.53) in her heat at the World Championships in Athens only to injure herself again warming down, causing her to scratch from the semis. That was her last serious race; she bade farewell to her fans a month later in a mixed 4x200m relay at Gateshead.

COLIN JACKSON

Born: 18.2.1967 Cardiff (Wales).
Clubs: Cardiff AAC, Brecon AC

ALTHOUGH THE ULTIMATE distinction, an Olympic title, eluded him, Colin Jackson has a legitimate claim to be considered the world's greatest ever sprint hurdler. His world record of 12.91 in 1993 was equalled by China's Liu Xiang in 2004 but remains unsurpassed all these years later, while no one has got within 6/100ths of his world indoor 60m hurdles record of 7.30 set in 1994. The Olympics apart (and he was silver medallist in 1988), he has won every other title going – World, World Indoor, European, European Indoor, Commonwealth – and has won more major international championship medals (25) than any other British athlete. In one season alone (1992) he was inside 13.20 a record 15 times. At one point in his career he won 44 consecutive races and his longevity was remarkable, too. He was World Junior champion in 1986, European Indoor champion in 2002 and ranked in the world top ten for 17 seasons running. During that entire period he was coached by Malcolm Arnold, the man who had previously guided John Akii-Bua of Uganda to Olympic gold and world record in the 400m hurdles.

Jackson, born in Wales into a Jamaican family, was 14 when he joined Cardiff AAC and his talent was obvious from the start. His first title came in the 1981 Welsh Schools Junior 80m hurdles and he was Welsh Youths 100m hurdles champion in 1982. Just two years later, in his first season of tackling the men's 3ft 6in (1.067m) barriers, he clocked 13.95 and finished third in the British Olympic trials. He didn't make the team for Los Angeles but was awarded his first British senior vest, winning in a match against Yugoslavia.

His great rival in those early years was Jon Ridgeon, who was four days older than Jackson. For a few seasons Ridgeon held the advantage, rather like Graham Williamson had against his junior contemporary Steve Cram, but whereas Jackson and Cram went on to enjoy fabulous success in the senior ranks both Ridgeon and Williamson were so injury prone that sadly they were never able to fulfil their potential.

A fine sporting all-rounder (he played cricket for the Glamorgan under-15 team), who in addition to being a good sprinter jumped virtually his own height with 1.81 in 1982, long jumped 7.56 in 1985 and threw the javelin 56.86 in 1983, Jackson was considered possible decathlon material, Daley Thompson being one of his heroes. Those plans were shelved, permanently as it turned out, after he finished second at the 1985 European Junior Championships (in 13.69 behind Ridgeon's world under-18 best of 13.46) and progressed in 1986 to taking a silver medal at the Commonwealth Games and winning the World Junior title well clear of Ridgeon with a European junior record of 13.44. That year he also ran a 10.49 100m and long jumped a windy 7.96.

As Malcolm Arnold mused a few years later: "It was possible back then he could have been a very good long jumper, or decathlete, but it's a brave man who changes a 13.44 hurdler!" Arnold continued: "He is totally in control and he's such a good competitor. He's great to coach. We get on well together; he's a very perceptive athlete. He's always asking questions and wanting to know things."

Hamstring trouble hampered Jackson in 1987. He improved a little, clocking 13.37, but the ascendancy swung back to Ridgeon. In the three big events of the year Jackson finished second in the European Indoors, fourth in the World Indoors and third in the World Championships (13.38), one place behind Ridgeon whose time of 13.29 equalled his own UK record. That record fell to Jackson in June 1988 when he was timed at 13.23, and he has held it ever since. Despite a moderate start but deriving full benefit from the 2000m altitude of Sestriere in the Italian Alps he improved to 13.11, a European and Commonwealth record. That ranked Jackson as the fourth fastest sprint hurdler of all time behind the Americans Renaldo Nehemiah (12.93), Roger Kingdom (12.97 winning in Sestriere) and Greg Foster (13.03)

Kingdom confirmed his status as overwhelming favourite to retain the Olympic title in Seoul, winning by a full three metres in 12.98, but Jackson ran a splendid race too to take the silver medal in 13.28, becoming the first Welshman to win an individual Olympic medal since John Disley in the 1952 steeplechase. No Briton had reached the Olympic 110m hurdles final since Don Finlay in 1936 but this time all three representatives did, with Ridgeon – his season ruined by a virus – placing fifth and the even younger Tony Jarrett sixth.

Jackson won his first gold medal as a senior in the 1989 European Indoor 60m hurdles, and at the World Indoors went very close to beating Kingdom for the first time. He ran 7.45 to the American's 7.43. Kingdom went on to equal Foster's questionable world indoor record of 7.36 but two days later in Glasgow – at the eighth attempt – Jackson beat him at last, 7.44 to 7.46. Off to a tremendous start, Jackson was always in front but it was only his gravity-defying dip that enabled him to stay ahead. Kingdom remarked: "He can break 13 seconds. He has the ability, he has the speed and he has the talent."

Jackson didn't take long to fulfil that prophecy. He was timed at 12.99 in Birmingham in June 1989 and 12.95 at the World Cup in Barcelona in September, but on both occasions the wind was over the acceptable limit. In the World Cup race Jackson led until the ninth hurdle, when Kingdom zipped past to win in a staggering 12.87, still the fastest time ever registered although the following wind was 2.6m/sec. However, it should be noted that a strong tailwind is not always to the hurdler's advantage as it can carry him too close to the barriers.

Jackson began his 1990 campaign by equalling his European and Commonwealth record of 13.11 in a heat at January's Commonwealth Games in Auckland and trimming that to 13.08 in the final despite clipping several hurdles. Jarrett was runner-up in 13.34 and second again to Jackson in the European Championships, although this was a much closer affair as Jackson – running with his right knee bandaged – prevailed in 13.18 to Jarrett's English record of 13.21. Jackson became the first Briton to win that title since Finlay in 1938, and he also reached new heights as a sprinter, clocking 10.29 for a Welsh 100m record.

Having been ranked by *Athletics Today* as the world's no 2 behind Kingdom for three years, Jackson was hoping to become the top man in 1991 but surgery to his right knee soon after his European triumph led to a relatively modest season, although he did run 13.09 plus a world's best of 22.63 for 200m hurdles. The World Championships were a disaster as he had to scratch from his semi after pulling muscle fibres in his back while warming up, but after surgery on his other knee in September he returned to enjoy an almost flawless season in 1992 during which he broke 13.20 a record 15 times.

A European and Commonwealth record of 13.06 at Crystal Palace, a race in which he beat all three American Olympic representatives, confirmed him as favourite for the Olympic title in Barcelona. The only serious contender he didn't race before the Games was Canada's Mark McKoy, who had been training in Wales with Jackson under Arnold's coaching since November 1991. McKoy was good, with a best of 13.11, but even he acknowledged Jackson was better.

Jackson arrived in Barcelona in awesome shape and made no secret of it as he clocked the fastest ever heat time of 13.10, virtually walking across the line. As Jackson wrote in his autobiography: "I knew then I could win the Olympics, and break the world record while I was there. I felt this with certainty – not arrogance, but the clear knowledge of a professional who has done his work."

Deciding to conserve energy in the second round the same day, Jackson deliberately ran without his usual snap ... and his trail leg caught one of the early hurdles, twisting his body round and tearing his left oblique, a muscle in the hips. Next day he felt a stabbing pain in his side and although he qualified safely for the final the oblique began to seize up. His friend, McKoy, frantically massaged the problem area right up to the moment they had to walk out into the arena for the final. Any remaining chance that Jackson might yet get away with it was destroyed when teammate Hugh Teape false started.

That aggravated the injury, creating serious pain, and as he couldn't lift his leg high enough because of it Jackson smashed into hurdle after hurdle. Miraculously he still managed to run 13.46 but that was good only for seventh as McKoy took gold in 13.12. "I'm so sorry," he told Jackson. "I wouldn't have been here today but for Colin," he said. "I can't explain how much he's done for me and I'm dedicating part of this gold medal to him."

It wasn't much consolation that a recovered Jackson defeated McKoy three times out of three after the Games and in successive races clocked 13.07, 13.04 (European and Commonwealth record), 13.06 and 13.05 for the greatest ever sequence of races to that date. He was also merit ranked world no 1 for the first time. Interviewed by Duncan Mackay in *Athletics Today*, Jackson said: "It's one of the worst things I could ever have imagined, where I can be the best in the world in Olympic year but not win the title that really matters. If things had been right in the Games I could have run 12.85."

Jackson's sense of injustice was heightened when at the next major championship, the 1993 World Indoors in Toronto, home town hero McKoy was allowed to get away with a blatant flier (0.053 reaction time) to win narrowly, 7.41 to 7.43. He masked his feelings at the time, but Jackson wrote in his book: "I seriously considered giving up track. Again I was gutted; track was all I had done with my adult life and I genuinely didn't feel I could cope with this constant emotional disappointment." Happily, his mood changed in time, he resolved to train harder than ever for the much more important World Championships in Stuttgart that summer, and proceeded to make an indelible mark on athletics history.

That Jackson was ready to reach a new level in 1993 was apparent after he lowered his European and Commonwealth record to 12.97 in Sestriere in July, the altitude advantage being cancelled out by a 1.6m headwind. Three weeks later he produced a superlative display in Stuttgart. The first UK athlete ever to win a global title in this event he also became the first Briton to set a new world record in the 'highs' since his namesake, Clement Jackson, ran 16.0 for 120 yards back in 1865. Clocking 12.91, 1/100th inside Kingdom's figures, he posted a time which 12 years later has never been surpassed.

On a red letter day for British hurdling, Jarrett – probably Jackson's match in pure talent but lacking his ruthless competitive streak – finished second in an equally stunning 13.00, still unapproached as the English record and at the time making him the world's fourth fastest ever performer. It remains Britain's only one-two in any World Championships event. Jackson later won his only international relay medal, silver in the 4x100m. Literally for the record, Jackson – with a typically rapid reaction time to the gun of 0.122 sec – got to the first hurdle (13.72m) in 2.56 sec and reeled off the 9.14m between barriers in 0.98, 0.98, 0.98, 0.98, 0.98, 1.02, 1.00, 1.02 and 1.02 with a 1.39 sec run-in over the 14.02m to the line.

Jackson, who admits he was anorexic at that time ("how I managed to run so fast with no fuel in my body's tank is still beyond me"), was voted the IAAF's world athlete of the year and in 1994 he scaled a new peak indoors. First he equalled the world 60m hurdles record of 7.36 in Glasgow; then he completed an unique double at the European Indoors by winning both the flat 60m (with 6.49 becoming the world's fifth quickest ever) and 60m hurdles (7.41 after 7.39 semi); and he ended with a 7.30 clocking in Sindelfingen which still stands as the world record. The fastest time since has been 7.36 by Allen Johnson (USA) in 2004. Jackson carried all before him that summer too, world ranked no 1 for a third year thanks to such exploits as retaining both the European (13.08 after 13.04 semi) and Commonwealth (13.08) titles and having the six fastest times of the year topped by a 12.98 in Tokyo. In all, he ran inside 13.10 in nine wind-free races, as against three in 1993.

This golden patch came to an end in 1995. His hurdles win streak of 44 races was terminated when Johnson – who would continue to be his main rival for many seasons – edged him, 7.42 for both, in an indoor race in Madrid in February. The fact that he had to undergo surgery on both knees in November 1995 sheds light on some of the problems of that summer. He ran no faster than 13.17 and missed the chance to defend his world title following a row with the British Athletic Federation executive chairman Peter Radford, the former world record holder for 200m and 220y.

Deciding to withdraw from the AAA 100m semi-finals as he had tweaked a hamstring in his heat, there was consternation when Jackson won a hurdles race in Padua the next day. Jackson's explanation was that his massage therapist had advised him to fly to Italy, carry out a particularly long warm-up and then make a decision whether to race.

As Jackson felt all right he went ahead, but there was a furore back home with suggestions that Jackson pulled out of the AAA Championships in order to race for money and, Jackson has written, Radford "dragged me into the Federation offices in Birmingham for an hour-and-a-half lecture about how I'd let British athletics down."

A few days later Jackson pulled a hamstring in training and, unable to race in Sheffield as requested by Radford to prove his fitness, he was omitted from the World Championships team. "To drive home the injustice of it," Jackson wrote, "by the time Gothenburg came around I was as fit as a fiddle." Would he have kept the title? Johnson won in 13.00 with the perpetual silver medallist Jarrett clocking 13.04.

His image and self confidence somewhat damaged after that incident, Jackson had a lacklustre season in 1996 (best of 13.13) and admitted he felt strangely apathetic towards the Atlanta Olympics in which he finished fourth in 13.19, the title going to Johnson on home soil in 12.95.

Motivation returned in 1997 and he picked up silver medals in the World Championships both indoors (7.49 just behind Anier García's 7.48) and out with 13.05, his fastest for three years, behind the all-conquering Johnson's 12.93. Further knee surgery delayed training for the 1998 campaign, yet he became the first to win a third European 110m hurdles title. Lowering his championship record to 13.02 in his semi, he equalled that in the final 75 minutes later for the speediest ever one-day double clocking. However, he controversially rejected the chance of winning a third Commonwealth title for Wales, choosing a commercial race in Tokyo instead, which enabled Jarrett to strike gold at last.

By now some may have felt that Jackson, at 32, should be in the twilight of his career but 1999 proved to be one of his greatest years. After finishing a close second in 1989, 1993 and 1997 he finally became world indoor champion. It was tight again this time but a superb 0.111 reaction time and his spectacular dip helped him snatch the verdict over Reggie Torian (USA) in 7.38.

He suffered a grievous blow in June, though, when his young training colleague Ross Baillie (21), the Scottish record holder described by Jackson as his most likely successor, died after suffering an allergic reaction to taking a couple of bites from a chicken sandwich.

Jackson, in effect, dedicated the rest of the season to his young friend's memory. He notched up his ninth AAA 110m hurdles title since 1986, surpassing Finlay's admittedly war-interrupted record of eight between 1929 and 1949, and would finish up with eleven. Jackson then went on to regain the world title in 13.04 ahead of García (13.07), the Cuban who would be crowned Olympic champion a year hence.

Defending champion Johnson strained a calf muscle warming up for his semi. "Lots of people had written me off as past it but I knew I still had another championship in me," said Jackson, who became the first Briton in any track and field event to win a second world title.

A hamstring injury sustained while weight training in March seriously affected his Olympic preparations in 2000 and it became a race against time for him to be fully fit in time for Sydney. He did run 13.10 that summer but at the Games he could place only fifth in 13.28 with García timed at 13.00 for victory. "I made mistakes during the race and paid the penalty," he admitted. "It looks like I'm the World Championships man, not the Olympics man."

Following further knee surgery and an Achilles tendon injury he opted not to defend his world title in 2001 (his best for the year was 13.32) but came back strongly one last time in 2002. He won the European indoor title in 7.40, a championship record and his best for three years; he placed second in the Commonwealth Games, a race he would surely have won had he not smacked into the first hurdle, never fully recovering his rhythm; and he signed off his outdoor championship career a winner in 13.11 at the Europeans, making history as the first track athlete to win four golds in the same event. Peter Matthews, in his UK Merit Rankings, rated him no 1 for a 15th year – a record for any event.

That would have been a fitting climax to a fabulous career but he carried on for a few more months, bowing out with fifth place (and a standing ovation) at the 2003 World Indoors in Birmingham. That was his 71st appearance in a British vest, a men's record, although shot putter Judy Oakes piled up 87 full internationals between 1976 and 2000. As IAAF President, Lamine Diack, said on the occasion of his retirement: "Colin Jackson has fully earned his place in the history books. He is a superb technician over the hurdles but above all else he has always been a fantastic ambassador for athletics."

The man voted in 1999 Britain's most popular athlete remains in the public eye as an analyst for BBC Television's athletics coverage and in 2005 he won new acclaim as a ballroom and Latin dancer on television.

STEVE BACKLEY

Born 12.2.1969 Sidcup (Kent). Club: Cambridge H

ARTHUR ROWE, Lynn Davies, Geoff Capes and Keith Connor went fairly close, but the distinction of becoming the first British male to set a world record in a field event fell to the man with the golden arm, Steve Backley. His date with history came in Stockholm's Olympic Stadium on 2 July 1990. Everything clicked for the 21 year-old on his first attempt. Flying high and true, into the wind, the Sandvik javelin touched down at 89.58, bettering the listed world record of 87.66 by Ján Zelezny of Czechoslovakia and the pending mark of 89.10 by Sweden's own Patrik Bodén, who threw nine metres less than Backley on this occasion.

Backley, whose policeman father John clocked a 4:10.8 mile in 1964 and 1:52.2 880y in 1965, had started off as a cross country runner but at 14 decided that chucking a javelin was more fun, even though he recalls his first throw travelled only about 22 metres! Within four years, coached by John Trower (an 81.06 performer with the old specification model in 1980), he was European Junior champion and had a best of 78.16, an astonishing improvement over his 64.98 of the previous year. The following season (1988) he set a world junior record of 79.50 but, to his disappointment, placed second in the World Junior Championships.

Expecting to advance to around 82-83m in 1989, the 1.96m (6ft 5in) tall sports science student at Loughborough University progressed at such a rate that he ended up ranked as world's no 1. Admirably consistent, he won seven consecutive Grand Prix contests, including the Grand Prix Final, together with victories at the European Cup, World University Games and World Cup. More often than not he destroyed the opposition with a thunderbolt of an opening throw, as at the World Cup where he set a Commonwealth record of 85.90.

He started 1990 brilliantly by taking the Commonwealth Games title with 86.02 in the sixth round (but his 84.90 opener effectively won him the gold medal) and after improving to 88.46 at the UK Championships he went on to become world record holder with that 89.58. His reign was brief, for only 12 days later Zelezny defeated him in Oslo, 89.66 (final round) to 87.94 (second round). At that stage of his career Zelezny was known as a man who could throw prodigious distances but had yet to capture a major title, so in retrospect it was ironic that in 1989 Backley had told an interviewer: "Winning titles means more to me than records. I would rather be a Seppo Räty [Finland's 1987 world champion] than a Ján Zelezny." Backley would go on to enjoy a glittering career, including four European titles, but had it not been for Zelezny's presence he would also have been world champion in 1995, Olympic champion in 1996 and 2000 and consequently a strong contender for the title of Britain's most successful athlete ever!

Within six days Backley struck back. It was like a dream come true. Here he was at Crystal Palace, just a few miles from his home, the main attraction at London's prestigious Grand Prix meeting. The stadium was filled with 17,000 spectators, all of them willing him not only to beat Zelezny but to break the world record into the bargain. And he did ... with the added bonus of crashing through the 90-metre barrier. Zelezny's best for the evening was 85.84 in the final round but Backley was in great form from the outset. Throwing his usual Sandvik implement, he opened with 86.40 and 85.88, but for his third attempt he borrowed from Zelezny the controversial javelin designed by Hungary's 1976 Olympic champion and ex-world record holder Miklos Németh. It flew out to 89.20. He tried it again in the fourth round and this time it travelled clearly beyond the 90m arc ... and the stadium erupted. There was another roar when the figures of 90.98 were flashed up.

Although the IAAF ratified Zelezny's 89.66 and Backley's 90.98 as world records, plus subsequent marks of 91.98 and 96.96 by Räty in 1991, the world governing body subsequently banned the Németh javelin for contravening the specification rules and Backley's 89.58 from 1990 was reinstated as the listed world record.

Meanwhile, the Németh spear was not allowed at the 1990 European Championships, a competition Backley had won from his first throw of 85.78, reaching 87.30 in the final round, while Zelezny didn't even make the final. Backley ended the season with a rare defeat by his predecessor as British record holder, Mick Hill, who threw a personal best of 85.88, but he had done more than enough to rank as world's no 1 javelin thrower for a second year ... and as a bonus a worldwide poll conducted by the IAAF voted him male athlete of the year.

Backley has likened javelin throwing to the swing in golf (he's a seven handicap player) – "all about timing". Unfortunately that timing was off at his next big test, the 1991 World Championships. Hampered by an adductor muscle injury, he – together with Zelezny – failed to qualify for the final. "I didn't get the rhythm," he explained. "You talk about the music of the event but I couldn't hear a thing." Having gone into the championship third on the world list that year with 88.46 he threw just 78.24. Actually, he would have needed to be at his very best in the final as Finland's Kimmo Kinnunen won with 90.82. Later in the season in Sheffield, his injury cured after cortisone injections, Backley clicked with a first-round Commonwealth record of 91.36, followed by 90.48 with his second throw. Zelezny reached 89.58 with Kinnunen fifth at 85.90. That would be the last time Backley used a Sandvik 'spiral' model as they, along with other 'rough surface' implements, were banned the following week.

Olympic year of 1992 was less than four weeks old when, during a warm weather training trip to New Zealand with Hill and their coach Trower, Backley threw a smooth Sandvik spear 91.46 in competition to break the official world record which had reverted to his own 89.58. That was over 300 feet or about the length of a football pitch. "Conditions were perfect with the tailwind coming in from just the right quarter," said Backley, who had been expecting to throw around 86m, not 91m! Nine years would elapse before he crossed the 90m line again.

Confusion continued to reign over javelin specifications that summer. In July, Zelezny threw a mighty 94.74 in Oslo, an obscene distance ahead of Backley (second at 85.06), but it transpired that he was using a newly designed Németh model that consisted of four components instead of the allowable three and thus it could not count as a world record. Backley's feeling was that "90 metres will win the Olympic Games and I am on course for that." He was half right. Throwing an approved Sandvik, Zelezny took the title in Barcelona with 89.66 ahead of Räty's 86.60 with Backley third at 83.38.

The 1993 season was virtually a write-off for Backley due to shoulder and adductor injuries but he was back in business the following year, retaining the European (ahead of Räty and Zelezny) and Commonwealth titles and being ranked world no 2 by *Athletics International*. Zelezny got his own back at the 1995 World Championships (89.58 to 86.30) but Backley was a much closer second in the Atlanta Olympics of 1996. He opened with 87.44, which might have been good enough to win, but Zelezny's response came in the second round. He threw 88.16 for his second Olympic gold medal and was well on his way to becoming the greatest javelin thrower who ever lived. It was a remarkable performance all the same by Backley, for he had undergone an operation to repair a ruptured Achilles tendon in April 1996, was still on crutches in early June and had only been able to start competing on June 30. Yet here he was, less than five weeks later, claiming Olympic silver. As he related to Bob Frank of *Athletics Weekly*: "I hardly did any training. I did a lot of psychological work rather than physical – a lot of visualisation of throws and mental imagery, but very little physical training."

Another silver medal came his way at the 1997 World Championships. On this occasion Zelezny placed a lowly ninth, but out of the woodwork came South Africa's Marius Corbett, the 1994 World Junior champion whose lifetime best prior to 1997 was a mere 77.98. During the season he raised that to a more respectable 83.90 but no one would have expected him to challenge for first place. Even he later remarked:

"I thought I might find a big throw in the final, but maybe fourth or fifth. I never thought of gold." But in round 2, to gasps of astonishment (his included), he reached 88.40. Backley, only fifth with 84.74 until the final round, rallied with an 86.80 which won him the silver but had the unfortunate side effect of knocking his good friend Hill (86.54) out of the medals. To be fair, Corbett's throw was not a complete fluke as two weeks later, at Crystal Palace, he beat Backley again, 87.46 to 87.14.

Having in the meantime hooked up in training with Zelezny and his coach Ján Pospisil, Backley made an auspicious start to 1998, throwing a remarkable 87.58 in snowy, freezing cold conditions in Finland, while in Gateshead a couple of months later he came up with his longest distance (89.89) for six years. Again, at the European Championships, he struck top form and needed just two throws to notch up his third title. In the qualifying round he raised his own 1990 championship record to 87.45 and he opened his account in the final with an 89.72 delivery which withstood all assaults. Silver went to Hill at 86.92, just 2cm short of his 1993 personal best, and a British one-two was unprecedented in an event which, within living memory, used to be one of the nation's weakest.

The Commonwealth Games in Kuala Lumpur looked the easier option, particularly as Corbett didn't win a single competition in Europe and had been throwing only between 74 and 81m whereas Backley had been over 88m in four contests. Yet, at the Games, Corbett found inspired form again in setting an African record of 88.75 to wrest the crown from Backley (87.38). However, Backley beat Corbett 6-1 during the year, including an easy win at the World Cup, and with Zelezny out injured all season the Briton was world ranked no 1 for 1998.

A five-year sequence of winning a medal in every major championship came to an end at the 1999 World Championships where, hindered by a knee injury, Backley could place only eighth, but the 2000 Olympics in Sydney would be one of his finest moments.

Bidding for a record third Olympic javelin title despite a rib injury sustained in training the previous month, Zelezny opened with a daunting 89.41, but in round 2 Backley threw an Olympic record (current implement) 89.85, a riposte which he might reasonably have expected to merit the coveted gold medal. But Zelezny, irritated at having to hold fire while the women's 100m victory ceremony was being staged, poured all his frustration as well as strength, skill and speed into his third round effort. It landed at 90.17 and Backley knew he was destined to finish second best once more to the maestro who at 34 became the oldest ever Olympic javelin winner. Instead Backley was able to console himself with the thought that yet again he had raised his game on the big occasion and had become the first Briton in any event to win an Olympic medal in three Games. "Ján's a true champion," he acknowledged. "I take my hat off to the guy. I thought 89 would be enough."

Backley's next attempt to win a global title, at the 2001 World Championships, was looking very promising after he threw 90.81 at Crystal Palace in July – his second longest ever. But disaster lay ahead in Edmonton, Alberta. A throw of 81.50 placed him only 14th in the qualifying round and he did not advance to a final for the first time in a decade. While Zelezny (again!) went on to win with a great throw of 92.80, Backley was at a loss to explain his performance. "I didn't get hold of one; it was as simple as that."

He bounced back in 2002 with two more shiny gold medals. With the first throw of the competition he effectively ended the contest at the Manchester Commonwealth Games with 86.81, winning by a record margin of nearly eight metres, but he had to work much harder for his fourth European title in Munich. Sergey Makarov, world leader that season with a Russian record of 92.61, got in front with an 88.05 opener and it was not until the fifth round that everything fell into place and Backley threw his season's best of 88.54. As he quipped after placing only sixth (82.49) at Crystal Palace shortly afterwards: "I am 33 years old; in Munich I felt like 23 years old and today I felt like 43 years old!"

He was world ranked no 2 behind Makarov in 2002 but from then on he went into gentle decline. A knee operation prior to the 2003 season limited him to a best throw of 85.69 and he could place only ninth in the World Championships, but he bowed out next year in some style by placing fourth in the Athens Olympics with his season's best of 84.13. Clearly Britain's greatest ever male thrower, he equalled Colin Jackson's record of being ranked by Peter Matthews as UK no 1 in his event for a 15th time.

KELLY HOLMES

Born 19.4.1970 Pembury (Kent). Clubs: Tonbridge AC, Middlesex Ladies, Ealing, Southall & Middlesex AC

THE YEAR IS 1983. The English Schools Championships are being staged in Plymouth and among the winners is Sally Gunnell in the Senior Girls 100m hurdles (13.7w). Nine years later she will be crowned Olympic 400m hurdles champion. She is one of the stars of the meeting, which is more than can be said for Jonathan Edwards – ninth in the Senior Boys triple jump with 13.84. Twelve years later he will astound everyone by setting a world record which looks like standing for a long time yet and another five years after that he takes the Olympic gold medal. But there is a third youngster on view in Plymouth who will take all of 21 years to realise her Olympic dream. Reporting for *Athletics Weekly*, Barry Trowbridge wrote: "Kent's Kelly Holmes (who?) produced one of the major upsets of the meeting." She, an unknown 13 year-old, won the Junior Girls 1500m in 4:37.8.

The daughter of a white English mother and Jamaican father, she was – as she puts it in her autobiography *Black, White and Gold* – "an accident that no one wanted to happen." She had begun her running career the year before at cross country and joined Tonbridge AC where she was coached by Dave Arnold. In 1984 she ran 2:15.1 for 800m and 4:35.3 for 1500m and finished a close second in the English Schools 1500m, but just as significant was that she watched the Los Angeles Olympics on TV and Seb Coe became her hero. "He was an aggressive runner who didn't give up and his determination was obvious. I identified with that even then."

By 1987 her times were down to 2:09.45 and 4:26.10 and that summer she won the English Schools Senior Girls 1500m and represented Britain at junior level. And that, as is sadly the case with so many talented young athletes, could well have been that. Once she had left school, athletics was no longer a priority. Kelly's ambition was to join the Army and when she did so in February 1988, aged 17, her military career came first. She didn't run at all in 1988 and it was only at the urging of the Army's star athlete, Kriss Akabusi, that she resumed training in 1989. She did win the Inter-Services 1500m that year but her times were mediocre and at that point no one – least of all Kelly herself – ever expected her to make a real name for herself on the track.

The turning point was when, in her barracks, she watched the 1992 Olympics on TV and recognised Lisa York running in the 3000m – an athlete she had often raced during their schooldays. "It dawned on me," Kelly reflected in her book. "If she could make it to the Olympics, then maybe I could too. Why not? The dream that I'd had as a junior athlete started to take shape again."

By now a corporal and physical training instructor, Kelly started to train seriously. She switched clubs to Middlesex Ladies and for a while was coached by Wes Duncan. Seemingly back from the dead, she took British athletics by storm in 1993. Short but well muscled after working hard on her upper body strength, she was a revelation at 800m. In 1992 she had improved to 2:03.94 but at the 1993 British Championships she won in 2:00.86, while at the World Championships she only just missed making the final with a time of 1:58.64, an English record.

Dave Arnold took over her coaching again following that breakthrough season and in 1994 she burst forth as a world class 1500m runner. She hadn't run faster than 4:17.3 until then, but a road mile in Sydney in April 1994 signalled her potential when she finished 5 sec ahead of Hassiba Boulmerka, the Algerian Olympic 1500m champion, in 4:29.0. Two months later she narrowly won the AAA 1500m title, after a tremendous scrap with Yvonne Murray (the 1993 World Indoor 3000m champion), in 4:01.41 and followed that with a 1:59.43 800m victory over Holland's Olympic champion Ellen van Langen which was notable also for the speed (28.5) of her final 200m.

Even Kelly's fierce kick was insufficient to hold Lyudmila Rogachova in an otherwise slowly run European Championships 1500m, the Russian covering the last lap in 56.5, but Kelly herself was inside 57 sec and to win a silver medal in her first season of serious racing at the distance was a considerable achievement. Her first gold medal, and it would prove to be the only one for eight often frustrating years, came at the 1994 Commonwealth Games, a race she won in 4:08.86. However, medals of other denominations would continue to come her way even though her career would be constantly interrupted by various setbacks.

It was in 1995 that Kelly, now promoted to sergeant, became a truly world class performer at 800m as well as 1500m. She lowered the English record to 1:57.56 when winning the AAA title (with Paula Radcliffe sharpening her speed with a personal best 2:05.22 in fifth), while at the World Championships she not only finished second to Boulmerka in the 1500m (4:03.04) but also took third place over 800m in 1:56.95, breaking Kirsty Wade's 10 year-old Commonwealth and UK record of 1:57.42. She went faster still in the Grand Prix Final with 1:56.21 behind the 1:55.72 of Mozambique's Maria Mutola.

The 1996 AAA Championships saw her complete a double which had not been achieved since Diane Leather in 1957 as she took both the 800m (1:57.84) and 1500m (4:08.14) but her Olympic hopes were dashed when just prior to the Games she developed a hairline fracture in her lower left leg and for a time was unable even to jog. In Atlanta, injections helped numb the pain and it was a remarkable performance on her part that she should finish fourth in the 800m (1:58.81), a race won by Svetlana Masterkova of Russia in 1:57.73. She was in no shape really to tackle the 1500m but typically had a go, leading at the bell before fading to 11th place in 4:07.46. She travelled home on crutches with her leg encased in plaster for seven weeks.

Kelly's luck was even worse in 1997. The same weekend that she announced she was leaving the Army to concentrate full-time on athletics she smashed the Commonwealth 1500m record in cold and windy Sheffield with 3:58.07, making her clear favourite for the world title in Athens. Next fastest on the world list was Regina Jacobs (USA) at 4:03.42, although Masterkova – with no current form – could pose a threat. In fact, the clash never materialised. Agonisingly, in her final training session before flying to Athens, Kelly ran her swiftest ever 200m of 23.7 – only to feel a slight pull in the back of her left heel. Hoping for the best, she encountered the worst in her heat. Feeling excruciating pain, she broke down, eventually walking in tears to the finish. It transpired that she had torn the Achilles tendon and ruptured a calf muscle. Masterkova didn't fare much better, her Achilles injury reducing her to limping home last in her semi. Carla Sacramento of Portugal won the much devalued title in 4:04.24 with a 60.8 last lap, which hardly bore comparison with Kelly's 59.7 closing 400m in her 3:58.07.

Following surgery in January 1998 and a long wait while the leg healed, Kelly returned to racing short of training but just in time to take her place in the late season Commonwealth Games. She may have lost her 1500m title but she won much admiration for her fighting second place in 4:06.10. She deserved a lucky break but 1999 was virtually a write-off. It was a year of personal upheaval and ill health and she was eliminated in the 800m semi-finals at the World Championships. She flirted with the idea of retirement after further setbacks and her prospects of doing well at the 2000 Olympics were pretty dim as she was unable to start racing until mid-August. That was the AAA 800m, which she won in 2:02.08, a modest enough time but vastly encouraging in the circumstances. "Four weeks ago I really didn't think I would be able to run at all, let alone today," she declared. "I'm relieved I'm still in one piece. I'm back running and injury free."

Kelly went on to provide an amazing sight in Sydney. So short of training that making the Olympic team had for most of the year seemed a forlorn hope and with a pre-Olympic season's best of 2:00.35, there she was well clear of the field entering the finishing straight in the Olympic 800m final! It was the stuff of dreams. Okay, Mutola (1:56.15) and her arch-rival Stephanie Graf (Austrian record of 1:56.64) did steam past to take gold and silver as anticipated but Kelly could not have been more delighted with her bronze. Stating "I had nothing to lose," she had taken the field by surprise with an early strike and led until 50m out, finishing in an admirable 1:56.80, second only to her 1995 UK record of 1:56.21. Placing seventh in the 1500m (4:08.02) was an anti-climax, but as she admitted: "My mind was somewhere else. I wanted to go out and celebrate winning my bronze properly."

What, one wondered, was Kelly capable of if only she ever had a full year of injury-free training and racing. We would have to wait the four years of another Olympiad to find out.

For the first time in a decade, Kelly raced exclusively at 800m in 2001. A long-term stomach problem, for which she underwent surgery at the end of the year, prevented her reaching top form in time for the World Championships and she faded from fourth to sixth (1:59.76) in the finishing stages of a race won by Mutola (1:57.17) just ahead of Graf (1:57.20). In later season races, though, Kelly was much stronger, splitting the pair in four races and clocking a best of 1:57.88.

She reverted to 1500m in 2002 and that year began on a high note as she reclaimed the Commonwealth title in Manchester in 4:05.99. "I'm not afraid to say I was crying my eyes out," she said. "There have been so many ups and downs in my career that last week I was so scared to train in case I was injured again." She did get her time down to 4:01.91, her best for five years, but was too tired in her heat at the European Championships to avoid elimination after having finished third in the 800m in 1:59.83. Shortly afterwards she lost a record of sorts when Helen Pattinson (now Clitheroe) finished ahead of her in a 1500m race – the first time she had been beaten at the distance by a Briton since 1987!

The year of 2003 was noteworthy for various reasons: she trained with Mutola at altitude in South Africa and came under the coaching influence of Mutola's American trainer, Margo Jennings, and she embarked upon her first indoor season since her schooldays. An early dividend was a British indoor 800m record of 1:59.21 behind Mutola, while at the World Indoor Championships in Birmingham she astounded herself by clocking a UK 1500m record of 4:02.66 for a silver medal behind Jacobs (4:01.67), the 39 year-old American who would three months later fail a drugs test.

Full of hope that the summer would see her crowned world 1500m champion at last, she returned to South Africa, only to sustain a very painful injury to the left knee. Over-compensating for that, she proceeded to cause damage to her right calf. So, while Mutola was flying in training, Kelly was restricted to working out in the pool or gym. It was all very disheartening. Later, in Font Romeu – the Pyrenees training base favoured by Paula Radcliffe – everything just got too much for Kelly. She had unsuccessfully tried jogging and, as she revealed in her book: "After one particularly frustrating day I suddenly felt as if I couldn't cope any longer. I stood in the bathroom, locked the door and stared in the mirror, feeling utterly miserable. I was crying uncontrollably. There was a pair of nail scissors on a shelf. To this day, I don't know what made me do this, but I picked them up, opened them and started to cut my left arm with one of the blades. One cut for every day that I had been injured."

From the pit of despair, hope returned as gradually the leg responded to treatment. She would be able to compete in the World Championships after all ... but in what event? In her last 1500m race, in Zürich, she had been beaten out of sight, finishing ninth in 4:05.24 with Turkey's Süreyya Ayhan the winner in 3:55.60, the world's fastest time for six years. Alarmingly unacquainted with the rules, Kelly told the media that although her original aim had been the 1500m she would first see how she felt in the 800m and then opt out of that event after one or two rounds. Advised that she couldn't do that with impunity, she decided to concentrate exclusively on the 800m.

It proved a wise decision. She ran 1:58.86 behind Mutola in her semi, while in a slow final the training companions finished one-two. Kelly led into the straight but Mutola was always in command and slipped past to win in 1:59.89, covering the last 200m in 27.57, with Kelly showing 2:00.18. There were accusations after the race that the pair had somehow ganged up to prevent anyone else getting past, but both denied any such collusion. Later in the season Kelly set a UK 600m best of 85.41, impressive speed for someone who had earlier in the summer clocked a 3000m personal best of 9:01.91 after reaching the bell in 7:47.0. Her fastest 400m, by the way, was 53.8 in 1996 although she was timed at 52.7 for a relay leg the year before that.

And so to 2004, the year in which Kelly's long-held and seemingly never to be fulfilled dream of becoming an Olympic gold medallist became a reality. What's more, she proved lightning can strike twice!

Of course, even in her *annus mirabilis*, not everything ran smoothly. After posting a European indoor 1000m record of 2:32.96 she looked all set for her first global title at the World Indoor Championships, but once more the fates were against her. With just over 600m to run she fell as she was moving through the field. She hared off in pursuit but the effort of regaining contact took its toll and she faded to last place as Ethiopia's Kutre Dulecha claimed the title in 4:06.40.

Outdoors, her season leading up to the Athens Olympics was curiously uneven. She won all her 800m races: 1:58.71 (58.8 for the second lap) in San Sebastián ahead of one of her main rivals, Hasna Benhassi of Morocco; 1:59.39 (58.53 last 400m) for a record seventh AAA title at the distance; and 2:00.46 to beat another serious contender, Jolanda Ceplak of Slovenia, in Birmingham. It was a different story in what she always considered her stronger event, the 1500m. Of six races before the Games she won in Gateshead (4:06.83) and London (4:04.06) but was second in Eugene (4:03.73), Madrid (4:05.27) and Zürich (4:03.48), third in Ostrava (4:04.18).

Consequently, although normally the most self assured of athletes Kelly found herself oddly indecisive. As she has written: "By the time I reached the Olympic trials in July I was feeling strangely unsure of myself. I kept panicking that everything was going to go wrong again." She faced a dilemma. Should she run the 800m first and thus probably have three races in her legs before embarking upon the heats of the 1500m, or should she put all her eggs in one basket and simply opt for the 1500m? An added complication about going also for the 800m was the fact that her coach's first loyalty in that event was towards defending champion Mutola. In the best of all possible worlds Kelly would win the 1500m and her friend the 800m, but obviously that could not be guaranteed and in the final analysis every athlete must take their chances as they see fit. In fact, Kelly's mind was made up when a particularly good speed session at the British Olympic team's holding camp in Cyprus convinced her she was ready to run a great 800m.

In Athens on August 20 she won her heat in 2:00.81 and next day, barely out of breath at the finish, she clocked the quickest semi-final time of 1:57.98, her best for three years. It was looking promising and in the final on August 23 she ran the most tactically astute race of her long career. Content to run near the back (57.6) while Jearl Miles Clark (USA) blazed through the first lap in 56.37, she followed Mutola as she clawed her way towards the front along the back straight. Into the final stretch it was Miles Clark, Mutola and Holmes. Normally when Mutola moves ahead early in the straight the race is over, but this was an occasion which saw her in a vulnerable state and Kelly in inspired form.

"Suddenly I was side by side with Maria," she reflected. "I've never beaten her in a major race and normally in that situation I would buckle but there was something magical about this race. I just had to win it." The two women slogged it out and until a few strides from the finish Mutola was still just in front, but ultimately there was no resisting her opponent. Out in lane 3 Kelly was even more resolute than Mutola, the most bemedalled female 800m runner in history. Indeed, Mutola faltered to such an extent that Benhassi and Ceplak, both running even wider than Kelly, snatched the other medals as Kelly crossed the line first in 1:56.38, her fastest since setting the UK record nine years earlier. Her 200m segments of 28.7, 28.9, 29.2 and 29.6 proved the value of even pace running ... Tom Hampson would have been proud of her. Television pictures of her look of disbelief, turning to wonderment and delight when she realised she had indeed won, will forever remain in the memory. Benhassi was second in a Moroccan record of 1:56.43, the same time as Ceplak, with Mutola out of the medals in 1:56.51.

With her feet barely touching the ground, Kelly was back next day to finish second in her 1500m heat in 4:05.58; two days after that she placed second in her semi in 4:04.77. Having discovered her most effective way of racing, she ran with assurance in both those races, holding back until the finishing straight, and that's how she ran – and won – the final too on August 28.

While Tatyana Yevdokimova dashed straight to the front, Kelly sauntered at the back of the field and was still one from last at 400m, reached by the Russian in a swift 63.59. Kelly moved a little closer to the leader (2:08.64) by 800m and at the bell Yevdokimova (2:57.45) was ahead of Poland's Lidia Chojecka and Russian world champion Tatyana Tomashova, with Kelly lurking in eighth place. Yevdokimova, whose brave front running led to a personal best of 3:59.05 but no medal, was still ahead at 1200m in 3:12.82. With 200m to go Kelly was up to fifth and by the time Yevdokimova led into the finishing straight the Briton was second and no power on earth was going to deprive her of a second golden moment. Running inside 60 sec for her last lap, she moved into the lead 60m from the finish, looked round to assess the danger, and held on grimly. Her winning time of 3:57.90, which astonished her, broke her 1997 UK record. Tomashova placed second in 3:58.12 with Maria Cioncan of Romania third in 3:58.39.

It completed a double that had been achieved twice before by a woman, by Tatyana Kazankina (USSR) in 1976 and Masterkova in 1996, but it was a feat which had eluded her hero Seb Coe as well as Steve Ovett. The only British man who had doubled successfully was Albert Hill back in 1920. Kelly also went into the record books as, at 34, the oldest man or woman to have won either title and she became the only British woman to win two Olympic gold medals.

"The feeling was indescribable," Kelly wrote in her autobiography. "I had achieved my lifetime's dream twice over. It had taken years of dedication, commitment, focus, emotional struggle and pain but now I had done it. I was double Olympic champion. And yes, it was worth all the wait." Ever since, she has become one of Britain's most recognisable and feted citizens, and in the 2005 New Year Honours she became the first active athlete to be made a Dame (or be knighted for that matter) ... "the ultimate accolade".

ASHIA HANSEN

Born 5.12.1971 Evansville, Indiana (USA).
Clubs: Essex Ladies, Shaftesbury Barnet H

SHE FAILED TO reach the final at the 1994 European Indoor and Outdoor Championships and at the 1995 World Championships, she came last or almost last at the 1996 European Indoors, 1999 World Championships and 2000 Olympics, and didn't even get to the World Championships of 2003 and 2005 or the 2004 Olympics. A failed international athlete, right? Wrong, because the same athlete – Ashia Hansen – has proved herself one of the world's greatest triple jumpers with victories in the 1998 European Indoors (with a world indoor record), 1998 Commonwealth, 1999 World Indoors, 2002 Commonwealth and Europeans, and 2003 World Indoors to her name. Who knows what more she would have achieved but for a seemingly endless series of serious injuries.

Born Ashia Nana Korandima in the USA, she was adopted at the age of three months by a British woman, Elaine Hansen, and her Ghanaian husband. She was taken to Ghana when she was two and to London at eight. Like her upbringing, Ashia's early forays into athletics were less than straightforward. She started off, without success, as an 800m/1500m runner before switching to the sprints, high jump and long jump (she was a junior international in 1989) and discovering – "for a bit of a laugh" – that the triple jump was her forte.

In her first year at the newly established event, aged 18 in 1990, she registered 10.84 but made a big leap forward in 1991 (12.68) as she started to come to terms with the discipline's demands and continued to progress steadily up the British rankings with 13.31 in 1992 and 13.48 indoors plus a windy 13.55 in 1993 before reaching international level with 14.22 (no wind gauge) and 14.09 for her first official UK record in 1994. However, her first two European Championship appearances that year proved a big disappointment as indoors she wound up 16th with 13.30 and outdoors 15th with 13.45 ("I was so nervous I just froze"), each time being eliminated in the qualifying competition.

It was in 1995 that she became a significant player on the international triple jump stage. After triumphing at the European Cup, she looked forward to challenging the elite at the World Championships, but flopped so badly (21st with 13.61) that, aged only 23, she thought about retiring from the sport. She persevered and soon after the Gothenburg debacle she set a Commonwealth record of 14.66, a distance which would have placed sixth at the World Championships where Inessa Kravets of the Ukraine set a fabulous world record of 15.50.

Her first real opportunity of a major medal went begging at the 1996 European Indoors. She jumped 14.58 that winter and even her qualifying round mark of 14.32 would have given her third place in the final, won by Bulgaria's Iva Prandzheva at 14.54, but she fouled three times. She had better luck, of sorts, at the Atlanta Olympics that summer. Her leap of 14.49 was a creditable performance but she wound up in that most frustrating of positions, fourth, in the inaugural Olympic women's triple jump. To be fair, though, a higher placing would have been beyond her at that stage as Kravets won with 15.33, which remains the Olympic record, while silver and bronze went at 14.98. Later in the season Ashia improved her Commonwealth record to 14.67 and 14.78.

Having in the meantime switched coaches from one former triple jumper (Frank Attoh, best of 15.98 in 1980) to another (ex-UK record holder Aston Moore, best of 16.86 in 1981), Ashia started her medal collection at the 1997 World Indoors. Originally she had not been selected for the team, as she had been in South Africa at the time of the trials, and was added to the squad only after threats of legal action. Like other professional athletes, Ashia needed to compete for prize money and there was $50,000 on offer by the IAAF for first place, $20,000 for second. She opened with a Commonwealth indoor record of 14.70 but the lead passed to Inna Lasovskaya with 14.72 in the second round and the Russian made it a clearcut victory by reaching 15.01 in the third round.

Outdoors, she raised the Commonwealth record to 14.94 and looked capable of bringing home a medal from the Athens World Championships. She led the qualifying contest with 14.77 only to suffer a back injury after the first round of the final. She placed a crestfallen fifth with 14.49, the bronze medal going at 14.67. Way ahead, though, were Sarka Kaspárková of the Czech Republic (15.20) and Romania's Rodica Mateescu (15.16). There was still a big gap to bridge, it seemed, but Ashia had the ability and desire, for in the late season Grand Prix Final in Fukuoka she beat all three Athens medallists with a magnificent 15.15. That distance not only elevated her to fifth on the world all-time list but ranked her among the top 20 British *men* that year! The *Athletics International* world rankings panel voted her no 3.

The year of 1998 was all too typical for its highs and lows. Prior to the European Indoors she raised her indoor record to 14.85 and in Valencia she reached one of the peaks of her career. No one could now accuse her of under-performing on big occasions. Kaspárková had taken the lead in the fourth round with a Czech record of 14.76 but Ashia's immediate response was sensational. Following a very fast approach and hitting the board perfectly, she was only 60cm away from the sand when she took off for the jump phase. She landed at 15.16, smashing the world indoor record of 15.03 by Russia's Iolanda Chen.

There was a price to pay. She injured her heel in the process, causing her to miss practically the entire outdoor season. On her return at the end of August and after only three weeks of training she jumped a highly tentative 13.39 and yet another three weeks later, in Kuala Lumpur, she became the inaugural Commonwealth Games champion. It was an anxious competition for her. She fouled her first two attempts and so on her third try she took off way before the board. From take-off to landing it must have been around 14.60 but 14.32, as it was measured, was more than good enough against a modest field.

A much more prestigious title came her way at the 1999 World Indoors in Maebashi, thanks to her grand opening effort of 15.02, but it was all going too well to last. She sustained a foot injury soon afterwards and underwent surgery to remove a floating bone. That put back her training for the outdoor season and she suffered a disaster at the World Championships in Seville. Again she opened with two fouls but her third attempt, a despairing effort from a vast distance behind the board ("I didn't have the confidence to take a risk"), measured just 13.39 and she was 12th and last as the title went to Paraskevi Tsiamita of Greece at 14.88. Later that summer she displayed her true form, winning the Grand Prix Final with 14.96 and comfortably defeating Tsiamita.

The next two seasons proved non-productive. Further injury problems meant that the Sydney Olympics was her first outdoor competition of 2000. She jumped an encouraging 14.29 to qualify but in the final the nightmare scenario of two fouls plus an inadequate 'safety' jump came back to haunt her and she finished down in 11th place (13.44) as Tereza Marinova of Bulgaria was crowned champion with a leap of 15.20.

Turmoil in her private life didn't help in 2001 and after deciding not to defend her world indoor title she fared poorly in the outdoor World Championships. She produced her best jump for two years (14.51) in the qualifying round but managed only 14.10 for seventh in the final. Tatyana Lebedeva of Russia won with 15.25, silver going at 'only' 14.60.

The upswing came in 2002. At the European Indoors she finished a close second to Marinova (14.81) with 14.71, and during the summer she came away with two shining gold medals. In each case victory was won at the final gasp. First came the Commonwealth Games in Manchester. With the penultimate jump of the contest Francoise Mbango from Cameroon soared to an African record of 14.82, her demeanour suggesting she felt the competition was over.

That, in turn, fired up Ashia even more for her final attempt. She would need to conjure up her longest jump for three years but the moment after she landed she bounded out of the pit, waving excitedly to the crowd, convinced she had done it. She had ... but it was frighteningly close. The distance was 14.86.

Even better was to follow just ten days later at the European Championships in Munich. The challenge this time came unexpectedly from Finland's Heli Koivula, whose legal personal best was only 14.36 but had opened with an only just wind assisted 14.83. Ashia was from the outset a safe second with jumps of 14.54 and 14.60 but nothing less than gold was acceptable to her. A run-through in round 3 followed by two other fouls (one a marginal no-jump in the region of 15.20) meant that it was all down to her final attempt. She would need at least 14.84 for the chance of victory (Koivula had her last jump to come) ... and Ashia, now gloriously restored to peak physical and emotional strength, responded. She broke the sand at exactly 15 metres (with 3.1m/sec wind assistance), the first time she had reached that level for five long years, and she became the first British woman to win a European jumping title since Thelma Hopkins (high jump) and Jean Pickering (long jump) in 1954. For the first time she was ranked the world's number one triple jumper.

She enjoyed another momentous success on home ground when the 2003 World Indoors were staged in Birmingham. Of course there had to be drama on the way. It started in the qualifying round. Suffering from a heel injury she could only compete after being injected with an anaesthetic, and even then she was in pain while jumping 14.61. In the final she opened promisingly with 14.77 but Mbango concluded the first round with an African record of 14.88. To add to her distress, Ashia found her runway marker had been moved, causing a lengthy delay and much expenditure of nervous energy as she 'dolly-stepped' her run-up again. In round 5 everything came together at last ... a splendid effort of 15.01, a distance only she and Chen had ever bettered indoors.

It was all too good to last and sure enough that has proved to be Ashia's last international championship appearance to date. She was selected for the outdoor World Championships in 2003 but, following an Achilles tendon operation, she was not fit enough to accept. She jumped 14.47 in February 2004, decided to skip the World Indoors in order to concentrate on her Olympic build-up and found the sacrifice was in vain. Having finally regained full fitness after a long, hard slog, and competing outdoors for the first time in nearly two years, she suffered an horrendous injury to her left knee while competing in the 2004 European Cup. A series of operations on the ruptured patella tendon followed and although she missed the whole of 2005 she was hopeful of returning in time for the 2006 Commonwealth Games only to have to withdraw from the England team following further surgery to remove scar tissue.

Now 34, the age at which Kelly Holmes achieved Olympic immortality after a comparable number of injury setbacks, Ashia vows to return. As her coach Aston Moore has stated: "She is still determined to come back. She says she has unfinished business with the Olympics in 2008."

DENISE LEWIS

Born 27.8.1972 West Bromwich.
Clubs: Wolverhampton & Bilston AC, Birchfield H

ALTHOUGH SHE WAS never a world record breaking all-rounder like Daley Thompson or Mary Peters, Denise Lewis thoroughly deserved her heptathlon gold medal in Sydney in 2000 as she struggled bravely against injuries which came so close to shattering her Olympic dream. Her career was one of long-term consistency, encompassing also a European title, two Commonwealth Games successes, a pair of World Championship silver medals and an Olympic bronze.

Born to a Jamaican mother who arrived in England in 1966, Denise first saw the light of day just a week before the Olympic pentathlon triumph of the woman who would become her inspiration, Mary Peters. So keen was she on athletics that she was only nine when she joined the local Wolverhampton & Bilston club. Honours came early in her career, winning the English Schools Junior Girls long jump in 1986, aged 13. The following year she had to make an important decision. Just as Sally Gunnell once had to choose between gymnastics and athletics, so Denise opted to drop her other passion, dancing, in order to concentrate on long jumping. At 15 she joined Birchfield and began to be coached by Darrell Bunn, the man who would steer her to top world class.

She added further English Schools titles in 1986 and 1988, and it was in the latter year when just turned 16 that she entered her first heptathlon. It was the Midland Championship, she won and "from that moment Darrell and I knew the heptathlon would be my number one event." There was an early setback, though. Her 1989 target was the European Junior heptathlon but a few weeks before that she injured her right knee when her foot slipped on the take-off board when long jumping. It was so serious that she had to undergo surgery in February 1990 and learn to walk again. Crucially, it was her take-off leg which had been damaged and Bunn suggested she try jumping off the other leg as he thought it would take too long to regain full strength in her right leg. It was a difficult transition but she persevered and in 1991 she placed fifth in the next European Juniors with a score of 5476, eight points below her best.

Although she improved to 5812 in 1992 she didn't qualify for the Olympic team and she missed the following year's World Championships too, but in 1994 she made a huge breakthrough at the Commonwealth Games. Although she had withdrawn from the European Championships in order to concentrate on this contest, little did she dream that she would obliterate her previous highest score of 6069 with a total of 6325. Not for the last time, it was the javelin which made all the difference. With a previous best of 48.58 she couldn't believe it when the spear touched down at a colossal 53.68! As she recalled in her autobiography *Personal Best*: "I think it is the only time that I have completely lost my composure. I was running around, excited, dancing and smiling, jumping up and down, unable to fully digest what I had done." What she had done was to turn a 197 point deficit against Australia's Commonwealth record holder Jane Flemming into a 27 point lead ... and a personal best 800m of 2:17.60 enabled her to take the gold medal with a score which hoisted her to second on the UK all-time list behind clubmate Judy Simpson's 6623.

The following season was one of consolidation, scoring 6299 both when winning in the European Cup and when placing seventh in the World Championships, but in 1996 she moved up several notches among the world elite. She was a revelation at the annual multi-events classic staged in Götzis (Austria) in May. On the way to setting a British record of 6645 she registered no fewer than five individual personal bests, three of them by a massive margin: from 13.47 to 13.18 in the 100m hurdles, 1.84 high jump, 14.36 shot (up from 13.58), windy 24.06 200m (compared to her best legal time of 24.80) and 2:16.84 800m.

World champion Ghada Shouaa, a statuesque Syrian, won with 6942 and it was she who triumphed at the Atlanta Olympics with 6780. Denise was only sixth after the first day and dropped to eighth after a modest long jump of 6.32, far down on her best of 6.67. At that stage she was so despondent that she was tempted to drop out but a timely personal best of 54.82 with the javelin moved her all the way up to third overall and she clung on to the bronze medal with her score of 6489. Later in the season, she improved her javelin still further to 56.50, ranking her fourth in Britain that year. She was also the nation's top long jumper and equal second at 100m hurdles.

Her development continued in 1997. She won at Götzis with a Commonwealth record of 6736, including a 200m best of 24.10 and a windy long jump of 6.77, and claimed silver (6654) behind Germany's Sabine Braun (6739) in the World Championships. Denise got off to a frustrating start. Heading for a hurdles time of close to 13.10 she hit the eighth barrier, lost her impetus and clocked only 13.43, well behind Braun's 13.16. She tied her high jump best of 1.84, put the shot farther than ever with 14.55 and was close to her fastest 200m with 24.13, yet after day one Braun led with 4009 and Denise was fourth at 3888. A 6.47 long jump took her into second place and a 52.70 throw also closed the gap a little but Braun was still 82 points ahead before the 800m and eventually won by 85.

Now coached by the Dutchman, Charles van Commenee (who pointed out that her mistake in the hurdles had cost her the world title), Denise became the world's number one in 1998. She won both of the year's major titles with the two highest scores of what was admittedly not a vintage season for the event.

With Braun below her best due to a toe injury, the main challenge at the European Championships was expected to come from Olympic silver medallist Natalya Sazanovich of Belarus. The shot proved to be a vital event this time. Benefitting from the extra strength training she undertook while restricted by an ankle injury, Denise raised her personal best from 14.72 to 15.27 to take the lead after three events. After a disappointing 200m she fell back to second with 3842 behind Sazanovich's 3870, but the next two events ensured her victory (6559) while Urszula Wlodarczyk of Poland (6460) overhauled Sazanovich for the silver medal.

Denise went on to emulate Mary P by collecting a second Commonwealth Games gold. She led on day one by 85 points and was 222 clear prior to the 800m. A tight thigh muscle, necessitating physiotherapy before the race, caused some anxiety but she got around unscathed to claim victory with 6513 points.

A calf injury sustained early in 1999, which meant that for ten weeks she could work only on strength training, compromised her participation in the World Championships but she recovered in time to score 6724 for second place to the Sierra Leone-born Eunice Barber, whose score of 6861 was a French record and with her surname was an appropriate winner in Seville. Shouaa placed a distant third and Braun fourth. Barber immediately established a huge 185-point advantage over Denise in the hurdles, 12.89 to 13.61, and both high jumped lifetime bests: 1.93 for Barber, 1.87 for Denise. However, the shot brought a dramatic turnabout. While Barber could manage only a pathetic 12.37, Denise produced three successive personal bests of 15.41, 15.95 and 16.12 (which ranked her equal fourth in Britain) to give her a 65-point lead. Barber, much the faster at 200m, led overnight by 3994 to 3993. A 6.86 long jump was just fine for Barber but Lewis had only 6.20 on the board until her final leap of 6.64, her longest since having to switch her take-off leg back to the right the previous year due to the weakness of her left ankle. Barber eventually won by 137 points.

The year ended in surgery for Denise; she was on crutches for four weeks and had ten weeks of rehabilitation. It was hardly the introduction to Olympic year she would have chosen. Nevertheless, despite having managed barely five weeks of uninterrupted training since the start of the year she scored 6831, which remains the Commonwealth record, for victory in Talence (France) in late July. It was made up of 13.13 (personal best), 1.84, 15.07, 24.01w (windy personal best), 6.69 (personal best), 49.42 (her best with the new specification javelin) and a big personal best of 2:12.20 in the 800m.

She was in the shape of her life ... only to receive an immense blow to her Olympic hopes seven weeks before the Games when she injured her left Achilles tendon. It took intensive physiotherapy to get her to the point where, only ten days before leaving for Sydney, she was able to start running again. Barber had also been beset by injuries and no one quite knew what to expect from the two favourites for the title.

The French star looked to be in good condition after all with a 12.97 hurdles, while Denise clocked a creditable 13.23, commenting: "I was really pleased ... the best I had run in a championship by a long way." Barber then jumped 1.84, a modest result for her, but Denise made a potentially disastrous decision to pass at 1.78 after clearing 1.75 and then proceeded to fail three times at 1.81. "My heart sank, and I realised I had probably just kissed goodbye to the gold medal," was how she described that moment in her book. She sank to eighth place, 152 points behind Barber. But, as in the previous year's World Championships, the shot transformed the situation. Denise threw it over four metres further than Barber and the positions after day one were: 1, Sazanovich 3903; 2, Natalya Roshchupkina of Russia 3872; 3, Lewis 3852 with Barber seventh on 3707.

It was completely over for Barber when, next morning, she took only one mediocre long jump before retiring injured. But Denise was having serious problems too with her Achilles tendon. She managed a decent 6.48 leap, taking her into second overall, before feeling such intense pain that she could hardly walk. She very nearly didn't make it to the javelin. She took some painkillers in the hope that she could unleash one good throw and despatched the implement 48.49. Not bad, but she felt she could do better and took a chance by throwing again ... and improved to 50.19 to take the lead with 5717 to 5654 by Sazanovich and 5571 by Russia's Yelena Prokhorova. Offered another injection before the 800m, she declined. Instead she pluckily toughed it out, doing enough to ensure victory with a score of 6584. Prokhorova totalled 6531, Sazanovich 6527. "It's not a great score," Denise admitted. "It was simply about winning."

Although she was keen to extend her career and defend the title in Athens in 2004, Denise's glory days in the heptathlon were effectively over. Irritable Bowel Syndrome which had continually plagued her for ten years led to her withdrawing on the eve of the 2001 World Championships, by which time she was pregnant by Belgian sprinter Patrick Stevens. Their daughter was born in April 2002.

By that time van Commenee had ceased coaching her, feeling he could not guide her to further titles now she had a child to raise. In terms of her career, he noted "Darrell [Bunn] baked the cake and I put a little bit of cream on top." As she prepared for her comeback in 2003 Denise was caught up in a bitter controversy over the coaching involvement of Dr Ekkart Arbeit, who had been linked with the GDR's notorious state doping programme for athletes. She scored 6282 in the 2003 European Cup, far behind the new sensation Carolina Klüft's 6692, and placed fifth (6254) in the World Championships in which the young Swede scored a fabulous 7001.

Denise did get to the Athens Olympics, having set a personal best of 51.48 with the current specification javelin that summer, but she ended the first day limping in ninth place. A dreadful long jump of 5.89 relegated her to 18th position and she dropped out ... a sad conclusion to a notable career. She subsequently became better known to the British general public than she ever was as an athlete when she became one of the stars of the *Strictly Come Dancing* series on BBC television at the end of 2004, as did Colin Jackson a year later.

PAULA RADCLIFFE

Born 17.12.1973 Barnton, near Northwich (Cheshire). Clubs: Frodsham H, Bedford & County AC

BEFORE SURVEYING THE life and times of Paula Radcliffe I shall make my position clear. Unlike Mary Rand, Ann Packer, Mary Peters, Tessa Sanderson, Sally Gunnell, Denise Lewis or Kelly Holmes, Paula has yet to strike Olympic gold, but in my view she is the greatest female athlete this country has ever produced. Others have broken world records too, but no one has pushed out the frontiers of performance in the way that Paula has in the marathon or been so far ahead of the world's second best in their event. In 2003 she was Britain's fastest marathon runner, male or female! True, that fact also reflected the dire state of men's distance running in the UK that year but Paula's time of 2:15:25 was a truly phenomenal achievement. No woman in the world, other than herself, has yet run faster than 2:18:47 ... a gap representing one kilometre of road. Her record time is over seven minutes quicker than Emil Zátopek's when he famously won the 1952 Olympic title and only a few seconds slower than Abebe Bikila's world record equalling run at the 1960 Games. Like Jim Peters half a century earlier, Paula has revolutionised the marathon; unlike him she has a global title to her name besides being a fabulous track and cross country runner.

Another reason why I am so besotted by Paula the athlete is her uncompromising attitude. Not for her the Ethiopian way of sitting in during long distance track races and kicking to victory. Admittedly, she doesn't possess the finishing speed to employ those tactics, but even if she did she wouldn't run her races that way. Her fulfilment comes from running eyeballs out right from the start, challenging her rivals to keep pace with her. The flaw is that with a self appointed pacemaker to follow, the Ethiopians get a free ride, but that does not deter her. The perpetual challenge is that maybe next time she will be able to maintain such a strong pace – as in most of her marathons – that no one on earth would be able to stay in contact. It takes a lot of courage and self belief to commit in that fashion.

Paula was blessed with good sporting genes in her family (great aunt Lottie was a 1920 Olympic silver medallist in the 4x100m freestyle swimming relay) and it was no surprise that, tall and skinny, she should take to running. Shortly after moving from the north of England to Bedford she found herself on the starting line of the 1986 English National Girls Cross Country Championship at Leicester. Aged 12 she finished 299th out of 607 starters and 596 finishers. A disaster? Hardly. "To come in the first half of the country I was really chuffed."

Just one year later she showed she was one of the nation's best in her age group by placing fourth in the same race, with her Bedford club winning the team title which pleased her coaches, Alex and Rosemary Stanton, even more. In the next three years she finished second, third and third, while in 1991 she became national cross country champion at last, taking the Intermediates title. That won her selection for the World Championships, in which she placed 15th. That summer she was fourth in the European Junior 3000m, a race won by Romania's tiny Gabriela Szabo, who nine years later would become Olympic 5000m champion. A significant pointer to Paula's future occurred that autumn when she tackled a 10 miles road race, clocking 60:06, but many years would pass before she moved up seriously to that sort of distance.

In a rare indoor race in February 1992 Paula had a long-range view of Liz McColgan when she ran 16:16.77 way behind the Scot's world indoor 5000m record of 15:03.17, prompting Paula to state: "In the long term 3000m is my distance. As the races get longer I tend to fade." She would prove to be better as a runner than as a prophet!

An anaemia sufferer on iron tablets at the time, Paula travelled to snowy Boston for the World Cross Country Championships hoping for a top ten placing in the Junior 4km event. "Not in my wildest dreams did I expect this," she gasped after winning the title, 5 sec ahead of China's Wang Junxia, who just the following year would set world records at 3000m (8:06.11) and 10,000m (29:31.78) that remain unapproached but are viewed with suspicion by many, this writer included. At this early stage of her career, Paula was running only 25-30 miles per week, fitted around her A-level studies, and that summer she became the year's fastest European junior at 3000m with 8:51.78 when finishing fourth in the World Junior Championships.

As a student at Loughborough University in 1993, she improved to 8:40.40 for seventh place in the World Championships. Injury virtually blanked out 1994 and she encountered other problems at the 1995 World Cross Country Championships. She was excelling herself by holding third place with 800m to go before fading drastically to finish 18th, collapsing and losing consciousness. It was a frightening experience, diagnosed as due to a chronic depletion of blood sugar. In fact she had suffered since age 14 from occasional blackouts for that reason and was also found to be an exercise-induced asthmatic.

She made a notable outdoor 5000m debut in Hengelo in June 1995. Not only did she win the race, overtaking Olympic 10,000m champion Derartu Tulu of Ethiopia on the final bend, but her time of 15:02.87 was the fastest yet by an English-born runner. A few days later she just missed Zola Budd's UK record of 14:48.07 with a time of 14:49.27. At the World Championships, won by Ireland's Sonia O'Sullivan in 14:46.47, she placed fifth in 14:57.02.

Paula was again fifth in the 1996 Olympics (15:13.11), victory going to Wang Junxia in 14:59.88, but the year was noteworthy also in that as well as succeeding Budd as UK record holder with 14:46.76 she graduated from Loughborough with first class honours in Modern European Studies, French and German being her specialist languages.

A professional athlete now, Paula won her first major medal as a senior in the 1997 World Cross Country, splitting the Ethiopian pair of Tulu and Gete Wami, but at the World Championships in Athens that summer an all too familiar scenario was established: leading at the bell, she was outrun on the last lap. Szabo's 29.35 last 200m carried her to victory in 14:57.68 with Paula a crestfallen fourth in 15:01.74. Later she ran the Romanian much closer in Brussels, setting a UK record of 14:45.51.

By 1998 she felt ready to move up to 10,000m and two weeks after finishing second to O'Sullivan in the World Cross Country she made the world's fastest debut in the event. Narrowly outkicked by Olympic champion Fernanda Ribeiro (Portuguese record of 30:48.06) in the European Challenge race, Paula ran 30:48.58 for a Commonwealth record. One week after that she established world road bests of 24:45 for 8km and 24:54 for 5 miles at Balmoral.

But heartbreak lay ahead in the European 10,000m championship. Leading for much of the race, she launched her strike for home with five laps to go but to her frustration couldn't find the pace she was seeking. She slipped back to fifth (31:36.51) as

O'Sullivan – uncorking a 28.1 last 200m which Paula could only dream about – won ahead of Ribeiro in 31:29.33. Paula finished in tears, feeling totally drained. As she explained in her autobiography *Paula: My Story So Far*: "Blood tests showed the existence of a virus that had attacked and depleted my red cells, lowering my haemoglobin to a level that fully explained why there had been so little energy." Consequently she withdrew from the Commonwealth Games 5000m, which was won in a time over a minute slower than Paula's best that season. Determined to salvage something from a year which had started so promisingly, and despite being far from fully fit, she won the European cross country title in December.

Another medal, bronze this time, came her way at the 1999 World Cross Country. Wami ran out an easy winner but Paula was disappointed to lose silver in the last few strides to another Ethiopian, Merima Denboba. "I'll keep coming back to this race until I win it," she vowed. "It's not going to beat me." Nor did it, as we shall see later. Again she began her track season with the European Challenge 10,000m and led all the way for a Commonwealth record of 30:40.70, a time that among non-Chinese only her idol, Norway's Ingrid Kristiansen, had ever bettered. And again she collected world road bests at Balmoral with 24:38 at 8km, 24:47 at 5 miles.

During the summer Paula set Commonwealth records at all three of her main distances. She clocked 14:43.54 for 5000m and 8:27.40 for 3000m but the main event was the World Championships 10,000m in Seville. As I wrote in *Athletics International*: "They don't award medals for courage in athletics but if they did there should be one for Radcliffe, who enabled this to be the greatest ever distance race for women. Despite 30°C+ heat she led for most of the race at incredible speed for the conditions and smashed the Commonwealth record by over 13 sec. The only problem was that despite her herculean efforts she could not shake off Wami who proceeded to outkick the Briton over the last 200m, having not led for a single stride until then." The 5000m splits were 15:25.24 and 14:59.32 as Wami won with an Ethiopian record of 30:24.56 with Paula second on 30:27.13. The year ended with Paula making an auspicious half marathon debut, finishing third in the Great North Run with an English record of 69:37.

Olympic year of 2000 was notable for her wedding in April to Northern Irish 1500m record holder (3:34.76 in 1995) Gary Lough, but again she just missed out in the big races. She ran herself to a state of collapse to finish fifth in the World Cross Country Championship at 8km, returning next day to place fourth over 4km one second behind the winner. Her track season started late after arthroscopic surgery on her knee in June, which cost her 13 weeks of training, but in August she came up with good runs at 5000m (14:44.36) and 3000m (8:28.85). Her speed was never better, for a few days before the Olympics husband Gary paced her to a 4:01 1500m time trial, way inside her racing best of 4:05.81.

Once more, in Sydney, she ran herself into the ground with, heartbreakingly, no medal to show for it. I wrote in *Athletics International*: "Long after many a medallist from Sydney is forgotten, the vision of Radcliffe's brave front running will remain. In Seville she burned off everyone except Wami. This time she ran even faster with

30:26.97, and yet came fourth. She led through 5000m in a searing 15:05.70. Just before 7800m the Ethiopians went ahead in order to slow it down but before long Radcliffe was in charge again. The heroic Radcliffe went from first to fourth as her three remaining opponents accelerated approaching the bell." Tulu produced a 60.26 last lap to win with an African record of 30:17.49; Wami (30:22.48) and Ribeiro (Portuguese record of 30:22.88) followed. Paula described her fourth place as an "overwhelming disappointment."

As she put it in her book: "There was a desire to show people I was a winner, not just some plucky English girl who tried hard but couldn't get there. I believed that each year I was getting stronger and better and with perseverance and patience I could get to where I wanted to be. Until those results and titles came I could do nothing about the perception of the gallant front-runner, and anyhow it never really hurt or upset me."

Still, she wanted something tangible to ease her Olympic disappointment and she ended the year with two impressive half marathons. She won the Great North Run in 67:07, surpassing McColgan's European best, and in hot and humid conditions in Mexico captured the world championship in 69:07, her first global title as a senior.

In her next major race, the 2001 World Cross Country in Ostend, she finally realised her dream – at the eighth attempt – of winning the senior 8km title. A muddy course where strength rather than blazing speed was needed for success played into her hands. With a kilometre remaining it was between Radcliffe and Wami. Momentarily there was a sense of *déjà vu* when Wami moved ahead in sight of the finish, until it became apparent to Paula that her rival was at full stretch and not pulling away. Paula had enough left to produce a counterstrike and there was a beatific smile on her face as she crossed the line ahead. "This is the one I've always really wanted. For me, winning this is as good as winning the Olympics." Next day, in the 4km event, the pair slugged it out again. This time Wami moved ahead with 80m to go and held Paula at bay by one second.

It was looking good for the World Championships 10,000m in Edmonton, particularly after a Commonwealth 3000m record of 8:26.97 and a 1500m personal best of 4:05.37. In the big race, though, she departed from her usual tactics yet the outcome remained more or less the same: fourth place (31:50.06) behind the Ethiopian trio of Tulu (31:48.81), Berhane Adere (31:48.85) and Wami (31:49.98). As she wrote: "It was the same gut-wrenching result as Sydney, only this time I'd made mistakes. I felt I hadn't given every last ounce of energy." Following a very slow first half of 16:29.89 (Edmonton is at 2000ft altitude) she had intended to make a decisive move but didn't feel physically or mentally strong enough and by the time she went, with less than four laps remaining, it was too late.

Earlier, Paula had caused a stir in Edmonton when she and some British teammates were so incensed by the decision to allow Olga Yegorova to run in the 5000m that they displayed a banner proclaiming "EPO Cheats Out". Because of irregular procedure with her EPO test in Paris the previous month the Russian had her suspension overturned by the IAAF. Booed as she crossed the finish, she easily won the world title. Paula herself has always been among the strongest advocates for ridding athletics of doping and wears a red ribbon on her vest to signify her support for blood testing.

She ended the season in style. She slashed over 11 sec from her Commonwealth 5000m record with 14:32.44 behind Yegorova (European record of 14:29.32) and Wami (14:31.69), tied McColgan's world 5km road best of 14:57 and retained her world half marathon title in Bristol with a European record 66:47. En route she was timed at 63:26 for 20km, which was later ratified as an official world record.

Enter Paula Radcliffe, prospective marathon runner. Excitement ran high as she completed her preparations for the 2002 London Marathon with a 30:43 road 10km in Puerto Rico, astonishing running in 30°C heat and windy conditions, and another deeply satisfying victory in the World 8km Cross Country.

The date of Paula's momentous marathon debut was 14 April 2002. The conventional wisdom was that she would stay with more experienced runners until 20-22 miles before making a move if still feeling comfortable. But that's not Paula's style. She felt so easy that by 9 miles she was the only runner still in contact with the pacemaker and before halfway (71:04) she was on her own. Her second half was just awesome. She covered it in 67:52 and her final time of 2:18:56 was hailed as the fastest ever in a women-only race and broke every other record in the book except for the world and Commonwealth best of 2:18:47 by Kenya's Christine Ndereba. She even managed to better the Radcliffe family record, which had stood to her father's name with 3:30 in 1985! Paula also entered the stratosphere in terms of earnings; she collected $255,000 in prize money and record/time bonuses, never mind her appearance fee and shoe sponsor's bonus. Other lucrative marathon successes to come would make her a seriously wealthy young woman.

In July she embarked upon her track season; just three races, each one a gem. First she pushed Szabo to a European 3000m record of 8:21.42 in Monaco, herself setting a Commonwealth record of 8:22.22 ... fabulous speed for someone who had been training for the marathon. Next came the Commonwealth Games 5000m in Manchester, close to her Cheshire birthplace, where she not only won her first international track title but came within 3.33 sec of the world mark with a Commonwealth record of 14:31.42. Better still was her continental record of 30:01.09 nine days later when winning the European 10,000m title in Munich, the second fastest ever behind Wang's controversial world record. She was in front by the second lap, quickly dropped all opposition (despite setting an Irish record O'Sullivan finished 300m behind in second place) and reached 5000m in 14:57.65, easily the fastest ever halfway split and well inside O'Sullivan's European Championships record for that distance!

There was more to come. Tuning up for the Chicago Marathon she set a European 10km road best of 30:38 and in the Windy City on October 13 she carved almost a minute and a half off the world record with 2:17:18, leaving Ndereba over two minutes adrift in the race. With the confidence gained from her London run,

Paula set a devilish pace from the outset of this mixed race. She reached halfway, with Ndereba for company, in 69:05 – only to cover the second half even faster in 68:13. Not surprisingly, Paula won every athlete of the year award going. No longer was she the good loser; now she was a superlative winner.

She began 2003 as she finished 2002 ... breaking world records. Racing 10km in Puerto Rico she ran 30:21 on a hilly course in warm, humid and windy conditions, reportedly passing 5km in 14:48 and 8km in 24:05 for further world bests. "I'm in way better shape than before London last year," she claimed, having been covering up to 140 miles a week in high altitude Albuquerque, and so it proved.

Theoretically, world records should be progressively harder to beat as an event develops, yet Paula's stunning run in London on 13 April 2003 represented the biggest single improvement since the breakthrough by Joan Benoit (USA) to 2:22:43 20 years earlier. Since then Kristiansen had clocked 2:21:06 in 1985, Tegla Loroupe of Kenya 2:20:47 in 1998 and 2:20:43 in 1999, Naoko Takahashi of Japan 2:19:46 and Ndereba 2:18:47 in 2001, Paula 2:17:18 in 2002 ... and now the astonishing figures of 2:15:25. Until Paula entered the marathon picture the women's world record had always been at least 13 minutes slower than the men's; now the difference was a mere 9 min 47 sec.

Not surprisingly, no one could live with her unprecedented pace in London; her third mile was covered in 4:57 and she flashed past 10km in 32:01, 10 miles in 51:48 and halfway in 68:02. At 30km her time of 1:36:36 was way inside the world record but could not be recognised as the course from the start to that point falls by about 40 metres, which is over the 1/1000th (30m) allowable for record purposes. At 20 miles her time was a world best of 1:43:33. Finishing second in 2:19:55 was Ndereba, with Deena Drossin (now Kastor) third in an American record of 2:21:16.

Frustratingly, a combination of a shin injury and bronchitis caused her to sit out the entire 2003 track season, thus missing another chance for the world 10,000m title, won by Adere in the African record time of 30:04.18. Again, though, Paula produced a strong finish to the year. A week apart, she set world bests at 5km (14:51) in London's Hyde Park and at half marathon (65:40) in the Great North Run from Newcastle to South Shields. On the way she passed 15km in 46:41, 10 miles in 50:01 and 20km in 62:21 but because of the downhill nature of the point to point course none of those times could be officially accepted. Two weeks later she won her third world half marathon title, in Portugal, in 67:35, and to round off the year nicely she claimed a second European cross country title, leading Britain to team victory.

What a rollercoaster of a year 2004 turned out to be. She had two tremendous front-running track races a week apart in June. First she won over 5000m at the European Cup in Bydgoszcz in 14:29.11, a Commonwealth record and third fastest ever time, and then at Gateshead – in her first 10,000m on a British track – she lapped Ribeiro with a time of 30:17.15 (15:00.67 at 5000m) which, considering the exceedingly windy weather, must have been worth inside 30 minutes on a still day.

So much has been written about Paula's excruciating Olympic experience in Athens that there is little to add except to state that in my opinion certain British sportswriters (the ones that know nothing about athletics but feel qualified once every four years to pontificate on Olympic competition) were an absolute disgrace. To accuse Paula of all people of being a quitter, of dropping out when the going got too tough or the prospect of a medal had disappeared, would be laughable if the comments had not been so hurtful, damaging and ignorant. Nobody in athletics can surpass Paula for sheer guts and determination, and the fact that she was unable to complete either the marathon or 10,000m was because her body – not her spirit – would not permit her to.

She was in such a bad way before she even started the marathon on August 22 that had it been any competition other than the Olympics she would have withdrawn. As Paula explained in *The Daily Telegraph,* the problem was that anti-inflammatories used in the treatment of a leg injury shortly before the Games upset her bowel so that she was unable to absorb enough energy and nutrients. "My fuel tank was very low before I began the race. This meant I had to break down body tissue for fuel while I was running. Had I pushed further I would have damaged my body further. As it is, tests showed my liver was struggling to cope and I lost a lot of weight." As for the 10,000m five days later: "I don't have any regrets about trying. At least I won't always be wondering if I could have raced it. My legs were just unable to recover from the trauma." For the record, Mizuki Noguchi of Japan won the marathon in 2:26:20, Xing Huina of China the 10,000m in 30:24.36.

In her book, Paula states: "One deep disappointment is not a reason to change long-term plans or give up on my dreams. What happened at the Olympics makes me all the more determined to keep working and inspires me to try even harder. I know that I am not a quitter. I will learn from the experience and come back tougher. I still have so much left to achieve and have not become a lesser athlete."

To the surprise of many, Paula chose to contest the 2004 New York City Marathon on November 7 for her first race since Athens, and bounced back magnificently with a hard fought victory over Kenya's Susan Chepkemei, 2:23:10 to 2:23:13. It may have been the slowest of her four completed marathons but it was the win which mattered ... of huge importance to her morale.

Her rehabilitation was completed at the 25th running of the Flora London Marathon on 17 April 2005. Following the smoothest build-up to any of her marathons, this saw her back to her sparkling best as she won by a full mile from Constantina Tomescu (Romanian record of 2:22:50) with Chepkemei third in 2:24:00. Her time of 2:17:42 was her – and the world's – third fastest ever and constituted a world best for a women-only race. By posting four of the five sub-2:19 marks in history, she had now achieved a degree of global supremacy unprecedented in marathon annals. The halfway time was 68:27 and her second half would have been quicker than 69:15 had she not had to stop in the 22nd mile to answer an urgent call of nature.

Undecided for a while as to which event to run at the World Championships in Helsinki, she eventually opted for both although the marathon was the main goal. She was disappointed with her 10,000m (ninth in 30:42.75 with Ethiopia's Tirunesh Dibaba producing a 58.4 last lap to win in 30:24.02) but "on the positive side I came out of the race feeling no ill effects and had had a good hard workout at well above marathon pace." She was thus able to start the marathon, eight days later on August 14, mentally and physically ready for the challenge.

It was no occasion (or course) for world record attempting heroics and she contented herself with running the first half well within her comfort zone, which for her – uniquely – is around 70 minutes, and then be guided by how she felt. Leading from the start, Paula reached the half in 69:49 and pulled clear of her nearest pursuer at 27km to win in 2:20:57, easily the fastest ever time in a global championship race, and becoming the first Briton of either sex to win a world or Olympic marathon title. Ndereba was second in 2:22:01, Tomescu third in 2:23:19 and her old rival Tulu fourth in 2:23:30. By winning the world title so convincingly she strengthened her claim to be considered the greatest of all women marathon runners but we shall have to wait to see whether she can fulfil her ultimate ambition of becoming Olympic champion in Beijing in 2008.

BRITISH HONOURS LIST

This unique "honours list" features more than 500 British athletes who have achieved particular international distinction between 1900 and 2005. It also underlines the huge contribution the UK has made to the highest levels of athletic endeavour.

The criteria for inclusion: placing in the first three in the Olympics, World Championships (including cross country since it became an IAAF event in 1973 and road races) and World Indoor Championships; winner (individual events only) in European Championships, European Indoor Games/Championships, Empire/Commonwealth Games, International (pre-IAAF) Cross Country Championships and World Race Walking Cup, plus world record setters in the more commonly contested or significant events. * = record not ratified by IAAF and/or FSFI (Women's World Federation; marks set between 1921 and 1934).

Clearly the top family in British athletics has been the Stewarts. The two brothers, Ian and Peter, plus sister Mary all won European indoor titles, while Ian and Mary were Commonwealth champions with Ian's other honours including a world cross country title, European outdoor gold and an Olympic bronze medal. Among the married couples listed: Robbie and Ann Brightwell, Garry and Kathy Cook, John and Sylvia Disley, Gary and Heather Oakes, John and Dorothy Parlett, Alan and Della Pascoe, Howard and Rosemary Payne (later Chrimes), Gordon and Shirley Pirie, and John and Sheila Sherwood. Both Godfrey Brown and his sister Audrey made the list, as did Janet Simpson and her mother Violet Webb, and brothers Con and Patrick Leahy (Irish athletes who competed for Gt Britain and Ireland have been included in this section).

Abbreviations: CG = Commonwealth Games (previously Empire Games); Eur = European Championships; Eur Ind = European Indoor Championships; Int CC = International Cross Country Championships; Oly = Olympic Games; World = World Championships; World CC = World Cross Country Championships; World Ind = World Indoor Championships; World Walk Cup = World Race Walking Cup (previously Lugano/Eschborn Trophy); WR = World Ranking (no 1 as assessed by *Track & Field News*, men 1947-87 & women 1956-87, and *Athletics Today/Athletics International* since 1988).

A

ABRAHAMS Harold: 1 1924 Oly 100 (2 4x100); world record – 4x100 (42.0 – 1924)
ACHIKE Larry: 1 1998 CG TJ
ADAM Marcus: 1 1990 CG 200
ADCOCKS Bill: WR (Mar) 1968
AHEARNE Tim (GBR/IRL): 1 1908 Oly TJ; world record – TJ (14.92 – 1908)
AINSWORTH-DAVIS John: 1 1920 Oly 4x400
AKABUSI Kriss: 2 1984 Oly 4x400, 2 1987 World 4x400, 1 1990 CG & Eur 400H, 3 1991 World 400H (1 4x400), 3 1992 Oly 400H (3 4x400)
ALDER Jim: 1 1966 CG Mar; world records – 30,000m (1:34:01.8 – 1964, 1:31:30.4 – 1970)
ALDRIDGE Albert: 1 1905 Int CC
ALEXANDER Sheila: see under LERWILL
ALFORD Jim: 1 1938 CG 1M
ALLDAY Sue: 1 1958 CG DT
ANDERSON Gerard: World record – 440yH (56.8 – 1910)
ANDERSON Tim: 1 1950 CG PV
APPLEBY Fred: World records – 20,000m (1:06:42.2* – 1902), 15M (1:20:04.6 – 1902)
APPLEGARTH Willie: 3 1912 Oly 200 (1 4x100); world records – 200m/220y (21.2 – 1914), 4x100 (43.0* – 1912)
ARCHER Jack: 1 1946 Eur 100, 2 1948 Oly 4x100
ARDEN Daphne: 3 1964 Oly 4x100; world record – 4x110y (45.2 – 1963)
ARMITAGE Heather: see under YOUNG
ASHURST Andy: 1 1986 CG PV
ATTWOOD Pauline: World record – 4x400 (3:37.6 – 1969)
AUGEE Myrtle: 1 1990 CG SP

B

BACKLEY Steve: (JT) 1 1990 CG, 1 1990 Eur, 3 1992 Oly, 1 1994 CG & Eur, 2 1995 World, 2 1996 Oly, 2 1997 World, 1 1998 Eur, 2 2000 Oly, 1 2002 CG & Eur; world records – (89.58 & 90.98 – 1990, 91.46 – 1992); WR 1989, 1990 & 1998
BAILEY George: 1 1930 CG 8 laps steeple-chase
BAILEY McDonald: 3 1952 Oly 100; world record – 100 (10.2 – 1951); WR (200) 1951
BAKER Philip: 2 1920 Oly 1500
BALL Valerie: World records – 880y (2:14.5 – 1952), 4x220y (1:43.4 – 1951), 3x800m/ 3x880y (7:07.8 – 1949)
BANNISTER Roger: 1 1954 CG 1M, 1 1954 Eur 1500; world records – 1500 (3:43.0* – 1954), 1M (3:59.4 – 1954), 4x1M (16:41.0 – 1953); WR (1500/1M) 1951, 1954
BAPTISTE Joan: 2 1983 World 4x100
BARRETT Henry: World best – Mar (2:42:31 – 1909)

BARRY Steve: 1 1982 CG 30k Walk
BARTHOLOMEW Phyllis: 1 1934 CG LJ
BATTY Mel: World record – 10M (47:26.8 – 1964)
BAULCH Jamie: 2 1996 Oly 4x400, 2 1997 World Ind 400, 2 1997 World 4x400, 1 1999 World Ind 400 (3 4x400), 3= 2003 World Ind 400 (3 4x400)
BEACHAM Margaret: 1 1971 Eur Ind 1500; world indoor records – 1500 (4:20.5*, 4:17.4* & 4:17.2* – 1971)
BEATTIE Phil: 1 1986 CG 400H
BEAVERS Walter: 1 1934 CG 3M
BEDFORD Dave: 1 1971 Int CC; world record – 10,000 (27:30.80 – 1973); WR (10,000) 1970
BELASCO Joan: World record – HJ (1.575* & 1.625* – 1920)
BELL Chris: see under PERERA
BENJAMIN Tim: 3 2003 World Ind 4x400
BENNETT Ainsley: 3 1983 World 4x400
BENNETT Charles: 1 1900 Oly 1500 & 5000 team race (first individual finisher), 2 4000mSC; world records – 1500 (4:06.2* – 1900), 5000 (15:29.8* – 1900)
BENNETT Todd: 3 1983 World 4x400, 2 1984 Oly 4x400, 1 1985 Eur Ind 400, 2 1985 World Ind 400, 1 1987 Eur Ind 400; world indoor record – 400 (45.56* – 1985)
BERNARD Verona: see under ELDER
BIGNAL Mary: see under RAND
BILLY Ikem: 3 1985 World Ind 800
BLACK Roger: 1 1986 CG & Eur 400, 2 1987 World 4x400, 2 1991 World 400 (1 4x400), 3 1992 Oly 4x400, 2 1996 Oly 400 (2 4x400), 2 1997 World 4x400
BLAGROVE Mike: World record – 4x1M (16:30.6 – 1958)
BLEWITT Charles: 2 1920 Oly 3000 team race, 1 1923 Int CC
BOARD Lillian: 2 1968 Oly 400, 1 1969 Eur 800 (1 4x400); world records – 4x110y (45.0 – 1968), 4x400 (3:37.6 & 3:30.8 – 1969), 4x800 (8:27.0 – 1970)
BOOTHE Lorna: 1 1978 CG 100H
BORN Doris: World record – 3x800m/3x880y (7:07.8 – 1949)
BOULTER John: World record – 4x880y (7:14.6* – 1966); world best – 1000y (2:06.2 – 1967)
BOXER Chris: 1 1982 CG 1500
BRADFORD Carole: 3 1984 World 10k road, 3 1985 World 15k
BRADSTOCK Roald: World record – JT (81.74* – 1986)
BRAITHWAITE Darren: 3 1991 World 4x100, 2 1995 World Ind 60, 3 1997 World 4x100; world indoor record – 4x200 (1:22.11 – 1991)
BRASHER Chris: 1 1956 Oly 3000SC; WR 1956

BRIAN Margaret: World record – 4x220y
(1:41.4 – 1951)
BRIDGE Robert: World records – 15M Walk
(1:56:41.4* – 1914), 2 hours (24,781m*
– 1914)
BRIGHTWELL Ann: see under PACKER
BRIGHTWELL Robbie: 1 1962 Eur 400, 2
1964 Oly 4x400
BROWN Audrey: 2 1936 Oly 4x100
BROWN Godfrey: 2 1936 Oly 400 (1 4x400),
1 1938 Eur 400
BROWN Jon: 1 1996 Eur CC
BROWN Phil: (4x400) 3 1983 World, 2 1984
Oly, 2 1987 World
BUCKNER Jack: (5000) 1 1986 Eur, 3 1987
World
BUDD Zola: 1 1985 & 1986 World CC; world
records – 2000 (5:33.15* – 1984), 5000
(14:48.07 – 1985); world indoor record
– 3000 (8:39.79 – 1986)
BULL Mike: 1 1970 CG PV, 1 1974 CG Dec
BUNNEY Elliot: 2 1988 Oly 4x100
BURGHLEY Lord: 1 1928 Oly 400H, 1 1930
CG 120yH & 440yH, 2 1932 Oly 4x400;
world record – 440yH (54.2 – 1927)
BURKE Barbara (GBR/S Africa): 2 1936 Oly
4x100; world records – 100y (11.0 – 1935),
220y (24.8 – 1935), 80mH (11.6 – 1937)
BUTLER Guy: 2 1920 Oly 400 (1 4x400),
3 1924 Oly 400 (3 4x400); world record
– 300y (30.6 – 1926)

C

CAHILL Chris: see under BOXER
CAINES Daniel: 1 2001 World Ind 400, 2
2003 World Ind 400 (3 4x400)
CALLEBOUT Nora: World record – 4x100m/
4x110y (51.4/51.8 – 1922)
CALLENDER Bev: (4x100) 3 1980 Oly, 2
1983 World, 2 1984 Oly
CAMPBELL Darren: 3 1997 World 4x100, 1
1998 Eur 100, 2 1999 World 4x100, 2 2000
Oly 200, 3 2003 World 100, 1 2004 Oly
4x100
CAPES Geoff: (SP) 1 1974 Eur Ind, 1 1974
CG, 1 1976 Eur Ind, 1 1978 CG; WR 1975
CAREY Sheila: World records – 4x800 (8:27.0
& 8:25.0 – 1970)
CARTER Chris: World record – 4x880y
(7:14.6* – 1966)
CAST Alice: World records – 200 (27.8
– 1922), 4x200m/4x220y (1:53.0 – 1921)
CAWLEY Shirley: 3 1952 Oly LJ
CHAMBERS Dwain: 3 1999 World 100 (2
4x100)
CHARLES Diane: see under LEATHER
CHATAWAY Chris: 1 1954 CG 3M; world
records – 3M (13:32.2 – 1954, 13:23.2
– 1955), 5000 (13:51.6 – 1954), 4x1M
(16:41.0 – 1953)

CHEESEMAN Sylvia: 3 1952 Oly 4x100;
world records – 4x200 (1:39.7 – 1952),
4x220y (1:43.9, 1:43.4 & 1:41.4
– 1951)
CHIPCHASE Ian: 1 1974 CG HT
CHRISTIE Linford: 1 1986 Eur Ind 200, 1
1986 Eur 100, 3 1987 World 100, 1 1988
Eur Ind 60, 2 1988 Oly 100 (2 4x100), 1
1990 Eur Ind 60, 1 1990 CG & Eur 100, 2
1991 World Ind 60 & 200, 2 1991 World
4x100, 1 1992 Oly 100, 1 1993 World 100
(2 4x100), 1 1994 CG & Eur 100; world
indoor records – 200 (20.25 – 1995), 4x200
(1:22.11 – 1991); WR (100) 1992, 1993 &
1994
CHRISTMAS Ruth: World record – 1M
(5:27.5* – 1932)
CHURCHER Harry: World records – 5M Walk
(35:43.4 – 1948, 35:33.0 – 1949)
CLARK Duncan: 1 1950 CG HT
CLARK Peter: World record – 4x1M (16:30.6
– 1958)
CLOVER Charles: 1 1974 CG JT
COALES Bill: 1 1908 Oly 3M team race (3rd
indiv)
COBB Madeleine: World records – 4x110y
(45.3 – 1958, 45.2 – 1963)
COE Seb: 1 1977 Eur Ind 800, 1 1980 Oly
1500 (2 800), 1 1984 Oly 1500 (2 800), 1
1986 Eur 800; world records – 800 (1:42.33
– 1979, 1:41.73 – 1981), 1000 (2:13.40 –
1980, 2:12.18 – 1981), 1500 (3:32.1/3:32.03
– 1979), 1M (3:48.95 – 1979, 3:48.53 &
3:47.33 – 1981), 4x800 (7:03.89 – 1982);
world indoor records – 800 (1:46.0* – 1981,
1:44.91 – 1983), 1000 (2:18.58* – 1983);
WR (800) 1979, 1981 & 1982, (1500/1M)
1979 & 1981
COLE Billy: 1 1986 CG SP
COLEBROOK Jane: see under FINCH
COLYEAR Sharon: World record – 4x200
(1:31.6 – 1977)
CONDON Allyn: 3 1999 World Ind 4x400
CONNOR Keith: (TJ) 1 1978 CG, 1 1982
CG & Eur, 3 1984 Oly; world indoor record
– (17.31* – 1981); WR 1982
COOK Garry: (4x400) 3 1983 World, 2 1984
Oly; world record – 4x800 (7:03.89 – 1982)
COOK Kathy: 3 1980 Oly 4x100, 3 1983
World 200 (2 4x100), 3 1984 Oly 400 (3
4x100)
COOPER Bert: World records – 3000 Walk
(12:38.2 – 1935), 5000 (21:52.4 – 1935)
COOPER John: 2 1964 Oly 400H (2 4x400)
CORNELL Muriel: World records – 80mH
(12.2* – 1930), LJ (5.48 & 5.57* – 1926, 5.57
– 1927)
CORNES Jerry: 2 1932 Oly 1500; world
record – 4x1500 (15:55.6 – 1931)
COTTERELL Joe: 1 1924 & 1929 Int CC

COTTRILL William: 3 1912 Oly CC team race

CRAIG Georgena: World record – 4x800 (8:25.0 – 1970)

CRAM Steve: 1 1982 CG & Eur 1500, 1 1983 World 1500, 2 1984 Oly 1500, 1 1986 CG 800 & 1500, 1 1986 Eur 1500; world records – 1500 (3:29.67 – 1985), 1M (3:46.32 – 1985), 2000 (4:51.39 – 1985), 4x800 (7:03.89 – 1982); WR (1500/1M) 1982, 1983, 1985, 1986 & 1988

CRITCHLEY Muriel: World record – 3x880y (7:00.6 – 1952)

CROPPER Pat: see under LOWE

D

DALY John (GB/IRL): 2 1904 Oly 2590mSC

D'ARCY Vic: 1 1912 Oly 4x100; world record – 4x100 (43.0* – 1912)

DAVIES John: World indoor record – 1000 (2:20.9* – 1970)

DAVIES Lynn: (LJ) 1 1964 Oly, 1 1966 CG & Eur, 1 1967 Eur Ind, 1 1970 CG

DEAKIN Joe: 1 1908 Oly 3M team race (individual winner)

DENMARK Rob: 3 1991 World Ind 3000, 1 1994 CG 5000

DESFORGES Jean: 3 1952 Oly 4x100, 1 1954 Eur LJ

DEVONISH Marlon: 2 1999 World 4x100, 1 2003 World Ind 200, 1 2004 Oly 4x100, 3 2005 World 4x100

DISLEY John: 3 1952 Oly 3000SC

DISLEY Sylvia: see under CHEESEMAN

DOUGLAS Sandra: 3 1992 Oly 4x400

DRIVER Peter: 1 1954 CG 6M

DRYDEN Joan: World record – 3x880y (7:00.6 – 1952)

DUNKLEY Ralph: World record – 4x1500 (15:27.2 – 1953)

DYSON Maureen: see under GARDNER

DYSON Sandra: World record – 400H (61.1* – 1971)

E

EAST Michael: 1 2002 CG 1500

EATON William: 1 1936 Int CC

ECKERSLEY Harry: 1 1928 Int CC

EDWARD Harry: 3 1920 Oly 100 & 200

EDWARDS Eileen: World records – 100y (11.3* – 1924), 200 (26.0 – 1926, 25.4 – 1927), 200m/220y (26.2 – 1924, 25.8* – 1926 & 1927), 400m/440y (60.8 – 1924), 4x100m/4x110y (50.2* & 49.8 – 1926), 4x200m/4x220y (1:51.6/1:52.4 – 1923)

EDWARDS Jonathan: (TJ) 3 1993 World, 1 1995 World, 2 1996 Oly, 2 1997 World, 1 1998 Eur Ind, 1 1998 Eur, 3 1999 World, 1 2000 Oly, 2 2001 World Ind, 1 2001 World, 1 2002 CG; world records – (17.98, 18.16 &

18.29 – 1995); WR 1995, 1996, 1998, 1999, 2000, 2001 & 2002

ELDER Verona: 1 1973, 1975 & 1979 Eur Ind 400; world record – 4x200 (1:31.6 – 1977)

ELDON Stan: 1 1958 Int CC

ELLIOTT Geoff: 1 1954 & 1958 CG PV

ELLIOTT Gladys: World records – 200m/220y (26.8* – 1924), 4x200m/4x220y (1:51.6/1:52.4 – 1923)

ELLIOTT Peter: 2 1987 World 800, 2 1988 Oly 1500, 1 1990 CG 1500; world record – 4x800 (7:03.89 – 1982); world indoor record – 1500 (3:34.20 – 1990)

ELLIOTT-LYNN Sophie: World record – HJ (1.485 – 1923)

ELLIS Cyril: World record – 1000y (2:11.2 – 1929)

ELLIS Mike: 1 1958 CG HT

EMERY Jack: 1 1938 Int CC

ENGELHART Stan: 1 1930 CG 220y

EVANS Frank: World record – 4x880y (7:30.6 – 1951)

EVENSON Tom: 1 1930 & 1932 Int CC, 2 1932 Oly 3000SC

EYRE Len: 1 1950 CG 3M

F

FAWKES Marion: 1 1979 World Walk Cup 5k; world records – 10,000 (48:37.6* & 48:11.4* – 1979)

FENN Jo: 3 2004 World Ind 800

FERRIS Sam: 2 1932 Oly Mar

FINCH Jane: (800) 1 1977 Eur Ind, 2 1985 World Ind; world indoor record – 800 (2:01.12* – 1977)

FINLAY Don: 3 1932 Oly 110H, 1 1934 CG 120yH, 2 1936 Oly 110H, 1 1938 Eur 110H

FITZSIMONS John: 1 1966 CG JT

FLOCKHART Jim: 1 1937 Int CC

FLYNN Olly: 1 1978 CG 30k Walk

FORD Bernie: 3 1976 World CC

FORSTER Evelyne: World record – 1M (5:15.3* – 1939)

FOSTER Barbara: World record – 4x220y (1:41.4 – 1951)

FOSTER Brendan: 1 1974 Eur 5000, 3 1976 Oly 10,000, 1 1978 CG 10,000; world records – 3000 (7:35.1 – 1974), 2M (8:13.68 – 1973); WR (10,000) 1975 & 1977

FOULDS June: see under PAUL

FOWLER Roy: 1 1963 Int CC

FRASER Donna: 3 2005 World 4x400

FREEMAN Walter: 1 1921 Int CC

FRITH Bob: World indoor record – 50 (5.5* – 1963)

FUDGE Paula: 1 1978 CG 3000; world record – 5000 (15:14.51 – 1981); world indoor record – 3000 (8:56.4* – 1981)

G

GARDENER Jason: 3 1999 World Ind 60, 2 1999 World 4x100, 1 2000 & 2002 Eur Ind 60, 3 2003 World Ind 60, 1 2004 World Ind 60, 1 2004 Oly 4x100, 1 2005 Eur Ind 60, 3 2005 World 4x100
GARDINER Charles: World professional best – Mar (2:37:02 – 1909)
GARDNER Maureen: 2 1948 Oly 80mH
GARRITT Eileen: World record – 3x800m/3x880y (7:07.8 – 1949)
GARTON Agnes: World record – 4x200m/4x220y (1:53.0 – 1921)
GILL Cyril: 3 1928 Oly 4x100
GLOVER Ernest: 3 1912 Oly CC team race
GODDARD Bev: see under CALLENDER
GODDARD Tracy: 3 1993 World 4x400
GOLDING Julian: 3 1997 World 4x100, 1 1998 CG 200
GOLLEY Julian: 1 1994 CG TJ
GOODWIN Reginald: 2 1924 Oly 10,000 Walk
GRAHAM Tim: 2 1964 Oly 4x400
GRANT Dalton: (HJ) 1 1994 Eur Ind, 1 1998 CG
GRANT Graeme: World record – 4x880y (7:14.6* – 1966)
GREEN Freddie: World record – 3M (13:32.2 – 1954)
GREEN Harry: World records – 2 hours (33,057m – 1913), 25M (2:29:04.0 – 1913); world best – Mar (2:38:16.2 track – 1913)
GREEN Phyllis (1): World records – HJ (1.52 – 1925, 1.55 – 1926, 1.58* – 1927)
GREEN Phyllis (2): see under PERKINS
GREEN Tommy: 1 1932 Oly 50k Walk
GREENWOOD Dora: World record – HJ (1.65* – 1933)
GREGORY Jack: 2 1948 Oly 4x100
GREIG Dale: World best – Mar (3:27:45 – 1964)
GRIFFITHS Cecil: 1 1920 Oly 4x400
GRINDLEY David: 3 1992 Oly 4x400
GUNN Charles: 3 1920 Oly 10,000 Walk
GUNN Muriel: see under CORNELL
GUNNELL Sally: 1 1986 CG 100H, 1 1989 Eur Ind 400, 1 1990 CG 400H, 2 1991 World 400H, 1 1992 Oly 400H (3 4x400), 1 1993 World 400H (3 4x400), 1 1994 CG & Eur 400H; world record – 400H (52.74 – 1993); WR 1991, 1992, 1993 & 1994

H

HALL Dorothy: see under MANLEY
HALL Olive: World record – 880y (2:17.4 – 1936)
HALL Phyllis: World record – 800m/880y (2:43.0* – 1922)
HALLOWS Norman: 3 1908 Oly 1500

HALSTEAD Nellie: 3 1932 Oly 4x100; world records – 100y (11.0* – 1931), 220y (25.2* – 1930), 400m/440y (58.8* – 1931, 58.8* & 56.8* – 1932), 800 (2:15.6* – 1935)
HALSWELLE Wyndham: 2 1906 Oly 400 (3 800), 1 1908 Oly 400
HAMPSON Tom: 1 1930 CG 880y, 1 1932 Oly 800 (2 4x400); world record – 800 (1:49.70 – 1932)
HAMPTON Shirley: World records – 4x200 (1:39.7 – 1952), 4x220y (1:39.9 – 1953)
HANSEN Ashia: (TJ) 2 1997 World Ind, 1 1998 Eur Ind, 1 1998 CG, 1 1999 World Ind, 1 2002 CG & Eur, 1 2003 World Ind; world indoor record – (15.16 – 1998); WR 2002
HARDING Enid: World records – 880y (2:14.4* – 1952), 1M (5:09.8* – 1953)
HARDY Roland: World records – 5M Walk (35:24.0 – 1951, 35:15.0 – 1952)
HARPER Ernie: 1 1926 Int CC, 2 1936 Oly Mar; world records – 25,000m (1:23:45.8 – 1929), 2 hours (33,653m – 1933)
HARRIS Aubrey: World record – 4x1500 (15:55.6 – 1931)
HARRISON Rob: 1 1985 Eur Ind 800
HARTLEY Donna: 1 1978 CG 400, 3 1980 Oly 4x400; world record – 4x200 (1:31.6 – 1977)
HATT Hilda: World record – 4x100m/4x110y (51.8 – 1921)
HAWTREY Henry: 1 1906 Oly 5M
HAYNES Florence: World records – 440y (60.8* – 1928), 4x100m/4x110y (50.2* & 49.8 – 1926)
HEARD Steve: 1 1989 Eur Ind 800
HEARNSHAW Sue: (LJ) 1 1984 Eur Ind, 3 1984 Oly
HEATLEY Basil: 1 1961 Int CC, 2 1964 Oly Mar; world record – 10M (47:47.0 – 1961), world best – Mar (2:13:55 – 1964)
HEDGES Harry: World record – 4x1500 (15:55.6 – 1931)
HEGARTY Frank: 2 1920 Oly CC team race
HEMERY David: 1 1966 CG 120yH, 1 1968 Oly 400H, 1 1970 CG 110H, 3 1972 Oly 400H (2 4x400); world record – 400H (48.12 – 1968); WR (400H) 1968
HENLEY Ernest: 3 1912 Oly 4x400
HENRY Cori: 3 2003 World Ind 4x400
HERBERT John: 1 1986 CG TJ
HERRIOTT Maurice: 2 1964 Oly 3000SC
HEWSON Brian: 1 1958 Eur 1500; world record – 4x1M (16:30.6 – 1958); world bests – 1000y (2:08.0 – 1955, 2:07.5 – 1956), 3/4M (2:55.4 – 1955, 2:55.2 – 1958)
HIBBINS Fred: 3 1912 Oly CC team race
HICKS Nelly: World record – 800m/880y (2:45.0 – 1922)
HIGGINS Peter: 3 1956 Oly 4x400

HILL Albert: 1 1920 Oly 800 & 1500 (2 3000 team race)

HILL Mick: 3 1993 World JT

HILL Ron: (Mar) 1 1969 Eur, 1 1970 CG; world records – 10M (47:02.2 & 46:44.0 – 1968), 15M (1:12:48.2 – 1965), 25,000m (1:15:22.6 – 1965); WR (Mar) 1970

HISCOCK Eileen: 3 1932 Oly 4x100, 1 1934 CG 100y & 220y, 2 1936 Oly 4x100; world records – 100y (11.0* – 1931), 220y (25.0* – 1934)

HISCOX Molly: World record – 440y (55.6 – 1958)

HODGE Percy: 1 1920 Oly 3000SC

HOGAN Jim: 1 1966 Eur Mar; world record – 30,000m (1:32:25.4 – 1966)

HOLDEN Jack: 1 1933, 1934, 1935 & 1939 Int CC, 1 1950 CG & Eur Mar; WR (Mar) 1950

HOLMES Cyril: 1 1938 CG 100y & 220y

HOLMES Kelly: 1 1994 CG 1500, 2 1995 World 1500 (3 800), 3 2000 Oly 800, 1 2002 CG 1500, 2 2003 World Ind 1500, 2 2003 World 800, 1 2004 Oly 800 & 1500; WR (800 & 1500) 2004

HOPKINS Thelma: (HJ) 1 1954 CG & Eur, 2= 1956 Oly; world record (1.74 – 1956)

HORGAN Dennis (GBR/IRL): 2 1908 Oly SP; world best (from 7ft square) – (14.88 – 1904)

HOSKIN Sheila: 1 1958 CG LJ; world record – 4x100 (45.2* – 1956)

HOYTE-SMITH Joslyn: 3 1980 Oly 4x400

HUMPHREYS Tom: 3 1912 Oly CC team race

HUNTE Heather: see under OAKES

HUNTER Alan: 1 1934 CG 440yH

HUTCHINGS Tim: 2 1984 & 1989 World CC

HUTSON George: 3 1912 Oly 5000 & 3000 team race

HYMAN Dorothy: 2 1960 Oly 100 (3 200), 1 1962 Eur 100, 1 1962 CG 100y & 220y, 3 1964 Oly 4x100; world records – 4x110y (45.3 – 1958, 45.2 – 1963); WR (100) 1962 & 1963, (200) 1963

I

IBBOTSON Derek: 3 1956 Oly 5000; world records – 1M (3:57.2 – 1957), 4x1M (16:30.6 – 1958); WR (1500/1M) 1957

INKPEN Barbara: see under LAWTON

J

JACKSON Arnold: 1 1912 Oly 1500

JACKSON Colin: (110H) 3 1987 World, 2 1988 Oly, 1 1989 Eur Ind 60H, 1 1989 World Ind 60H, 1 1990 CG & Eur, 2 1993 World Ind 60H, 1 1993 World (2 4x100), 1 1994 Eur Ind 60 & 60H, 1 1994 CG & Eur, 2 1997 World

Ind 60H, 2 1997 World, 1 1998 Eur, 1 1999 World Ind 60H, 1 1999 World, 1 2002 Eur Ind 60H, 1 2002 Eur; world record – 110H (12.91 – 1993), world best – 200H (22.63 – 1991), world indoor records – 60H (7.36 & 7.30 – 1994); WR 1992, 1993 & 1994

JACOBS David: 1 1912 Oly 4x100; world record – 4x100 (43.0* – 1912)

JACOBS Simmone: 3 1984 Oly 4x100

JAMES Della: World record – 4x200 (1:33.8 – 1968)

JARRETT Tony: (110H) 3 1991 World (3 4x100), 2 1993 World (2 4x100), 3 1995 World Ind 60H, 2 1995 World, 1 1998 CG

JENKINS David: 1 1971 Eur 400, 2 1972 Oly 4x400; WR 1975

JOHNSON Ann: World records – 4x200 (1:39.7 – 1952), 4x220y (1:39.9 – 1953)

JOHNSON Derek: 1 1954 CG 880y, 2 1956 Oly 800 (3 4x400)

JOHNSON Ethel: World record – 100y (11.0* – 1932)

JOHNSTON Johnny: 2 1924 Oly 3000 team race

JOHNSTON Tim: World record – 30,000m (1:32:34.6 – 1965)

JONES Berwyn: World record – 4x110y (40.0 – 1963)

JONES David: 3 1960 Oly 4x100; world record – 4x110y (40.0 – 1963)

JONES Ken: 2 1948 Oly 4x100

JONES Mick: 1 2002 CG HT

JONES Pat: World record – 200H (27.3* – 1967)

JONES Ron: World record – 4x110y (40.0 – 1963)

JONES Steve: 3 1984 World CC; world best – Mar (2:08:05 – 1984); WR (Mar) 1985

JORDAN Joy: World record – 880y (2:06.1 – 1960)

K

KELLY Barrie: 1 1966 Eur Ind 60

KEOUGH Linda: 3 1993 World 4x400

KIELY Tom (GBR/IRL): 1 1904 Oly 'Decathlon'

KILBY Brian: 1 1962 Eur & CG Mar; WR 1962

KINCH Bev: 1 1984 Eur Ind 60

KING Marion: World records – 220y (25.8* – 1928), 440y (60.6* & 59.2* – 1929)

L

LADEJO Du'aine: (400) 1 1994 Eur Ind, 1 1994 Eur, 1 1996 Eur Ind

LANE Gladys: World record – 800m/880y (2:24.8* – 1925)

LANNAMAN Sonia: 1 1978 CG 100, 3 1980 Oly 4x100; world record – 4x200 (1:31.6 – 1977)

LARNER George: 1 1908 Oly 3500m & 10M Walks; world records included – 2M (13:11.4 – 1904), 5M (36:00.2 – 1905), 7M (50:50.8 – 1905), 10M (1:15:57.4 – 1908) and 1 hour (13,275m – 1905)

LAW David: World record – 4x1500 (15:27.2 – 1953)

LAWTON Barbara: 1 1974 CG HJ

LEACH Daisy: World record – 4x100m/ 4x110y (51.4/51.8 – 1922)

LEAHY Con (GBR/IRL): 1 1906 Oly HJ (2 TJ), 2= 1908 Oly HJ

LEAHY Patrick (GBR/IRL): 2 1900 Oly HJ (3 LJ)

LEATHER Diane: World records – 440y (56.6* – 1954), 880y (2:09.0 – 1954), 1500 (4:30.0* & 4:29.7* – 1957), 1M (5:02.6* – 1953, 5:00.2* & 4:59.6* – 1954, 4:50.8* & 4:45.0* – 1955), 3x880y (6:49.0 – 1953, 6:46.0 – 1954); WR (800) 1957

LERWILL Alan: 1 1974 CG LJ

LERWILL Sheila: (HJ) 1 1950 Eur, 2 1952 Oly; world record (1.72 – 1951)

LEWIS Denise: (Hep) 1 1994 CG, 3 1996 Oly, 2 1997 World, 1 1998 Eur & CG, 2 1999 World, 1 2000 Oly; WR 1998 & 2000

LEWIS-FRANCIS Mark: 3 2001 World Ind 60, 1 2004 Oly 4x100, 3 2005 World 4x100

LIDDELL Eric: 1 1924 Oly 400 (3 200)

LINDSAY Robert: 1 1920 Oly 4x400

LINES Mary: World records – 60 (7.8* – 1922), 100y (11.8 – 1921, 11.6 – 1922), 100m (12.8 – 1922), 200m/220y (26.8 – 1922), 400m/440y (64.4 – 1922, 62.4 – 1923), 800m/880y (2:26.6 – 1922), 4x100m/4x110y (51.4/51.8 – 1922), 4x200m/4x220y (1:53.0 – 1921, 1:51.6/1:52.4 – 1923)

LIVINGSTON Jason: 1 1992 Eur Ind 60

LLOYD JOHNSON Tebbs: 3 1948 Oly 50k Walk

LOCK Betty: World record – 60m (7.4* – 1938)

LONDON Jack: 2 1928 Oly 100 (3 4x100)

LOWE Douglas: 1 1924 & 1928 Oly 800; world record – 600y (1:10.4 – 1926)

LOWE Pat: World records – 4x400 (3:30.8 – 1969), 3x800 (6:20.0 – 1967), 3x880y (6:25.2 – 1967), 4x800 (8:27.0 & 8:25.0 – 1970)

LOWMAN Ivy: World records – HJ (1.47* – 1923)

LUCKING Martyn: 1 1962 CG SP

LUNN Gladys: 1 1934 CG 880y & JT; world records – 880y (2:18.2* – 1930), 1000 (3:04.4 – 1931, 3:00.6 – 1934), 1M (5:24.0* & 5:23.0* – 1936, 5:20.8* & 5:17.0* – 1937)

LYNCH Andrea: 1 1975 Eur Ind 60; world record – 60 (7.2 – 1974)

M

MACDONALD Bernard: 2 1924 Oly 3000 team race (3rd indiv)

MACDONALD Linsey: 3 1980 Oly 4x400

MACEY Dean: (Dec) 2 1999 World, 3 2001 World

MACINTOSH Henry: 1 1912 Oly 4x100; world record – 4x100 (43.0* – 1912)

MAFE Ade: (200) 2 1985 World Ind, 1 1989 Eur Ind & World Ind, 3 1991 World Ind; world indoor record – 4x200 (1:22.11 – 1991)

MALCOLM Christian: 1 2000 Eur Ind 200, 2 2001 World Ind 200, 3 2005 World 4x100

MANLEY Dorothy: 2 1948 Oly 100; world record – 4x220y (1:41.4 – 1951)

MARTIN Eamonn: 1 1990 CG 10,000

MATTHEWS Ken: (20k Walk) 1 1961 World Walk Cup, 1 1962 Eur, 1 1963 World Walk Cup, 1 1964 Oly

MAYOCK John: 1 1998 Eur Ind 3000

McCOLGAN Liz: 1 1986 CG 10,000, 2 1987 World CC, 2 1988 Oly 10,000, 2 1989 World Ind 3000, 1 1990 CG 10,000, 3 1991 World CC, 1 1991 World 10,000, 1 1992 World Half Mar; world indoor record – 5000 (15:03.17 – 1992); world road bests – 5k (14:57 – 1991), 10k (30:38 – 1989), Half Mar (67:11 – 1992); WR (10,000) 1991

McCONNELL Lee: 3 2005 World 4x400

McCORQUODALE Alistair: 2 1948 Oly 4x100

McDERMOTT Kirsty: see under WADE

McFARLANE Mike: 1= 1982 CG 200, 1 1985 Eur Ind 60, 2 1988 Oly 4x100

McGHEE Joe: 1 1954 CG Mar

McGOUGH John (GBR/IRL): 2 1906 Oly 1500

McKEAN Tom: (800) 1 1990 Eur Ind, 1 1990 Eur, 1 1993 World Ind

McLEOD Mike: 2 1984 Oly 10,000

MERRY Katharine: 3 2000 Oly 400

METCALFE Adrian: 2 1964 Oly 4x400; WR (400) 1961

MILLIGAN Bill: World record – 4x880y (7:50.4 – 1920)

MITCHELL Roy: 1 1978 CG LJ

MODAHL Diane: 1 1990 CG 800

MONTAGUE Edwin: World record – 600y (1:11.0* – 1908)

MOORCROFT Dave: 1 1978 CG 1500, 1 1982 CG 5000; world record – 5000 (13:00.41 – 1982); WR (5000) 1982

MOORE Betty (GBR/AUS): World record – 80mH (10.5 – 1962)

MORGAN Nathan: 1 2002 CG LJ

MORLEY Kay: 1 1990 CG 100H

MOUNTAIN Edgar: World record – 500 (65.6* – 1921)

MURRAY Yvonne: 1 1987 Eur Ind 3000, 3 1988 Oly 3000, 1 1990 Eur 3000, 1 1993 World Ind 3000, 1 1994 CG 10,000; WR (3000) 1990

N

NANKEVILLE Bill: World records – 4x880y (7:30.6 – 1951), 4x1500 (15:27.2 – 1953), 4x1M (16:41.0 – 1953)

NEIL Anita: World record – 4x110y (45.0 – 1968)

NEUFVILLE Marilyn: 1 1970 Eur Ind 400; world indoor record – 400 (53.01* – 1970); later representing Jamaica: 1st 1970 CG 400; world record – 400 (51.02 – 1970); WR 1970

NEWBOULT Jean: World record – 4x220y (1:39.9 – 1953)

NICHOL William: 2 1924 Oly 4x100; world record – 4x100 (42.0 – 1924)

NICHOLS Alfred: 1 1914 Int CC, 3 1920 Oly CC team race

NICOL George: 3 1912 Oly 4x400

NIHILL Paul: 2 1964 Oly 50k Walk, 1 1969 Eur 20k

NOEL-BAKER Philip: see under BAKER

NOKES Malcolm: (HT) 3 1924 Oly, 1 1930 & 1934 CG

NORRIS Fred: 1 1959 Int CC

NUTTING Pat: World records – 100H (14.3* – 1966), 200H (28.3* – 1961)

O

OAKES Gary: 3 1980 Oly 400H

OAKES Heather: 3 1980 & 1984 Oly 4x100, 2 1985 World Ind 60, 1 1986 CG 100

OAKES Judy: 1 1982, 1994 & 1998 CG SP

O'CONNOR Peter (GBR/IRL): 1 1906 Oly TJ (2 LJ); world record – LJ (7.61 – 1901)

ODAM Dorothy: see under TYLER

OHURUOGU Christine: 3 2005 World 4x400

OLADAPO Joyce: 1 1986 CG LJ

OLIVER Anne: World records – 1M (5:11.0* – 1952, 5:08.0* – 1953), 3x880y (6:46.0 – 1954)

OLNEY Violet: 2 1936 Oly 4x100

OTTLEY Dave: (JT) 2 1984 Oly, 1 1986 CG

OVETT Steve: 1 1978 Eur 1500, 1 1980 Oly 800 (3 1500), 1 1986 CG 5000; world records – 1500 (3:32.1/3:32.09 & 3:31.36 – 1980, 3:30.77 – 1983), 1M (3:48.8 – 1980, 3:48.40 – 1981), 2M (8:13.51* – 1978); world bests – 3/4M (2:51.0 – 1980, 2:50.4 – 1981); WR (1500/1M) 1977, 1978 & 1980

OWEN Edward: 2 1908 Oly 5M

P

PACKER Ann: 1 1964 Oly 800 (2 400); world record – 800 (2:01.1 – 1964)

PALMER Vera: World record – 4x200m/ 4x220y (1:51.6/1:52.4 – 1923)

PARLETT Dorothy: see under MANLEY

PARLETT John: 1 1950 CG 880y, 1 1950 Eur 800; world record – 4x880y (7:30.6 – 1951)

PASCOE Alan: 1 1969 Eur Ind 50H, 2 1972 Oly 4x400, 1 1974 CG & Eur 400H; WR (400H) 1975

PASCOE Della: see under JAMES

PASHLEY Anne: 2 1956 Oly 4x100; world records – 4x100 (45.2* – 1956), 4x220y (1:39.9 – 1953)

PATERSON Alan: 1 1950 Eur HJ; WR 1949

PATRICK Adrian: 3 1999 World Ind 4x400

PAUL June: (4x100) 3 1952 Oly, 2 1956 Oly; world records – 4x100 (45.2* – 1956), 4x110y (45.3 – 1958), 4x200 (1:39.7 – 1952), 4x220y (1:43.9 & 1:43.4 – 1951)

PAWSEY Jenny: World record – 4x400 (3:37.6 – 1969)

PAYNE Howard: 1 1962, 1966 & 1970 CG HT

PAYNE Rosemary: 1 1970 CG DT

PAYNE Lewis: 1 1927 Int CC

PEAT Val: World record – 4x200 (1:33.8 – 1968)

PENNY Arthur: 1 1934 CG 6M

PERERA Chris: World record – 100H (13.7* – 1967)

PERKINS Phyllis: World records – 1500 (4:35.4* – 1956), 3x880y (7:00.6 – 1952)

PETERS Jim: World bests – Mar (2:20:43 – 1952, 2:18:41 & 2:18:35 – 1953, 2:17:40 – 1954); WR 1953

PETERS Mary: 1 1970 CG SP & Pen, 1 1972 Oly Pen, 1 1974 CG Pen; world record – Pen (4801 – 1972), world indoor record – 60H (8.5* – 1970); WR (Pen) 1972

PICKERING Jean: see under DESFORGES

PIERCY Pam: World records – 3x800 (6:20.0 – 1967), 3x880y (6:25.2 – 1967)

PIERCY Violet: World best – Mar (3:40:22 – 1926)

PIRIE Gordon: 2 1956 Oly 5000; world records – 3000 (7:55.5 & 7:52.7 – 1956), 5000 (13:36.8 – 1956), 6M (28:19.4 – 1953), 4x1500 (15:27.2 – 1953)

PIRIE Shirley: see under HAMPTON

PLATT Sue: 1 1962 CG JT

PLUMB Arthur: World record – 20M Walk (2:43:38.0 – 1932)

POPE Alf: World records – 5M Walk (35:47.2 – 1932), 10,000 (44:42.4 – 1932), 7M (50:28.8 – 1932), 1 hour (13,308m – 1932)

PORTER Cyril: 3 1912 Oly CC team race

PORTER Gwendoline: 3 1932 Oly 4x100

PORTER Muriel: World record – 4x100m/ 4x110y (51.4/51.8 – 1922)

POTTER Edna: World record – 220y (25.8* – 1928)

PRICE Berwyn: 1 1978 CG 110H

PRITCHARD Norman: (GBR/IND) 2 1900 Oly 200

PROBERT Michelle: 3 1980 Oly 4x400
PRYCE Pat: see under NUTTING
PUGH Derek: 1 1950 Eur 400

Q

QUINTON Carole: 2 1960 Oly 80mH

R

RADCLIFFE Paula: 2 1997 World CC, 2 1998 World 8k CC, 1 1998 Eur CC, 3 1999 World 8k CC, 2 1999 World 10,000, 1 2000 World Half Mar, 1 2001 World 8k CC (2 4k CC), 1 2001 World Half Mar, 1 2002 World 8k CC, 1 2002 CG 5000, 1 2002 Eur 10,000, 1 2003 World Half Mar, 1 2003 Eur CC, 1 2005 World Mar; world road records – 10k (30:21 – 2003), 20k (63:26 – 2001), Mar (2:17:18 – 2002, 2:15:25 – 2003); world road bests include – 5k (14:51 – 2003), 8k (24:38 – 1999), 5M (24:47 – 1999), 10M (50:01 – 2003), 15k (46:41 – 2003), Half Mar 65:40 (2003); WR (10,000) 2002, (Half Mar) 2000, 2001 & 2003; (Mar) 2002, 2003 & 2005
RADFORD Peter: 3 1960 Oly 100 (3 4x100); world records – 200m/220y (20.5 – 1960), 4x110y (40.0 – 1963), world indoor record – 50m (5.5* – 1958)
RAMPLING Godfrey: 2 1932 Oly 4x400, 1 1934 CG 440y, 1 1936 Oly 4x400
RAND Mary: 1 1964 Oly LJ (2 Pen, 3 4x100), 1 1966 CG LJ; world records – LJ (6.76 – 1964), 4x110y (45.2 – 1963); world indoor record – LJ (6.35* – 1965); WR (LJ) 1959, 1960, 1963 & 1964
RANGELEY Walter: 2 1924 Oly 4x100, 2 1928 Oly 200 (3 4x100); world record – 4x100 (42.0 – 1924)
RAWLINSON Chris: 1 2002 CG 400H
RAWSON Mike: 1 1958 Eur 800
REDMAN Frank: World record – 10M Walk (1:14:30.6 – 1934)
REDMOND Derek: (4x400) 2 1987 World, 1 1991 World
REEVE Sue: 1 1978 CG LJ
REGIS John: 3 1987 World 200, 2 1988 Oly 4x100, 1 1989 World Ind 200, 1 1990 Eur 200, 1 1991 World 4x400 (3 4x100), 3 1992 Oly 4x400, 2 1993 World 200 (2 4x100); world indoor record – 4x200 (1:22.11 – 1991)
REITZ Colin: 3 1983 World 3000SC
RENWICK George: 3 1924 Oly 4x400
REYNOLDS Martin: 2 1972 Oly 4x400
RICHARDS Tom: 2 1948 Oly Mar
RICHARDSON Mark: (4x400) 2 1996 Oly, 2 1997 World
RIDGEON Jon: 3 1985 World Ind 60H, 2 1987 World 110H

RIDLEY Rita: 1 1970 CG 1500, 3 1974 World CC
RIMMER John: 1 1900 Oly 5000 team race (2nd indiv) & 4000mSC
RIPLEY Richard: 3 1924 Oly 4x400
RITCHIE Meg: 1 1982 CG DT
ROBERTS Bill: 1 1936 Oly 4x400, 1 1938 CG 440y
ROBERTSON Archie: 1 1908 Int CC, 1 1908 Oly 3M team race (2nd indiv) (2 3200mSC); world record – 5000 (15:01.2* – 1908)
ROBINS Valerie: World records – 4x220y (1:43.9 & 1:43.4 – 1951)
ROBINSON Sidney: 1 1900 Oly 5000 team race (2 2500mSC, 3 4000mSC)
ROSE Nick: 3 1980 World CC
ROSS Harold: World records – 15M Walk (1:59:12.6 – 1911), 2 hours (24,256m – 1911)
ROWE Arthur: 1 1958 CG & Eur SP
ROWLAND Mark: 3 1988 Oly 3000SC
ROYLE Lancelot: 2 1924 Oly 4x100; world record – 4x100 (42.0 – 1924)
RUFF Janet: World record – 440y (56.5* – 1956)
RUSSELL Arthur: 1 1908 Oly 3200mSC

S

SALISBURY John: 3 1956 Oly 4x400
SANDERS Nicola: 3 2005 World 4x400
SANDERSON Tessa: (JT) 1 1978 CG, 1 1984 Oly, 1 1986 & 1990 CG
SANDO Frank: 1 1955 & 1957 Int CC
SAUNDERS Geoff: 1 1951 Int CC
SAVIDGE John: 1 1954 CG SP
SCARSBROOK Stan: 1 1934 CG 2MSC
SCHOFIELD Sidney: World record – 25M Walk (3:37:06.8 – 1911)
SCOULER Doris: World records – 4x100m/ 4x110y (50.2* & 49.8 – 1926)
SCRIVENS Jean: 2 1956 Oly 4x100; world record – 4x100 (45.2* – 1956)
SEAGROVE William: 2 1920 Oly 3000 team race
SEAMAN Don: World record – 4x1M (16:41.0 – 1953)
SEARLE Vera: see under PALMER
SEEDHOUSE Cyril: 3 1912 Oly 4x400
SEGAL Dave: 3 1960 Oly 4x100
SHARPE David: 1 1988 Eur Ind 800
SHAW Lorraine: 1 2002 CG HT
SHENTON Brian: 1 1950 Eur 200
SHERWOOD John: (400H) 3 1968 Oly, 1 1970 CG
SHERWOOD Sheila: (LJ) 2 1968 Oly, 1 1970 CG
SHIRLEY Dorothy: 2= 1960 Oly HJ
SHRUBB Alf: 1 1903 & 1904 Int CC; world records – 2M (9:11.0* – 1903, 9:09.6 – 1904), 3M (14:17.6 – 1903, 14:17.2*

– 1904), 6M (29:59.4 – 1904), 10,000 (31:02.4* – 1904), 10M (50:40.6 – 1904), 1 hour (18,742m – 1904)

SIMMONS Tony: 2 1976 World CC

SIMPSON Alan: World indoor record – 5000 (13:58.4* – 1965)

SIMPSON Janet: 3 1964 Oly 4x100; world records – 4x110y (45.0 – 1968), 4x200 (1:33.8 – 1968), 4x400 (3:37.6 & 3:30.8 – 1969); world best – 500m (1:11.7 – 1968)

SIMPSON Judy: 1 1986 CG Hep

SIMSON Matt: 1 1994 CG SP

SLATER Daphne: see under ARDEN

SLEMON Chris: World record – 3x880y (6:49.0 – 1953)

SLY Wendy: 1 1983 World 10k road, 2 1984 Oly 3000

SMALLEY Norah: World records – 3x880y (6:49.0 – 1953, 6:46.0 – 1954)

SMITH Anne: World records – 1500 (4:17.3* – 1967), 1M (4:39.2* & 4:37.0 – 1967); WR (800) 1965

SMITH Colin: 1 1958 CG JT

SMITH David: 1 1986 CG HT

SMITH Joyce: 1 1972 Int CC, 2 1973 World CC; world record – 3000 (9:23.4* – 1971)

SMITH Phylis: (4x400) 3 1992 Oly, 3 1993 World

SMITH Steve: (HJ) 3 1993 World Ind, 3 1993 World, 3 1996 Oly

SMOUHA Edward: 3 1928 Oly 4x100

SOLLY Jon: 1 1986 CG 10,000

SOTHERTON Kelly: 3 2004 Oly Hep

SOUTTER James: 3 1912 Oly 4x400

SPEDDING Charlie: 3 1984 Oly Mar

SPENCER Edward: 3 1908 Oly 10M Walk

STALLARD Henry: 3 1924 Oly 1500; world record – 4x880y (7:50.4 – 1920)

STEWART Ian: 1 1969 Eur Ind 3000, 1 1969 Eur 5000, 1 1970 CG 5000, 3 1972 Oly 5000, 1 1975 Eur Ind 3000, 1 1975 World CC; WR (5000) 1970

STEWART Lachie: 1 1970 CG 10,000

STEWART Mary: (1500) 1 1977 Eur Ind, 1 1978 CG; world indoor record (4:08.1* – 1977)

STEWART Peter: 1 1971 Eur Ind 3000

STIRLING Rosemary: 1 1970 CG 800; world records – 4x400 (3:30.8 – 1969), 3x800 (6:20.0 – 1967), 3x880y (6:25.2 – 1967), 4x800 (8:27.0 & 8:25.0 – 1970)

STONE Anne: World record – 440y (59.2* – 1929)

STONELEY Crew: 2 1932 Oly 4x400

STOUTE Jennifer: 3 1992 Oly 4x400

STRANG David: (1500) 2 1993 World Ind, 1 1994 Eur Ind

STRAW Charlie: 1 1906 Int CC

STRODE-JACKSON Arnold: see under JACKSON

STRONG Shirley: (100H) 1 1982 CG, 2 1984 Oly

SWEENEY Arthur: 1 1934 CG 100y & 220y

T

TAGG Mike: 1 1970 Int CC

TAITT Laurie: World indoor records – 60H (7.9* & 7.8* – 1963)

TATHAM Wilfrid: World record – 4x880y (7:50.4 – 1920)

THACKERY Carl: 3 1993 World Half Mar

THOMAS Iwan: 2 1996 Oly 4x400, 2 1997 World 4x400, 1 1998 Eur & CG 400

THOMAS Reggie: 1 1930 CG 1M; world record – 4x1500 (15:55.6 – 1931)

THOMAS Shirley: 2 1983 World 4x100

THOMPSON Daley: (Dec) 1 1978 Comm, 1 1980 Oly, 1 1982 Comm & Eur, 1 1983 World, 1 1984 Oly, 1 1986 Comm & Eur; world records – (8648 – 1980, 8730 & 8774 – 1982, 8847 – 1984); WR 1980, 1982, 1983, 1984 & 1986

THOMPSON Don: 1 1960 Oly 50k Walk

THOMPSON Ian: 1 1974 CG & Eur Mar; WR 1974

THOMPSON Rose: World records – 100y (11.4 – 1922), 4x100m/4x110y (50.2* & 49.8 – 1926), 4x200m/4x220y (1:51.6/1:52.4 – 1923)

TOMLIN Stan: 1 1930 CG 3M

TOMS Edward: 3 1924 Oly 4x400

TOOBEY Angela: 2 1998 World CC

TRANTER Maureen: World records – 4x110y (45.0 – 1968), 4x200 (1:33.8 – 1968)

TRAVIS David: 1 1970 CG JT

TREMEER Jimmy: 3 1908 Oly 400H; world record – 100 (10.8* – 1906)

TRICKEY Edith: World records – 880y (2:26.6* & 2:24.0* – 1925), 1000 (3:08.2 – 1924)

TULLETT Hayley: 3 2003 World 1500

TULLOH Bruce: 1 1962 Eur 5000

TURNER Bettie: World record – 4x220y (1:43.9 – 1951)

TYLER Dorothy: (HJ) 2 1936 Oly, 1 1938 CG, 2 1948 Oly, 1 1950 CG; world records – (1.65* – 1936, 1.66 – 1939)

TYSOE Alfred: 1 1900 Oly 800 & 5000 team race

TYSON Carol: World records – 3000 Walk (13:25.2* – 1979), 5000 (23:11.2* – 1979)

U

UNDERWOOD Adam: 1 1907 Int CC

V

VARAH Mike: World record – 4x880y (7:14.6* – 1966)

VERNON Judy: 1 1974 CG 100H; world record – 400H (60.4* – 1973)

VICKERS Stan: (20k Walk) 1 1958 Eur, 3 1960 Oly

VOIGT Emil: 1 1908 Oly 5M

W

WADE Kirsty: 1 1982 CG 800, 1 1986 CG 800 & 1500

WALKER Doug: 3 1997 World 4x100, 1 1998 Eur 200

WALKER Ivy: World records – 100y (11.0* – 1930), 220y (25.4* – 1930)

WALKER Nigel: 3 1987 World Ind 60H

WALLACE Andrea: 2 1991 World 15k

WALLWORK Ron: 1 1966 CG 20M Walk

WARHURST John: 1 1974 CG 20M Walk

WARISO Solomon: 3 1999 World Ind 4x400

WEBB Ernest: 2 1908 Oly 3500m & 10M Walks, 2 1912 Oly 10,000

WEBB Violet: 3 1932 Oly 4x100

WEBBER George: 2 1924 Oly 3000 team race

WEBSTER Albert: World record – 4x880y (7:30.6 – 1951)

WEBSTER Jack: 1 1925 Int CC

WEIR Robert: 1 1982 CG HT, 1 1998 CG DT

WELLS Allan: 1 1978 CG 100 (1= 200), 1 1980 Oly 100 (2 200), 1 1982 CG 100; WR (200) 1981

WESTON Madeleine: see under COBB

WHEELER Mike: 3 1956 Oly 4x400

WHETTON John: (1500) 1 1966, 1967 & 1968 Eur Ind, 1 1969 Eur

WHITBREAD Fatima: (JT) 2 1983 World, 3 1984 Oly, 1 1986 Eur, 1 1987 World, 2 1988 Oly; world record (77.44 – 1986); WR 1986 & 1987

WHITEHEAD Nick: 3 1960 Oly 4x100

WHITLOCK Harold: (50k Walk) 1 1936 Oly, 1 1938 Eur; world record – 30M (4:29:31.8 – 1935)

WILDE Ricky: 1 1970 Eur Ind 3000; world indoor record – 3000 (7:46.85* – 1970)

WILLIAMS Simon: 1 1990 CG SP

WILLIAMSON Audrey: 2 1948 Oly 200

WILMSHURST Ken: 1 1954 CG LJ & TJ

WILSON Harold: 2 1908 Oly 1500 & CC team race; world record – 1500 (3:59.8* – 1908)

WILSON Jim: 1 1920 Int CC, 3 1920 Oly 10,000

WINN Valerie: see under BALL

WINT Arthur (representing JAM): 1 1948 Oly 400 (2 800), 1 1952 Oly 4x400 (2 800); world record – 4x400 (3:03.9 – 1952); WR (800) 1951

WINTER Neil: 1 1994 CG PV

WISE Jo: 1 1998 CG LJ

WOLFF Freddie: 1 1936 Oly 4x400

WOOD Ted: 1 1909 & 1910 Int CC

WOODERSON Sydney: 1 1938 Eur 1500, 1 1946 Eur 5000; world records – 800m/880y (1:48.4/1:49.2 – 1938), 1M (4:06.4 – 1937); world best – 3/4M (2:59.5 – 1939)

WRIGHT Daisy: World record – 4x200m/ 4x220y (1:53.0 – 1921)

WRIGHT Dunkie: 1 1930 CG Mar

WRIGHT Rosemary: see under STIRLING

WRIGHTON John: 1 1958 Eur 400

Y

YATES Matthew: 1 1992 Eur Ind 1500

YOUNG Heather: 3 1952 Oly 4x100, 2 1956 Oly 4x100, 1 1958 Eur 100; world record – 4x110y (45.3 – 1958)